Student Study Guide

to accompany

Essentials of Understanding Psychology

Fourth Edition

Robert S. Feldman
University of Massachusetts, Amherst

Prepared by
Robert S. Feldman, Christopher R. Poirier,
Joshua M. Feldman, and John G. Graiff
University of Massachusetts

Boston   Burr Ridge, IL   Dubuque, IA   Madison, WI   New York   San Francisco   St. Louis
Bangkok   Bogotá   Caracas   Lisbon   London   Madrid
Mexico City   Milan   New Delhi   Seoul   Singapore   Sydney   Taipei   Toronto

McGraw-Hill Higher Education

*A Division of The **McGraw-Hill** Companies*

Student Study Guide to accompany
ESSENTIALS OF UNDERSTANDING PSYCHOLOG, FOURTH EDITION

Copyright ©2000 by The McGraw-Hill Companies, Inc. All rights reserved.
Previous edition(s) ©1997, 1994 by The McGraw-Hill Companies, Inc.
Printed in the United States of America.

The contents of, or parts thereof, may be reproduced for use with
ESSENTIALS OF UNDERSTANDING PSYCHOLOGY by Robert S. Feldman, provided
such reproductions bear copyright notice and may not be reproduced in any form for any
other purpose without permission of the publisher.

 This book is printed on recycled, acid-free paper
containing 10% postconsumer waste.

1 2 3 4 5 6 7 8 9 0 QPD QPD 9 0 3 2 1 0 9

ISBN 0-07-228537-0

www.mhhe.com

Table of Contents

Preface

This *Student Study Guide* has been prepared with several very important student concerns in mind. First, the students' need for a comprehensive guide that is meant to supplement Robert Feldman's *Essentials of Understanding Psychology 4th Edition* in such a way as to take advantage of the many features in the book that support effective study habits. Second, students need practice and drill work that focuses on the full content of each chapter and presents practice questions that are similar to those provided in the instructor's *Test File*. In order to provide a study guide that responds to both of these concerns, the chapter summaries have been organized using the key terms (both the bold-faced and italicized terms) and concepts in the text and the student learning objectives have been carefully page referenced to the text. These summaries are presented as a "guided review." In addition, the definitions in the text of the key terms were used to develop the key term drills found throughout the study guide.

Three practice multiple choice tests have been created for each chapter. The first two tests are composed of questions that are primarily factual in nature. The third test is composed of difficult factual, applied, and conceptual questions. Each chapter has between 45 and 70 practice multiple choice questions. I have added a complete set of answer explanations for both the right and wrong answers to all these multiple choice questions.

You will also find two practice essay questions for each chapter. These questions are intended to provide opportunities to practice writing and critical analysis skills. In the answer key at the back of the *Study Guide*, a list of points that should be covered in your answer to each question has been provided. These questions are meant to be difficult and to require you to draw on both conceptual and factual knowledge. Some require that you apply concepts to situations, and others may require that you compare several ideas. New in this edition, students will discover a section called "Cultural Idioms." Quite a few idiomatic uses are explained in detail for the reader who may be less experienced in American usages of the English language.

The introduction explains the organization of the *Study Guide* and offers tips on how to use the features of the *Study Guide* to improve your study skills and make your time spent with the text more effective.

Introduction

Using
Essentials of Understanding Psychology, 4th Edition:
Strategies for Effective Study

Essentials of Understanding Psychology, 4th Edition, has been written with the reader in mind, and it therefore includes a number of unique features that will help you to maximize your learning of the concepts, theories, facts, and other kinds of information that make up the field of psychology. To take advantage of these features, there are several steps that you should take when reading and studying the book. The *Student Study Guide* was designed to help the student take full advantage of the features in the textbook, and the steps recommended for the text have been incorporated into this *Study Guide*. By following these steps, you will not only get the most from reading and studying *Essentials of Understanding Psychology, 4th Edition,* but you will also develop habits that will help you to study other texts more effectively and to think critically about material you are learning. Among the most important steps to follow:

■ *Familiarize yourself with the logic of the book's structure.* Begin by reading the Table of Contents. It provides an overview of the topics that will be covered and gives a sense of the way the various topics are interrelated. Next, review the Preface, which describes the book's major features. Note how each chapter is divided into three or four self-contained units; these provide logical starting and stopping points for reading and studying. Also note the major highlights of each chapter: a chapter-opening outline, a Prologue, a Looking Ahead section that includes chapter objectives, Recaps and Reviews of key information following each of the major units, and—at the end of every chapter—a Looking Back section, a list of key terms and concepts, and the Epilogue. Because every chapter is structured in the same way, you are provided with a set of familiar landmarks as you chart your way through new material, allowing you to organize the chapter's content more readily. This *Study Guide* is designed to lead you through each of these steps.

■ *Use a study strategy.* Although we are expected to study and ultimately to learn a wide array of material throughout our schooling, we are rarely taught any systematic strategies that permit us to study more effectively. Yet, just as we wouldn't expect a physician to learn human anatomy by trial and error, it is the unusual student who is able to stumble upon a truly effective studying strategy.

Psychologists, however, have devised several excellent (and proven) techniques for improving study skills, two of which are described here. By employing one of these procedures—known by the initials "SQ3R" and "MURDER"—you can increase your ability to learn and retain information and to think critically, not just in psychology classes but in all academic subjects.

The SQ3R method includes a series of five steps, having the initials S-Q-R-R-R. The first step is to *survey* the material by reading the chapter outlines, chapter headings, figure captions, recaps, and Looking Ahead and Looking Back sections, providing yourself with an overview of the major points of the chapter. The next step—the "Q" in SQ3R—is to *question*. Formulate questions—either aloud or in writing—prior to actually reading a section of the material. For instance, if you had first surveyed this section of the book, you might jot down in the margin, "what do 'SQ3R' and 'MURDER' stand for?" The reviews that end each section of the chapter are also a good source of questions. But it is important not to rely on them entirely; making up your own questions is critical. *Essentials of Understanding Psychology, 4th Edition,* has wide margins in which you can write out your own questions. Such questioning helps you to focus in on the key points of the chapter, while putting you in an inquisitive frame of mind as well.

It is now time for the next, and most crucial, step: to *read* the material. Read carefully and, even more importantly, actively and critically. For instance, while you are reading, answer the questions you have asked yourself. You may find yourself coming up with new questions as you read along; that's fine since it shows you are reading inquisitively and paying attention to the material. Critically evaluate material by considering the implications of what you are reading, thinking about possible exceptions and contradictions, and examining the assumptions that lie behind the assertions made by the author.

The next step—the second "R"—is the most unusual. This "R" stands for *recite*, in which you look up from the book and describe and explain to yourself, or to a friend, the material you have just read and answer the questions you have posed earlier. Do it aloud; this is one time when talking to yourself is nothing to be embarrassed about. The recitation process helps you to clearly identify your degree of understanding of the material you have just read. Moreover, psychological research has shown that communicating material to others (even imaginary others, if you are reciting aloud to yourself and not a friend) aids you in learning it in a different—and deeper—way than material that you do not intend to communicate. Hence, your recitation of the material is a crucial link in the studying process.

The final "R" refers to *review*. As we will discuss in Chapter 6, reviewing is a prerequisite to fully learning and remembering material you have studied. Look over the information, reread the Recaps and Looking Back summaries, answer in-text review questions; and use this *Student Study Guide*. Reviewing should be an active process, in which you consider how different pieces of information fit together and develop a sense of the overall picture.

An alternative approach to studying—although not altogether dissimilar to SQ3R—is provided by the MURDER system of Dansereau (1978). Despite the unpleasant connotations of its title, the MURDER system is a useful study strategy.

In MURDER, the first step is to establish an appropriate *mood* for studying by setting goals for a study session and choosing a time and place in which you will not be distracted. Next comes reading for *understanding*, in which careful attention is paid to the meaning of the material being studied. *Recall* is an immediate attempt to recall the material from memory, without referring to the text. *Digesting* the material comes next; you should correct any recall errors, and attempt to organize and store newly learned material in memory.

You should work next on *expanding* (analyzing and evaluating) new material, and try to apply it to situations that go beyond the applications discussed in the text. By incorporating what you have learned into a larger information network in memory, you will be able to recall it more easily in the future. Finally, the last step is *review*. Just as with the SQ3R system, MURDER suggests that systematic review of material is a necessary condition for successful studying.

Both the SQ3R and MURDER systems provide a proven means of increasing your study effectiveness. It is not necessary, though, to feel tied to a particular strategy; you might want to combine other elements into your own study system. For example, learning tips and strategies for critical thinking will be presented throughout *Essentials of Understanding Psychology, 4ᵗʰ Edition*, such as in Chapter 6 when the use of mnemonics (memory techniques for organizing material to help its recall) are discussed. If these tactics help you to successfully master new material, stick with them.

■ *The Study Guide is designed for use of the SQ3R system.* In addition to directions between major sections that suggest a systematic way of using the features of the text, the major sections of the *Study Guide* chapters include a check box to the right of the page that will help remind you of the type of activity that the section involves. As you work through the text and the *Study Guide*, you will find the reminders in the *Study Guide*. These contain the appropriate steps of the SQ3R approach for the section of the *Study Guide* to which they are attached. You may wish to check each box as you complete the section. Here are a few samples:

Chapter Guided Review

This title identifies a summary of each section (established the *Recap, Review, and Rethink* sections of the chapters). The summary has the key terms removed and blanks provided to make your study more active. To the right, the word "Survey" reminds you that the material is designed to help with this phase of the SQ3R system.

Survey ❑

Practice Questions

Test your knowledge of the chapter material by answering the **Multiple Choice Questions**. These questions have been placed in three Practice Tests. The first two tests are composed of questions that will test your recall of factual knowledge. The third test contains questions that are challenging and primarily test for conceptual knowledge and your ability to apply that knowledge. Check your

Recite ❑
Review ❑

answers and review the feedback using the Answer Key in the back of the *Study Guide*. Again, "Recite and Review" are placed on the right to remind you of the SQ3R activity.

Each chapter is divided by title bars like these, and each provides recommendations for what can be done with the material provided.

■ *Find a location and time.* The last aspect of studying that warrants mention is that *when* and *where* you study are in some ways as important as *how* you study. One of the truisms of the psychological literature is that we learn things better - and are able to recall them longer - when we study material in small chunks over several study sessions rather than massing our study into one lengthy period. This implies that all-night studying just prior to a test is going to be less effective—and a lot more tiring—than employing a series of steady, regular study sessions.

In addition to carefully timing your studying, you should seek out a special location to study. It doesn't really matter where it is, as long as it has minimal distractions and is a place that you use *only* for studying. Identifying a special "territory" allows you to get in the right mood for study as soon as you begin.

A Final Comment

By using the proven study strategies presented above, as well as by making use of the pedagogical tools integrated in the text, you will maximize your understanding of the material in this book and you will master techniques that will help you learn and think critically in all your academic endeavors. More importantly, you will optimize your understanding of the field of psychology. It is worth the effort: The excitement, challenge, and promise that psychology holds for you is immense.

Robert Feldman

1 Introduction to Psychology

Detailed Chapter Outline

This detailed outline contains all the headings in Chapter 1: Introduction to Psychology. If you are using the SQ3R method, then an examination of the outline is the best way to begin your survey of the chapter.

Survey ❑
Question ❑

Prologue: From Terrorism to Heroism

Looking Ahead

Psychologists at Work

The Branches of Psychology: Psychology's Family Tree

The Demographics of the Discipline

Recap, Review and Rethink

A Science Evolves: The Past, the Present, and the Future

The Roots of Psychology

Women in Psychology: Founding Mothers

Today's Perspectives

Applying Psychology in the 21st Century:
Psychology and the Reduction of Violence

Connections: Psychology's Unifying Themes

The Links Between Psychology's Branches and Perspectives

Psychology's Future

Recap, Review, and Rethink

Research in Psychology

Posing Questions: The Scientific Method
Finding Answers: Psychological Research

> **Pathways Through Psychology:** Mary Garrett, AIDS Researcher

Recap, Review, and Rethink

Research Challenges: Exploring the Process

The Ethics of Research

> **Exploring Diversity:** Choosing Participants Who Represent the Scope of Human Behavior

Should Animals Be Used in Research?
Threats to Experiments: Experimenter and Participant Expectations

> **The Informed Consumer of Psychology:** Thinking Critically about Research

Recap, Review, and Rethink
Looking Back
Key Terms and Concepts

► Now that you have surveyed the chapter, read **Looking Ahead**, pages 4–6. Focus on the questions on page 6. Note that in this chapter the introductory remarks provide a description of the basic format of the book (on page 6).

Survey ❑
Read ❑

Concepts and Learning Objectives

These are the concepts and the learning objectives for Chapter 1. Read them carefully as part of your preliminary survey of the chapter.

Survey ❑

Concept 1: Psychology is a diversified scientific approach to the understanding of human and animal behavior. Psychologists explore ways of understanding behavior and mental processes as they are manifest in biology, sensation, perception, language, thought, memory, feelings, and many other processes.

1. Define psychology and explain what makes it a science.

2. Name and describe the different branches of psychology and distinguish between them by giving examples of the work and workers in each field.

3. Identify and describe the emerging fields of psychology.

4. Identify the significant demographic trends of the profession, including place of employment, international and gender distribution, and educational background.

Concept 2: Psychology dates its beginning with the foundation of a research laboratory in 1879 by Wilhelm Wundt. The major historical perspectives have been structuralism, functionalism, and gestalt psychology. The five contemporary conceptual perspectives are biological, psychodynamic, cognitive, behavioral, and humanistic.

5. Discuss the history of the science of psychology and the approaches taken by early psychologists.

6. Define the term "model," and name each of the five models of psychology.

7. Outline the key characteristics of each of the five models, and discuss how proponents of each model investigate a particular topic.

Concept 3: The scientific method is crucial to the way psychologists study phenomena of interest to psychology. The scientific method allows for careful, organized, and meaningful research, and using the method, psychologists develop formal theories and testable hypotheses.

8. Describe the scientific method approach.

9. Distinguish between theory and hypothesis, and describe the role of each in scientific inquiry.

Concept 4: When conducting research, psychologists must remain aware of a number of factors that may influence the outcome or affect the participants in the study. The ability to evaluate and make critical judgments about research findings is an important one. for our society.

10. Describe the ethical concerns involving the welfare of human and animal participants in scientific research.

11. Identify the possible sources of experimental bias, and discuss techniques used to safeguard against them.

12. Discuss the importance of statistical techniques used to establish whether or not the outcome of an experiment is significant.

13. Apply knowledge of scientific methods to evaluate how well research supports particular findings.

Chapter Guided Review

There are several ways you can use this guided review as part of your systematic study plan. Read the corresponding pages of the text, and then complete the review by supplying the correct missing key word. Or, you may want to complete the guided review as a means of becoming familiar with the text. Complete the review and then read the section thoroughly. As you finish each section, complete the Recap and Review questions that are supplied in the text.

Survey ❑
_____

Concept 1: Psychologists at Work

- *What is psychology, and why is it a science?*
- *What are the different branches of the field of psychology?*
- *Where are psychologists employed?*

_____
Survey ❑
Read ❑
Recite ❑
_____

Pages 6-12

[a] _____ is defined as the scientific study of behavior and mental processes. Psychologists investigate what people do, as well as their thoughts, feelings, perceptions, reasoning processes, and memories. They also investigate the biological foundations of these processes. Psychology relies upon the scientific method to discover ways of explaining, predicting, modifying, and improving behavior. The study of behavior and mental processes involves examining animal as well as human subjects to find the general laws that govern the behavior of all organisms.

Contrary to the mistaken view held by many people that psychology is interested only in abnormal behavior, psychologists examine a wide array of behaviors and mental processes. The specialty areas are described in the order in which they appear throughout the text.

[b] _____ explores the relationship between fundamental biological

processes and behavior. The study is focused on the brain and the nervous system, and both diseases and healthy functions are examined for their contribution to the understanding of behavior.

[c] _____ *psychology* is both a specialty and a task undertaken by most psychologists. The scientific work of psychology requires experimental methods to be applied wherever possible. [d] _____ *psychology* is a specialty within experimental psychology that focuses on higher mental functions like thought, language, memory, problem solving, reasoning, and decision making, among other processes.

[e] _____ *psychology* examines how a person changes and grows throughout life, and [f] _____ *psychology* seeks to explain how a person's behavior is consistent through time and why different people respond differently to the same situation.

Several types of psychologists study ways of improving health and assessing and treating mental illness. [g] _____ *psychology* explores the relationship between physical and mental health and, especially, the role of stress in health. [h] _____ *psychology* is primarily involved with the assessment, diagnosis, and treatment of abnormal behavior. [i] _____ *psychology* focuses on the problems of adjustment to challenges that everyone faces in life. [j] _____ *psychology* examines how educational processes occur, with close examination, for instance, of the student-teacher interaction. [k] _____ *psychology* is devoted to the assessment and remedy of problems encountered in education, including both learning disabilities and emotional problems.

[l] _____ *psychology* studies the way people's thoughts, feelings, and actions are affected by others. Social psychologists may examine the problem of aggression or the nature of friendship. [m] _____ *psychology* applies psychological principles to the workplace and studies topics like job satisfaction and productivity.

[n] _____ *psychology* applies psychological principles to consumer behavior in order to test advertising strategies and to improve products. To determine similarities and differences between groups, [o] _____ *psychology* examines topics common to a number of psychological specialties in different cultural and ethnic settings.

Emerging areas of psychology include: [p] _____ *psychology*, an area that seeks to identify behavior patterns that are a result of our genetic inheritance; [q] _____, an area that focuses on identifying which biological factors relate to psychological disorders; [r] _____ *psychology*, the study of how physical environments influence behavior; [s] _____ *psychology*, the study of law and psychology; **[t]** _____ *psychology*, the branch investigating applications of

psychology to sports and athletic activity; and **[u]** _____ evaluation, the

application of psychologically based assessment principles to large programs.

Concept 2: A Science Evolves: The Past, the Present, and the Future

Survey ❑
Read ❑
Recite ❑

- **What are the historical roots of the field of psychology?**
- **What major approaches are used by contemporary psychology?**

Pages 13–21

Trephining (drilling holes in the skull to let evil spirits escape), Hippocrates' theory of humors, Gall's "science" of phrenology (the association of bumps on the head with traits), and Descartes' concept of animal spirits reflect some of the most forward thought of past times. The era of scientific psychology is usually dated from the establishment by Wilhelm Wundt of an experimental psychology laboratory in 1879. Today psychology is based on a number of systems of interrelated ideas and concepts called conceptual perspectives, or

[a] _____ .

The model associated with Wundt's laboratory is called **[b]** _____ .

Structuralism utilized a technique called **[c]** _____ to examine the basic elements of thought, consciousness, and emotions. Introspection required the subject to report

how a stimulus was experienced. A model called **[d]** _____ replaced structuralism, and instead of focusing on the structure of mental elements, it focused on how the mind works and how people adapt to environments. William James was the leading functionalist in the early 1900s, and one of the leading educators, John Dewey, took a functionalist approach

in his development of school psychology. **[e]** _____ was another reaction to structuralism that developed in the early 1900s. The gestalt approach examines phenomena in terms of the whole experience rather than the individual elements, and gestalt psychologists are identified with the maxim "the whole is greater than the sum of the parts."

Two early female contributors to the field of psychology were Leta Stetter Hollingsworth, known for the term "gifted" and for an early focus on women's issues, and June Etta Downey, who studied personality traits in the 1920s.

The field of psychology is now dominated by five major conceptual perspectives. The

[f] _____ perspective is focused on the study of the relationship between

biological processes and behavior. The **[g]** _____ perspective views behavior as motivated by inner and unconscious forces over which the individual can exert little control. The psychodynamic perspective, developed by Sigmund Freud in the early 1900s, has been a major influence in twentieth-century thinking and continues to have an influence in the treatment of mental disorders. The **[h]** _____ perspective has evolved the structuralists' concern with trying to understand the mind into a study of how we internally represent the outside world and how this representation influences behavior. The

[i] _____ perspective began as a reaction to the failure of other early perspectives to base the science of psychology on observable phenomena. John B. Watson developed behaviorism as a study of how environmental forces influence behavior. The newest perspective, the **[j]** _____ perspective, rejects the deterministic views of the other perspectives and instead focuses on the unique ability of humans to seek higher levels of maturity and fulfillment and to express **[k]** _____ . All the major perspectives have active practitioners and continuing research programs.

CONCEPT 3: Research in Psychology

Survey ❑
Read ❑
Recite ❑

- *What is the scientific method, and how do psychologists use theory and research to answer questions of interest?*
- *What are the different research methods employed by psychologists?*
- *How do psychologists establish cause-and-effect relationships in research studies?*

Pages 22–34

The cases of Abner Louima and Kitty Genovese illustrate the complex task of conducting research in order to explain phenomena that otherwise appear inexplicable. Research into the question of why bystanders fail to help—and under what conditions they are more likely to offer help—is used throughout the chapter to illustrate research methods.

A major aim of research in psychology is to discover which of our assumptions about human behavior is correct. First, questions that interest psychologists must be set into the proper framework so that a systematic inquiry may be conducted to find the answer to the question.

Psychologists use an approach called the **[a]** _____ to conduct their inquiry. The scientific method has three main steps: (1) identifying questions of interest; (2) formulating an explanation; and (3) carrying out research designed to lend support or refute the explanation.

[b] _____ are broad explanations and predictions about phenomena that interest the scientist. Because psychological theories grow out of diverse models, they vary in breadth and detail. Psychologists' theories differ from our informal theories by being formal and focused. Latané and Darley proposed a theory of *diffusion of responsibility* to account for why bystanders and onlookers did not help Kitty Genovese.

After formulating a theory, the next step for Latané and Darley was to devise a way of testing the theory. They began by stating a **[c]** _____, a prediction stated in a way that allows it to be tested. Latané and Darley's hypothesis was: The more people who witness an emergency situation, the less likely it is that help will be given to a victim. Formal theories and hypotheses allow psychologists to organize separate bits of information and to move beyond the facts and make deductions about phenomena not yet encountered.

Research is systematic inquiry aimed at the discovery of new knowledge. It is a central ingredient of the scientific method. Research is the means of actually testing hypotheses and theories. In order to research a hypothesis, the hypothesis must be stated in a manner that is testable. **[d]**_____ refers to the translation of a hypothesis into specific, testable procedures that can be observed and measured. If we examine scientific methods closely, we can then make more critically informed and reasoned judgments about everyday situations.

[e] _____ requires examining existing records and collecting data regarding the phenomena of interest to the researcher. Latané and Darley would have begun by examining newspaper clippings and other records to find examples of situations like those they were studying. The problem with the archival data is that it may be incomplete, collected in the wrong form, or collected haphazardly.

[f] _____ involves the researcher observing naturally occurring behavior without intervening in the situation. Unfortunately, the phenomena of interest may be infrequent. Furthermore, when people know they are being watched, they may act differently.

In **[g]** _____, participants are chosen from a larger population and asked a series of questions about behavior, thoughts, or attitudes. Techniques are sophisticated enough now that small samples can be drawn from large populations to make predictions about how the entire population will behave. For instance, the sampling technique is used to predict how the population will vote in a presidential election. The potential problems are that some people may not remember how they felt or acted at a particular time, or they may give answers they believe that the researcher wants to hear. Also, survey questions can be formulated in such a way as to bias the response.

When the phenomena of interest is uncommon, psychologists may use a **[h]**_____, an in-depth examination of an individual or small group of people. The application of insight gained through a case study must be done carefully because the individuals studied may not be representative of a larger group.

[i] _____ examines the relationship between two factors and the degree to which they are associated, or correlated. The correlation is measured by a mathematical score ranging from +1.0 to -1.0. A positive correlation says that when one factor *increases*, the other correlated factor also *increases*. A negative correlation says that as one factor *increases*, the other negatively correlated factor *decreases*. When little or no relationship exists between two factors, the correlation is close to 0. Correlation can show that two factors are related and that the presence of one predicts another, but it cannot prove that one causes the other. Correlation research cannot rule out alternative causes when examining the relationship between two factors.

Experiments must be conducted in order to establish cause-and-effect relationships. A formal **[j]** _____ examines the relationship of two or more factors in a setting that is deliberately manipulated to produce a change in one factor and then to observe how the change affects other factors. This **[k]** _____ allows psychologists to detect the relationship between these factors. These factors, called **[l]**_____ _____, can be behaviors, events, or other characteristics that can change or vary in some way. The first step in developing an experiment is to operationalize a hypothesis (as did Latané and Darley). At least two groups of participants must be observed. One group receives the **[m]**_____, the manipulated variable, and is called the

[n] _____. The other group is called the **[o]** _____ and is not exposed to the manipulated variable. Latané and Darley created a bogus emergency and then varied the number of bystanders present, in effect creating several different treatment groups.

The variable that is manipulated is the **[p]** _____ —the condition that distinguishes the treatment groups—and in this example it was the number of people present.

The **[q]** _____ is the variable that is measured to reveal the effect of the manipulation. In this example, the dependent variable was how long it took the participant to offer help.

In order to be assured that some characteristics of the participant do not influence the outcome of an experiment, a procedure called **[r]** _____ must be used to assign participants to treatment or control groups. The objective of random assignment is to make each group comparable.

Latané and Darley utilized a trained *confederate*, who feigned an epileptic seizure, to create the bogus emergency. The results of their experiment suggested that the size of the audience did indeed influence the time it took for participants to offer help. To be sure, they had to analyze their results according to statistical procedures to prove that it was unlikely that their results were caused by chance. Also, to be certain of their results, other psychologists must try to repeat the experiment under the same or similar circumstances and test other variations of the hypothesis. This process is called **[s]** _____.

CONCEPT 4:   Research Challenges: Exploring the Process

Survey ❑
Read ❑
Recite ❑

● *What are the major issues that underlie the process of conducting research?*

Pages 35-39

Issues other than the quality of research are of concern to psychologists. The ethics of certain research practices come into question when there exists a possibility of harm to a participant. The use of deception—like that of the Latané and Darley experiment—and similar tactics has led to the need to assure participants and the scientific community that no harm will come to the participants. Guidelines have been developed for the treatment of human and animal participants, and most proposed research is now reviewed by a panel to assure that guidelines are being met. The concept of **[a]** _____ has become a key ethical principle. Prior to participating in an experiment, participants must sign a form indicating that they have been told of the basic outlines of the study and what their participation will involve.

A problem with psychology experiments is that the participants are often college students. The advantage of using college students is their availability, and the major disadvantage is that they may not be representative of the population—they tend to be middle class, white, and hold better-informed attitudes. However, for proper and meaningful generalizations of research results, a selection of participants that reflects the diversity of human behavior is necessary.

The ethical guidelines call for assurance that animals in experiments do not suffer as a consequence of being participants in the experiment. Not only is physical discomfort avoided, but psychological discomfort is avoided as well. The need for using animals in experiments has become a controversial topic. The advantages of using animals include the fact that they have a shorter life span, that their behavior may be less complex than human behavior, and finally, that circumstances can be manipulated that could not be manipulated with humans.

Another problem that researchers face is that of **[b]** _____, the factors that distort the experimenter's understanding of the relationship between the independent and dependent variables. **[c]** _____ expectations occur when the experimenter unintentionally conveys cues about how the participants should behave in the experiment.

[d] _____ expectations are the participant's expectations about the intended goal of the experiment. The participant's guesses about the hypothesis can influence behavior and thus the outcomes. One approach is to disguise the true purpose of the experiment. Another is to use a **[e]** _____ with the control group so that the participants remain unaware of whether or not they are being exposed to the experimental condition. The *double-blind procedure* guards against these two biases by informing neither the experimenter nor the participant about which treatment group the participant is in.

Psychologists utilize statistical procedures to determine if the results of a research study are significant. A **[f]** _____ means that the results of the experiment were not likely to be a result of chance. It does not imply that the outcome has real-life significance. *Meta-analysis* is a technique that allows researchers to use statistical procedures on the data that has been reported by other researchers, thereby combining the results of several research reports.

➤ Now that you have surveyed, questioned, and read the chapter and completed the guided review, review **Looking Back**, pages 40-41.

Review ❏

➤ For additional practice through recitation and review, test your knowledge of the chapter material by answering the questions in the *Key Word Drill*, the *Practice Questions*, and the *Essay Questions*.

Key Word Drill

The following **Matching Questions** test the boldfaced and italicized key words from the text. Check your answers with the Answer Key in the back of the *Study Guide*.

Recite ❏

MATCHING QUESTIONS

1. biopsychology

2. experimental psychology

3. cognitive psychology

4. developmental psychology

5. personality psychology

a. The branch that studies the processes of sensing, perceiving, learning, and thinking about the world.

b. The branch that studies consistency and change in a person's behavior over time as well as the individual traits that differentiate the behavior of one person from another when each confronts the same situation.

c. The branch that specializes in the biological basis of behavior.

d. The branch that studies how people grow and change throughout the course of their lives.

e. The branch that focuses on the study of higher mental processes, including thinking, language, memory, problem solving, knowing, reasoning, judging, and decision making.

6. health psychology

7. clinical psychology

8. counseling psychology

9. educational psychology

10. school psychology

a. The branch of psychology that explores the relationship of psychological factors and physical ailments or disease.

b. The branch of psychology devoted to assessing children in elementary and secondary schools who have academic or emotional problems, and to developing solutions to such problems.

c. The branch of psychology that focuses on educational, social, and career adjustment problems.

d. The branch of psychology that deals with the study, diagnosis, and treatment of abnormal behavior.

e. The branch of psychology that considers how the educational process affects students.

---

11. industrial-organizational psychology

12. consumer psychology

13. cross-cultural psychology

14. evolutionary psychology

15. clinical neuropsychology

a. The branch of psychology that investigates the similarities and differences in psychological functioning in various cultures and ethnic groups.

b. The emerging area that relates biological factors to psychological disorders.

c. The branch of psychology that seeks to identify behavior patterns that are a result of our genetic inheritance.

d. The branch of psychology that considers our buying habits and the effects of advertising on buyer behavior.

e. The branch of psychology that studies the psychology of the workplace, considering productivity, job satisfaction, and decision making.

---

16. Sigmund Freud   a. The first laboratory

17. Hippocrates   b. Giftedness

18. Franz Josef Gall   c. The four temperaments

19. Wilhelm Wundt   d. Psychoanalysis

20. William James   e. Phrenology

21. Leta Stetter Hollingsworth   f. Functionalism

---

22. biological perspective

     a. The psychological perspective that suggests that observable behavior should be the focus of study.

23. psychodynamic perspective

     b. The psychological perspective that views behavior from the perspective of biological functioning.

24. cognitive perspective

     c. The psychological perspective based on the belief that behavior is motivated by inner forces over which the individual has little control.

25. behavioral perspective

26. humanistic perspective

     d. The psychological perspective that suggests that people are in control of their lives.

     e. The psychological perspective that focuses on how people know, understand, and think about the world.

---

27. scientific method

28. theories

29. hypothesis

30. research

31. operationalization

32. random assignment to condition

a. Systematic inquiry aimed at discovering new knowledge.

b. The assignment of participants to given groups on a chance basis alone.

c. A prediction stated in a way that allows it to be tested.

d. The process of translating a hypothesis into specific testable procedures that can be measured and observed.

e. The process of appropriately framing and properly answering questions, used by scientists to come to an understanding about the world.

f. Broad explanations and predictions concerning phenomena of interest.

---

33. experimental manipulation

34. variable

35. treatment

36. experimental group

37. control group

38. independent variable

39. dependent variable

a. The variable that is manipulated in an experiment.

b. The group receiving the treatment or manipulation.

c. A behavior or event that can be changed.

d. The change deliberately produced in an experiment to affect responses or behaviors in other factors to determine causal relationships between variables.

e. The manipulation implemented by the experimenter to influence results in a segment of the experimental population.

f. The variable that is measured and is expected to change as a result of experimenter manipulation.

g. The group receiving no treatment.

---

40. archival research

41. naturalistic observation

42. survey research

43. case study

44. correlational research

45. experiment

a. A study carried out to investigate the relationship between two or more factors by deliberately producing a change in one factor and observing the effect that change has upon other factors.

b. Observation without intervention, in which the investigator records information about a naturally occurring situation and does not intervene in the situation.

c. The examination of existing records for the purpose of confirming a hypothesis.

d. An in-depth interview of an individual in order to understand that individual better and to make inferences about people in general.

e. Research to determine whether there is a relationship between two sets of factors, such as certain behaviors and responses.

f. Sampling a group of people by assessing their behavior, thoughts, or attitudes, then generalizing the findings to a larger population.

Practice Questions

Test your knowledge of the chapter material by answering these **Multiple Choice Questions**. These questions have been placed in three Practice Tests. The first two tests are composed of questions that will test your recall of factual knowledge. The third test contains questions that are challenging and primarily test for conceptual knowledge and your ability to apply that knowledge. Check your answers and review the feedback using the Answer Key in the back of the *Study Guide*.

Recite ❑
Review ❑

MULTIPLE CHOICE QUESTIONS

PRACTICE TEST I:

1. Which of the following techniques distinguishes the kind of inquiry used by scientists from that used by professionals in nonscientific areas like literature, art, and philosophy?
    a. intuitive thought
    b. scientific methods
    c. common sense
    d. construction of new theoretical models

2. Biopsychology is the branch of psychology that specializes in:
    a. the biological basis of behavior.
    b. how people grow and change both physically and socially throughout their lives.
    c. how people's thoughts, feelings, and actions are affected by others.
    d. the study, diagnosis, and treatment of abnormal behavior.

3. Which of the following psychological specialty areas would be considered a **model**?
    a. psychodynamic psychology
    b. cross-cultural psychology
    c. experimental psychology
    d. counseling psychology

4. Which of the following psychologists would most likely be involved primarily in administering tests and utilizing evaluative instruments for the assessment of abnormal behavior?
    a. counseling psychologist
    b. health psychologist
    c. personality psychologist
    d. clinical psychologist

5. The focus of developmental psychology is on:

    a. applications such as improving the parenting skills of adults.

    b. understanding growth and changes occurring throughout life.

    c. development and maintenance of healthy interpersonal relationships as in friendships, co-worker relationships, and marriages.

    d. identifying behavioral consistencies throughout life.

6. The effectiveness of government programs such as Head Start and Medicaid would be the focus of psychologists interested in:

    a. experimentation.   c. forensics.

    b. evaluation.   d. cognition.

7. Psychology was established formally in 1879 when:

    a. Sigmund Freud began psychoanalysis.

    b. the American Psychological Association was founded.

    c. William James, an American, published his first major book.

    d. Wilhelm Wundt founded his psychology laboratory in Germany.

8. According to the discussion in the text, the problem that psychology faces of losing its diversity as a discipline can best be corrected by:

    a. social psychologists becoming more active trainers of psychologists.

    b. more studies in cultural psychology based on demonstrating the importance of diversity.

    c. increasing the ethnic sensitivity of counseling and clinical psychologists.

    d. increasing the number of minorities in the profession.

9. "The whole is greater than the sum of the parts" is a postulate of:

    a. structuralism.   c. gestalt psychology.

    b. functionalism.   d. behaviorism.

10. Leta Stetter Hollingsworth is known for her contribution of:

    a. the concept of a kindergarten.

    b. the concept of giftedness.

    c. the idea that males and females were psychologically different.

    d. the study of personality traits.

11. The influence of inherited characteristics on behavior would be studied with the:

    a. cognitive model.   c. behavioral model.

    b. psychodynamic model.   d. biological model.

12.   In the example of Kitty Genovese, how many bystanders probably heard her call for help?

    a.   38   c.   1

    b.   2   d.   107

13.   According to the text, formulating an explanation is one of the steps of:

    a.   naturalistic explanation.   c.   ethics review panel.

    b.   experimenter bias.   d.   scientific method.

14.   Theories tend to be _____ while hypotheses are _____.

    a.   general statements; specific statements   c.   provable; impossible to disprove

    b.   specific statements; general statements   d.   factual; based on speculation

15.   Scientific research begins with:

    a.   formulating an explanation.   c.   identifying a research question.

    b.   beginning the data-collection exercise.   d.   confirming or disconfirming a hypothesis.

16.   Operationalization requires that:

    a.   data always be useful.

    b.   procedures are followed exactly.

    c.   variables are correctly manipulated.

    d.   predictions be made testable.

17.   The technique of conducting an in-depth interview of an individual in order to understand that individual better and to make inferences about people in general is called a:

    a.   focused study.   c.   case study.

    b.   generalization study.   d.   projection study.

18.   When the strength of a relationship is represented by a mathematical score ranging from +1.0 to -1.0, we are dealing with a:

    a.   dependent variable.   c.   correlation.

    b.   manipulation.   d.   treatment.

19.   Researchers like to do experiments whenever feasible because experiments:

    a.   impress the public that psychology is really scientific.

    b.   identify causal relationships.

    c.   permit the application of statistical analyses to the data.

    d.   are required in order for the study to get government funding.

20. In an experiment with two groups, the group that receives no treatment serves as:
    a. a control.
    b. a case.
    c. an independent variable.
    d. a measured variable.

21. The event that is measured and is expected to change as a result of the experiment is called:
    a. dependent variable.
    b. independent variable.
    c. control variable.
    d. confounding variable.

22. The document signed by the participant in an experiment that affirms that the participant knows generally what is to happen is called:
    a. "in loco parentis."
    b. participant expectations.
    c. informed consent.
    d. experimenter expectations.

23. A participant's interpretation of what behaviors or responses are expected in an experiment is called:
    a. the placebo effect.
    b. experimenter expectations.
    c. participant expectations.
    d. treatment condition.

24. A pill without any significant chemical properties that is used in an experiment is called:
    a. a control.
    b. a placebo.
    c. a dependent variable.
    d. an independent variable.

25. When the results of a study cannot be replicated, then:
    a. the claimed effect is regarded with skepticism.
    b. cheating by the experimenter should be presumed.
    c. psychics have probably worked mischievously against the research.
    d. the data have probably been analyzed incorrectly.

———————

PRACTICE TEST II:

26. Although their interests are diverse, psychologists share a common:
    a. concern for applying their knowledge to social situations.
    b. interest in mental processes or behavior.
    c. respect for the ideas of psychoanalyst Sigmund Freud.
    d. interest in the study of animals' behavior.

27. The relationship of experimental psychology and cognitive psychology might best be described as:
    a. only experimental psychology conducts experiments.
    b. cognitive psychology is not interested in studying learning.
    c. cognitive psychology is a specialty area of experimental psychology.
    d. experimental psychology is a specialty of cognitive psychology.

28. Guests on a TV talk show include a panel of obese women whose average weight is 450 pounds. This program will be especially interesting to:
    a. forensic psychologists.   c. cognitive psychologists.
    b. social psychologists.   d. health psychologists.

29. Questions concerning such topics as how we are influenced by others and why we form relationships with each other are studied by:
    a. counseling psychologists.   c. clinical psychologists.
    b. social psychologists.   d. health psychologists.

30. During legislative hearings to review the state's insanity laws, lawmakers are likely to seek the advice of:
    a. social psychologists.   c. clinical psychologists.
    b. counseling psychologists.   d. forensic psychologists.

31. Of the following, an environmental psychologist would be most likely to study:
    a. the impact of smoking on health.
    b. experimental ethics.
    c. the effects of crowding on behavior.
    d. program effectiveness.

32. The largest proportion of psychologists are employed:
    a. privately at their own independent practices.
    b. in hospitals or mental institutions.
    c. at colleges or universities.
    d. in private businesses or industries.

33. Which of these questions would most interest a functionalist?
    a. What are the best human values?
    b. What are the contents of the mind?
    c. How do nerves work?
    d. How do a person's thoughts help her to get along in daily life?

34. Gestalt psychology was developed:
    a. around 1850.
    c. during the early 1900s.
    b. in 1879.
    d. in the 1950s.

35. John B. Watson was the first American psychologist to follow the:
    a. behavioral perspective.
    c. cognitive perspective.
    b. humanistic perspective.
    d. psychodynamic perspective.

36. "Slips of the tongue" are seen by _____ psychologists as revealing the unconscious mind's true beliefs or wishes.
    a. cognitive
    c. biological
    b. psychodynamic
    d. humanistic

37. Sigmund Freud believed that behavior is motivated by:
    a. subconscious inner forces.
    b. a desire to achieve personal fulfillment.
    c. the natural tendency to organize data through perception.
    d. inherited characteristics.

38. According to the text, identifying questions of interest is one of the steps of:
    a. survey research.
    c. scientific method.
    b. case study methods.
    d. experimental design.

39. Hypotheses are to predictions as:
    a. explanations are to theories.   c. explanations are to operationalizations.
    b. theories are to explanations.   d. operationalizations are to explanations.

40. Telephoning large numbers of people to gather information concerning their attitudes toward television is a form of:
    a. case study research.   c. experimental research.
    b. survey research.   d. archival research.

41. Suppose that a psychology professor dresses in old clothes and joins the homeless on city streets in order to study them. Which research method is being applied?
    a. archival research   c. naturalistic observation
    b. correlational research   d. experimentation

42. Which of the following statements is **not** true?
    a. A correlation of 1.0 means that there is a strong positive relationship between two factors.
    b. A correlation of 0.0 means that there is no systematic relationship between two factors.
    c. Correlations describe a relationship between two factors.
    d. Correlations tell us that one factor is caused by another.

43. A variable is:
    a. the experimental group receiving no treatment.
    b. the experimental group receiving treatment.
    c. a behavior or event that can be changed.
    d. a participant in research.

44. In order for proper assignment of participants to the conditions in an experiment, the assignment must be by:
    a. someone who does not know the participants.
    b. chance.
    c. someone who does know the participants.
    d. factors relevant to the experiment.

45. The variable that is manipulated by the experimenter is called the:
    a. dependent variable.   c. control variable.
    b. independent variable.   d. confounding variable.

46. Whether a behavioral scientist uses human or animal participants in an experiment, there are _____ that the scientist must satisfy in order not to violate the rights of the participants.
    a. moral obligations   c. professional standards
    b. religious principles   d. ethical guidelines

47. Deception—disguising the true nature of a study—is sometimes used in experiments in order to:
    a. eliminate participant expectations.   c. eliminate experimenter expectations.
    b. confuse the participant.   d. confuse the experimenter.

48. The double-blind procedure is used to:
    a. keep the confederate from influencing other participants.
    b. eliminate dependent variables.
    c. control the placebo effect.
    d. eliminate participant and experimenter expectations.

PRACTICE TEST III: Conceptual, Applied, and Challenging Questions

49. What kind of psychologist would have a special interest in studying the aspects of an earthquake that people are most likely to recall?
    a. social psychologist   c. educational psychologist
    b. consumer psychologist   d. cognitive psychologist

50. A motorist's car stalls on the highway on a cold, windy, and snowy night. Which type of psychologist would be most interested in whether other motorists offered assistance?
    a. a social psychologist   c. a clinical psychologist
    b. an environmental psychologist   d. an industrial-organizational psychologist

51. Professor Greenland has identified a trait he calls persistence, and he has begun to conduct research on the consistency of this trait in various situations. Dr. Greenland is most likely:
    a. a social psychologist.   c. an educational psychologist.
    b. a cross-cultural psychologist.   d. a personality psychologist.

52. An architect interested in designing an inner-city apartment building that would not be prone to vandalism might consult with:
    a. a clinical psychologist.   c. a forensic psychologist.
    b. a school psychologist.   d. an environmental psychologist.

53. Structuralists trained people to describe carefully, in their own words, what they experienced upon being exposed to various stimuli. This procedure for studying the mind is called:

   a. cognition.

   b. mind expansion.

   c. perception.

   d. introspection.

54. According to the text, the major distinction between educational and school psychology is that:

   a. educational psychology is devoted to improving the education of students who have special needs, and school psychology is devoted to increasing achievement in all students.

   b. school psychology is devoted to improving the schooling of students who have special needs, and educational psychology is devoted to better understanding of the entire educational system.

   c. school psychology attempts to examine the entire educational process, and educational psychology looks at individual students.

   d. educational psychology attempts to examine the entire educational process, and school psychology is devoted to assessing and correcting academic and school-related problems of students.

55. Today's scientists believe that the purpose of trephining was to:

   a. enable one person to read another's mind.

   b. allow evil spirits to escape.

   c. increase telekinetic powers.

   d. heal the patient of mental illness.

56. Which pair of individuals has been associated with functionalism?

   a. Leta Stetter Hollingsworth and June Etta Downey

   b. Sigmund Freud and Wilhelm Wundt

   c. William James and John Dewey

   d. Wilhelm Wundt and William James

57. Of the following, the _____ perspective of psychology places the greatest emphasis on the environment.

   a. biological

   b. psychodynamic

   c. behavioral

   d. humanistic

58.   In the past, Professor Chung has conducted research on topics that include how genetics may influence particular behaviors and personality traits, such as shyness. Which of the following best describes Professor Chung's research interests?

    a.   program evaluation

    b.   industrial-organizational psychology

    c.   cross-cultural psychology

    d.   evolutionary psychology

59.   Jose, Maria, and Carla have volunteered to be subjects in a study. They are each, in turn, asked to concentrate on creating an image of a geometric shape. After forming the image, they are then required to describe how the image came to them. The researcher then asks them to imagine a triangle, then a square, and then several more complicated shapes. Which of the following have they been doing?

    a.   experimental psychology   c.   gestalt psychology

    b.   introspection   d.   functionalism

60.   Based on what you have read in the text, which of the following would be least interested in cross-cultural studies?

    a.   the biological perspective   c.   the cognitive perspective

    b.   the psychodynamic perspective   d.   the behavioral perspective

61.   Professor Mansfield is particularly interested in explanations of an individual's ability to make decisions based on free choice. She is exploring a number of factors that may influence or determine choices, but she is very hopeful that she can illustrate that some non-determined choices can be demonstrated. Which of the following combinations best represents the two perspectives that would be supported by her research?

    a.   the psychoanalytic and biological perspectives

    b.   the behavioral and the humanistic perspectives

    c.   the humanistic and cognitive perspectives

    d.   the cognitive and behavioral perspectives

62.   Studies of violence that suggest a cycle of violence - that is, violence in one generation is correlated with violence in the next generation - support which of the following sides in the key issues examined by psychology?

    a.   determinism   c.   individual differences

    b.   nature   d.   conscious control of behavior

63.   The method of sampling the attitudes of a small group of persons to use the information to predict those of the general population is called:

    a.   situational research.   c.   survey research.

    b.   archival research.   d.   experimentation.

64. A psychologist studies wedding photos from the early 1900s in an effort to understand wedding customs of that era. This research is:

    a.   delayed naturalistic observation.   c.   a survey.

    b.   a case study.   d.   archival.

65. Freud based his theory of psychoanalysis on in-depth examinations of the patients he was treating for psychological problems. This method of research relies on the use of:

    a.   case studies.   c.   dependent variables.

    b.   correlational data.   d.   naturalistic observation.

66. A prospective executive may undergo intensive interviews and extensive psychological testing. The executive may also have to provide references from previous and current occupational and personal sources. This process is most similar to:

    a.   a survey.   c.   naturalistic observation.

    b.   an experimental study.   d.   a case study.

67. A researcher finds a positive correlation between a student's Scholastic Assessment Test (SAT) score and the income of the student's parents. This correlational finding means:

    a.   larger incomes cause better SAT scores.

    b.   parents with larger incomes can provide experiences which boost SAT scores.

    c.   income and SAT scores are somewhat related, so one can be roughly predicted from the other.

    d.   the SAT gives an advantage to upper-middle-class students.

68. For several years, Professor Taylor has been studying the effects of light on the ability of monkeys to tolerate stress. Each experiment varies the conditions slightly, but usually only one factor is altered each time. Dr. Taylor is most likely trying to:

    a.   develop a new statistical test.

    b.   operationalize her hypothesis.

    c.   formulate a new hypothesis.

    d.   test the limits of her theory.

69. Research volunteers must be told in advance about any important details of a research project that might influence whether they want to serve. This is called the principle of:

    a.   subject protection.   c.   informed consent.

    b.   behavioral privacy.   d.   prevention of deception.

70.   A researcher uses a different tone of voice while speaking to groups of subjects in a problem-solving study: She speaks encouragingly to students in a class for the gifted, and with a discouraging voice to a remedial class. This shows the experimental bias of:

    a.   experimenter expectations.
    b.   the double-blind procedure.
    c.   randomization.
    d.   the placebo effect.

71.   Professor Wright is convinced that his theory claiming that voters are more easily influenced by negative campaign messages is a correct theory. Which of the following would be his first step in demonstrating the theory's claims to be correct?

    a.   Professor Wright must find ways to measure the negativity of messages and voter behavior.
    b.   Professor Wright must define the correlation coefficients.
    c.   Professor Wright must collect data about voters and campaigns.
    d.   Professor Wright must select the appropriate statistical analyses to utilize.

72.   Which of the following statements requires the least modification in order to produce testable predictions?

    a.   Intelligence declines dramatically as people age.
    b.   Disgruntled employees are likely to steal from their employers.
    c.   Smiling can make you feel happy.
    d.   Increases in physical exercise are associated with declines in heart-related diseases.

73.   In an experiment, participants are placed in one of several rooms, each with a different color scheme. In each setting, the participants are given a problem-solving task that has been shown to be challenging and often results in increased tension while the problem-solver attempts to solve the problem. Researchers have hypothesized that some colors may reduce stress and improve problem solving. In this study, the color schemes of the rooms would be considered:

    a.   irrelevant.
    b.   the independent variable.
    c.   the dependent variable.
    d.   the confounding variable.

74.   In an experiment, participants are placed in one of several rooms, each with a different color scheme. In each setting, the participants are given a problem-solving task that has been shown to be challenging and often results in increased tension while the problem-solver attempts to solve the problem. Researchers have hypothesized that some colors may reduce stress and improve problem solving. In this study, the levels of stress experienced by the participants would be considered:

    a.   a combination of the problem and the color schemes.
    b.   the confounding variable.
    c.   the independent variable.
    d.   irrelevant.

Essay Questions

Essay Question 1.1: *Conceptual Perspectives*

Recite ❑
Review ❑

Describe the perspective—or conceptual model—that best fits your
current understanding of why people behave the way that they do. Be sure to explain why
you selected this particular perspective. Which perspectives do you reject? Why?

Essay Question 1.2: *Deceptive Practices*

Imagine yourself in the Latané and Darley experiment as one of the participants who delays
responding because of the diffusion of responsibility (you thought there were others around
to help). After the experiment, you discover that your behavior has been deceptively
manipulated and that the epileptic seizure was staged. What are your reactions to this
deception? What are the ethical constraints on the researchers? Can you suggest
alternatives to this kind of research? Is it justified?

Activities and Projects

1.   Use the following chart to create a time line of psychology's recent past. Include other major social and political events (wars, depressions and recessions, etc.) to broaden your perspective and to give the events in psychology greater context.

Recite ❑
Review ❑
_____

ERA	MAJOR EVENTS IN PSYCHOLOGY	OTHER EVENTS
1850		
1875		
1900		
1925		
1950		
1975		

2. Using naturalistic observation, select a person or group to observe. You might observe students immediately before taking an examination, someone on a bus or train, or a child. When you record your observations, make sure you write down behaviors—only what can be seen—do not make any inferences about what the behaviors might mean or what the person might be feeling. Recording behaviors appropriately, without making inferences, takes practice. The following chart can be used to focus your observations.

Naturalistic Observation: Recording Chart		
Conditions of Observation:		
Place of Observation:		
Starting Time: _____ **Ending Time:** _____ **Length:** _____		
Behavior	**Number of People engaging in Behavior**	**Number of Repetitions of Observed Behavior**

3.   Go to the library and select an article from a psychology journal in which an experiment is described. What is the format of the article? What is the investigator trying to discover? What are the independent and dependent variables? What are the treatment and control groups? What are the results and implications?

Format:

Stated Hypothesis:

Variables:

   Independent:

   Dependent:

Participants:

   Treatment Group:

   Control Group:

Results:

Were any aspects of the hypothesis not confirmed? Why?

Cultural Idioms

Recite ❑
Review ❑

p. 4

Superman: an American comic book hero with "super" powers, that is, abilities beyond the human realm

appearances are deceiving: what something looks like may not be the truth

the triumph of the human spirit: people are capable of doing very difficult, or "impossible," things when they want something with a great passion

the first stirrings: the beginning

p. 5

box, boxes: a sidebar. In this book, a "box" is a short section of writing that is separate from the main text. Each chapter has several boxes that add interesting information.

p. 6

critical analysis: thinking very carefully and logically about something

pinky: an informal word for the little finger

p. 7

family tree: a diagram of all your ancestors on both your mother and your father's side, going back as many generations as the family can remember

p. 8

losing touch with reality: when a person is very disoriented and cannot distinguish reality from fantasy, we say that this person has "lost touch with reality."

p. 9

child-rearing practices: the ways that a group or an individual raises children

genetic inheritance: what gets passed down from biological parents to their offspring, such as hair color

p. 10

home court advantage: the idea that it is easier to win a sports game (for example, basketball or baseball) if you are playing it on your own court or field

Head Start program: an educational program for three- and four-year-old children, paid for by the United States government. It serves children from low-income families.

Medicaid: a health insurance program for poor Americans

Help Wanted: a sign that means that an employer wants to find an employee. This is also a section of the newspaper where people look for jobs.

substance abuse: addiction to, or problems with, drugs or alcohol

p.11

not-for-profit, non-profit: an organization or company that doesn't try to make a profit (money); its main focus is to educate or help people

minorities, minority population, racial and ethnic minorities: In the U.S., the "majority" of the population is white. "Minorities" refers to members of other groups, such as African-Americans, Asians, Hispanics, Native Americans, and so forth. Members of the white population, such as women and Jewish people, can also be considered minorities.

p. 12

marriage counseling: When a couple has problems in their relationship, sometimes they seek the advice of a psychologist trained to help couples learn to communicate better, or to help them decide whether they should stay together or get a divorce.

assembly plant: a factory

p. 14

new kid on the block: a recent arrival

a set of pathways: a map

major landmarks: important events

building blocks: the pieces, like bricks, that are used to build something; the smaller units that go into something.

p. 15

Founding Mothers: This is the female counterpart to the phrase "Founding Fathers," which refers to the men who started this country—George Washington, Thomas Jefferson, John Hancock, Ben Franklin, and so forth. The Founding Mothers here refers to the women who were important in the beginnings of psychology.

p. 16

Blood, Sweat and Fears: Here, the author is making a pun about the ways that biology influences our reactions. Many English speakers know the phrase "blood, sweat, and tears," which refers to very hard work—work that is so hard that it makes you bleed, perspire, and cry.

Inner Person: your thoughts and feelings, your secrets

Outer Person: only what can be observed

slips of the tongue: when you say one word, but mean to say another word. For example, you say "wife" when you mean to say "life" or "refrigerator" when you mean to say "oven."

seething cauldron: Traditionally, a big pot where witches cooked up potions using mysterious ingredients like snakes. This means that our feelings are hard to know and perhaps dangerous.

p. 17

Homo sapiens: the Latin word for human being

p. 18

it shows little sign of letting up: it doesn't appear to be stopping.

p. 20

only skin deep: only on the surface, not inside. Differences that are only skin deep are not real differences.

p. 22

toilet plunger: a device with a long wooden handle and a suctioning head, used to unclog drains and toilets.

"bad Samaritanism": Good Samaritanism is acting to help strangers who are in trouble. (The Good Samaritan was a biblical figure who helped a stranger.) The author is reversing this phrase: "bad Samaritanism" is not helping others who obviously are in need of help".

p. 24

cramming for an exam: to stay up all night studying for an exam, usually because a student hasn't done any school work all semester.

p. 27

The New York Times **Business Poll:** *The New York Times* is one of the top newspapers in the United States. A poll is a survey, where pollsters (people who conduct the survey) telephone people and ask their opinions about different political issues. This cartoon is making fun of polls.

p. 32

right on target: 100 percent correct

"er" and "um": These are not words, but rather sounds that someone makes when they are struggling to speak.

p. 36

to violate the rights of participants: In U. S. culture, it is believed that human beings have certain basic human rights (you can't torture or experiment on people), and not to respect these rights is considered unethical.

authority figures: people with power and authority, such as police officers, parents, and teachers.

disproportionately white and middle class: For example, in the whole population of the U.S., white middle-class people are a certain percentage, but in the population of college students the percentage of white and middle-class students is much highert. If you want to represent the whole population, college students do not reflect the actual population, which consists of more low-income people and more members of minority groups.

p. 37

to ensure that animals do not suffer: In U. S. culture, where many people have pets such as cats and dogs, people believe that animals should be well treated.

"Even the best-laid experimental plans . . .": "best-laid plans" means projects or experiments that have been very carefully planned. The author means that even experiments that been very carefully designed can still have problems. He is making a reference to a famous saying: "Even the best laid plans of mice and men often go astray."

p. 38

"drug": In the United States the word "drug" can mean legal, prescribed medication as well as illegal, recreational drugs such as cocaine and heroin.

"Blind" as to the nature of the drug: here, "blind" means that the patients don't know whether they are getting a placebo or the real drug, and neither does the experimenter.

p. 39

a handful of respondents: only a few people

Brand X: When people want to talk about a specific product (for example, a well-known brand of aspirin) without actually naming the product, they say "Brand X." Advertisers use this phrase to avoid naming their competitors.

animals as subjects: See note above for "to ensure that animals do not suffer."

p. 40

welfare programs: these are government programs that help the low-income population, primarily unmarried women and their young children.

2 The Biology Underlying Behavior

Detailed Chapter Outline

This detailed outline contains all the headings in Chapter 2: The Biology Underlying Behavior. If you are using the SQ3R method, then an examination of the outline is the best way to begin your survey of the chapter.

Survey ❑
Question ❑

Prologue: Damage Control
Looking Ahead

Neurons: The Elements of Behavior
The Structure of the Neuron
Firing the Neuron
Where Neuron Meets Neuron: Bridging the Gap
Neurotransmitters: Multitalented Chemical Couriers

Recap, Review, and Rethink

The Nervous System: Structure and Evolutionary Foundations
Central and Peripheral Nervous Systems
  Activating the Autonomic Nervous System
The Evolutionary Foundations of the Nervous System
Behavioral Genetics

Recap, Review, and Rethink

The Brain
Studying the Brain's Structure and Functions: Spying on the Brain

Applying Psychology in the 21st Century: Your Wish
Is Its Command

The Central Core: Our "Old Brain"
The Limbic System: Beyond the Central Core
Recap, Review, and Rethink
The Cerebral Cortex: Our "New Brain"

The Motor Area of the Cortex
 The Sensory Area of the Cortex
 The Association Areas of the Cortex
 Mending the Brain

> **Pathways Through Psychology:** Ching-Yune Chen,
> Brain Laboratory Researcher

 The Specialization of the Hemispheres: Two Brains or One?

> **Exploring Diversity:** Human Diversity and the Brain

 The Split Brain: Exploring the Two Hemispheres
Brain Modules: The Architecture of the Brain

The Endocrine System: Of Chemicals and Glands

> **The Informed Consumer of Psychology:** Learning to Control Your
> Heart—and Mind—through Biofeedback

Recap, Review, and Rethink
Looking Back
Key Terms and Concepts

➤ Now that you have surveyed the chapter, read **Looking Ahead**, pages
46-47. What questions does the Chapter seek to answer?

Question ❑
Read ❑

Concepts and Learning Objectives

These are the concepts and the learning objectives for Chapter 2. Read them
carefully as part of your preliminary survey of the chapter.

Survey ❑

Concept 1: The biology of the organism affects its behavior. The brain and its basic building
blocks, the neurons, are the biological components that have the greatest influence on
behavior. Neurotransmitters are critical to various functions because they are the means by
which the neural message is communicated from one neuron to another.

 1. Understand the significance of the biology that underlies behavior, and identify reasons
why psychologists study these biological underpinnings, especially the brain and the
nervous system.

 2. Describe the structure of the neuron and its parts.

3. Describe the action and resting potential of the neuron, as well as the complete transmission of a message from initial stimulation to transmission across the synapse.

4. Name key neurotransmitters and their functions, and describe their known or suspected roles in behavior, as well as in illnesses.

Concept 2: The major divisions of the nervous system include the central and peripheral divisions, the autonomic and somatic divisions, and the sympathetic and parasympathetic divisions.

5. Describe the major divisions of the nervous system, including the central and peripheral, the autonomic and somatic, and the sympathetic and parasympathetic divisions.

6. Outline the major developments in the evolution of the nervous system, and describe the associated fields of evolutionary psychology and behavioral genetics.

Concept 3: The central core and the limbic system control and monitor basic life functions, as well as self-preservation needs.

7. Name the techniques used to map and study the brain, and describe some of the anatomical differences between the male and female brain that have been identified using these techniques.

8. Name the components of the central core and the limbic system, and describe the functions of their individual parts.

Concept 4: The higher brain functions are associated with the cerebral cortex. The role of the endocrine system is to communicate hormones that control growth and behavior through the bloodstream.

9. Name the major areas of the cerebral hemispheres, especially the lobes and the cortex areas, and describe the roles of each area in behavior.

10. Discuss the issues involved with brain specialization, brain lateralization, and the split-brain operation, including what has been learned about the two hemispheres from that procedure.

11. Name the major hormones and describe the function of the endocrine system.

12. Describe how biofeedback can be used to control some of the basic biological processes.

Chapter Guided Review

Survey ❑

There are several ways you can use this guided review as part of your systematic study plan. Read the corresponding pages of the text and then complete the review by supplying the correct missing key word. Or, you may want to complete the guided review as a means of becoming familiar with the text. Complete the review and then read the section thoroughly. As you finish each section, complete the **Recap and Review** questions that are supplied in the text.

CONCEPT 1:   Neurons: The Elements of Behavior

Survey ❑
Read ❑
Recite ❑

- ● *Why do psychologists study the brain and the nervous system?*
- ● *What are the basic elements of the nervous system?*
- ● *How does the nervous system communicate electrical and chemical messages from one part to another?*

Pages 47-54

Psychologists' understanding of the brain has increased dramatically in the past few years. *Neuroscientists* examine the biological underpinnings of behavior, and

[a] _____ explore the ways the biological structures and functions of the body affect behavior.

Specialized cells called **[b]** _____ are the basic component of the nervous system. There may be one trillion neurons involved in behavior. Every neuron has a nucleus, a cell body, and special structures for communicating with other neurons.

[c] _____ are the receiving structures and **[d]** _____ are the sending structures. At the ends of the axons are **[e]** _____ that serve to connect with other neurons. The message is communicated in one direction from the dendrites, through the cell body, and down the axon to the terminal buttons. A fatty substance

known as the **[f]** _____ surrounds the axons of most neurons and serves as an insulator for the electrical signal being transmitted down the axon. It also speeds up the signal. Certain substances necessary for the maintenance of the cell body travel up the axon to the cell body in a reverse flow. Amyotrophic lateral sclerosis (ALS), or Lou Gehrig's disease, is a failure of the neuron to work in this reverse direction.

The neuron communicates its message by "firing," which refers to its changing from a

[g] _____ to an **[h]** _____ . Neurons express the

action potential following the **[i]** _____ law, that is, firing only when a certain level of stimulation is reached. The stimulation involves a reversal of the electrical charge inside the neuron from -70 millivolts to a positive charge. This reversal flows very rapidly through the neuron, and the neuron quickly returns to its resting state. Just after the action potential has passed, the neuron cannot fire again for a brief period. The thickness of the myelin sheath and the diameter of the axon determine the speed of the action potential, with action potentials traveling down thicker axons much more rapidly. A neuron can fire as many as 1,000 times per second if the stimulus is very strong. However, the communicated message is a matter of how frequently or infrequently the neuron fires, not the intensity of the action potential, since the action potential is always the same strength.

The message of a neuron is communicated across the **[j]** _____ to the receiving neuron by the release of **[k]** _____ . The synapse is the small space between the terminal button of one neuron and the dendrite of the next. Neurotransmitters can either excite or inhibit the receiving neuron. The exciting neurotransmitter makes

[l] _____ , and the inhibiting neurotransmitter makes **[m]** _____ . A neuron must summarize the excitatory and inhibitory messages it receives in order to fire. Once the neurotransmitters are released, they lock into special sites on the receiving neurons.

They must then be reabsorbed through **[n]** _____ into the sending neuron or deactivated by enzymes.

About 100 neurotransmitters have been found. Neurotransmitters can be either exciting or inhibiting, depending on where in the brain they are released. The most common neurotransmitters are _acetylcholine_ (_ACh_), _gamma-amino butyric acid_ (_GABA_), _dopamine_ (_DA_), _serotonin_, _adenosine triphosphate_ (_ATP_), and _endorphins_.

CONCEPT 2:   The Nervous System

- **_In what way are the structures of the nervous system tied together?_**

Survey ❑
Read ❑
Recite ❑

Pages 55-59

The nervous system is divided into the **[a]** _____—composed of the brain and the spinal cord—and the peripheral nervous system. The **[b]** _____ is a bundle of nerves that descend from the brain. The main purpose of the spinal cord is as a pathway for communication between the brain and the body. Some involuntary behaviors, called

[c] _____ , involve messages that do not travel to the brain but instead stay

entirely within the spinal cord. **[d]** _____ neurons bring information from

the periphery to the brain. **[e]** _____ neurons carry messages to the

muscles and glands of the body. **[f]** _____ , a third type of neuron, connect the sensory and the motor neurons, carrying messages between them. The spinal cord is the major carrier of sensory and motor information. Its importance is evident in injuries that result in _quadriplegia_ and _paraplegia_. The **[g]** _____ branches out from the spinal

cord. It is divided into the **[h]** _____ , which controls muscle movement,

and the **[i]** _____ , which controls basic body functions like heartbeat, breathing, glands, and lungs.

The role of the autonomic nervous system is to activate the body through the

[j] _____ and then to modulate and calm the body through the

[k] _____. The sympathetic division prepares the organism for stressful situations; and the parasympathetic division returns the organism to help the body recover after the emergency has ended.

The branch of psychology known as **[l]** _____ attempts to provide answers concerning how our genetic inheritance from our ancestors influences the structure and function of our nervous system and influences everyday behavior. The new field known as

[m] _____ studies the effects of heredity on behavior.

CONCEPT 3: The Brain

- _How do researchers identify the major parts and functioning of the brain?_
- _What are the major parts of the brain, and what are the behaviors for which each part is responsible?_

Survey ❏
Read ❏
Recite ❏

Pages 60-66

Some knowledge of the structure and function of the brain has been gained by studying the results of injuries to the brain, and today, much additional knowledge is being added by using brain scans, techniques that picture the brain without having to perform an autopsy. The _electroencephalogram (EEG)_ records the electrical activity of the brain by using electrodes placed outside the skull. _Computerized axial tomography (CAT) scan_ utilizes computer imaging to construct an image that is made by combining thousands of separate x-rays taken from different angles. _Functional magnetic resonance imaging (fMRI) scan_ uses powerful magnets to create a picture of the brain. _Superconducting quantum interference device (SQUID) scan_ uses a powerful magnetic field to detect tiny changes in magnetic fields when neurons fire. _Positron emission tomography (PET) scan_ records the location of radioactive isotopes in the brain during brain activity, thus allowing a picture of the activity.

Because it evolved very early, the **[a]** _____ of the brain is referred to as the old brain. It is composed of the _medulla_, which controls functions like breathing and heartbeat; the _pons_, which transmits information helping to coordinate muscle activity on the

right and left halves of the body; and the **[b]** _____, which coordinates

muscle activity. The **[c]** _____ is a group of nerve cells extending from the medulla and the pons that serve to alert other parts of the brain to activity. The central core also

includes the **[d]** _____, which transmits sensory information, and the

[e] _____, which maintains _homeostasis_ of the body's environment. The hypothalamus also plays a role in basic survival behaviors like eating, drinking, sexual behavior, aggression, and child-rearing behavior.

The **[f]** _____ is a set of interrelated structures that includes pleasure centers and structures that control eating, aggression, reproduction, and self-preservation. Intense pleasure is felt through the limbic system, and rats with electrodes implanted in their limbic systems will often stimulate their pleasure centers rather than eat. The limbic system also plays important roles in learning and memory. The limbic system is sometimes called the "animal brain" because its structures and functions are so similar to those of other animals.

CONCEPT 4: **The Brain (continued)** **The Endocrine System: Of Chemicals and** **Glands**	*Survey* ❑ *Read* ❑ *Recite* ❑

Pages 66-79

The **[a]** _____ is identified with the functions that allow us to think and remember. The cerebral cortex is deeply folded in order to increase the surface area of the

covering. The cortex is divided into four main sections, or **[b]** _____.
They are the *frontal lobes*, the *parietal lobes*, the *temporal lobes*, and the *occipital lobes*. The lobes are separated by deep groves called sulci. The cortex and its lobes have been divided into three major areas: the motor area, the sensory area, and the association area.

The **[c]** _____ area of the brain is responsible for the control and direction of voluntary muscle movements. There are three areas devoted to the

[d] _____ area, that of touch, called the *somatosensory area*; that of sight, called the *visual area*; and that of hearing, called the *auditory area*. The

[e] _____ area takes up most of the cortex and is devoted to mental processes like language, thinking, memory, and speech. The condition called *apraxia* results when a person cannot integrate activities rationally or logically. An *aphasia* occurs when a person has difficulty with verbal expression. *Broca's aphasia* refers to difficulty with the production of speech. *Wernicke's aphasia* refers to brain damage that involves the loss of the ability to understand the speech of others.

The two halves of the brain are called **[f]** _____. The left hemisphere controls the right side of the body, and the right hemisphere controls the left side. Since each hemisphere appears to have functions that it controls, it is said that the brain is lateralized. The left hemisphere concentrates on verbally based skills, like thought and reason. The right half

deals with spatial understanding and pattern recognition. This **[g]** _____
appears to vary greatly with individuals, and there may be general differences between the brains of males and females, as males appear to have language more lateralized. The two halves of the brain are, however, quite interdependent on each other. The major difference that has been discovered is that the connecting fibers between the two hemispheres, called the *corpus callosum*, have different shapes in men and women.

Roger Sperry pioneered the study of the surgical separation of the two hemispheres for cases of severe epilepsy. Those who have had the procedure are called **[h]** _____.

The **[i]** _____ is a chemical communication network that delivers **[j]** _____ into the bloodstream which, in turn, influence growth and behavior. Sometimes called the "master gland," the **[k]** _____ gland is the major gland of the endocrine system. The hypothalamus regulates the pituitary gland.

"The Informed Consumer of Psychology" discusses the use of **[l]** _____ to control a variety of body functions. It has been successfully applied to the control of headaches, blood pressure, and other medical and physical problems.

➤ Now that you have surveyed, questioned, and read the chapter and completed the guided review, review **Looking Back**, pages 80-81.

Review ❑

➤ For additional practice through recitation and review, test your knowledge of the chapter material by answering the questions in the _Key Word Drill_, the _Practice Questions_, and the _Essay Questions_.

Key Word Drill

The following **Matching Questions** test the boldfaced and italicized key words from the text. Check your answers with the Answer Key in the back of the _Study Guide_.

Recite ❑

MATCHING QUESTIONS

_____ 1. neurons

_____ 2. dendrites

_____ 3. axon

_____ 4. terminal buttons

_____ 5. myelin sheath

a. Specialized cells that are the basic elements of the nervous system that carry messages.

b. Small branches at the end of an axon that relay messages to other cells.

c. A long extension from the end of a neuron that carries messages to other cells through the neuron.

d. An axon's protective coating, made of fat and protein.

e. Clusters of fibers at one end of a neuron that receive messages from other neurons.

_____ 6. neurotransmitter

_____ 7. excitatory message

_____ 8. inhibitory message

_____ 9. synapse

_____ 10. acetylcholine

_____ 11. endorphins

_____ 12. GABA

a. A chemical secretion that makes it more likely that a receiving neuron will fire and an action potential will travel down its axons.

b. A class of chemical secretions that behave such as pain-killing opiates.

c. A chemical messenger that inhibits behaviors like eating and aggression.

d. A chemical secretion that prevents a receiving neuron from firing.

e. A chemical that carries the message from one neuron to another when secreted as the result of a nerve impulse.

f. The gap between neurons across which chemical messages are communicated.

g. A chemical secretion that transmits messages relating to skeletal muscles and may also be related to memory.

_____ 13. peripheral nervous system

_____ 14. somatic division

_____ 15. autonomic division

_____ 16. sympathetic division

_____ 17. parasympathetic division

a. The part of the autonomic division of the peripheral nervous system that calms the body, bringing functions back to normal after an emergency has passed.

b. All parts of the nervous system _except_ the brain and the spinal cord (includes somatic and autonomic divisions).

c. The part of the nervous system that controls involuntary movement (the actions of the heart, glands, lungs, and other organs).

d. The part of the autonomic division of the peripheral nervous system that prepares the body to respond in stressful emergency situations.

e. The part of the nervous system that controls voluntary movements of the skeletal muscles.

_____ 18. central core

_____ 19. medulla

_____ 20. pons

_____ 21. cerebellum

_____ 22. reticular formation

_____ 23. thalamus

_____ 24. hypothalamus

_____ 25. corpus callosum

a. The part of the brain that joins the halves of the cerebellum, transmitting motor information to coordinate muscles and integrate movement between the right and left sides of the body.

b. A bundle of fibers that connects one half of the brain to the other and which is thicker in women than in men.

c. The part of the brain's central core that transmits messages from the sense organs to the cerebral cortex and from the cerebral cortex to the cerebellum and medulla.

d. The part of the central core of the brain that controls many important body functions, such as breathing and heartbeat.

e. The part of the brain that controls bodily balance.

f. The "old brain," which controls such basic functions as eating and sleeping and is common to all vertebrates.

g. A group of nerve cells in the brain that arouses the body to prepare it for appropriate action and screens out background stimuli.

h. Located below the thalamus of the brain, its major function is to maintain homeostasis.

_____ 26. limbic system

_____ 27. cerebral cortex

_____ 28. frontal lobes

_____ 29. temporal lobes

_____ 30. occipital lobes

_____ 31. motor area

_____ 32. somatosensory area

_____ 33. association area

a. The brain structure located at the front center of the cortex, containing major motor, speech, and reasoning centers.

b. The structures of the brain lying behind the temporal lobes; includes the visual sensory area.

c. The area within the cortex corresponding to the sense of touch.

d. One of the major areas of the brain, the site of the higher mental processes, such as thought, language, memory, and speech.

e. The "new brain," responsible for the most sophisticated information processing in the brain; contains the lobes.

f. The portion of the brain located beneath the frontal and parietal lobes; includes the auditory sensory areas.

g. One of the major areas of the brain, responsible for voluntary movement of particular parts of the body.

h. The part of the brain located outside the "new brain" that controls eating, aggression, and reproduction.

Practice Questions

Test your knowledge of the chapter material by answering these **Multiple Choice Questions**. These questions have been placed in three Practice Tests. The first two tests are composed of questions that will test your recall of factual knowledge. The third test contains questions that are challenging and primarily test for conceptual knowledge and your ability to apply that knowledge. Check your answers and review the feedback using the Answer Key in the back of the *Study Guide*.

Recite ❑
Review ❑

MULTIPLE CHOICE QUESTIONS

PRACTICE TEST I:

1. The function of a neuron's dendrites is to:
   a. frighten potential cellular predators.
   b. make waves in the liquid that bathes the neurons.
   c. give personality or uniqueness to each neuron.
   d. receive incoming signals relayed from other neurons.

2. Neurons communicate with each other through specialized structures known as:
   a. glial cells.
   b. myelin sheaths.
   c. somas.
   d. dendrites and axons.

3. The gap between neurons is called the:
   a. terminal button.
   b. cell body.
   c. synapse.
   d. refractory period.

4. A neurotransmitter affects particular neurons, but not others, depending upon whether:
   a. the receiving neuron expects a message to arrive.
   b. a suitable receptor site exists on the receiving neuron.
   c. the nerve impulse acts according to the all-or-none law.
   d. the receiving neuron is in its resting state.

5. The neural process of reuptake involves:
   a. the production of fresh neurotransmitters.
   b. the release of different neurotransmitter types by message-sending neurons.
   c. chemical breakdown of neurotransmitters by the receiving cell.
   d. soaking up of surplus neurotransmitters by the terminal button.

6. The portion of the nervous system that is particularly important for reflexive behavior is the:
   a. brain.
   b. spinal cord.
   c. sensory nervous system.
   d. motor nervous system.

7. Reflexes:
   a. are learned from infancy.
   b. involve the peripheral nervous system.
   c. always involve both the peripheral and central nervous systems.
   d. do not involve the cerebral cortex at all.

8. The autonomic nervous system controls:
   a. habitual, automatic movements such as applying the brakes of an automobile.
   b. the functions of the spinal cord.
   c. the body's response to an emergency or crisis.
   d. most of the spinal reflexes.

9. Which of the following is **not** likely to happen during activation of the sympathetic division of the nervous system?
   a. increase in digestion
   b. increase in heart rate
   c. increase in sweating
   d. increase in pupil size

10. Although "pleasure centers" are found at many brain sites, the most likely place to find them is in the:
    a. association areas of the cerebral cortex.
    b. limbic system.
    c. medulla.
    d. cerebellum.

11. Which of the following controls important bodily functions such as heartbeat and breathing?
    a. medulla
    b. cerebellum
    c. thalamus
    d. hypothalamus

12. _____ in the cerebral cortex enhance(s) the most sophisticated integration of neural information by providing for much greater surface area and complex interconnections among neurons.
    a. Convolutions
    b. Mapping
    c. Lateralization
    d. Hemispheric dominance

13. The area of the brain associated with thinking, language, memory, and speech is called the:
    a. sensory area.
    b. somatosensory area.
    c. motor area.
    d. association area.

14. When a person is unable to undertake purposeful, sequential behaviors, the condition is known as:
    a. dyslexia.
    b. aphasia.
    c. apraxia.
    d. paraplegia.

15. Sequential information processing is a characteristic of:
    a. the left cerebral hemisphere.
    b. the right cerebral hemisphere.
    c. the frontal lobes.
    d. the occipital lobes.

16. Which statement about the cerebral hemispheres does **not** apply to most right-handed people?
    a. The left hemisphere processes information sequentially.
    b. The right hemisphere processes information globally.
    c. The right hemisphere is associated with language and reasoning.
    d. Women display less hemispheric dominance than men, particularly with skills such as language.

17. Which response listed below is **least** likely to be treated with biofeedback?
    a. impotence
    b. headaches
    c. high blood pressure
    d. problems with maintaining optimal skin temperature

_____

PRACTICE TEST II:

18. Neurons share many structures and functions with other types of cells, but they also have a specialized ability to:
    a. be active, yet to consume almost no cellular energy.
    b. regenerate themselves even if injured very seriously.
    c. send messages to specific targets over long distances.
    d. live for a long time even after the official death of the body.

19. When an action potential has been fired, the neuron cannot fire again until:
    a. the resting state has been restored.
    b. the rising phase of the action potential has reached its peak.
    c. the reuptake of neurotransmitters has been blocked.
    d. the direction of the nerve impulse within the axon has been reversed.

20. Generally, neural impulses travel:
    a. electrically between and within each neuron.
    b. chemically between and within each neuron.
    c. electrically between neurons and chemically within each neuron.
    d. chemically between neurons and electrically within each neuron.

21. A deficiency of acetylcholine is associated with:
    a. depression.   c. Parkinson's disease.
    b. Alzheimer's disease.   d. Huntington's chorea.

22. According to the text, the main function of the endorphins is:
    a. contraction of muscle tissue.   c. smooth and coordinated motor movements.
    b. reduction of pain in the body. d. alertness and emotional expression.

23. Muscle tremors and rigidity result from _____ in neural circuits.
    a. excessive ACh   c. excessive dopamine
    b. not enough ACh   d. not enough dopamine

24. The peripheral nervous system consists of:
    a. the spinal cord and brain.
    b. all neurons with myelin sheath.
    c. all neurons other than those in the spinal cord or brain.
    d. entirely efferent neurons.

25. Sympathetic division is to parasympathetic division as:
    a. fight is to flight.   c. arousing is to calming.
    b. central is to peripheral.   d. helpful is to hurtful.

26. The _____ records the brain's ongoing neural activities via electrodes attached externally to the skull.
    a. electroencephalogram (EEG)   c. computerized axial tomography (CAT) scan
    b. magnetic resonance imaging (MRI) d. positron emission tomography (PET) scan

27. Which of the following structures is **not** directly involved in the control of motor function?
    a. cerebellum   c. pons
    b. medulla   d. spinal cord

28. The capacities to think and remember probably best distinguish humans from other animals. These qualities are most closely associated with the function of the:
    a. cerebral cortex.   c. cerebellum.
    b. medulla.   d. limbic system.

29. The diagram with parts of the "little man" on the surface of the motor cortex of a cerebral hemisphere shows that:
    a. body structures requiring fine motor movements are controlled by large amounts of neural tissue.
    b. major motor functions are controlled by the right hemisphere.
    c. large body parts on the diagram (e.g., fingers on a hand) receive little motor input.
    d. certain areas of the body are more responsive to touch, temperature, and other stimulation.

30. Which area has the largest portion of the cortex?
    a. motor area
    b. somatosensory area
    c. sensory area
    d. association area

31. Appreciation of music, art, and dance, and understanding of spatial relationships are more likely to be processed in the:
    a. right side of the brain.
    b. left side of the brain.
    c. occipital lobes.
    d. temporal lobe.

32. Damage to which of the following areas is most likely to cause people to have difficulty with pattern recognition tasks and spatial memory?
    a. frontal lobe
    b. left hemisphere
    c. right hemisphere
    d. temporal lobe

33. Injury to the _____ will disrupt the actions of many other glands of the endocrine system.
    a. ovaries or testes
    b. pancreas
    c. pituitary gland
    d. thyroid

34. Biofeedback is a technique to control internal biological states by:
    a. following the suggestions and strategies of a biologically trained facilitator or therapist.
    b. thinking positively about the biological responses to be modified.
    c. listening to a soothing audiocassette containing biorhythmic signals that alter biological responses in the brain.
    d. electronically monitoring biological responses so that adaptive tactics for changing those responses can be applied.

PRACTICE TEST III: Conceptual, Applied, and Challenging Questions

35. In multiple sclerosis, the _____ deteriorates, exposing parts of the _____. The result is a short circuit between the nervous system and muscle, which leads to difficulties with walking, vision, and with general muscle coordination.
    a. cell body; nucleus
    b. dendrite; terminal button
    c. terminal button; nucleus
    d. myelin sheath; axon

36. The purpose of reverse flow of some substances from the axon to the cell body is to:
    a. release neurotransmitters.
    b. clear metabolites from the cell.
    c. bring nourishment to the cell.
    d. regenerate an action potential after firing.

37. In **most** cases, after neurotransmitters have sent their message to the receiving neuron, they are:
    a. deactivated by enzymes.
    b. reabsorbed by the terminal buttons.
    c. absorbed into the body and filtered through the kidneys.
    d. absorbed into the receiving neuron.

38. The word most closely associated with the function of the limbic system is:
    a. thinking.
    b. waking.
    c. emergency.
    d. emotion.

39. According to the text, which of the following may be the most critical structure for maintaining homeostasis, a steady internal state of the body?
    a. hippocampus   c. hypothalamus
    b. cerebral cortex   d. cerebellum

40. Damage to or lesions in which of the following brain structures would be most likely to cause dramatic changes in emotionality and behavior?
    a. pons   c. cerebellum
    b. medulla   d. limbic system

41. Which of the following is true of both the sensory and motor areas of the cortex?
    a. They both contain pleasure centers.
    b. More cortical tissue is devoted to the most important structures.
    c. Electrical stimulation produces involuntary movement.
    d. Destruction of any one area affects all the senses.

42. Phineas was a shrewd, energetic business executive who persistently carried out all his plans of operation. After an injury to his head, he was no longer able to make plans or complete them. The dramatic changes in him following his accident suggest which area of his cerebral cortex was injured?
    a. neuromuscular   c. sensory-somatosensory
    b. association   d. motor

43. Which of the following is characterized by difficulty understanding the speech of others and producing coherent speech?
    a. Wernicke's aphasia   c. Broca's aphasia
    b. Lou Gehrig's disease   d. Phineas Gage's disease

44. Left hemisphere is to _____ function as right hemisphere is to _____ function.
    a. sequential; successive   c. successive; sequential
    b. sequential; global   d. global; sequential

45. Wernicke's aphasia is to _____ as Broca's aphasia is to _____.
    a. spasticity, flaccidity
    b. motor cortex; sensory cortex
    c. overeating, irregular gait
    d. difficulty in comprehending words; searching for the correct word.

46. One primary difference in the organization of male and female brains is that:
    a. logical abilities are on the opposite sides in males and females.
    b. language abilities are more evenly divided between the two hemispheres in females.
    c. the right hemisphere is almost always dominant in females.
    d. spatial abilities are on the opposite sides in males and females.

47. In all cases, a split-brain patient has had:
    a. a stroke.   c. damage to one of the hemispheres.
    b. the nerves between the hemispheres cut. d. epilepsy.

48. George has just been diagnosed with a disease that causes his neurons to die of starvation because they are unable to get chemical substances necessary for cell function to flow up the axon toward the cell body. The diagnosis is most likely:
    a. Alzheimer's disease.
    c. multiple sclerosis.
    b. Parkinson's disease.
    d. amyotrophic lateral sclerosis.

49. In the middle of a sentence, Dan becomes rigid and stares into space. After few minutes he shakes a little bit and then seems to return to the discussion. He explains that he has a common neural disorder related to a shortage of a neurotransmitter. His disorder is probably:
    a. Alzheimer's disease.
    c. multiple sclerosis.
    b. Parkinson's disease.
    d. amyotrophic lateral sclerosis.

50. Professor Evans records the activity of a set of neurons. As the neurons in the set increase their activity, surrounding neurons seem to slow down. What kind of messages are the neurons in the set most likely sending?
    a. sensory
    c. inhibitory
    b. motor
    d. autonomic

51. After a stroke, Janet could no longer tie her shoes, write, or make a tight fist. These deficits would be known as:
    a. Wernicke's aphasia.
    c. apraxia.
    b. Lou Gehrig's disease.
    d. Korsakoff's syndrome.

Essay Questions

Essay Question 2.1: *The Benefits of Knowledge about the Brain*

Recite ❑
Review ❑

Describe the specific benefits of our knowledge of brain function and the effect of injury on the brain. What are the possible consequences of research in neurotransmitters, biofeedback, and even sex differences in the brain?

Essay Question 2.2: *Ethics and Brain Research*

Several recent developments raise important questions for ethical consideration. What are the problems that arise when surgery separates the two hemispheres? What are the potential dangers of transplanting fetal tissue into the brain? Discuss these ethical and moral issues. Are there other issues?

Activities and Projects

Recite ❑
Review ❑

1. Fill in the labels that are missing from the following diagram of a neuron.

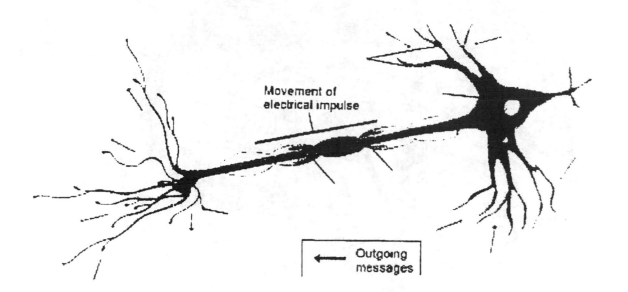

2. Fill in the labels that are missing from the diagram of the cortex of the left hemisphere of the brain.

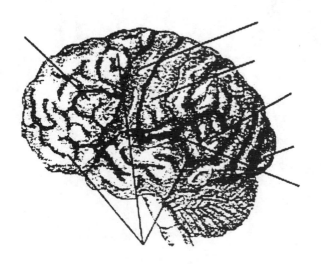

3.   Fill in the labels that are missing from the diagram of the brain.

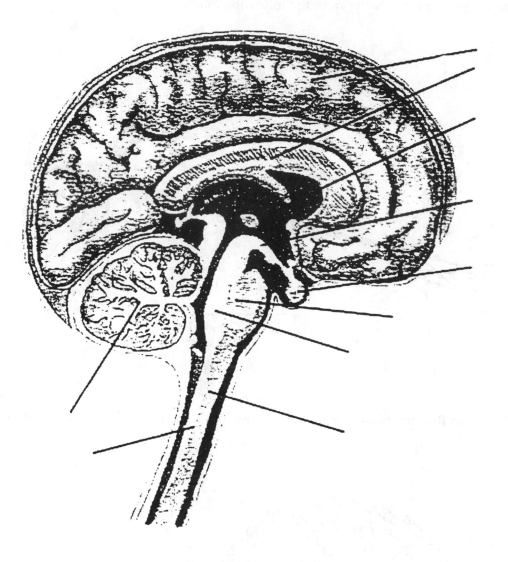

4. Fill in the labels and functions that are missing from this flowchart describing the parts of the nervous system.

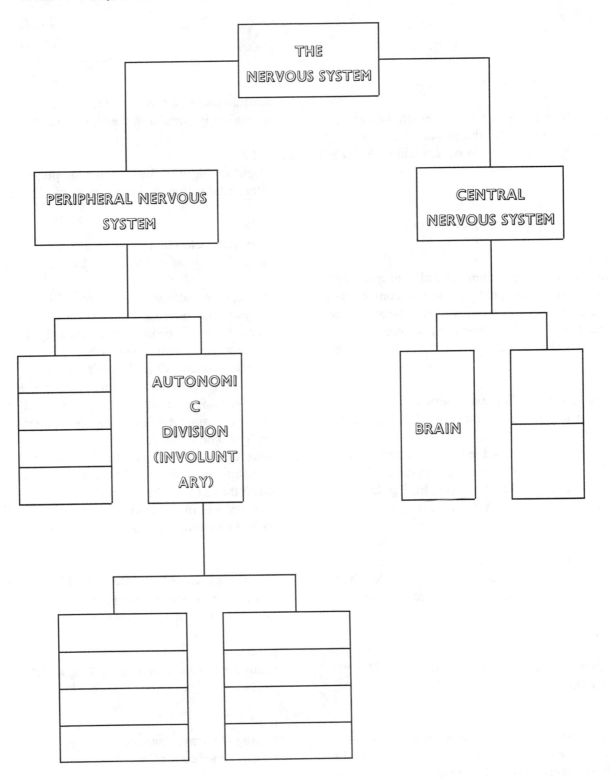

Cultural Idioms

Recite ❏
Review ❏

p. 46
culprit: literally, the guilty person; here, it means the reason for the stroke
little short of miraculous: amazing; almost a miracle

p. 47
executes a performance: performs

p. 48
short-circuiting, a short circuit: in electricity, when wires accidentally come into contact, they cause an electrical problem; here, the axons are like wires, and they must not interfere accidentally with each other.

p.49
Lou Gehrig: a famous American baseball player who played on the New York Yankees team
batting average: in the game of baseball, a player's batting average is a statistic that tells how successful the player is at hitting the ball.
dizzying speeds: extremely fast

p. 50
bridging the gap: creating a connection
radio kit: all the pieces and parts needed for a radio, with instructions how to put the pieces together to build it.

p. 52
lightning speed: as fast as a bolt of lightning; very fast.

p. 54
Mohammed Ali: American athlete who was the heavyweight boxing champion of the world. He now suffers from Parkinson's disease.
in its infancy: very new
joggers: people who run for sport or exercise

acupuncture: a form of Chinese medicine, increasingly popular in the United States

p. 57
"fight or flight": the human body prepares to either take action (fight) or run away (flight)

p. 58
everyday behavior: the way that human beings act under regular conditions in their day-to-day life
sexual orientation: whether an individual is heterosexual, homosexual, or bisexual
level of family conflict: how much fighting or how many problems a family has
learning disabilities: difficulty using, processing, and understanding language. People with learning disabilities can have normal or above average intelligence, but find situations such as school difficult.
general sociability: sociability is how much a person likes to be around other people; how much they enjoy other people
novelty-seeking behavior: constantly needing to find new things to do and experience

p. 59
a caution is in order: "Be careful." This is a warning to the student to understand that behavior is not simple; it is complex.

p, 60
scanning; brain scanning: taking a picture of the brain

p. 61
paving the way: leading
harnessing: controlling

p. 62

Your wish is its command: In folk legends, a magic character such as a genie often says, "Your wish is my command," meaning that the genie will do whatever you ask. Here, "your wish is its command" means that through thought alone (a "wish"), a person will be able to get a computer to do something.

mind-over-cursor: On a computer screen, the cursor is the blinking line that shows your place on the screen. Mind-over-cursor, a pun on the common English phrase "mind over matter," implies that a person can have the same control over the computer as they do over their body.

ever-vigilant guard: a person who is always awake and watching and protecting something valuable or an important person

p. 63

relay station: a place where messages pass through on their way to somewhere else; an intermediary place, not the final destination

basic survival; the Four Fs: fight (aggression), flight (running away), feeding (food), fornication (sex)

science fiction: stories and novels that take place in the future and involve ideas about how humans and life will be different in the future

p. 64

belligerent savages: wild and aggressive humans

p. 65

at a loss to describe: unable to describe

p. 68

lined up neatly: placed in a row; placed in order

p. 69

the senses: sight, hearing, taste, touch, and smell are the major senses

p. 70

wild schemes: unrealistic ideas

tip-of-the-tongue phenomenon: When you can't find the right word to use, but you know the word, you say, "It's on the tip of my tongue." This is normal, but with people suffering from Broca's aphasia, it happens all the time.

p. 71

rambling reply: an answer that doesn't directly answer the question. In U. S. culture when someone asks you a question, you are expected to answer the question directly. Thus, this patient's answer is inappropriate and an example of Wernicke's aphasia.

unraveling the brain's knotty mysteries: understanding the many complicated things about the brain. The image is of untying a big tangled ball of string.

an institution: a special school where children with serious disabilities go to live

p. 72

the gamble paid off: if you take a risk and you succeed.

test tube environment: in the laboratory, in glass jars (test tubes). This means that the cells were taken out of the mice's brains and looked at in a test tube.

p. 73

thorny ethical issues: difficult moral questions. (The difficult question here is that the cells that help people with Parkinson's disease come from abortions.)

mirror-image: exactly the same, but reversed, as though you were looking in a mirror. A person's right and a left hand are mirror images of each other.

p. 74

unearthed evidence: discovered

p. 76

last-ditch measure: the last possible thing you can try; a big risk

Nobel Prize: annual international prizes given for excellence in various fields (for example, chemistry, medicine, literature, peace). A Nobel Prize is the most important prize you can win in science.

blindfolded subjects: participants whose eyes were covered so they could not see.

p. 77

richness of thought: the wonderful and complex ways that humans can think and use their brains.

not strictly a one-way street: a one-way street is a road where a car can only travel in one direction. This means that the relationship is not completely in one direction.

p. 78

cruising: riding in a car

New York State Thruway: a highway in the state of New York

"I can bench-press 100 pounds": This refers to weight lifting. Bench press is when a person lies on their back and lifts barbells over their head with their arms. To bench press 100 pounds a person must have strong arms.

stationary bike: a bicycle that doesn't move because it has no wheels; it is a form of exercise equipment, to exercise the legs as though a person were riding a bicycle.

p. 79

hooked up to an apparatus: attached to a machine.

curvature of the spine: a medical problem of the back; when the main bones of a person's back bend or curve in a way that is not normal.

p. 80

snapshot: a photograph

p. 81

hallmarks of being human: the main characteristics of being human; what separates us from other creatures

Sensation and Perception

Smell

Taste

The Skin Senses: Touch, Pressure, Temperature, and Pain

	Pathways Through Psychology: James C. Willcockson, Pain Management Center Coordinator

Recap, Review, and Rethink

Perceptual Organization: Constructing Our View of the World

The Gestalt Laws of Organization

Feature Analysis: Focusing on the Parts of the Whole

Top-Down and Bottom-Up Processing

Perceptual Constancy

Depth Perception: Translating 2-D to 3-D

Motion Perception: As the World Turns

Perceptual Illusions: The Deceptions of Perceptions

	Exploring Diversity: Culture and Perception

Subliminal Perception and Other Perceptual Controversies

Extrasensory Perception (ESP)

	The Informed Consumer of Psychology: Managing Pain

Recap, Review, and Rethink
Looking Back
Key Terms and Concepts

➤ Now that you have surveyed the chapter, read **Looking Ahead**, pages 84-85. What questions does the Chapter seek to answer?

Question ❑
Read ❑

Concepts and Learning Objectives

These are the concepts and the learning objectives for Chapter 3. Read them carefully as part of your preliminary survey of the chapter.

Survey ❑

Concept 1: Sensation is the means by which information from the world around us is conveyed to the brain. The study of sensation requires examining the nature of physical stimuli and its relationship to the kinds of sensory responses they can evoke.

1. Define sensation and stimulus.

2. Distinguish among absolute threshold, signal detection theory, just noticeable difference, and sensory adaptation.

Concept 2: Vision is the most studied of the five-plus senses, and the details of the transfer of a light image from its entrance into the eye, through its transformation into a neural message, to its destination in the visual cortex, illustrates the complexity of sensation.

3. Describe the structural components of the eye, the initial processing of light, and adaptation to different light levels.

4. Discuss how an image is conveyed from the eye to the brain, and the role of feature detection in processing visual information.

5. Explain the trichromatic and opponent-process theories, and how they account for color vision.

Concept 3: The ear is responsible for detecting sound, body position, and movement. Smell and taste are detected through chemical contact. The skin senses include touch, pressure, temperature, and pain.

6. Describe the structural parts of the ear, the role of each part in detecting sound, and the basic physical properties of sound.

7. Describe how semicircular canals detect motion and produce the sense of balance.

8. Describe the sensory mechanisms of smell and taste.

9. Describe the skin senses of touch, pressure, and temperature, and explain the gate-control theory of pain.

Concept 4: Perception is the means of organizing and giving meaning to sensory information. The gestalt approach begins with perceptual organization founded on basic laws of organization. Feature analysis identifies the components of sensory information and combines them into complex perception.

10. Define perception and distinguish it from sensation.

11. Distinguish between the gestalt approach and feature analysis.

12. Distinguish between top-down and bottom-up processing.

13. Explain perceptual constancy, depth perception, and motion perception.

14. Describe and illustrate the major perceptual illusions, especially the Müller-Lyer and the Poggendorf illusions.

15. Discuss the evidence for the existence of subliminal perception and extrasensory perception.

Chapter Guided Review

There are several ways you can use this guided review as part of your systematic study plan. Read the corresponding pages of the text and then complete the review by supplying the correct missing key word. Or, you may want to complete the guided review as a means of becoming familiar with the text. Complete the review and then read the section thoroughly. As you finish each section, complete the **Recap and Review** questions that are supplied in the text.

Survey ❑

CONCEPT 1:   Sensing the World Around Us

- *What is sensation and how do psychologists study it?*
- *What is the relationship between the nature of a physical stimulus and the kinds of sensory responses that result from it?*

Survey ❑
Read ❑
Recite ❑

Pages 85-89

A **[a]** _____ is the activity of the sense organ when it detects a stimulus. The difference between perception and sensation is that sensation involves the organism's first encounter with physical stimuli, and **[b]** _____ is the process of interpreting, analyzing, and integrating sensations.

We detect the world around us through our senses. A **[c]** _____ is any physical energy that can be detected by a sense organ. Stimuli vary in type and intensity.

Intensity refers to the physical strength of the stimulus. **[d]** _____ studies the relationship between the strength of a stimulus and the nature of the sensory response it creates.

[e] _____ refers to the smallest amount of energy, the smallest intensity, needed to detect a stimulus. The absolute threshold for sight is illustrated by a candle burning at 30 miles away on a dark night; for hearing, the ticking of a watch 20 feet away in a quiet room; for taste, one teaspoon of sugar in two gallons of water; for smell, one drop of perfume in three rooms; and for touch, a bee's wing falling one centimeter onto a cheek. *Noise* refers to the background stimulation for any of the senses.

The ability to detect a stimulus is influenced not only by the stimulus but also by conditions like expectations and experience. **[f]** _____ attempts to explain the role of psychological factors in detecting stimuli. Two errors can be made while a subject is detecting stimuli: one, that a stimuli is present when it is not, and the other, that the stimuli is not present when it actually is. Signal detection theory has great practical importance, ranging from helping people who must distinguish various items on radar screens to improving how witnesses identify suspects in a police lineup.

The smallest noticeable difference between two stimuli is called the **[g]** _____, or the **[h]** _____. The amount of stimulus required for the just noticeable difference depends upon the level of the initial stimulus. **[i]** _____ states that the just noticeable difference is a constant proportion for each sense. Weber's law is not very accurate at extreme high or low intensities.

After prolonged exposure to a sensory stimulus, the capacity of the sensory organ adjusts to the stimulus in a process called **[j]** _____. The sensory receptor cells are most responsive to changes in stimuli because constant stimulation produces adaptation. Context also affects judgments about sensory stimuli. People's reactions to sensory stimuli do not always accurately represent the physical stimuli that cause it.

CONCEPT 2: Vision: Shedding Light on the Eye

Survey ❑
Read ❑
Recite ❑

- *What are the basic processes that underlie the sense of vision?*
- *How do we see colors?*

Pages 90-99
The stimulus that produces vision is light. Light is the electromagnetic radiation that our visual apparatus is capable of detecting. The range of visible light is called the
[a] _____.

Light enters the eye through the **[b]** _____, a transparent, protective window. It then passes through the **[c]** _____, the opening in the

[d] _____. The iris is the pigmented muscle that opens and closes the pupil depending on how much light is in the environment. The narrower the pupil is, the greater is the focal distance for the eye. After the pupil the light passes through the *lens*, which then bends and focuses the light on the back of the eye by changing its thickness, a process called

accommodation. The light then strikes the **[e]** _____, a thin layer of nerve cells at the back of the eyeball. The retina is composed of light-sensitive cells called

[f] _____, which are long and cylindrical, and

[g] _____, which are shorter and conical in shape. The greatest concentration of cones is in the *fovea*, an area that is extremely sensitive. Cones are responsible for color vision, and rods are insensitive to color and play a role in *peripheral vision*, the ability to see objects to our side, and in night vision.

When a person goes into a dark room from a well-lit space, the person becomes, after a time, accustomed to the dark and experiences **[h]** _____, an adjustment by the eyes to low levels of light. The changes that make this adjustment are chemical changes in the rods and cones.

Rods contain **[i]** _____, a complex substance that changes chemically when struck by light. This chemical change sets off a reaction. The response is then transmitted to two other kinds of cells, first to the *bipolar cells* and then to *ganglion cells*. The ganglion cells

organize and summarize the information and then convey it to the **[j]** _____. Where the optic nerve goes from the retina back through the eyeball there are no rods or cones, which results in the blind spot. The optic nerves from both eyes meet behind the eyes at the

eyes meet behind the eyes at the [k] _____ where each optic nerve splits. Nerve impulses from the right half of each eye go to the right side of the brain, and nerve impulses from the left half of each eye go to the left half of the brain. The disease called *glaucoma* is a restriction of the nerve impulses across the optic nerve. The restriction is caused by buildup of fluid in the eye, and as the pressure increases, the vision becomes more restricted,

resulting in [l] _____.

The visual message is processed from the beginning by ganglion cells, and continues to the visual cortex, where many neurons are highly specialized. Their roles are specialized to detect

certain visual features, and the process is called [m] _____.

A person with normal color vision can distinguish about seven million different colors. Color vision involves two processes. The first of these processes is called the

[n] _____. This theory says that there are three types of cones: one sensitive to blue-violet colors, another sensitive to green, and another sensitive to red-yellow. This theory does not explain how two colors mix to make gray, and it does not explain

afterimages. [o] _____ explains afterimages as the result of the opposing color of linked pairs of cones continuing to compensate for the stimulation of the first color. Apparently, the trichromatic process is at work at the level of the retina, and the opponent processes are at work at the retinal level and at later stages in the processing of visual information. The processing of visual information takes place in all parts of the visual system.

CONCEPT 3: Hearing and the Other Senses

- *What role does the ear play in the senses of sound, motion, and balance?*
- *How do smell and taste function?*
- *What are the skin senses, and how do they relate to the experience of pain?*

Survey ❏
Read ❏
Recite ❏

Pages 100-109

[a] _____ is the movement of air that results from the vibration of objects. The *outer ear* collects sounds and guides them to the internal portions of the ear. Sounds are funneled into the *auditory canal* toward the [b] _____. Sound waves hit the eardrum, which in turn transmits its vibrations into the [c] _____. The middle ear contains three small bones, the *hammer*, the *anvil*, and the *stirrup*. These three bones transmit the vibrations to the [d] _____. Each step of the way amplifies the sound waves that reach the ear. The *inner ear* contains the organs for transmitting the sound waves into nerve impulses as well as the organs for balance and position. The [e] _____ is a coiled tube that contains the [f] _____. The basilar membrane is covered with [g] _____ that vibrate. Sound may also enter the cochlea through the bones that surround the ear.

Sound is characterized by *frequency*, or the number of waves per second, and *pitch* is our experience of this number as high or low. *Intensity* may be thought of as the size of the waves—how strong it is. Intensity is measured in *decibels*. The **[h]** _____ is based on the fact that parts of the basilar membrane are sensitive to different pitches. The **[i]** _____ suggests that the entire basilar membrane vibrates in response to any sound, and the nerves send signals that are more frequent for higher pitches and less frequent for lower pitches. Both of these theories appear to have merit. The auditory cortex appears to be like a map of frequencies, with cells that respond to frequencies close to each other.

The inner ear is also responsible for the sense of balance. The disturbance of the sense of balance is called *vertigo*. The structures responsible for balance are the **[j]** _____, three tubes filled with fluid that moves around in the tubes when the head moves. The fluid affects **[k]** _____, small motion-sensitive crystals in the semicircular canals.

We are able to detect about 10,000 different smells, and women have a better sense of smell than do men. Some animals can communicate using odor. Odor is detected by molecules of a substance coming into contact with the *olfactory cells* in the nasal passages. Each olfactory cell responds to a narrow band of odors. **[l]** _____ are chemicals that can produce a reaction in members of a species. These chemicals have a role in sexual activity and identification. Taste is detected by *taste buds* on the tongue. Taste buds detect sweet, sour, salty or bitter flavors. The experience of taste also includes the odor and appearance of food.

The **[m]** _____ include touch, pressure, temperature, and pain. Receptor cells for each of these senses are distributed all over the body, though each sense is distributed in varying concentrations. The major theory of pain is called the **[n]** _____. This theory states that nerve receptors send messages to the brain areas related to pain, and whenever they are activated, a "gate" to the brain is opened and pain is experienced. The gate can be shut by overwhelming the nerve pathways with non-painful messages. It can also be closed by the brain producing messages to reduce or eliminate the experience of pain. *Acupuncture* may be explained by the first option, in which the needles shut off the messages going to the brain. Endorphins may also close the gate.

CONCEPT 4: Perceptual Organization: Constructing Our View of the World

Survey ❑
Read ❑
Recite ❑

- *What principles underlie our organization of the visual world, allowing us to make sense of our environment?*
- *How are we able to perceive the world in three dimensions when our retinas are capable of sensing only two-dimensional images?*
- *What clues do visual illusions give us a about our understanding of general perceptual mechanisms?*

Pages 110-123

Errors in perception occur because perception is an *interpretation* of sensory information. The distinction between *figure* and *ground* is crucial to perceptual organization. The tendency is to form an object in contrast to its ground, or background. This is illustrated by the two faces versus a single vase.

Through perception we try to simplify complex stimuli in the environment. This tendency toward simplicity and organization into meaningful wholes follows basic principles called the

[a] _____. *Gestalt* refers to a "pattern." Basic patterns identified by the gestalt psychologists are: (1) *closure*, groupings tend to be in complete or enclosed figures; (2) *proximity*, elements close together tend to be grouped together; (3) *similarity*, elements that are similar tend to be grouped together; and (4) *simplicity*, the tendency to organize patterns in a basic, straightforward manner. The gestalt psychologists argued that perception goes beyond combining individual elements and that when we organize the elements, we actively make the result more than the parts.

The recent approach called **[b]** _____ suggests that we perceive first the individual components and then formulate an understanding of the overall picture. Specific neurons respond to highly specific components of stimuli, suggesting that each stimuli is composed of a series of component features. In this view, our perception involves matching new stimuli to components in memory. One theory has identified 36 fundamental components that form the basic components of complex objects. Treisman has proposed that perception requires a two-stage process; first a *preattentive stage,* and then a *focused-attention stage*.

Perception proceeds in two ways, though top-down or through bottom-up processing. In

[c] _____ perception is controlled by higher-level knowledge, experience, expectations, and motivation. Top-down processing helps sort through ambiguous stimuli or missing elements. Context is critical for filling in missing information. Isolated stimuli illustrate how context is important for top-down processing. **[d]** _____ consists of recognizing and processing information about individual components. If we cannot recognize individual components, recognizing the complete picture would be very difficult.

One phenomena that contributes to our perception of the world is that of

[e] _____, the tendency for objects to be perceived as unvarying and consistent even as we see them from different views and distances. The rising moon is one example of how perceptual constancy works. The moon illusion is explained as resulting from the intervening cues of landscape and horizon that give it context. When it rises, there are no context cues. Perceptual constancies occur with size, shape, and color.

The ability to view the world in three dimensions is called **[f]** _____.
The two slightly different positions of the eyes give rise to minute differences in the visual

representation in the brain, a phenomenon called **[g]** _____. Discrepancy between the two images from the retinas gives clues to the distance of the object or the distance between two objects. The larger the disparity, the larger the distance. Other cues for visual depth perception can be seen with only one eye, and so they are called

[h] _____. *Motion parallax* is a monocular cue in which the position of distant objects moves on the retina slower than does the position of closer objects when the head moves. *Relative size* depends on the distant object having a smaller retinal image. *Linear perspective* is the phenomena in which railroad tracks appear to join together.

Motion perception judges the movement of objects relevant to stable objects. However, our perception compensates for head and eye movements. When objects move too fast for the eye to follow, we tend to anticipate the direction and speed of movement.

The importance of our knowledge about perception has been evident since the time of the ancient Greeks. The Parthenon in Athens is built with an intentional illusion to give the building a greater appearance of straightness and stability. **[i]** _____ are physical stimuli that produce errors in perception. The *Poggendorf illusion* and the *Müller-Lyer illusion* are two of the more well-known illusions. Explanations of the **[j]** _____ focus on the apparatus of the eye and the interpretations made by the brain. The eye-based explanation suggests that the eyes are more active where the arrow tips point inward, giving the illusion of greater length. The brain-base explanation suggests that we interpret the lines with the inward arrows as being interior spaces and the outward pointing lines as closed exterior spaces. In comparison, the inside corner then seems larger. Cultural differences play an important role also. We have difficulty drawing the "devil's tuning fork" because it is contradictory to our expectations. However, for individuals for whom the picture has no meaning, it is easy to draw by simply copying the lines.

[k] _____ is the process of perceiving messages without our awareness of their being presented. Research has shown that the subliminal message does not lead to attitude or behavior change. Another controversial area is that of *extrasensory perception* (*ESP*). Claims of ESP are difficult to substantiate.

A number of methods for dealing with pain have been developed. They include drug therapy, hypnosis, biofeedback, relaxation techniques, surgery (cutting the nerve fiber that carries the pain message), nerve and brain stimulation (using *transcutaneous electrical nerve stimulation*, or *TENS*), and psychological counseling.

➤ Now that you have surveyed, questioned, and read the chapter and completed the guided review, review **Looking Back**, pages 124-126.

Review ❑

➤ For additional practice through recitation and review, test your knowledge of the chapter material by answering the questions in the **Key Word Drill**, the **Practice Questions**, and the **Essay Questions**.

Key Word Drill

The following **Matching Questions** test the boldfaced and italicized key words from the text. Check your answers with the Answer Key in the back of the *Study Guide*.

Recite ❑

MATCHING QUESTIONS

_____ 1. sensation

_____ 2. intensity

_____ 3. absolute threshold

_____ 4. noise

_____ 5. difference threshold

a. The strength of a stimulus.

b. The smallest detectable difference between two stimuli.

c. The process of responding to a stimulus.

d. The smallest amount of physical intensity by which a stimulus can be detected.

e. Background stimulation that interferes with the perception of other stimuli.

_____ 6. pupil

_____ 7. cornea

_____ 8. iris

_____ 9. lens

_____ 10. retina

_____ 11. fovea

_____ 12. rhodopsin

_____ 13. rods

_____ 14. cones

_____ 15. ganglion cells

_____ 16. optic nerve

a. The colored part of the eye.

b. The part of the eye that converts the electromagnetic energy of light into useful information for the brain.

c. A complex reddish-purple substance that changes when energized by light, causing a chemical reaction.

d. A dark hole in the center of the eye's iris that changes size as the amount of incoming light changes.

e. A very sensitive region of the retina that aids in focusing.

f. A transparent, protective window into the eyeball.

g. The part of the eye located behind the pupil that bends rays of light to focus them on the retina.

h. Light-sensitive receptors that are responsible for sharp focus and color perception, particularly in bright light.

i. Nerve cells that collect and summarize information from rods and carry it to the brain.

j. Light-sensitive receptors that perform well in poor light but are largely insensitive to color and small details.

k. A bundle of ganglion axons in the back of the eyeball that carry visual information to the brain.

_____ 17. outer ear

_____ 18. auditory canal

_____ 19. eardrum

_____ 20. middle ear

_____ 21. oval window

a. The visible part of the ear that acts as a collector to bring sounds into the internal portions of the ear.

b. A tiny chamber containing three bones—the hammer, the anvil, and the stirrup—that transmit vibrations to the oval window.

c. The part of the ear that vibrates when sound waves hit it.

d. A thin membrane between the middle ear and the inner ear that transmits vibrations while increasing their strength.

e. A tubelike passage in the ear through which sound moves to the eardrum.

_____ 22. cochlea

_____ 23. basilar membrane

_____ 24. hair cells

_____ 25. frequency

_____ 26. pitch

_____ 27. decibel

_____ 28. otoliths

a. A measure of sound loudness or intensity.

b. The number of wave crests occurring each second in any particular sound.

c. A structure dividing the cochlea into an upper and a lower chamber.

d. A coiled tube filled with fluid that receives sound via the oval window or through bone conduction.

e. Crystals in the semicircular canals that sense body acceleration.

f. The characteristic that makes sound "high" or "low."

g. Tiny cells that, when bent by vibrations entering the cochlea, transmit neural messages to the brain.

_____ 29. gestalts

_____ 30. closure

_____ 31. proximity

_____ 32. similarity

_____ 33. simplicity

_____ 34. figure/ground

a. The tendency to group together those elements that are similar in appearance.

b. Patterns studied by the gestalt psychologists.

c. The tendency to perceive a pattern in the most basic, straightforward, organized manner possible—the overriding gestalt principle.

d. The tendency to group together those elements that are close together.

e. Figure refers to the object being perceived, whereas ground refers to the background or spaces within the object.

f. The tendency to group according to enclosed or complete figures rather than open or incomplete ones.

_____ 35. perceptual constancy

_____ 36. depth perception

_____ 37. binocular disparity

_____ 38. monocular cues

_____ 39. motion parallax

_____ 40. relative size

_____ 41. linear perspective

_____ 42. visual illusion

a. The ability to view the world in three dimensions and to perceive distance.

b. The change in position of the image of an object on the retina as the head moves, providing a monocular cue to distance.

c. The phenomenon by which, if two objects are the same size, the one that makes a smaller image on the retina is perceived to be farther away.

d. The phenomenon by which physical objects are perceived as unvarying despite changes in their appearance or the physical environment.

e. Signals that allow us to perceive distance and depth with just one eye.

f. The difference between the images that reach the retina of each eye; this disparity allows the brain to estimate distance.

g. The phenomenon by which distant objects appear to be closer together than nearer objects, a monocular cue.

h. A physical stimulus that consistently produces errors in perception (often called an optical illusion).

Practice Questions

Test your knowledge of the chapter material by answering these **Multiple Choice Questions**. These questions have been placed in three Practice Tests. The first two tests are composed of questions that will test your recall of factual knowledge. The third test contains questions that are challenging and primarily test for conceptual knowledge and your ability to apply that knowledge. Check your answers and review the feedback using the Answer Key in the back of the *Study Guide*.

Recite ❑
Review ❑

MULTIPLE CHOICE QUESTIONS

PRACTICE TEST I:

1. A focus of interest on the biological activity of the sense organ is typical in:
   a. sensory psychology.
   b. perceptual psychology.
   c. gestalt psychology.
   d. illusionary psychology.

2. Psychophysicists define absolute threshold as the:
   a. minimum amount of change in stimulation that is detectable.
   b. range of stimulation to which each sensory channel is sensitive.
   c. maximum intensity that is detectable to the senses.
   d. minimum magnitude of stimulus that is detectable.

3. On the day after his wedding, a groom is very conscious of the feeling of his wedding band on his finger, but two months later he does not notice the ring at all. This change has occurred because of the principle of:
   a. the difference threshold.
   b. sexual experience.
   c. bottom-up perceptual processing.
   d. sensory adaptation.

4. As the available light diminishes, the pupil:
   a. gets larger.
   b. gets smaller.
   c. remains the same.
   d. changes according to the wavelength of the light.

5. The process that causes incoming images to be focused in the eye is called:
   a. accommodation.
   b. constriction.
   c. adaptation.
   d. contraction.

6. Which of the following are found primarily in the fovea of the retina?
   a. ganglion cells
   b. rods
   c. bipolar cells
   d. cones

7. Which type of receptor is used in peripheral vision?
   a. cone
   b. rod
   c. fovea
   d. rhodopsin

8. Feature detection is best described as the process by which specialized neurons in the cortex:
    a. identify fine details in a larger pattern.
    b. see things clearly that are far away.
    c. discriminate one face from another.
    d. recognize particular shapes or patterns.

9. The contemporary view of color vision is that the _____ theory is true only for early stages of visual processing, but the _____ theory applies correctly to both early and later stages.
    a. trichromatic; gate-control   c. place; gate-control
    b. trichromatic; opponent-process   d. opponent-process; trichromatic

10. The function of the three tiny bones of the middle ear is to:
    a. add tension to the basilar membrane.
    b. prevent the otoliths from becoming mechanically displaced.
    c. amplify sound waves being relayed to the oval window.
    d. minimize the disorienting effects of vertigo.

11. Compared with high-frequency sound, low-frequency sound:
    a. has more peaks and valleys per second.
    b. generates an auditory sensation of low pitch.
    c. has a lower decibel value.
    d. is heard by pets such as cats or dogs but not by humans.

12. The sense of taste and the sense of smell are alike in that they both:
    a. have four basic qualities of sensation.
    b. depend on chemical molecules as stimuli.
    c. use the same area of the cortex.
    d. utilize opponent processes.

13. Which of the following theories holds that certain nerve receptors lead to specific areas of the brain that sense pain?
    a. endorphin   c. opponent process
    b. opiate   d. gate control

14. The gestalt laws of organization are best described as:
    a. patterns of perceiving determined by specific functions of neural receptors.
    b. principles that describe how people perceive.
    c. an explanation for how neural networks in the sensory system operate.
    d. explanations of how people determine the quality of a work of art.

15. The fact that a number of instruments all blend together to form a symphony orchestra demonstrates:
    a. a figure/ground relationship.
    b. the law of similarity.
    c. that the whole is more than the sum of its parts.
    d. the law of perceptual constancy.

16. Perception that is guided by higher-level knowledge, experience, expectations, and motivations is called:
    a. top-down processing.
    b. bottom-up processing.
    c. perceptual constancy.
    d. feature analysis.

17. Suppose that a person's racial prejudices influenced whether she perceived people as workers or vagrants. This would best demonstrate:
    a. preattentive perceptual processing.
    b. bottom-up processing.
    c. gestalt perceptual organization.
    d. top-down perceptual processing.

18. Binocular disparity refers to the fact that:
    a. the world looks different with prescription glasses than without.
    b. objects appear closer when they are larger.
    c. the visual image on the retina of each eye is slightly different.
    d. objects progressing into the distance, such as railroad tracks, appear to converge.

19. Railroad tracks appear to come closer together as they move away from the observer as a result of:
    a. linear perspective.
    b. figure/ground.
    c. binocular disparity.
    d. motion parallax.

20. The perception of messages about which the person is unaware is called:
    a. extrasensory perception.
    b. subliminal perception.
    c. cognition in the Ganzfeld.
    d. otolithic preprocessing.

PRACTICE TEST II:

21. The study of the relationship between the physical nature of stimuli and a person's sensory responses to them is called:
    a. introspection.
    b. operationalization.
    c. psychophysics.
    d. perception.

22. The objective of signal detection theory in psychophysics is to:
    a. determine absolute thresholds.
    b. explain the role of psychological factors.
    c. explain magnitude estimation.
    d. determine the nature of the stimulus.

23. A dog's nose is more sensitive to smells than is a human's nose. It then would be expected that the absolute threshold for smell will be _____ amount of odorant for a dog than for a person.
    a. a much larger
    b. a moderately larger
    c. about the same
    d. a smaller

24. The organ that gives your eyes their identifying color is:
    a. the retina.
    b. the pupil.
    c. the cornea.
    d. the iris.

25. The function of the retina is to:
    a. turn the image of the object upside down.
    b. redistribute the light energy in the image.
    c. convert the light energy into neural impulses.
    d. control the size of the pupil.

26. The visual receptors most useful for night vision are called:
    a. buds.   c. ossicles.
    b. cones.   d. rods.

27. Glaucoma may lead to blindness through:
    a. deterioration of the cones.
    b. deterioration of the rods.
    c. buildup of the myelin sheaths around the optic nerve.
    d. buildup of pressure within the eye.

28. Dark adaptation refers to the fact that:
    a. our eyes are less sensitive to a dim stimulus when we look directly at it rather than slightly to the side of it.
    b. the color of objects changes at dusk as light intensity decreases.
    c. the eyes become many times more sensitive after being exposed to darkness.
    d. some people have great difficulty seeing things under low levels of illumination.

29. According to the text, afterimages can best be explained by the:
    a. opponent-process theory of color vision.
    b. trichromatic theory of color vision.
    c. place theory of color vision.
    d. receptive-field theory of color vision.

30. People hear the sound of their own voice differently from the way others hear it primarily because of:
    a. bone conduction.
    b. tympanic vibrations.
    c. low-frequency vibrations.
    d. gradual hearing loss associated with age.

31. Chemical molecules that promote communication between members of a species are called:
    a. pheromones.   c. hormones.
    b. neurotransmitters.   d. odorants.

32. Which statement about the taste buds is accurate?
    a. Each receptor is able to respond to many basic tastes and to send the information to the brain.
    b. Over twelve types of receptors for different basic tastes have been described.
    c. Taste receptors on the tongue, the sides and roof of the mouth, and the top part of the throat send complex information about taste to the brain, where it is interpreted.
    d. Receptors for the four basic tastes are located on different areas of the tongue.

33. In the study of perception, "gestalts" refers to:
   a. patterns.
   b. colors.
   c. monochromatic stimuli.
   d. auditory stimuli.

34. Closure refers to:
   a. the basic element.
   b. filling in gaps.
   c. constancy.
   d. grouping together like elements.

35. Look at these letters: *ppp ppp ppp ppp*. You see four groups, each containing three *p*'s, rather than a single row of twelve *p*'s because of the gestalt principle known as:
   a. similarity.
   b. proximity.
   c. closure.
   d. constancy.

36. Which principle of perceptual organization is used when we group items together that look alike or have the same form?
   a. proximity
   b. similarity
   c. figure/ground
   d. closure

37. Making sense of a verbal message by first understanding each word and then piecing them together is:
   a. top-down processing.
   b. bottom-up processing.
   c. selective attention.
   d. perceptual constancy.

38. When we perceive the characteristics of external objects as remaining the same even though the retinal image has changed, _____ has been maintained.
   a. sensory adaptation
   b. bottom-up processing
   c. subliminal perception
   d. perceptual constancy

39. The brain estimates the distance to an object by comparing the different images that it gets from the right and left retinas using:
   a. the gestalt principle of figure/ground.
   b. binocular disparity.
   c. monocular cues.
   d. motion parallax.

40. The Parthenon in Athens looks as if it:
   a. is leaning backward from the viewer.
   b. is completely upright with its columns formed of straight lines.
   c. has bulges in the middle of the columns.
   d. is ready to fall over.

_____

PRACTICE TEST III: Conceptual, Applied, and Challenging Questions

41. _____ is to pinprick as _____ is to sharp pain.
   a. Threshold; just noticeable difference
   b. Stimulus; sensation
   c. Difference threshold; context
   d. Sensory adaptation; short-duration stimulation

42. An antiaircraft operator watching a radar scope may fail to identify the blips signaling the presence of an aircraft because they occur so infrequently. This suggests that:
a.   expectations about the frequency of events influence detection.
b.   detection of a stimulus depends only upon sensory factors.
c.   radar operators are highly atypical in their sensitivity to stimulation.
d.   past exposure is relatively unimportant in stimulus detection.

43. Sam rented an apartment just across the street from the fire station. At first, he woke up every time the siren went off at night. After a few weeks, however, Sam failed to notice the siren and slept right through it. This example illustrates:
a.   signal detection theory.   c.   a just noticeable difference.
b.   Weber's law.   d.   absolute thresholds.

44. Which statement about the rods and the cones of the retina is accurate?
a.   The rods are concentrated in the fovea of the retina; the cones are in the periphery.
b.   The rods are the receptors for dim illumination; the cones are for high illumination levels.
c.   The rods are responsible for the first 0–10 minutes of the dark adaptation curve; the cones are responsible for the remaining 11–40 minutes.
d.   Cones are found in larger numbers on the retina than are rods.

45. One of the most frequent causes of blindness is:
a.   an underproduction of rhodopsin.
b.   a restriction of impulses across the optic nerve.
c.   tunnel vision.
d.   an inability of the pupil to expand.

46. Suppose you could hear nothing but your own voice. Of the following, which might your physician suspect as the source of the problem?
a.   the cochlea.   c.   the auditory cortex.
b.   the basilar membrane.   d.   the middle ear.

47. On a piano keyboard, the keys for the lower-frequency sounds are on the left side; the keys for the higher-frequency sounds are on the right. If you first pressed a key on the left side of the keyboard, and then a key on the right side, you might expect that:
a.   pitch would depend on how hard the keys were struck.
b.   the pitch would be lower for the first key that was played.
c.   the pitch would be lower for the second key that was played.
d.   the pitch would be identical for each.

48. Intensity is to _____ as frequency is to _____.
a.   resonance; loudness   c.   acoustic nerve; auditory canal
b.   loudness; pitch   d.   external ear; consonance

49. Which of the following would refer to the number of wave crests that occur in one second when a tuning fork is struck?
a.   pitch   c.   decibel level
b.   intensity   d.   frequency

50. Loudness is to _____ as frequency is to _____.
    a. decibels; cycles per second
    b. millimicrometers; loudness
    c. cycles per second; wavelength
    d. cochlea; auditory nerve

51. When a person suffers from vertigo, the symptoms would probably be:
    a. a strange taste in the mouth, described as garlic and seaweed.
    b. persistently heard voices, typically shouting for help.
    c. dizziness or motion sickness.
    d. phantom skin sensations, such as insects crawling up the arm.

52. The figure-ground principle:
    a. was formulated by gestalt psychologists to describe how objects seem to pop out from the background against which they are seen.
    b. states that figures are obscured by their backgrounds.
    c. suggests that elements that are located near to each other tend to be seen as part of the same perceptual unit, in most cases.
    d. states that individuals with attractive figures are likely to be viewed with interest.

53. An interesting reversible figure/ground stimulus for perceptual demonstrations:
    a. has a predominant ground.
    b. has a predominant figure.
    c. always gives the same dramatic visual image, no matter how it is viewed.
    d. has a figure and a ground that can alternate when viewed in certain ways.

54. A shopper sorts a large pile of grocery coupons into similar groupings, such as dairy items, vegetables, and fruits. This activity illustrates the gestalt principle of:
    a. figure/group.
    b. closure.
    c. proximity.
    d. similarity.

55. As you look at a car, you can see only the last part of the make, reading "mobile." You determine that the car is probably an Oldsmobile. This illustrates:
    a. top-down processing.
    b. bottom-up processing.
    c. selective attention.
    d. feature analysis.

56. Which one of the following statements concerning depth perception is true?
    a. It is not always necessary to use two eyes to perceive depth.
    b. Distant objects appear smaller because of linear perspective.
    c. The greater the discrepancy between two retinal images, the more difficult it is to reconcile depth.
    d. If two objects are the same size, the one that projects the smaller image on the retina is closer.

57. Suppose that you happened upon two buffalo grazing in an open field, and one looked substantially larger than the other. Now suppose that the image of the smaller buffalo began to expand. You would probably assume that:
    a. it was growing.
    b. it was running toward you.
    c. it was moving away from you.
    d. it was turning sideways.

58. According to the text, which of the following processes is most important in order for major league baseball players to be able to hit the ball when it reaches the plate?
    a. tracking
    b. focusing
    c. anticipation
    d. eye coordination

59. Jeff is interested in learning to speak Russian, so he purchases some tapes that he is supposed to play while he is asleep. The concept that supports the notion of being able to learn in this manner is called _____. According to the text, will his tapes work?
    a. selective attention; yes
    b. selective attention; no
    c. subliminal perception; yes
    d. subliminal perception; no

60. According to the text, which alternative below is **not** an important factor that influences illusions?
    a. amount of formal education
    b. cultural experiences
    c. structural characteristics of the eye
    d. interpretive errors of the brain

Essay Questions

Essay Question 3.1: *The Problem of Extra Senses*

Recite ❑
Review ❑

Consider what it would be like if our senses were not within their present limits. What visual problems might we face? What would we hear if our hearing had a different range? What if we were more sensitive to smell? What about the other senses?

Essay Question 3.2: *Gestalt versus Feature Analysis*

What are the basic differences between the gestalt organizational principles and the feature analysis approach to perception? Are there some phenomena that one or the other explains better? Are there phenomena that would be difficult for one to explain?

Activities and Projects

1. Fill in the labels that are missing from this diagram of the eye.

Recite ❑
Review ❑

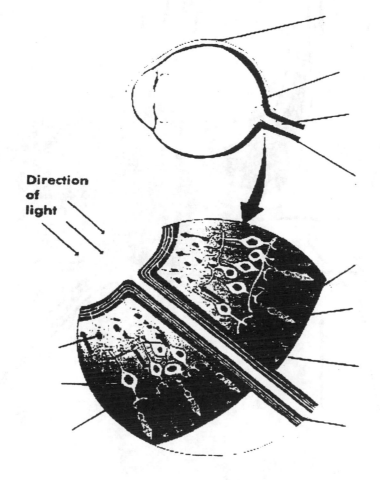

**Direction
of
light**

2.   Fill in the labels that are missing from this diagram of the ear.

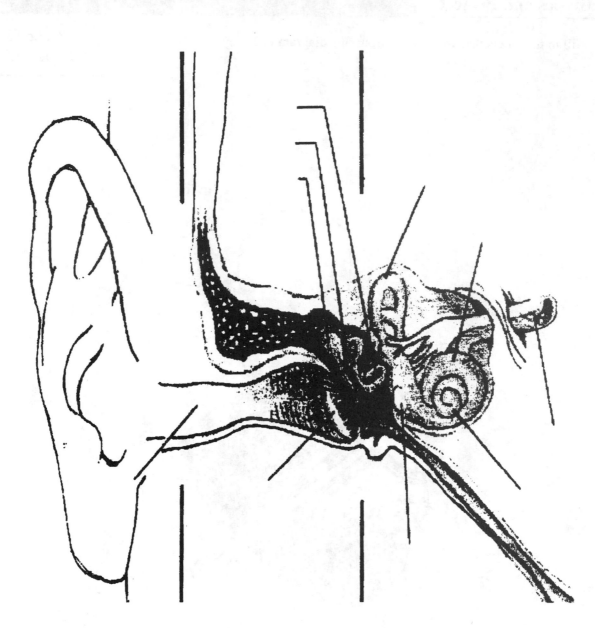

3.   Look at the Necker cube below. Stare at it until it reverses. What makes this illusion work?

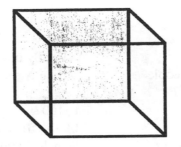

4.   Look at the following figures. They are ambiguous figures. What do you see? How long did it take to see the images? (You may wish to time yourself and others to see how long it takes to see both images.)

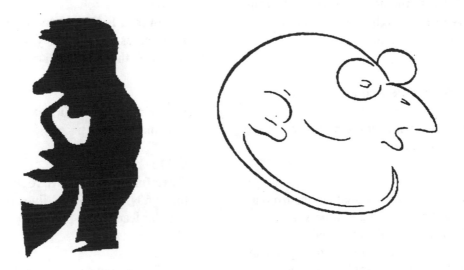

Cultural Idioms

Recite ❏
Review ❏

p. 84
barreled: went very fast
the busy commuter lines: trains that people use to get to work

p. 85
Thanksgiving: U. S. holiday in November; Thanksgiving is celebrated by families, who get together to eat a big meal of turkey.

p. 87
Will an impending storm strike?: Will bad weather arrive?
nuclear power plant: a way to make electricity that uses nuclear power, associated with the possible dangers of radiation escaping into the environment
black-and-white answer: yes and no are the only choices

p. 88
a lineup: a group of people standing in a line; witnesses to a crime are asked to look at a lineup and identify the person who did the crime
a three-way bulb: a light bulb that has three different levels of brightness

p. 91
camera buffs: people who love to take photographs
candlelight dinners: evening meals where the only light is from candles

p. 98
synthesized voice: a voice that comes from a computer; not the voice of a real person
code word: a word used as a signal
K-Mart: a popular U. S. store, where you can buy many things—for example, cameras, clothes, food, appliances, furniture, and so forth

p. 99
visually impaired: people who have great difficulty seeing, although they are not blind

p. 100
blast-off: when a rocket or space shuttle is launched into space

p. 102
stereo speaker that has no enclosure: the part of a sound system where the sound comes out; in this example, the speaker is not covered by a box

p. 104
the ups and downs of life: the good times and the bad times; here the author is making a joke about balance
I'd catch some off the end of my glove: in baseball a player wants to catch the ball in the center of the glove, not at the end of the glove; this shows that he was having difficulty

p. 107
a standard hole punch: a device used to make small holes in paper, so you can fit papers into a notebook that has metal rings

p. 109
the pain is in their heads: the pain is imaginary

p. 115
Grateful Dead: a U. S. rock group, begun in the 1960s, noted for its live concerts and its popular leader, the late Jerry Garcia

p. 117
and for my next trick ... : Magicians often use this phrase to announce the next illusion they will perform

p. 119
the Mona Lisa: one of the world's most famous paintings, painted by Leonardo da Vinci

p. 116
a paper-towel tube: the cardboard tube that paper towels are wrapped around; resembles a telescope

p. 117
As the world turns: the world is constantly turning, on its axis and around the sun; however, the author is also making a joke; *As the World Turns* is the name of a U. S. TV show.
When a batter tries to hit a pitched ball: in baseball, the pitcher pitches the ball at the batter, who tries to hit it
major-league games: the most important baseball teams are in the major leagues; the less important teams are in the minor leagues.

home plate: in baseball, where the hitter stands, and where a runner must cross to score a point.

p. 118
New Orleans Superdome: a large sports stadium in New Orleans, Louisiana
full house: every seat in an auditorium or stadium is filled by a person; no empty seats
toll booths: on highways, the place where you must stop and pay money in order to drive on the road

p. 119
pipe-like figure: a drawing in the shape of a tube

p. 120
mind-boggling: makes your mind puzzled

p. 123
rewrite the "script": to change the way you do something

4 States of Consciousness

Detailed Chapter Outline

This detailed outline contains all the headings in Chapter 4: States of Consciousness. If you are using the SQ3R method, then an examination of the outline is the best way to begin your survey of the chapter.

Survey ❏
Question ❏

Prologue: Beating the Blitz
Looking Ahead

Sleep and Dreams

The Stages of Sleep
REM Sleep: The Paradox of Sleep
Is Sleep Necessary?
Circadian Rhythms: Life Cycles
Psychology at Work Resetting the Body's Internal Clock: Staying Up as the Sun Goes Down
The Function and Meaning of Dreaming
   Do Dreams Represent Unconscious Wish Fulfillment?
   Reverse Learning Theory
   Dreams-for-Survival Theory
   Activation-Synthesis Theory
Daydreams: Dreams Without Sleep
Sleep Disturbances: Slumbering Problems
Pathways Through Psychology Thomas Roth

Pathways Through Psychology: James Covington, Sleep Laboratory Director

The Informed Consumer of Psychology: Sleeping Better

Recap, Review, and Rethink

Hypnosis and Meditation

Hypnosis: A Trance-Forming Experience?

A Different State of Consciousness?

Meditation: Regulating Our Own State of Consciousness

> **Exploring Diversity:** Cross-Cultural Routes to Altered States of Consciousness

Recap, Review, and Rethink

Drug Use: The Highs and Lows of Consciousness

Stimulants: Drug Highs

> **Applying Psychology in the 21st Century:** Just Say No—to DARE? Finding Anti-Drug Programs That Work

Cocaine

Amphetamines

Depressants: Drug lows

Alcohol

Barbiturates

Narcotics: Relieving Pain and Anxiety

Hallucinogens: Psychedelic Drugs

Marijuana

LSD and PCP

> **The Informed Consumer of Psychology:**
> Identifying Drug and Alcohol Problems

Recap, Review, and Rethink
Looking Back
Key Terms and Concepts

➤ Now that you have surveyed the chapter, read **Looking Ahead**, pages 130-131. What questions does the Chapter seek to answer?

Question ❑
Read ❑

Concepts and Learning Objectives

These are the concepts and the learning objectives for Chapter 4. Read them carefully as part of your preliminary survey of the chapter.   *Survey* ❑

Concept 1: Consciousness is a person's awareness of sensations, thoughts, and feelings that are being experienced at a given moment. Other than full alertness, sleep is one of the most important states of consciousness that we experience.

1. Discuss what is meant by consciousness and altered states of consciousness.

2. Explain the cycles of sleep and discuss the roles of circadian rhythms in our lives.

3. Identify the various theories of dreaming and daydreaming, and differentiate among them concerning the functions and meanings of dreams.

4. Describe the sleep disturbances of insomnia, sleep apnea, and narcolepsy, and discuss ways of improving sleep.

Concept 2: Hypnosis and meditation are two different states of consciousness that are achieved without the aid of any drugs or other substances. They represent two important and, sometimes, controversial areas of research into altered states of consciousness.

5. Discuss hypnosis, including its definition, therapeutic value, and the ongoing controversy regarding whether it represents an altered state of consciousness.

6. Describe how meditation works and the changes that occur during meditation.

Concept 3: The use of psychoactive drugs constitutes a major social problem. Psychologists study addiction, the consequences of drug abuse, and how to help people overcome drug dependency. Some psychoactive drugs, like caffeine and alcohol, have socially accepted uses.

7. Describe the characteristics, addictive properties, and psychological reactions to stimulants and depressants, as well as representative drugs from each category.

8. Describe the characteristics, addictive properties, and psychological reactions to narcotics and hallucinogens, as well as representative drugs from each category.

9. Identify the symptoms of drug abuse, and discuss current approaches to drug prevention.

Chapter Guided Review

There are several ways you can use this guided review as part of your systematic study plan. Read the corresponding pages of the text and then complete the review by supplying the correct missing key word. Or, you may want to complete the guided review as a means of becoming familiar with the text. Complete the review and then read the section thoroughly. As you finish each section, complete the **Recap and Review** questions that are supplied in the text.

CONCEPT 1:   Sleep and Dreams

- ● *What are the different states of consciousness?*
- ● *What happens when we sleep, and what are the meaning and function of dreams?*
- ● *How much do we daydream?*
- ● *What are the major sleep disorders and how can they be treated?*

Pages 131-144

[a] _____ is defined as our awareness of the sensations, thoughts, and feelings being experienced at any given moment. Consciousness can range from the perceptions during wakefulness to dreams. The variation in how we experience stimuli can be wide as well, and consciousness varies from active to passive states. Because of its personal nature, the use of introspection made early psychological approaches appear unscientific. Today, the study of consciousness depends on several approaches that have measurable, scientific basis, like the use of electrical recording, studying the effects of drugs, and other approaches.

Much of our knowledge of sleep itself comes from the use of the [b] _____ to record brain activity throughout the cycles of sleep. The amplitude and frequency of the wavelike patterns formed by the EEG during sleep show regular and systematic patterns of sleep.

These patterns identify four stages of sleep. The first stage, called [c] _____, is the stage of transition to sleep, and the brain waves are rapid, low-voltage waves.

[d] _____ is characterized by slower, more regular waves and by occasional sharply pointed waves called spindles. [e] _____ brain waves become even slower with higher peaks and lower valleys. [f] _____ has even slower wave patterns. Stage 4 is experienced soon after falling asleep, and through the night sleep becomes lighter and is characterized by more dreams.

The period of sleep associated with most of our dreaming is identified by the rapid back-and-forth movement of the eyes called [g] _____. REM sleep, which occupies about twenty percent of the total sleep time, is paradoxical because the body is in a state of paralysis even as the eyes are moving about rapidly. People who are deprived of REM sleep by being awakened whenever it begins to occur experience a *rebound effect* that is marked by a significant increase in the amount of REM sleep during subsequent sleep.

Sleep requirements vary from person to person, and, over time, individual sleep patterns change. Some people need very little sleep, others need much more. People deprived of sleep over long periods of time, up to 200 hours in some experiments, do not experience any long-term effects, but they do experience weariness, loss of concentration, decline in creativity, irritability, and tremors while they remain awake in the studies.

[h] _____ are the daily rhythms of the body, including the sleep and waking cycle, as well as the cycles of sleepiness throughout the day. Other functions, like body temperature, also follow circadian rhythms. People who work on night shifts experience difficulty in changing their basic rhythms. *Seasonal affective disorder* and premenstrual syndrome (PMS) are two examples of rhythmic changes that have cycles longer than twenty-four hours.

[i] _____ are unusually frightening dreams. They appear to occur frequently, perhaps about 24 times a year on average. Most dreams, however, involve daily, mundane events. According to Freud's [j] _____, dreams are guides into the unconscious. The true meaning of these wishes was disguised, and Freud used the label of [k] _____ because the meanings were too threatening. Freud called the story line of the dream the [l] _____. Freud sought to uncover the latent content by interpreting the symbols of the dream. Many psychologists reject this theory of dreams, instead preferring to interpret the content in terms of its more obvious references to everyday concerns. Another theory of dreams is called the [m] _____. This theory suggests that dreams flush away unnecessary information accumulated through the day. Dreams then have little meaning. Another theory is the [n] _____, which suggests that dreams involve a reconsideration and reprocessing of critical information from the day. Dreams in this theory have meaning as they represent important concerns drawn from daily experiences. Currently, the most influential theory is the [o] _____ which claims that dreams are by-products of biological processes. These processes are random firings related to changes in neurotransmitter production. Because these activities activate memories that have importance, what begins randomly becomes meaningful.

Another form of dreaming is [p] _____—fantasies produced while awake. Dreams of this type are under the control of individuals, and thus their content is relevant to current concerns and immediate events. Evidence suggests that people may daydream about 10 percent of the time. There is little relationship between daydreaming and psychological disturbances.

The most common sleep disturbance is [q] _____, the experience of difficulty in falling asleep. As many as one-quarter of the people in the United States experience this distubance. Affecting about 20 million people, [r] _____ is another sleep disturbance. In this type, a person has difficulty breathing and sleeping at the same time. In extreme cases a person may awaken as many as 500 times a night. *Sudden infant death syndrome*, a syndrome in which apparently healthy infants die in their sleep, may be related to sleep apnea. Finally, [s] _____, an uncontrollable urge to fall asleep, afflicts many people. With this affliction, the sleeper falls directly into REM sleep. Sleepwalking and sleeptalking are two usually harmless disturbances.

Tips for dealing with insomnia include exercising before bed, choosing a regular bedtime, using bed for sleep and not for watching TV or studying, avoiding caffeine drinks after lunch, drinking a glass of warm milk, avoiding sleeping pills, and if all else fails, trying not to go to sleep.

CONCEPT 2:   Hypnosis and Meditation

- *Are hypnotized people in a different state of consciousness, and can people be hypnotized against their will?*
- *What are the consequences of meditation?*

Survey ❑
Read ❑
Recite ❑

Pages 145-150

[a] _____ is a state of heightened susceptibility to the suggestions of others. When people are hypnotized, they will not perform antisocial behaviors, they will not carry out self-destructive acts, they will not reveal hidden truths about themselves, yet they are capable of lying. Between 5 and 20 percent of the population cannot be hypnotized at all, and about 15 percent are highly susceptible. Ernest Hilgard has argued that hypnosis does represent a state of consciousness that is significantly different from other states. The increased suggestibility, greater ability to recall and construct images, increased memories from childhood, lack of initiative, and ability to accept suggestions that contradict reality suggest that hypnotic states are different from other states. Some researchers have established that some people do pretend to be hypnotized. Moreover, adults do not have special ability to recall childhood events while hypnotized. Hypnotism has been used successfully for the following: 1) controlling pain; 2) ending tobacco addiction; 3) treating psychological disorders; 4) assisting in law enforcement; and 5) improving athletic performance

[b] _____ is a learned technique for refocusing attention that brings about the altered state. Transcendental meditation (TM), brought to the United States by the Maharishi Mahesh Yogi, is perhaps the best-known form of meditation. TM uses a *mantra*, a sound, word, or syllable, that is said over and over. In other forms, the meditator focuses on a picture, flame, or body part. In all forms the key is to concentrate intensely. Following meditation, people are relaxed, they may have new insights, and in the long term, they may have improved health. The physiological changes that accompany meditation are similar to relaxation: Heart rate declines, oxygen intake declines, and brain-wave patterns change. The simple procedures of sitting in a quiet room, breathing deeply and rhythmically, and repeating a word will achieve the same effects as trained meditation techniques.

The cross-cultural aspects of altered states of consciousness are examined in the Exploring Diversity section. The search for experiences beyond normal consciousness is found in many cultures, and it may reflect a universal need to alter moods and consciousness.

CONCEPT 3:   Drug Use: The Highs and Lows of Consciousness

Survey ❏
Read ❏
Recite ❏

- *What are the major classifications of drugs, and what are their effects?*

Pages 150-162

[a] _____ affect consciousness by influencing a person's emotions, perceptions, and behavior. Drug use among high school students has declined, as today about half of the seniors have used an illegal drug in their lives. The most dangerous drugs are those that are addictive. [b] _____ produce psychological or biological dependence in the user, and the withdrawal of the drug leads to cravings for it. The reasons for taking drugs range from taking them simply for the experience, to escaping the pressures of life, to seeking spiritual states, to the thrill of doing something illegal.

Any drug that affects the central nervous system by increasing its activity and by increasing heart rate, blood pressure, and muscle tension is called a [c] _____. An example of this kind of drug is *caffeine*, which is found in coffee, soft drinks, and chocolate. Caffeine increases attentiveness and decreases reaction time. Too much caffeine leads to nervousness and insomnia. Stopping caffeine can cause headaches and depression. *Nicotine* is the stimulant found in tobacco products. [d] _____ and its derivative, crack, are illegal stimulants. This drug produces feelings of well-being, confidence, and alertness when taken in small quantities. (See Table 5–3 in the text for a listing of illegal drugs and their effects.) Cocaine blocks the reuptake of excess dopamine, which in turn produces pleasurable sensations. Cocaine abuse makes the abusers crave the drug and go on binges of use.

[e] _____ are a group of very strong stimulants that bring about a sense of energy and alertness, talkativeness, confidence, and a mood "high." The amphetamines Dexedrine and Benzedrine are commonly known as speed, and excessive amounts of the drugs can lead to overstimulation of the central nervous system, convulsions, and death.

Drugs that slow the central nervous system are called [f] _____.

Feelings of *intoxication* come from taking small doses. [g] _____ is the most common depressant. The average person drinks about 200 alcoholic drinks a year (based on liquor sales). People's reactions to alcohol vary widely. The relaxation, feelings of happiness, and loss of inhibitions make people perceive the effects of alcohol as increasing sociability and well-being (the opposite of depression). *Alcoholics* are people who abuse alcohol, rely upon it, and continue to use it when they have serious problems. Alcoholism requires some people to drink just to be able to function normally. In some cases, alcoholics have sporadic binges and drink excessive quantities. The reasons for the tolerance to alcohol that leads to alcoholism are not clear, though there is evidence that there may be genetic factors. Environmental stressors are thought to play a role as well.

[h] _____ are a form of depressant drug used to induce sleep and reduce stress. They are addictive and can be deadly when combined with alcohol. Quaalude is an illegal drug similar to barbiturates.

[i] _____ increase relaxation and relieve pain and anxiety. *Morphine* and *heroin* are two powerful narcotics. Morphine is used to reduce pain, but heroin is illegal. Heroin effects include an initial rush followed by a sense of well-being. When the sense of well-being ends, the heroin user feels anxiety and the desire to use the drug again. With each use, more heroin is needed to have any effect. A successful treatment for heroin addiction is the use of *methadone*, a drug that satisfies the cravings but does not produce the high. Methadone is biologically addicting.

Drugs that produce hallucinations are called [j] _____. The most common is [k] _____, and its active ingredient is tetrahydrocannabinol. The effects of this drug include euphoria and well-being, and sensory experiences can be more intense. There is no scientific evidence for marijuana being addictive, and the short-term effects appear to be minor. It is now being used in some states for medical purposes. However, the long-term effects of heavy use include temporary decreases in the male sex hormone, decreased activity of the immune system, and damage to the lungs.

Vivid hallucinations are produced by *lysergic acid diethylamide*, or *LSD*. Perceptions of colors, sounds, and shapes are altered and time perception is distorted. The user may have a terrifying experience. After use, people can also experience flashbacks during which they hallucinate. *Phencyclidine*, or *PCP*, is similar to LSD, but can be more dangerous, with side effects that include paranoid and destructive behavior.

The Informed Consumer of Psychology section lists a number of signs that could indicate drug-abuse problems. Individuals with these symptoms should be encouraged to seek professional help.

➤ Now that you have surveyed, questioned, and read the chapter and completed the guided review, review **Looking Back**, pages 163-164.

Review ❏

➤ For additional practice through recitation and review, test your knowledge of the chapter material by answering the questions in the *Key Word Drill*, the *Practice Questions*, and the *Essay Questions*.

Key Word Drill

The following **Matching Questions** test the boldfaced and italicized key words from the text. Check your answers with the Answer Key in the back of the *Study Guide*.

Recite ❑
_____

MATCHING QUESTIONS

_____ 1. stage 1 sleep

_____ 2. stage 2 sleep

_____ 3. stage 3 sleep

_____ 4. stage 4 sleep

_____ 5. rapid eye movement
(REM) sleep

a. The deepest stage of sleep, during which we are least responsive to outside stimulation.

b. Sleep characterized by increased heart rate, blood pressure, and breathing rate; erections; and the experience of dreaming.

c. Characterized by sleep spindles.

d. The state of transition between wakefulness and sleep, characterized by relatively rapid, low-voltage brain waves.

e. A sleep characterized by slow brain waves, with greater peaks and valleys in the wave pattern.

_____ 6. latent content of dreams

_____ 7. manifest content of dreams

_____ 8. reverse learning theory

_____ 9. dreams-for-survival theory

_____ 10. activation-synthesis theory

a. According to Freud, the "disguised" meanings of dreams, hidden by more obvious subjects.

b. Hobson's view that dreams are a result of random electrical energy stimulating memories lodged in various portions of the brain, which the brain then weaves into a logical story line.

c. The view that dreams have no meaning in themselves, but instead function to rid us of unnecessary information that we have accumulated during the day.

d. The proposal that dreams permit information critical for our daily survival to be reconsidered and reprocessed during sleep.

e. According to Freud, the overt story line of dreams.

_____ 11. rebound effect

_____ 12. nightmares

_____ 13. daydreams

_____ 14. insomnia

_____ 15. sleep apnea

_____ 16. sudden infant death syndrome

_____ 17. narcolepsy

a. An inability to get to sleep or stay asleep.

b. A disorder in which seemingly healthy infants die in their sleep.

c. Unusually frightening dreams.

d. An uncontrollable need to sleep for short periods during the day.

e. An increase in REM sleep after one has been deprived of it.

f. Fantasies people construct while awake.

g. A sleep disorder characterized by difficulty in breathing and sleeping simultaneously.

_____ 18. caffeine

_____ 19. nicotine

_____ 20. cocaine

_____ 21. amphetamines

_____ 22. alcohol

_____ 23. intoxication

a. An addictive stimulant present in cigarettes.

b. Strong stimulants that cause a temporary feeling of confidence and alertness but may increase anxiety and appetite loss and, taken over a period of time, suspiciousness and feelings of persecution.

c. An addictive stimulant that, when taken in small doses, initially creates feelings of confidence, alertness, and well-being, but eventually causes mental and physical deterioration.

d. The most common depressant, which in small doses causes release of tension and feelings of happiness, but in larger amounts can cause emotional and physical instability, memory impairment, and stupor.

e. An addictive stimulant found most abundantly in coffee, tea, soda, and chocolate.

f. A state of drunkenness.

_____ 24. barbiturates

_____ 25. morphine

_____ 26. heroin

_____ 27. methadone

_____ 28. hallucinogen

_____ 29. marijuana

_____ 30. lysergic acid diethylamide
(LSD)

_____ 31. phencyclidine (PCP)

a. A powerful depressant, usually injected, that gives an initial rush of good feeling but leads eventually to anxiety and depression; extremely addictive.

b. Addictive depressants used to induce sleep and reduce stress, the abuse of which, especially when combined with alcohol, can be deadly.

c. A powerful hallucinogen that alters brain-cell activity and can cause paranoid and destructive behavior.

d. A chemical used to detoxify heroin addicts.

e. One of the most powerful hallucinogens, affecting the operation of neurotransmitters in the brain and causing brain cell activity to be altered.

f. A drug that is capable of producing changes in the perceptual process, or hallucinations.

g. A common hallucinogen, usually smoked.

h. Derived from the poppy flower, a powerful depressant that reduces pain and induces sleep.

Practice Questions

Test your knowledge of the chapter material by answering these **Multiple Choice Questions**. These questions have been placed in three Practice Tests. The first two tests are composed of questions that will test your recall of factual knowledge. The third test contains questions that are challenging and primarily test for conceptual knowledge and your ability to apply that knowledge. Check your answers and review the feedback using the Answer Key in the back of the *Study Guide*.

Recite ❑
Review ❑

MULTIPLE CHOICE QUESTIONS

PRACTICE TEST I:

1. Our experience of consciousness is mainly:
   a. our awareness of nervous system activity.
   b. actions observable by others.
   c. the deeply hidden motives and urges that influence our behavior in subtle ways but of which, for the most part, we are unaware.
   d. our own subjective mental activity of which we are aware.

2.   Which stage represents the transition from wakefulness to sleep?
     a.   stage 1   c.   stage 3
     b.   stage 2   d.   rapid eye movement (REM)

3.   Which sleep stage is characterized by electrical signals with the slowest frequency, by waveforms
     that are very regular, and by a sleeper who is very unresponsive to external stimuli?
     a.   rapid eye movement (REM)   c.   stage 3
     b.   stage 2   d.   stage 4

4.   REM sleep is considered paradoxical because:
     a.   brain activity is low but eye movement is high.
     b.   brain activity is low, but muscle activity is high.
     c.   eye movement becomes rapid and brain activity is high.
     d.   the brain is very active, but body muscles are paralyzed.

5.   The increase in REM sleep during periods after a person has been deprived of it is called:
     a.   paradoxical sleep.   c.   latent dreaming.
     b.   the rebound effect.   d.   somnambulism.

6.   According to Freud, dreams:
     a.   are reflections of day-to-day activities.
     b.   are reflections of conscious activity.
     c.   are reflections of unconscious wish fulfillment.
     d.   are remnants of our evolutionary heritage.

7.   The notion that dreams serve a "mental housecleaning" function is called:
     a.   the unconscious wish fulfillment theory. c.   the dreams-for-survival theory.
     b.   the activation-synthesis theory.   d.   the reverse-learning theory.

8.   According to studies, the average person daydreams about:
     a.   10 percent of the time.   c.   30 percent of the time.
     b.   20 percent of the time.   d.   40 percent of the time.

9.   Insomnia is a condition in which a person:
     a.   uncontrollably falls asleep.
     b.   sleeps more than twelve hours per night on a routine basis.
     c.   has difficulty sleeping.
     d.   exhibits abnormal brain wave patterns during rapid eye movement (REM) sleep.

10. Having difficulty sleeping and breathing simultaneously is called:
     a.   narcolepsy.   c.   hypersomnia.
     b.   sleep apnea.   d.   insomnia.

11. According to research discussed in the text, which of the following may account for sudden infant
     death syndrome?
     a.   narcolepsy   c.   somnambulism
     b.   sleep apnea   d.   insomnia

12. People who are easily hypnotized tend to:
    a. enroll in general psychology.
    b. be very aware of the outdoors.
    c. spend a lot of time daydreaming.
    d. be very good at biofeedback.

13. During transcendental meditation, a person repeats _____ over and over again.
    a. a mantra
    b. an allegory
    c. a banta
    d. an analogy

14. A psychoactive drug:
    a. affects a person's behavior only if he or she is receptive to "mind expanding" experiences.
    b. influences thoughts and perceptions and is usually physically addictive.
    c. affects a person's emotions, perceptions, and behavior.
    d. acts primarily on biological functions such as heart rate and intestinal mobility.

15. The most common central nervous system depressant is:
    a. phenobarbital.
    b. alcohol.
    c. Valium.
    d. Quaalude.

16. The most common hallucinogen in use in the United States is:
    a. PCP.
    b. LSD.
    c. cocaine.
    d. marijuana.

―――――――――

PRACTICE TEST II:

17. The deepest stages of sleep are generally experienced:
    a. during the first half of the sleep interval.
    b. during the second half of the sleep interval.
    c. during continuous periods averaging two hours each.
    d. while the sleeper dreams.

18. As we progress through the stages of sleep toward deepest sleep, within a single sleep cycle the EEG pattern gets:
    a. faster and more regular.
    b. faster and more irregular.
    c. slower and lower in amplitude.
    d. slower and more regular.

19. Which of the following stages of sleep is characterized by irregular breathing, increased blood pressure, and increased respiration?
    a. stage 1
    b. stage 2
    c. rapid eye movement (REM)
    d. non-rapid eye movement (non-REM)

20. The major muscles of the body act as if they are paralyzed during:
    a. stage 1 sleep.
    b. stage 3 sleep.
    c. stage 4 sleep.
    d. rapid eye movement (REM Sleep).

21. The viewpoint that dreams are the outcome of the random exercising of neural circuits in the brain is called the:
    a. unconscious wish fulfillment theory.
    b. dreams-for-survival theory.
    c. activation-synthesis theory.
    d. reverse learning theory.

22. Freud referred to the story line of a dream as its:
    a. libidinal content.
    b. unconscious content.
    c. manifest content.
    d. latent content.

23. Which of the following does **not** describe a common characteristic of daydreams?
    a. fantastic and creative
    b. mundane, ordinary topics
    c. a part of normal consciousness
    d. a predomination of sexual imagery

24. People pass directly from a conscious, wakeful state to REM sleep if they suffer from:
    a. narcolepsy
    b. insomnia
    c. somnambulism
    d. rapid eye movement (REM) showers

25. The uncontrollable need to sleep for short periods that can happen at any time during the day is called:
    a. narcolepsy.
    b. sleep apnea.
    c. hypersomnia.
    d. insomnia.

26. According to research discussed in the text, which of the following may account for sudden infant death syndrome?
    a. narcolepsy
    b. sleep apnea
    c. somnambulism
    d. insomnia

27. Generalizing from the text, all of the following are typical suggestions for overcoming insomnia **except**:
    a. Choose regular bedtimes.
    b. Don't try to go to sleep.
    c. Avoid drinks with caffeine.
    d. Watch TV in bed.

28. The procedure, introduced in the United States by Maharishi Mahesh Yogi, in which a person focuses on a mantra to reach a different state of consciousness is called:
    a. transactional analysis.
    b. Zen Buddhism.
    c. exorcism.
    d. transcendental meditation.

29. The problem doctors face with using methadone in drug therapy is that:
    a. the patient is likely to become addicted to methadone.
    b. methadone eventually causes mental retardation in the patient.
    c. methadone patients are at risk of becoming alcoholics.
    d. methadone users find the marijuana high to be very appealing.

30. Caffeine, nicotine, cocaine, and amphetamines are considered:
    a. anesthetic agents.
    b. central nervous system stimulants.
    c. anti-anxiety drugs.
    d. hallucinogens.

31. Nembutal, Seconal, and phenobarbital are all depressants and forms of:
    a. opiates.
    c. hallucinogens.
    b. barbiturates.
    d. hypnotics.

32. Which of the following are narcotic drugs?
    a. LSD and marijuana
    c. barbiturates and alcohol
    b. morphine and heroin
    d. amphetamines and cocaine

PRACTICE TEST III: Conceptual, Applied, and Challenging Questions

33. Sleep involves four different stages. What is the basis for differentiating these stages of sleep?
    a. They are defined according to the electrical properties recorded by an electroencephalogram (EEG) attached to the sleeper.
    b. They are defined by the amount of time elapsed from the onset of sleep.
    c. They are based on the mental experiences described when sleepers are awakened and asked what they are thinking.
    d. They are characterized by patterns of overt body movements recorded with a video camera that is positioned over the sleeper.

34. A friend comes to you concerned about his health after having stayed up for 36 hours straight studying. The most valid thing you could tell him is that:
    a. if he is going to stay up for so long, he should see a doctor regularly.
    b. if he continues to stay up for so long, he will probably get sick.
    c. there will most likely be rather severe long-term consequences of not sleeping for that amount of time.
    d. research has demonstrated that lack of sleep will affect his ability to study.

35. Sharon dreams that Jim climbs a stairway and meets her at the top. According to Freudian dream symbols described in the text, this would probably suggest:
    a. that Sharon would like to start a friendship with Jim.
    b. that Sharon is really afraid to talk to Jim, though she would like to start a friendship.
    c. that Jim and Sharon probably work together in a building where there are stairs.
    d. that Sharon is dreaming of sexual intercourse with Jim.

36. If you had a dream about carrying grapefruits down a long tunnel, Freud would interpret the grapefruit as a dream symbol suggesting a wish to:
    a. take a trip to the tropics.
    c. caress a man's genitals.
    b. caress a woman's body.
    d. return to the womb.

37. Suppose that a study were done to show that people who are in new surroundings and involved in major unfamiliar activities have more dreams per night than others whose lives have been stable through the same intervals of the study. This study aims to test:
    a. the unconscious wish fulfillment dream theory.
    b. the dreams-for-survival dream theory.
    c. the activation-synthesis dream theory.
    d. the reverse learning dream theory.

38. While in calculus class, Rob fantasized about sailing to Tahiti. He was experiencing a:
    a. nervous breakdown.
    b. daydream.
    c. diurnal emission.
    d. mantra.

39. Which of the following statements about sleepwalking is **not** true?
    a. Sleepwalkers should not be awakened.
    b. Sleepwalking occurs in stage 4 sleep.
    c. Sleepwalkers are somewhat aware of their surroundings.
    d. Sleepwalking occurs most frequently in children.

40. In what way are meditation and hypnosis similar?
    a. They are both accompanied by changes in brain activity.
    b. They both result in a decrease in blood pressure.
    c. They are both based on Eastern religious practices.
    d. They both result in total relaxation.

41. Which of the following statements about addiction to drugs is **not** true?
    a. Addiction may be biologically based.
    b. Addictions are primarily caused by an inherited biological liability.
    c. All people, with few exceptions, have used one or more "addictive" drugs in their lifetime.
    d. Addictions may be psychological.

42. You have just taken a tablet someone gave you. You feel a rise in heart rate, a tremor in the hands, and a loss of appetite. You have taken:
    a. a megavitamin.
    b. a stimulant.
    c. a depressant.
    d. a hallucinogen.

43. Which of the following is a hallucinogen?
    a. heroin
    b. cocaine
    c. marijuana
    d. morphine

44. Elizabeth dreams about wearing a man's leather jacket and parading around town. In Freud's view, the leather jacket and showing off are:
    a. latent content.
    b. manifest content.
    c. irrelevant to the meaning.
    d. day residues.

45. Elizabeth dreams about wearing a man's leather jacket and parading around town. If the leather jacket is seen as sexual encounter and the parade as a form of exhibitionism, then in Freud's view, they would have provided insight into:
    a. latent content.
    b. manifest content.
    c. activation processes.
    d. day residues.

46. Elena has just been hypnotized. Which of the following acts is she **least** likely to commit?
    a. Completely undress.
    b. Flirt with her escort.
    c. Recall a past life.
    d. Stand on a chair an crow like a rooster.

Essay Questions

Essay Question 4.1: *Dreams*

Recite ❑
Review ❑

Discuss the competing theories of dreams. Are the theories actually incompatible? Which appears most convincing? Defend your answer.

Essay Question 4.2: *Decriminalizing Psychoactive Drugs*

Debates regarding the legalization of drugs, especially marijuana, seem to come and go. If that debate were to arise today, what should psychology contribute? What are your feelings? Should some drugs be legalized or given through prescription? Defend your answer.

Activities and Projects

1. Go to a local drug store or to the section of the campus bookstore that has cold remedies, sleep aids, and other over-the-counter medications. Choose a product and record the active ingredients and the name of the product. Then go with the list to any medical reference and find the description of the active ingredient. This drug should also be classified according to what type of psychoactive drug it is. Is it a depressant or a stimulant? Is it related to a narcotic or hallucinogen? Is it classed as antianxiety or antidepressant (check Chapter 13 for a description of these two drug classes)?

   Recite ❑
   Review ❑

2. Your library should have a relaxation tape that you can check out. If not, ask your psychology instructor or someone in the campus counseling center. After locating a tape, find a quiet spot where you will not be disturbed and you can play the tape. Before playing the tape, take a pulse rate and count the number of breaths you take in a minute. Now play the tape. After the tape is over, wait a few moments and take your pulse and breathing rates again. How do you feel? In what way is this like meditation? In what way is it different?

3. Prepare a dream journal. Some people are able to record their dreams in the morning when they awaken, others will place a notepad and pencil next to their bed at night and record their dreams throughout the night by waking and writing a few notes immediately after the dream occurs. To use this second method, before you fall asleep you should give yourself the suggestion to awaken after each dream (you may wish to include in your suggestion that you will be able to record your dream and fall back to sleep without any problem). After about one week of keeping a journal, you should examine it for any patterns or recurrent themes (recurrent dreams will be very noticeable without keeping a journal). If other students in the class are doing this activity, you may wish to share a few of your dreams and discuss their possible meanings or other source. (This form is provided as a suggested format for recording your dreams. You may make copies of it if you wish.)

DREAM RECORD

Time of Dream: _____

Dream Narrative:

_____

_____

_____

_____

_____

_____

Significant events, characters, emotions about the dream
    (you may record these reflections at a later time):

_____

_____

_____

_____

_____

_____

_____

_____

Cultural Idioms

Recite ❑
Review ❑

p. 130
Green Bay Packers: a professional football team
quarterback: one of the positions on a football team
rehab: rehabilitation; a program, or a place, that helps people who have problems with drugs or alcohol
National Football League's Most Valuable Player: the best professional football player of the year

p. 131
knotty issues: complicated problems
running back; tackle; defensive lineman: three different positions on a football team
heck: this is a slang word for "hell".

p. 132
don't lose any sleep: the author is making a joke about sleep, using this common idiom that means "don't worry"
still photos: photographs (not movies or videos, which "move")

p. 134
safety hazard: a danger
pacemaker: a device that keeps a rhythm

p. 135
siesta: in the afternoon, time off from work to rest
night shift: when a person works at night, not during the day
near-meltdown: the nuclear reactor almost burned ("melted") after a malfunction
Three Mile Island: a nuclear power plant in Pennsylvania that almost melted down in 1979
Exxon Valdez: an oil-carrying ship owned by the Exxon Company

oil spill: a large quantity of oil got into the water, destroying the shoreline and killing wildlife
Chernobyl: a nuclear reactor in the Ukraine that malfunctioned and released radioactivity into the environment

p. 137
something on top of the bed: This cartoon reverses a typical childhood fear that there is a monster under the bed; here the monsters are afraid of something on top of the bed, that is, the child.
the popular press: magazines for general readers, such as *Time* magazine or *Newsweek*, or newspapers such as *U.S.A. Today*.
chemistry final: final exam in chemistry

p. 138
frozen with fear: unable to move because you are so afraid
locked up: imprisoned, jailed

p. 139
pierce the armor: to get through to the real meaning

p. 140
Madlibs: a word game that results in nonsense stories

p. 142
Sleep Lab: a laboratory where scientists study sleep

p. 143
tossing and turning: when people can't sleep they say that they "toss and turn" in the bed all night.
unwind: relax

p. 145
"flush away": get rid of (like a toilet flushing)

p. 145
A Trance-Forming experience: the author is making a pun here, on the word "transforming," which means something that changes you, and "trance," which is another word for being hypnotized.

p. 148
"OOOMMM": this is the sound, or mantra, often associated with meditation
"MMMOOOO": In English-speaking cultures, "moo" is the sound that cows makes; thus the cartoon is making a joke about meditation

p. 149
Sioux: a Native American people, or tribe
Aztec: A Central American culture, at its height during the early 16th century
consciousness-altering activities: things people do to change their consciousness

p. 150
butane-torch flame: a gas flame

p. 151
the dope: the drug
roach egg: the egg of a cockroach
over-the-counter: medicine that you can buy without a prescription from your doctor

p. 152
role models: people whom you admire or want to be like

p. 153
the pressures of peers: when your friends urge you to do something
substance abuse: problems with, or misuse of, drugs and alcohol

p. 153
the class cracks up: the class starts to laugh
gangs: groups of teenagers, associated with violence
to stem the use of drugs: to stop the use of drugs

p. 154
steep price: high penalty
"crash": when the drug wears off, a person feels awful

p. 155
street name: what people who use or sell the drug call it
face-picking: pulling at your skin with your fingers
altered body image: when you think that your body shape or size is different from how it really is

p. 156
"speed kills": This has two meanings; originally, it meant that it is dangerous to drive a car too fast; now it also means that it is dangerous to use the drug speed.
liquor sales: how much liquor is sold in the U.S.

p. 158
pass out: faint or lose consciousness

p. 160
"spaced out": vague

p. 161
the knots: the swirls that occur in wood
flashbacks: when you suddenly re-experience something that happened before
giving new life to "tired blood": giving you new energy
being high more often than not: being high most of the time

5 Learning

Detailed Chapter Outline

This detailed outline contains all the headings in Chapter 5: Learning. If you are using the SQ3R method, then an examination of the outline is the best way to begin your survey of the chapter.

Survey ❑
Question ❑

> **Pathways Through Psychology:** Lynne Calero,
> Dolphin Researcher

Biological Constraints on Learning: You Can't Teach an Old Dog Just Any Trick

Recap, Review, and Rethink

Cognitive Approaches to Learning

Latent Learning
Observational Learning: Learning Through Imitation

> **Applying Psychology in the 21st Century:** Fight
> Less, Talk More: Scripts for Reducing Violence

> **Exploring Diversity:** Does Culture Influence How We
> Learn?

The Unresolved Controversy of Cognitive Learning Theory

> **The Informed Consumer of Psychology:** Using
> Behavior Analysis and Behavior Modification

Recap, Review, and Rethink
Looking Back
Key Terms and Concepts

➤ Now that you have surveyed the chapter, read **Looking Ahead**, pages
168–169. What questions does the Chapter seek to answer?

Question ❑
Read ❑

Concepts and Learning Objectives

These are the concepts and the learning objectives for Chapter 5. Read them
carefully as part of your preliminary survey of the chapter.

Survey ❑

Concept 1: Learning is the relatively permanent change in behavior that results from
experience. Classical conditioning, the learning theory pioneered by Ivan Pavlov,
understands learning to be the substitution of a new stimulus for a preexisting stimulus in a
stimulus-response association.

1. Define learning and distinguish it from performance.

2. Define and describe the major principles of classical conditioning, including extinction, spontaneous recovery, generalization, discrimination, and higher-order conditioning.

3. Apply the concepts of classical conditioning to human behavior, and identify the challenges that have been made to the traditional views of classical conditioning.

Concept 2: Operant conditioning, developed by B. F. Skinner, utilizes the consequences of behavior to shape behavior. Reinforcement is the principle that accounts for the increase of particular behaviors. Most reinforcement of behavior follows schedules that provide partial reinforcement, which often leads to greater resistance to extinction.

4. Define and describe the major principles of operant conditioning, including primary and secondary reinforcers, positive and negative reinforcement, and punishment.

5. Outline the schedules of reinforcement, and define the operant view of generalization and discrimination, superstitious behavior, and shaping.

6. Apply the concepts of operant conditioning to human behavior.

7. Distinguish between classical and operant conditioning. Identify the limits of conditioning, such as biological constraints.

Concept 3: Cognitive approaches to learning focus on the role of cognitive processes, especially observation, in the learning of new behaviors.

8. Describe the cognitive-social learning concepts of latent learning, cognitive maps, and observational learning.

9. Discuss current learning topics such as the influence of television violence, cultural influences, and behavior modification.

Chapter Guided Review

There are several ways you can use this guided review as part of your systematic study plan. Read the corresponding pages of the text and then complete the review by supplying the correct missing key word. Or, you may want to complete the guided review as a means of becoming familiar with the text. Complete the review and then read the section thoroughly. As you finish each section, complete the **Recap and Review** questions that are supplied in the text.

Survey ❑

CONCEPT 1:   Classical Conditioning

- *What is learning?*
- *How do we learn to form associations between stimuli and responses?*

Pages 169-175

[a] _____ is distinguished from *maturation* on the basis of whether the resulting change in behavior is a consequence of experience (learning) or of growth (maturation). Short-term changes in performance, the key measure of learning, can also result from fatigue, lack of effort, and other factors that are not reflections of learning. According to some, learning can only be inferred indirectly.

Ivan Pavlov's studies concerning the physiology of digestive processes led him to discover the basic principles of [b] _____, a process in which an organism learns to respond to a stimulus that did not bring about the response earlier. An original study involved Pavlov training a dog to salivate when a tuning fork was sounded. In this process, the tuning fork's sound is considered the [c] _____ because it does not bring about the response of interest. The meat powder, which does cause salivation, is called the [d] _____. The salivation, when it occurs due to the presence of the meat powder (UCS), is called the [e] _____. The conditioning process requires repeated pairing of the UCS and the neutral stimulus. After training is complete, the neutral stimulus—now called the [f] _____—will now bring about the UCR, now called the [g] _____. Pavlov noted that the neutral stimulus had to precede the UCS by no more than several seconds for the conditioning to be the most effective.

One of the more famous applications of classical conditioning techniques with humans is the case of the 11-month-old infant, Albert. Albert was taught a fear of a laboratory rat, to which he had shown no fear initially, by striking a bar behind him whenever he approached the rat.

The process of ending the association of the UCS and the CS is called [h] _____, which occurs when a previously learned response decreases and disappears. If the tuning fork is repeatedly sounded without the meat powder being presented, the dog will eventually stop salivating. Extinction is the basis for the treatment principle called [i] _____, which is used to treat phobias. Systematic desensitization requires the repeated presentation of the frightening stimulus (a CS) without the presentation of the occurrence of the negative consequences.

When a CR has been extinguished, and a period of time has passed without the presentation of the CS, a phenomenon called [j] _____ can occur. The CS is presented and the previously extinguished response recurs, though it is usually weaker than in the original training and can be extinguished again more easily.

[k] _____ takes place when a conditioned response occurs in the presence of a stimulus that is similar to the original conditioned stimulus. In the case of baby Albert, the fear response was generalized to white furry things, including a white-bearded Santa Claus mask. [l] _____ occurs when an organism learns to differentiate (discriminate) one stimulus from another and responds only to one stimulus and not the others.

When a conditioned stimulus has been established and is then repeatedly paired with another neutral stimulus until the conditioned response becomes conditioned to the new stimulus, then [m] _____ has occurred. Some investigators have used the concept of higher-order conditioning to explain how people develop and maintain prejudices against members of racial and ethnic groups.

Many of the fundamental assumptions of classical conditioning have been challenged. One challenge has been to question the length of the interval between the neutral stimulus and the unconditioned stimulus. Garcia found that nausea caused by radiation, a state that occurred hours after exposure, could be associated with water drunk that has unusual characteristics or with water drunk in a particular place. Garcia's findings that the association could be made with delays as long as eight hours is a direct challenge to the idea that the pairing must be made within several seconds to be effective.

CONCEPT 2: Operant Conditioning

Survey ❑
Read ❑
Recite ❑

● **What is the role of reward and punishment in learning?**

Pages 176-187

[a] _____ is learning in which the response is strengthened or weakened according to whether it has positive or negative consequences. The term "operant" suggests that the organism *operates* on the environment in a deliberate manner to gain a desired result.

Edward L. Thorndike found that a cat would learn to escape from a cage by performing specific actions in order to open a door that allows it access to food, a positive consequence of the behavior. Thorndike formulated the [b] _____, stating that responses with satisfying results would be repeated, and those with less satisfying results would be less likely to be repeated.

B. F. Skinner took Thorndike's law of effect and suggested that chance behaviors that lead to desirable consequences are then repeated. Pigeons will accidentally peck a key that releases food pellets, and then begin to peck until satisfied, learning the contingency between the pecking and the food.

[c] _____ is the process by which a stimulus increases the probability that a preceding behavior will be repeated. Releasing the food by pecking is a reinforcement, and the food itself is called a [d] _____, which is any stimulus that increases the probability that a preceding behavior will be repeated. A [e] _____

satisfies a biological need without regard to prior experience. A **[f]** _____ is a stimulus that reinforces because of its association with a primary reinforcer.

Reinforcers are also distinguished as positive or negative. **[g]** _____ bring about an increase in the preceding response. **[h]** _____ lead to an increase in a desired response when they are *removed*. Negative reinforcement requires that an individual take an action to remove an undesirable condition. Negative reinforcement is used in **[i]** _____, where an organism learns to escape from an aversive situation, and in **[j]** _____, where the organism learns to act to avoid the aversive situation. **[k]** _____ refers to the use of an aversive stimulus by adding it to the environment in order to *decrease* the probability that a behavior will be repeated. Punishment includes the removal of something positive, such as the loss of a privilege.

The effectiveness of punishment depends greatly on how it is used. The use of punishment is usually an opportunity for reinforcing an alternate, preferred behavior. Also, in rare cases, such as autism, quick and intense physical punishment may be used to prevent or end self-destructive behavior. The disadvantages of punishment make its use questionable. It must be delivered shortly after the behavior or it will be ineffective. Physical punishment may convey the idea that physical aggression is an appropriate behavior. Punishment does not convey information about alternative behaviors.

The frequency and timing of reinforcement depends upon the use of **[l]** _____. With a **[m]** _____, the behavior is reinforced every time it occurs. **[n]** _____ describes the technique of using reinforcement some of the time but not for every response. Partial reinforcement schedules maintain behavior longer than continuous reinforcement before extinction occurs. A *cumulative recorder* automatically records the number of responses and the amount of time between responses. It also records the number of times a reinforcement is given (see Figure 6–5).

A **[o]** _____ delivers a reinforcement after a certain number of responses. A **[p]** _____ delivers reinforcement on the basis of a varying number of responses. The number of responses often remains close to an average. The fixed- and variable-ratio schedules depend upon a *number* of responses, and the fixed- and variable-interval schedules depend upon an *amount of time*. **[q]** _____ deliver reinforcements to the first behavior occurring after a set interval, or period of time.

[r] _____ deliver reinforcement after a varying interval of time. Fixed intervals are like weekly paychecks; variable intervals are like pop quizzes.

Discrimination and generalization are achieved in operant conditioning through

[s] _____. In stimulus control training , a behavior is reinforced only in the presence of specific stimuli. The specific stimulus is called a *discriminative stimulus*, a stimulus that signals the likelihood of a particular behavior being reinforced. Stimulus generalization occurs when an organism responds in situations similar to the original and expects reinforcement in the new situation just as the original was reinforced.

[t] _____ refers to a behavior that involves the repetition of elaborate rituals. Learning theory accounts for superstitious behavior as behavior that occurs prior to a reinforcement but is coincidental to the behavior that leads to the reinforcement. Also, these behaviors are strengthened because they are only partially reinforced.

When a complex behavior is desired, a trainer may *shape* the desired behavior by rewarding closer and closer approximations of the behavior. Initially, any similar behaviors are reinforced, and gradually the reinforcement is restricted to ever closer approximations. Many complex

human and animal skills are acquired through **[u]** _____.

Sometimes learning is constrained by behaviors that are biologically innate, or inborn. Not all behaviors can be taught to all animals equally well because of these *biological constraints*. Pigs might root a disk around their cages and raccoons might hoard and then clean similar disks.

CONCEPT 3: Cognitive Approaches to Learning

Survey ❑
Read ❑
Recite ❑

- *What is the role of cognition and thought in learning?*
- *What are some practical methods for bringing about behavior change, both in ourselves and in others?*

Pages 188-197

The approach that views learning in terms of thought processes is called **[a]**_____.
This approach does not deny the importance of classical and operant conditioning. It includes

the consideration of unseen mental processes as well. **[b]** _____ is behavior that is learned but not demonstrated until reinforcement is provided for demonstrating the behavior. Latent learning occurs when rats are allowed to wander about a maze without any reward at the end, but once they learn that a reinforcement is available, they will quickly find their way through the maze even though they had not been reinforced for doing so in the past.

The wandering around apparently leads them to develop a **[c]** _____ of the maze. Humans apparently develop cognitive maps of their surroundings based on landmarks.

Accounting for a large portion of learning in humans, **[d]** _____ is

learning that occurs by observing the behavior of another person, called the **[e]** _____.

The classic experiment involved children observing a model strike a Bobo doll, and then later those who had seen the behavior were more prone to act aggressively. Four processes are necessary for observational learning: (1) paying attention to critical features; (2) remembering the behavior; (3) reproducing the action; and (4) being motivated to repeat the behavior. We also observe the kinds of reinforcement that the model receives for the behavior. Observational learning has been related to how violence on television affects aggression and violence in children.

The Exploring Diversity section examines *learning styles* and how cultural differences are reflected in these different ways of approaching materials. Learning styles are characterized by cultural background and individual abilities.

[f] _____ refers to the formalized use of basic principles of learning theory to change behavior by eliminating undesirable behaviors and encouraging desirable ones. Behavior modification can be used to train mentally retarded individuals, to help people lose weight or quit smoking, and to teach people to behave safely. The steps of a typical behavior program include: 1) identifying goals and target behaviors; 2) designing a data recording system and recording preliminary data; 3) selecting a behavior change strategy; 4) implementing the program; 5) keeping careful records after the program has been implemented; and 6) evaluating and altering the ongoing program.

➤ Now that you have surveyed, questioned, and read the chapter and completed the guided review, review **Looking Back**, pages 198-199.

Review ❑

➤ For additional practice through recitation and review, test your knowledge of the chapter material by answering the questions in the *Key Word Drill*, the *Practice Questions*, and the *Essay Questions*.

Key Word Drill

The following **Matching Questions** test the boldfaced and italicized key words from the text. Check your answers with the Answer Key in the back of the *Study Guide*.

Recite ❑
_____

MATCHING QUESTIONS

_____ 1. classical conditioning

_____ 2. operant conditioning

_____ 3. escape conditioning

_____ 4. avoidance conditioning

_____ 5. cognitive-social learning theory

_____ 6. latent learning

_____ 7. observational learning

a. The study of the thought processes that underlie learning.

b. Learning that involves the imitation of a model.

c. A previously neutral stimulus comes to elicit a response through its association with a stimulus that naturally brings about the response.

d. A new behavior is acquired but not readily demonstrated until reinforcement is provided.

e. A voluntary response is strengthened or weakened, depending on its positive or negative consequences.

f. A response to a signal of an impending unpleasant event in a way that permits its evasion.

g. A response brings about an end to an aversive situation.

_____ 8. neutral stimulus

_____ 9. unconditioned stimulus
(UCS)

_____ 10. unconditioned response
(UCR)

_____ 11. conditioned stimulus
(CS)

_____ 12. conditioned response
(CR)

a. A stimulus that brings about a response without having been learned.

b. A stimulus that, before conditioning, has no effect on the desired response.

c. A once-neutral stimulus that has been paired with an unconditioned stimulus to bring about a response formerly caused only by the unconditioned stimulus.

d. A response that, after conditioning, follows a previously neutral stimulus (e.g., salivation at the sound of a tuning fork).

e. A response that is natural and needs no training (e.g., salivation at the smell of food).

_____ 13. extinction

_____ 14. systematic
desensitization

_____ 15. spontaneous recovery

_____ 16. stimulus generalization

_____ 17. stimulus discrimination

_____ 18. higher-order
conditioning

a. The weakening and eventual disappearance of a conditioned response.

b. The reappearance of a previously extinguished response after a period of time during which the conditioned stimulus has been absent.

c. Occurs when an already conditioned stimulus is paired with a neutral stimulus until the neutral stimulus evokes the same response as the conditioned stimulus.

d. Response to a stimulus that is similar to but different from a conditioned stimulus; the more similar the two stimuli, the more likely generalization is to occur.

e. The process by which an organism learns to differentiate among stimuli, restricting its response to one in particular.

f. A form of therapy in which fears are minimized through gradual exposure to the source of fear.

_____ 19. primary reinforcer

_____ 20. secondary reinforcer

_____ 21. positive reinforcer

_____ 22. negative reinforcer

_____ 23. punishment

_____ 24. aversive stimuli

a. An unpleasant or painful stimulus that is added to the environment after a certain behavior occurs, decreasing the likelihood that the behavior will occur again.

b. Unpleasant or painful stimuli.

c. A reward that satisfies a biological need (e.g., hunger or thirst) and works naturally.

d. A stimulus added to the environment that brings about an increase in the response that preceded it.

e. A stimulus that becomes reinforcing by its association with a primary reinforcer (e.g., money, which allows us to obtain food, a primary reinforcer).

f. A stimulus whose removal is reinforcing, leading to a greater probability that the response bringing about this removal will occur again.

_____ 25. continuous reinforcement schedule

_____ 26. partial reinforcement schedule

_____ 27. cumulative recorder

_____ 28. fixed-ratio schedule

_____ 29. variable-ratio schedule

_____ 30. fixed-interval schedule

_____ 31. variable-interval schedule

a. Reinforcement occurs after a varying number of responses rather than after a fixed number.

b. Reinforcing of a behavior every time it occurs.

c. A device that records and graphs the pattern of responses.

d. Reinforcement is given at various times, usually causing a behavior to be maintained more consistently.

e. Reinforcing of a behavior some, but not all, of the time.

f. Reinforcement is given at established time intervals.

g. Reinforcement is given only after a certain number of responses is made.

_____ 32. reinforcer

_____ 33. schedules of reinforcement

_____ 34. stimulus control training

_____ 35. discriminative stimulus

_____ 36. model

_____ 37. behavior modification

a. A formalized technique for promoting the frequency of desirable behaviors and decreasing the incidence of unwanted ones.

b. A person serving as an example to an observer; the observer may imitate that person's behavior.

c. Any stimulus that increases the probability that a preceding behavior will be repeated.

d. A stimulus to which an organism learns to respond as part of stimulus control training.

e. The frequency and timing of reinforcement following desired behavior.

f. Training in which an organism is reinforced in the presence of a certain specific stimulus, but not in its absence.

Practice Questions

Test your knowledge of the chapter material by answering these **Multiple Choice Questions**. These questions have been placed in three Practice Tests. The first two tests are composed of questions that will test your recall of factual knowledge. The third test contains questions that are challenging and primarily test for conceptual knowledge and your ability to apply that knowledge. Check your answers and review the feedback using the Answer Key in the back of the *Study Guide*.

Recite ❑
Review ❑

MULTIPLE CHOICE QUESTIONS

PRACTICE TEST I:

1. Which of the following statements concerning the relationship between learning and performance is correct?
    a. Learning refers to cognitive gains, whereas performance refers to gains in motor skills.
    b. Performance refers to permanent changes, whereas learning refers to temporary changes.
    c. Performance is synonymous with learning.
    d. Performance is measurable, whereas learning must be inferred.

2.　The changes in behavior brought about by learning:
　　a.　are hard to measure.
　　b.　are easily extinguished.
　　c.　must be measured indirectly.
　　d.　are generally maturational.

3.　In Pavlov's original experiment, the meat powder was the:
　　a.　unconditioned stimulus.
　　b.　conditioned stimulus.
　　c.　unconditioned response.
　　d.　conditioned response.

4.　Which of the following takes place after conditioning, when the conditioned stimulus is presented repeatedly without being paired with the unconditioned stimulus?
　　a.　learning
　　b.　perception
　　c.　systematic desensitization
　　d.　extinction

5.　Of the following, systematic desensitization would be most closely associated with:
　　a.　operant conditioning.
　　b.　token economy.
　　c.　spontaneous recovery.
　　d.　extinction.

6.　A classically conditioned response can be extinguished by:
　　a.　adding another conditioned stimulus to the pairing.
　　b.　no longer presenting the unconditioned stimulus after the conditioned response.
　　c.　using stimulus substitution.
　　d.　reintroducing the unconditioned stimulus.

7.　Garcia's behavioral investigations of rats that were treated with doses of radiation illustrate that:
　　a.　rats obey slightly different principles of classical conditioning than humans do.
　　b.　some research findings involving classical conditioning do not appear to obey Pavlov's conditioning principles.
　　c.　classical conditioning is a very robust form of learning, since it is not weakened even by large doses of medication.
　　d.　changes in classical conditioning are highly sensitive indicators of radiation effects.

8.　When we continue to act in a manner that will lead to pleasing consequences, we behave according to the:
　　a.　law of frequency.
　　b.　principle of similarity.
　　c.　law of effect.
　　d.　principle of contiguity.

9.　The distinction between primary reinforcers and secondary reinforcers is that:
　　a.　primary reinforcers satisfy some biological need; secondary reinforcers are effective because of their association with primary reinforcers.
　　b.　organisms prefer primary reinforcers to secondary reinforcers.
　　c.　primary reinforcers are not effective with all organisms.
　　d.　primary reinforcers depend upon the past conditioning of the organism; secondary reinforcers have a biological basis.

10. Any stimulus that increases the likelihood that a preceding behavior be repeated is called:
    a. a punisher.
    b. a reinforcer.
    c. a response.
    d. an operant.

11. Negative reinforcement:
    a. is a special form of punishment.
    b. is a phenomenon that results when reward is withheld.
    c. involves the decrease or removal of an aversive stimulus.
    d. occurs in both classical and instrumental conditioning.

12. Under variable schedules of reinforcement, the response rate is:
    a. always high.
    b. always constant and low.
    c. easily extinguished.
    d. highly resistant to extinction.

13. Since the number of responses made by a door-to-door salesperson before reinforcement in the form of a sale is not certain, he or she is working on a:
    a. variable-ratio schedule.
    b. fixed-ratio schedule.
    c. variable-interval schedule.
    d. fixed-interval schedule.

14. Superstitious behavior is thought to arise because of:
    a. continuously reinforced patterns of behavior that have led to results related to the behavior.
    b. universal biological constraints that guide specific kinds of behavior.
    c. religious dogma.
    d. partial reinforcement of the connection of incidental events to a specific consequence.

15. Given the opportunity to explore a maze with no explicit reward available, rats will develop:
    a. a cognitive map of the maze.
    b. an aversion to the maze.
    c. an increased interest in the maze.
    d. a superstitious fear of the maze.

PRACTICE TEST II:

16. Learning is best defined as:
    a. a change in behavior brought about by growth and maturity of the nervous system.
    b. a measurable change in behavior brought about by conditions such as drugs, sleep, and fatigue.
    c. a behavioral response that occurs each time a critical stimulus is presented.
    d. a relatively permanent change in behavior brought about by experience.

17. In classical conditioning, the stimulus that comes to elicit a response that it would not previously have elicited is called the:
    a. classical stimulus.
    b. unconditioned stimulus.
    c. conditioned stimulus.
    d. discriminative stimulus.

18. Prior to the conditioning trials in which Watson planned to condition fear of a rat in Baby Albert, the rat—which Albert was known not to fear—would have been considered:
    a. an unconditioned stimulus.
    b. an adaptive stimulus.
    c. a discriminative stimulus.
    d. a neutral stimulus.

19. Systematic desensitization is achieved by:
   a. no longer allowing the conditioned stimulus and the unconditioned stimulus to be paired in real-life situations.
   b. constructing a hierarchy of situations that produce fear and then gradually pairing more stressful situations with strategies to relax.
   c. identifying the situations that produce fear in order to modify or eliminate them.
   d. gaining exposure to the most fearful situations so that the unpleasant reactions can be extinguished quickly.

20. _____ occurs when the conditioned stimulus is presented repeatedly without being accompanied by the unconditioned stimulus.
   a. Escape conditioning
   b. Extinction
   c. Stimulus generalization
   d. Negative reinforcement

21. Pavlov's assumption that stimuli and responses were linked in a mechanistic, unthinking way has been challenged by:
   a. cognitive learning theorists.
   b. the animal trainers, the Brelands.
   c. Edward Thorndike's law of effect.
   d. operant conditioning.

22. A reinforcement given for the first correct or desired response to occur after a set period of time is called:
   a. a fixed-ratio reinforcement schedule.
   b. a continuous reinforcement schedule.
   c. a fixed-interval reinforcement schedule.
   d. a variable-interval reinforcement schedule.

23. Which alternative below is **not** an example of operant conditioning?
   a. A cat pushes against a lever to open a door on its cage.
   b. A student drives within the speed limit to avoid getting another parking ticket.
   c. A dog rolls over for a dog biscuit.
   d. A student's blood pressure increases when she anticipates speaking with her chemistry professor.

24. Which name below is **not** associated with classical conditioning or operant conditioning?
   a. Pavlov
   b. Skinner
   c. Wertheimer
   d. Thorndike

25. Typically, food is a _____, whereas money is a _____.
   a. discriminative stimulus; conditioned reinforcer
   b. need; motive
   c. primary reinforcer; secondary reinforcer
   d. drive reducer; natural reinforcer

26. According to the definition given in the text, which of the following is most likely to be considered a primary reinforcer?
   a. money
   b. water
   c. good grades
   d. a hammer

27. According to the text, in which of the following situations would the use of punishment be most effective in reducing the undesired behavior?
   a. An employee is demoted for misfiling a report.
   b. A child is spanked for hitting her sister.
   c. A teenager is denied the opportunity to attend the Friday dance for staying out late on Monday.
   d. A child is spanked for running into the street.

28. Piecework in a factory, where a worker is paid for three pieces made, is an example of a:
   a. fixed-interval schedule of reinforcement.
   b. variable-interval schedule of reinforcement.
   c. variable-ratio schedule of reinforcement.
   d. fixed-ratio schedule of reinforcement.

29. With a fixed-interval schedule, especially in the period just after reinforcement, response rates are:
   a. speeded up
   b. extinguished
   c. relatively unchanged
   d. relatively low

30. Rewarding each step toward a desired behavior _____ the new response pattern.
   a. inhibits
   b. shapes
   c. disrupts
   d. eliminates

PRACTICE TEST III: Conceptual, Applied, and Challenging Questions

31. Through conditioning, a dog learns to salivate at the sound of a bell because the bell signals that food is coming. In subsequent learning trials, a buzzer is sounded just prior to the bell. Soon the dog salivates at the sound of the buzzer. In this case, the bell acts as the:
   a. unconditioned stimulus.
   b. conditioned stimulus.
   c. unconditioned response.
   d. conditioned response.

32. In preparing food for her daughter, Joanna uses a juicer. Soon the baby knows that the sound of the juicer signals that food is on the way. In this case, the food acts as:
   a. an unconditioned stimulus.
   b. a conditioned stimulus.
   c. an unconditioned response.
   d. a conditioned response.

33. In preparing food for his young son, Ron uses a blender. Soon the baby knows that the sound of the blender signals that food is on the way. In this case, the blender acts as:
   a. an unconditioned stimulus.
   b. a conditioned stimulus.
   c. an unconditioned response.
   d. a conditioned response.

34. Rats are sometimes sickened by poisoned bait that resembles their favorite foods. Afterward, the rats avoid eating food that resemble the poisoned bait. The sickness caused by the poisoned bait is _____ in classical conditioning.
   a. an unconditioned response
   b. an unconditioned stimulus
   c. a conditioned response
   d. a conditioned stimulus

35. A child looks at her puppy; the puppy barks, and the child gently hugs the puppy. In this case, the puppy's bark is:
    a. evidence of stimulus generalization.
    b. an operant response, likely to be repeated
    c. a reinforcer for the girl's subsequent hug of the puppy.
    d. an aversive response established via classical conditioning.

36. Victor participates in aversive conditioning in order to stop smoking. Now he dislikes cigarettes and has also linked his dislike to the store where he used to buy them. This reaction illustrates:
    a. operant conditioning.   c. higher-order conditioning.
    b. stimulus discrimination.   d. systematic desensitization.

37. A 3-year-old is being taught colors and their names. When shown a red, pink, or yellow rose, the child correctly identifies the color of each flower. This is an example of:
    a. stimulus discrimination.   c. spontaneous generalization.
    b. stimulus generalization.   d. spontaneous recovery.

38. The U.S. Customs Service uses dogs at airports and docks to stop illegal drug shipments. Typically, the dogs are trained to sniff out a specific drug such as cocaine, and to ignore all other drugs. The ability of the dogs to respond only to the specific drug they were trained to detect is an example of:
    a. stimulus discrimination.   c. partial reinforcement.
    b. response generalization.   d. spontaneous recovery.

39. Students generally study very hard before midterms and then slack off immediately afterward, which is characteristic of behavior reinforced on:
    a. a fixed-ratio schedule.   c. a fixed-interval schedule.
    b. a variable-ratio schedule.   d. a variable-interval schedule.

40. Professor Chao has been conducting studies in which children are given an opportunity to explore a complicated play area for a time, and then they are asked to locate a specific item in the room. He claims that their speed and accuracy results from unseen mental processes that intervene in learning the area. Which of the following labels best describes Dr. Chao?
    a. personality psychologist.   c. cognitive psychologist.
    b. sensory psychologist.   d. biopsychologist.

41. The existence of _____ supports the idea that learning may occur even though it is not yet evident in performance.
    a. partial reinforcement   c. shaping
    b. classical conditioning   d. latent learning

42. Kachtia's roommate is playing her stereo with the volume turned almost all the way up. In order to study, she puts on her own headphones and plays softer music to block out the loud music. Since the headphones result in the removal of the aggravating sound, the action would be called:
    a. punishment by application.   c. negative reinforcement.
    b. positive reinforcement.   d. punishment by removal.

43. Research studies that show a positive relationship between hours of viewed TV violence and viewers' personal aggressiveness show a methodological weakness in the sense that:
   a. only a few hundred persons serve as subjects in the study.
   b. the researchers interpret the results with bias favoring their own theoretical viewpoints.
   c. people lie habitually on surveys regarding their viewing habits.
   d. correlational data cannot prove that the TV viewing caused the violent behavior.

44. Clyde tends to view information from the context of a broad perspective, usually taking an intuitive approach rather than a structured one in understanding information, and is also more task-oriented. Based on this information, which of the following best describes Clyde?
   a. He has a relational learning style.
   b. He tends to learn through classical conditioning.
   c. He will probably serve as a model in observational learning processes.
   d. He has a tendency toward implicit learning.

45. Raynard wants to improve his study skills. Which of the following options would he need to select before the others?
   a. He should determine how effective his strategies have been so far.
   b. He should identify specific tests and class projects on which he can show improvement.
   c. He should implement the program of skill improvement.
   d. He should select a study skill to change.

Essay Questions

Essay Question 5.1: *Using Physical Punishment*

Recite ❑
Review ❑

The use of physical punishment has become quite controversial. Most school systems now outlaw its use, and many parents try to find alternatives to it. Define the issues related to the use of punishment, and answer the question, "Is it wrong to use physical punishment to discipline children?" As you answer, consider whether there are circumstances that may require routine use, or if it should be rare. Describe alternatives for its use in normal disciplining of children.

Essay Question 5.2: *Which Approach Is Correct?*

Three approaches to learning are described in the text. Classical and operant conditioning rely on external determinants of behavior, and cognitive learning depends in part on internal, mental activity. How can the differences between these three approaches be reconciled?

Activities and Projects

1. Either write about or discuss with a friend a fear that you have—a fear of cats, mice, dogs, insects, spiders, heights, being home alone, or any other fear. How did you acquire the fear? Can you see any connection between acquiring the fear and the principles of classical conditioning? How might the fear be explained through conditioning? Has the fear extended to other stimuli through higher-order conditioning or through stimulus generalization? Why has your fear not been extinguished?

Recite ❏
Review ❏

Fear:

_____

_____

How acquired:

_____

_____

_____

_____

Possible original unconditioned stimulus/unconditioned response relationship:

_____

_____

_____

Any higher-order conditioning?

_____

_____

Reason extinction has not occurred:

_____

_____

2. Keep a record for several days of the activities that you undertake and the kinds of rewards and other reinforcements you give yourself or receive from others. Include the time you do the activity and whether anyone was with you. After several days, review the list and the related reinforcement. Are there any patterns? Do you tend to accept offers to do things that distract you from study (like going for pizza, going to the game room, or watching television or a movie) more readily than offers that distract you from other activities? What other patterns do you find? Do you reinforce your study time with food or with some other form of relaxation?

ACTIVITY CHART			
Activity/Time	**Reinforcement**	**Should it be changed?**	**Alternative Behavior**

Cultural Idioms

p. 168
golden retriever; labrador: two different types of dogs
Andre Agassi: famous tennis player

p. 169
national anthem: a country's song
golden arches: the symbol, or logo, of McDonald's fast food restaurants; the "golden arches" resemble a large rounded "M."
a bride walking down the aisle: In Christian wedding ceremonies, the bride walks down the aisle of a church, and the groom is waiting for her at the altar of the church
tuning fork: a device that makes a clear ringing sound

p. 170
a startle reaction: a feeling of being surprised

p. 172
rules of thumb: ideas that describe what is generally true

p. 173
the famous shower scene in *Psycho*: Alfred Hitchcock's movie *Psycho* contains a frightening scene where a person is murdered in a shower
"cured": the author uses quotation marks to suggest that perhaps the addicts are not really cured, but only called cured.
a rose is a rose is a rose: This is a line from the poet Gertrude Stein; here the author means that even though each rose is unique, it's still a rose.

p. 174
to brake at all red lights: to stop your car whenever you see a red traffic light
in uncomfortable straits: in a difficult situation

p. 176
getting the hang of it: understanding the subject
toiling industriously: working hard

p. 179
Hershey bar: a kind of chocolate candy
cold symptoms: the signs of being ill with a cold
hot radiator: a heater used in some homes; radiators can become very hot
"grounded": a taking away of privileges, such as driving or spending time with friends

p. 180
a treatment of last resort: the last thing you try

p. 181
folded for good: stopped playing the game of poker forever
missed a catch: when a fish that you think you are going to catch escapes
door-to-door salespeople: people who go from house to house trying to sell things

p. 182
soda vending machine: a machine where you put in money to buy a soda
Las Vegas slot machine: a gambling machine, where you put in a small amount of money and hope to win a lot of money

p. 183
x dollars: a certain amount of money, although the author is not specific
telephone salesperson: a person who sells things over the phone, by calling up strangers and offering them credit cards or a cheaper phone rate

p. 184
cram: to study intensely before an examination or test
surprise quizzes: a short test that the students do not know about in advance

p. 185
getting a single: in baseball, when a batter hits the ball well enough to get to first base
he is at bat: he is the batter, the person whose turn it is to hit the ball
automobile transmission: the part of a car that takes the power from the engine and makes the wheels turn; the gears
Model T: an early automobile, made by the Ford Motor Company
zither: a musical instrument

p. 186
back rub: a massage
You Can't Teach an Old Dog Just Any Trick: The author is making a joke, based on the common English proverb, "You can't teach an old dog new tricks." The original proverb means that once a person is old he or she can't learn anything new; here the author has changed the proverb to mean that animals can learn new behaviors, but what they can learn is limited because of their biology.

p. 187
unhealthy eating: eating food that is not nutritionally balanced

p. 188
get behind the wheel: to sit in the driver's seat, to drive a car
several quarters: several directions

p. 190
Fearless Peer: the friend who is not afraid

p. 191
media aggression: violence in the movies or on TV
MTV: Music Television, a cable TV channel that shows music videos
the mass media: TV, movies, newspapers, magazines, radio

p. 192
continual diet of aggression: constant exposure to violence

p. 193
treatment: a short written description of an idea for a movie
screenwriters: people who write movie scripts
television rating system: a TV labeling system that enables parents to tell how much violence or sex a TV show contains

p. 195
"black box analysis": this is a reference to B. F. Skinner's black boxes
the quality of their love life: their emotional/sexual relationship
dirty lunch dishes: in U. S. culture, it is now generally expected that men as well as women will do kitchen work

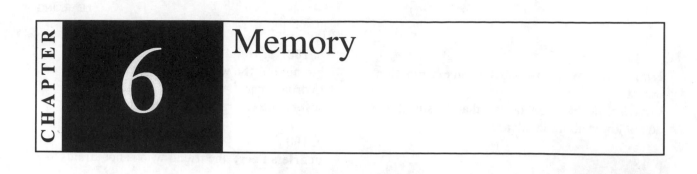

CHAPTER 6 Memory

Detailed Chapter Outline

This detailed outline contains all the headings in Chapter 6: Memory. If you are using the SQ3R method, then an examination of the outline is the best way to begin your survey of the chapter.

Survey ❑
Question ❑

Prologue: The Wife Who Forgot She Had a Husband
Looking Ahead

Encoding, Storage, and Retrieval of Memory
The Three Systems of Memory: Memory Storehouses
Sensory Memory
Short-Term Memory: Our Working Memory
Rehearsal
Working Memory: The Components of Short-Term Memory
Long-Term Memory: The Final Storehouse
The Modules of Memory
Levels of Processing

Recap, Review, and Rethink

Recalling Long-Term Memories
Retrieval Cues
Flashbulb Memories
Constructive Processes in Memory: Rebuilding the Past
Memory in the Courtroom: The Eyewitness on Trial
Repressed Memories: Truth or Fiction?
Autobiographical Memory: Where Past Meets Present

Exploring Diversity: Are There Cross-Cultural Differences in Memory?

Recap, Review, and Rethink

Forgetting: When Memory Fails

Proactive and Retroactive Interference: The Before and After of Forgetting

The Biological Bases of Memory: The Search for the Engram

The Site of the Engram

Recent Work on the Biological Bases of Memory

Memory Dysfunctions: Afflictions of Forgetting

Applying Psychology in the 21st Century: Are Memory Drugs on the Horizon?

Pathways Through Psychology: Janice McGillick, Alzheimer's Association

The Informed Consumer of Psychology: Improving Your Memory

Recap, Review, and Rethink

Looking Back

Key Terms and Concepts

➤ Now that you have surveyed the chapter, read **Looking Ahead**, pages 204–205. What questions does the Chapter seek to answer?

Question ❑
Read ❑

Concepts and Learning Objectives

Survey ❑

These are the concepts and the learning objectives for Chapter 6. Read them carefully as part of your preliminary survey of the chapter.

Concept 1: Memory involves three processes: encoding, storage, and retrieval of information. There are also three main systems of memory: sensory, short-term, and long-term, and these types are distinguished according to how long the information stays in them (storage), how they are acquired (encoded), and how they are recalled (retrieval).

1. Define memory and the basic processes of encoding, storing, and retrieving information.

2. Describe sensory memory, and discuss the characteristics of short-term memory.

3. Describe the characteristics of long-term memory, distinguishing between declarative and procedural, semantic and episodic, and implicit and explicit memories.

Concept 2: Recollection from long-term memory presents a number of issues regarding the accuracy of the memory, the way it was stored, and its specific nature.

4. Distinguish the levels of processing theory from the three memory stages of sensory, short-term, and long-term memory.

5. Define the means of recalling information from long-term memory, and the characteristics of memory that improve recall.

6. Define constructive processes. Consider issues regarding the accuracy of constructed memories, including autobiographical memory.

Concept 3: Forgetting is a normal process of memory, and some forgetting is required in order to make memory more efficient. The major forms of forgetting include the decay theory and the concept of interference. Memory dysfunctions can have biological and psychological causes.

7. Discuss how memories are forgotten, especially the roles of proactive and retroactive interference.

8. Describe the biological bases of memory, and distinguish among the common memory disorders.

9. Describe techniques for improving memory skills.

Chapter Guided Review

There are several ways you can use this guided review as part of your systematic study plan. Read the corresponding pages of the text and then complete the review by supplying the correct missing key word. Or, you may want to complete the guided review as a means of becoming familiar with the text. Complete the review and then read the section thoroughly. As you finish each section, complete the **Recap and Review** questions that are supplied in the text.

Survey ❏

CONCEPT 1:   Encoding, Storage, and Retrieval of Memory

Survey ❏
Read ❏
Recite ❏

- *What is memory?*
- *Are there different kinds of memory?*

Pages 205-216

Three processes comprise memory. **[a]** _____ is the process of placing information in a form that can be used by memory. **[b]** _____ is the process of retaining information for later use. **[c]** _____ is the process of recovering information from storage. By definition, then, **[d]** _____ is the sum of these three processes. Forgetting is an important part of memory because it allows us to make generalizations and abstractions from daily life.

The memory system is typically divided into three storage components or stages. The initial storage system is that of **[e]** _____, where momentary storage of sensory information occurs. **[f]** _____ includes information that has been given some form of meaning, and it lasts for 15 to 25 seconds. **[g]** _____ is the relatively permanent storage of memory. While there are no locations in the brain of these memory stages, they are considered abstract memory systems with different characteristics.

Sensory memories are considered to differ according to the kind of sensory information, and the sensory memory is thought of as several types of sensory memories based on the source of the sensory messages. Visual sensory memory is called **[h]** _____, and its source is the visual sensory system; auditory sensory memory is called

[i] _____, and its source is the auditory sensory system. Sensory memory stores information for a very short time. Iconic memory may last no more than a second, and echoic memory may last for three to four seconds. The duration of iconic memory was established by George Sperling's classic experiment in which subjects were unable to recall an entire array of letters but could, on a cue after the array was shown for one-twentieth of a second, recall any part of the array. Unless the information taken into the sensory memories is somehow transferred to another memory system, the sensory memories are quickly lost.

Sensory memories are raw information without meaning. In order to be transferred to the long-term memory, these sensory memories must be given meaning and placed in short-term memory. One view of this process suggests that the short-term memory is composed of verbal representations that have a very short duration. George Miller has identified the capacity of short-term memory as seven (plus or minus two) **[j]** _____, or meaningful groups of stimuli that are stored as a unit in the short-term memory. They can be several letters or numbers, or they can be complicated patterns, like the patterns of pieces on a chessboard. However, to be placed in a chunk, the board must represent a real or possible game for even chess masters to be able to make a chunk.

Memories can be held in short-term memory longer by **[k]** _____, the repetition of information already in the short-term memory. Rehearsal is also the beginning of transferring short-term memory into long-term memory. The kind of rehearsal influences the effectiveness of the transfer to long-term memory. **[l]** _____ occurs whenever the material is associated with other information through placement in a logical framework, connection with another memory, the formation of an image, or some other transformation. The strategies for organizing memories are called **[m]**_____. Mnemonics are formal techniques for organizing information so that recall is more likely.

[n] _____ comes from Baddeley's theory that short-term memory has three components: the *central executive*, the *visuospatial sketch pad*, and the *phonological loop*.

Two kinds of long-term memory have been identified, **[o]** _____ and

[p] _____. Procedural memory includes the memory for skills and habits, like walking, riding a bicycle, and other physical activity. Declarative memory includes

[q]_____, memories of specific events related to individual experiences,

and **[r]** _____, those that consist of abstract knowledge and facts about the

world. Psychologists use **[s]** _____ to suggest that semantic memories represent the associations between mental representations of various pieces of information. When we think about a particular thing, related ideas are activated because of the association.

[t]_____ refers to the activation of one item, thereby making recall of

related items easier. **[u]** _____ refers to intentional or conscious effort to

recall memory, and **[v]** _____ refers to memories of which people are not consciously aware but nevertheless affect later performance and behavior.

An alternative to the three-stage view of memory is the **[w]** _____. This theory suggests that the difference in memories depends on the depth to which particular information is processed, that is, the degree to which information is analyzed and considered. The more attention information is given, the deeper it is stored and the less likely it is to be forgotten. Superficial aspects of information are given shallow processing, but when meaning is given, the processing is at its deepest level. This approach suggests that memory requires more active mental processing than the three-stage approach involves.

CONCEPT 2: Recalling Long-Term Memories

Survey ❑
Read ❑
Recite ❑

- ● *What causes difficulties and failures in remembering?*

Pages 217-225

Retrieving information from long-term memory may be influenced by

many factors. The **[a]** _____ **phenomenon**, where one is certain of knowing something but cannot recall it, represents one difficulty. The simple number of items of information that has been stored may influence recall. We sort through this quantity with the

help of **[b]** _____. These are stimuli that allow recall from long-term memory. *Recall* consists of a series of processes—a search through memory, retrieval of potentially relevant information, then a decision whether the information is accurate, and a continuation of these steps until the right information is found. In contrast, *recognition* involves determining whether a stimulus that has been presented is correct, such as the selection of the stimulus from a list or determining whether the stimulus has been seen before.

In particularly intense events, we may develop [c] _____. A specific important or surprising event creates memories so vivid that they appear as a "snapshot" of the event. Research regarding flashbulb memories concerning President Kennedy's assassination has revealed common details, such as where the person was, who told the person, the person's own emotions, and some personal detail of the event. Harsh and Neisser asked students the day after the *Challenger* accident how they had heard about it, and then asked the same question three years later. One-third were wrong, a result suggesting that flashbulb memories may be inaccurate. Memories that are exceptional may be more easily retrieved than commonplace information.

Our memories reflect [d] _____, processes in which memories are influenced by the meaning we have attached to them. Guesses and inferences thus influence memory. Sir Frederic Bartlett first suggested that people remember in terms of

[e]_____, which are general themes without specific details. Schemas were based on an understanding of the event, expectations, and an understanding of the motivation of others. The process of *serial reproduction*, a process that requires people to pass information from one to another in a sequence, has shown the effect of schemas. The final story is much changed in comparison to the original version, and it reflects the expectations of those retelling the story. Apparently, prior knowledge and expectations influence how we initially store the information. How we understand peoples' motivation also influences memory. In the

[f]_____, knowledge about a person's motivation leads to an elaboration of past events involving that person.

The imperfection of memory has led to research into the accuracy of eyewitness testimony. The mistaken identification of individuals can lead to imprisonment. When a weapon is involved, the weapon draws attention away from other details. In research involving staged crimes, witnesses vary significantly in their judgment of the height of the perpetrator, with judgments differing by as much as two feet. The wording of questions can influence testimony. Children are especially prone to unreliable recollections.

The case of George Franklin illustrates the impact recovered memories can have (he was found guilty on the basis of these memories alone). While childhood recollections can be forgotten and then recovered, the evidence does suggest that much distortion can take place as well, even to the point of fabricating false memories from childhood.

[g] _____ are our collections of information about our lives. People tend to forget information about the past that is incongruent with the way they currently see themselves. Depressed people tend to recall sad events more readily than happy ones from their past. More recent information also appears to be more affected than recollections from earlier times.

CONCEPT 3: Forgetting: When Memory Fails

- *Why do we forget information?*
- *What are the biological bases of memory?*
- *What are the major memory impairments?*

Survey ❑
Read ❑
Recite ❑

Pages 226-235

Herman Ebbinghaus studied forgetting by learning a list of nonsense syllables and then timing how long it took him, at a later trial, to relearn the list. The most rapid forgetting occurs in the first nine hours. Two views concerning the forgetting of information have been developed. One theory explains forgetting by **[a]** _____, or the loss of information through nonuse. When a memory is formed, a **[b]** _____, or **[c]** _____, occurs. An engram is an actual physical change in the brain. The decay theory assumes that memories become more decayed with time, but the evidence does not support this happening, though there is support for the existence of decay. The other theory proposes that

[d]_____ between bits of information leads to forgetting. In interference, information blocks or displaces other information, preventing recall. Most forgetting appears to be the result of interference.

There are two kinds of interference. One is called **[e]** _____ which occurs when previously learned information blocks the recall of newer information. **[f]**

_____ is when new information blocks the recall of old information. Most research suggests that information that has been blocked by interference can eventually be recalled if appropriate stimuli are used.

The biological bases of memory at the level of the neuron point to the underlying process of

[g] _____, or the change in the excitability of a neuron at the synapse. As these changes occur, the work of **[h]** _____, or transfer of short-term memories to long-term memories, takes place. It was originally thought that memories were evenly distributed throughout the brain. However, the current view suggests that the areas of the brain that are responsible for processing information about the world also store that information.

[i] _____ includes severe memory problems as one of its many symptoms. Initially, the symptoms appear as simple forgetfulness, progressing to more profound loss of memory, even failure to recognize one's own name and the loss of language abilities. The protein beta amyloid, important for maintaining neural connections, has been implicated in the progress of the disease. **[j]** _____ is another memory problem. Amnesia is a loss of memory occurring without apparent loss of mental function.

[k]_____ is memory loss for memories that preceded a traumatic event.

[l]_____ is a loss for memories that follow a traumatic event. Long-term alcoholics who develop *Korsakoff's syndrome* also have amnesia. Korsakoff's syndrome is related to thiamine deficiency. A perfect memory, one with total recall, might actually be very discomforting. A case studied by Luria of a man with total recall reveals that the inability to forget becomes debilitating.

The Informed Consumer of Psychology section outlines several mnemonic techniques and how they can be applied to taking tests. They include the *keyword technique*, in which one pairs a word with a mental image, or in the case of learning a foreign language, the foreign word with a similar sounding English word. The *method of loci* requires that one imagine items to be remembered as being placed in particular locations. Another phenomenon that affects memory is called **[m]** _____ . Recall is best when it is attempted in conditions that are similar to the conditions under which the information was originally learned. The organization of text and lecture material may enhance memory of it. Practice and rehearsal also improve long-term recall. Rehearsal to the point of mastery is called *overlearning*. It should be noted that cramming for exams is an ineffective technique, and the better approach is to distribute practice over many sessions.

➤ Now that you have surveyed, questioned, and read the chapter and completed the guided review, review **Looking Back**, pages 235-236.

Review ❏

➤ For additional practice through recitation and review, test your knowledge of the chapter material by answering the questions in the *Key Word Drill*, the *Practice Questions*, and the *Essay Questions*.

Key Word Drill

The following **Matching Questions** test the boldfaced and italicized key words from the text. Check your answers with the Answer Key in the back of the *Study Guide*.

Recite ❏

MATCHING QUESTIONS

_____ 1. encoding

a. Locating and using information stored in memory.

_____ 2. storage

b. Relatively permanent memory.

_____ 3. retrieval

c. Information recorded as a meaningless stimulus.

_____ 4. sensory memory

d. Recording information in a form usable to memory.

_____ 5. short-term memory

e. Working memory that lasts about 15 to 25 seconds.

_____ 6. long-term memory

f. The location where information is saved.

_____ 7. iconic memory

_____ 8. echoic memory

_____ 9. episodic memories

_____ 10. semantic memories

_____ 11. declarative memory

_____ 12. procedural memory

a. Memory for skills and habits.

b. Stored information relating to personal experiences.

c. Stored, organized facts about the world (e.g., mathematical and historical data).

d. The storage of information obtained from the sense of hearing.

e. The storage of visual information.

f. Memory for facts and knowledge.

_____ 13. retrieval cue

_____ 14. recall

_____ 15. recognition

_____ 16. flashbulb memories

_____ 17. serial reproduction

_____ 18. soap opera effect

a. Drawing from memory a specific piece of information for a specific purpose.

b. The phenomena by which the memory of a prior event involving a person is more reliable when we understand that person's motivations.

c. Memories of a specific event that are so clear they seem like "snapshots" of the event.

d. Acknowledging prior exposure to a given stimulus, rather than recalling the information from memory.

e. A stimulus such as a word, smell, or sound that aids recall of information located in long-term memory.

f. The passage of interpretive information from person to person, often resulting in inaccuracy through personal bias and misinterpretation.

_____ 19. memory trace

_____ 20. proactive interference

_____ 21. retroactive interference

_____ 22. keyword technique

_____ 23. method of loci

_____ 24. encoding specificity

_____ 25. overlearning

a. The pairing of a foreign word with a common, similar sounding English word to aid in remembering the new word.

b. A physical change in the brain corresponding to the memory of material.

c. New information interferes with the recall of information learned earlier.

d. Rehearsing material beyond the point of mastery to improve long-term recall.

e. Assigning words or ideas to places, thereby improving recall of the words by envisioning those places.

f. Memory of information is enhanced when recalled under the same conditions as when it was learned.

g. Information stored in memory interferes with recall of material learned later.

_____ 26. rehearsal

_____ 27. associative models

_____ 28. priming

_____ 29. consolidation

_____ 30. long-term potentiation

_____ 31. autobiographical memory

_____ 32. engram

a. A technique of recalling information by having been exposed to related information at an earlier time.

b. Changes in sensitivity at the neuron's synapse.

c. The transfer of material from short- to long-term memory by repetition.

d. The process of creating long-term memories.

e. Recollections of the facts about our own lives.

f. A physical change in the brain corresponding to the memory of material.

g. A technique of recalling information by thinking about related information.

_____ 33. Alzheimer's disease

_____ 34. amnesia

_____ 35. retrograde amnesia

_____ 36. anterograde amnesia

_____ 37. Korsakoff's syndrome

a. An illness associated with aging that includes severe memory loss and loss of language abilities.

b. A memory impairment disease among alcoholics.

c. Memory loss unaccompanied by other mental difficulties.

d. Memory loss of the events following an injury.

e. Memory loss of occurrences prior to some event.

Practice Questions

Test your knowledge of the chapter material by answering these **Multiple Choice Questions**. These questions have been placed in three Practice Tests. The first two tests are composed of questions that will test your recall of factual knowledge. The third test contains questions that are challenging and primarily test for conceptual knowledge and your ability to apply that knowledge. Check your answers and review the feedback using the Answer Key in the back of the *Study Guide*.

Recite ❑
Review ❑

MULTIPLE CHOICE QUESTIONS

PRACTICE TEST I:

1. The process of recording information in a form that can be recalled is:
   a. encoding.
   b. storage.
   c. decoding.
   d. retrieval.

2. The process of identifying and using information stored in memory is referred to as:
   a. storage.
   b. retrieval.
   c. recording.
   d. learning.

3. _____ stores information for approximately 15 to 20 seconds.
   a. Sensory memory
   b. Short-term memory
   c. Iconic memory
   d. Long-term memory

4. Short-term memory can hold approximately:
   a. five items.
   b. seven items.
   c. ten items.
   d. eighteen items.

5. Rehearsal:
    a. facilitates neither short-term memory nor long-term memory.
    b. has no effect on short-term memory duration, yet it facilitates the transfer of material into long-term memory.
    c. helps to prolong information in short-term memory but has no effect on the transfer of material into long-term memory.
    d. extends the duration of information in short-term memory and also assists its transfer into long-term memory.

6. Recalling what we have done and the kinds of experiences we have had best illustrates:
    a. periodic memory.
    c. semantic memory.
    b. episodic memory.
    d. serial production memory.

7. If your episodic long-term memory were disabled, you would be unable to:
    a. remember details of your own personal life.
    b. recall simple facts such as the name of the U. S. president.
    c. speak, although you could still comprehend language through listening.
    d. maintain information in short-term memory via rehearsal.

8. Information from long-term memory is easier to access with the aid of:
    a. a retrieval cue.
    c. interpolated material.
    b. distractors.
    d. a sensory code.

9. The tip-of-the-tongue phenomenon exemplifies difficulties in:
    a. encoding.
    c. storage.
    b. decoding.
    d. retrieval.

10. Constructive processes are associated with all of the following **except**:
    a. episodic memory.
    c. procedural memory.
    b. motivation.
    d. organization.

11. After memorizing a series of nonsense syllables, Ebbinghaus discovered that forgetting was most dramatic _____ following learning.
    a. two days
    c. ten days
    b. an hour
    d. one day

12. Repeatedly reciting a verbal sequence of words:
    a. minimizes the effects of proactive interference.
    b. prevents trace decay from occurring.
    c. activates different brain areas than when the word sequence is spoken the first time.
    d. is a characteristic symptom of the disorder known as Korsakoff's syndrome; this symptom can, in most cases, be treated with drugs.

13. Memories lost under retrograde amnesia sometimes are recovered later; this implies that the amnesia interfered with the process of:
    a. encoding.
    c. retrieval.
    b. storage.
    d. association.

14. Which situation below is characteristic of anterograde amnesia?
    a. A person has loss of memory for events prior to some critical event.
    b. A person receives a physical trauma to the head and has difficulty remembering things after the accident.
    c. A person forgets simple skills such as how to dial a telephone.
    d. A person begins to experience difficulties in remembering appointments and relevant dates such as birthdays.

15. The keyword technique is a memory aid that can be helpful in learning a foreign language. The first step is to identify:
    a. a word that has similar meaning in a familiar language and pair it with the foreign word to be learned.
    b. a word that has a similar sound in a familiar language to at least part of the foreign word and pair it with the foreign word to be learned.
    c. a word that suggests similar imagery in a familiar language and pair it with the foreign word to be learned.
    d. the first word to come to mind in a familiar language and pair it with the foreign word to be learned.

PRACTICE TEST II:

16. Recording information in the memory system is referred to as:
    a. encoding.
    c. decoding.
    b. storage.
    d. retrieval.

17. Information deteriorates most quickly from:
    a. explicit memory.
    c. sensory memory.
    b. short-term memory.
    d. episodic declarative memory.

18. Information in short-term memory is stored according to its:
    a. meaning.
    c. length.
    b. intensity.
    d. sense.

19. The process of grouping information into units for storage in short-term memory is called:
    a. similarity.
    c. chunking.
    b. priming.
    d. closure.

20. In order to enhance consolidation of long-term memory, _____ may be necessary while information is in the short-term stage.
    a. massed practice
    c. interpolation
    b. elaborative rehearsal
    d. interference

21. Knowledge about grammar, spelling, historical dates, and other knowledge about the world best illustrates:
    a. periodic memory.
    c. semantic memory.
    b. episodic memory.
    d. serial production memory.

22. According to the levels-of-processing model, what determines how well specific information is remembered?
    a. the stage attained
    b. the meaning of the information
    c. the quality of the information
    d. the depth of processing

23. Finding the correct answer on a multiple choice test depends on:
    a. serial search.
    b. recall.
    c. mnemonics.
    d. recognition.

24. The detailed, vivid account of what you were doing when you learned of the *Challenger* disaster represents a:
    a. cognitive map.
    b. schema.
    c. flashbulb memory.
    d. seizure.

25. Your memory of how to skate is probably based on:
    a. procedural memory.
    b. semantic memory.
    c. elaborative rehearsal.
    d. declarative memory.

26. Which explanation has **not** been offered to account for how we forget information that was learned?
    a. decay
    b. interference
    c. retrieval cue loss
    d. spontaneous inhibition

27. All of the following have been associated with the biological basis of memory **except**:
    a. the hippocampus.
    b. sulci.
    c. neurotransmitters.
    d. long-term potentiation.

28. The fundamental issue surrounding the controversy about repressed memories is whether the memories:
    a. are retrieved from long-term memory or from other type of memory.
    b. can be counteracted by therapy.
    c. have any noticeable effect on mental activities or behavior.
    d. are genuine recollections from the past.

29. Which of the following syndromes is the **least** common?
    a. retrograde amnesia
    b. anterograde amnesia
    c. Alzheimer's disease
    d. Korsakoff's syndrome

30. Which alternative below is **least** likely to help you do well on your next psychology quiz?
    a. Use a prioritized strategy by studying the material only the day before the quiz and avoiding any other subjects which might interfere.
    b. Overlearn the material.
    c. Take brief lecture notes that focus on major points and that emphasize organization.
    d. Ask yourself questions about the material as you study.

PRACTICE TEST III: Conceptual, Applied, and Challenging Questions

31. As Bill listened to the television news, his young son talked excitedly about the new puppy next door. Somewhat frustrated, the boy exclaimed, "You're not paying attention to me!" At this point, Bill diverted his attention to his son and recited the last few things the boy had said. Which memory system is responsible for this ability?
    a. episodic memory
    b. echoic memory
    c. iconic memory
    d. short-term memory

32. Which of the following statements about sensory memory is true?
    a. The information is held until it is replaced by new information.
    b. The information is an accurate representation of the stimulus.
    c. The information is an incomplete representation of the stimulus.
    d. The information is lost if it is not meaningful.

33. When a story has been retold through several stages of serial reproduction, it is likely to be transformed as follows:
    a. Ambiguous details become regularized to fit the person's expectations.
    b. Distinctive features of the story are dropped out.
    c. Engrams that were located will become lost.
    d. The original story will become a "flashbulb," with excellent recall even after several serial reproductions.

34. Older computer monitor screens sometimes have a brief persistence of the old image when the image is changed. This persistence of the monitor image is analogous to:
    a. flashbulb memory.
    b. iconic memory.
    c. echoic memory.
    d. declarative memory.

35. Sherry's tennis coach instructs her to practice a basic stroke for about thirty hours in order to be proficient with the stroke. After she does what the coach has suggested, she discovers that she can execute the stroke without any thought and with complete confidence. This is a demonstration of what kind of memory?
    a. working memory
    b. declarative memory
    c. autobiographical memory
    d. procedural memory

36. After twenty years of not having been on a bicycle, the cycle-shop manager will allow Mark's son to test a cycle only if Mark rides one beside him. Within ten seconds, Mark has adjusted to the bicycle and is even more confident than his son, who has just learned to ride. This is a demonstration of which kind of memory?
    a. working memory
    b. procedural memory
    c. recovered, repressed memories
    d. autobiographical memory

37. Who was responsible for the concept of schemas?
    a. Sigmund Freud
    b. Jean Piaget
    c. Frederic Bartlett
    d. Eleanor Atwater

38. "The strength of a memory relates directly to the kind of attention given to it when the information was experienced." This statement supports most directly:
    a. the three-stage model of memory.
    b. the mental imagery model of memory.
    c. the levels-of-processing model of memory.
    d. the cultural diversity model of memory.

39. You are asked to write a definition of psychology that is based on text and lecture materials in your course. Instead, you write a definition based on materials learned prior to the course. You are experiencing:
    a. retroactive interference.
    b. fugue.
    c. amnesia.
    d. proactive interference.

40. John learns the word-processing program "Easy Word" on his personal computer. Then he learns a second program, "Perfect Word," at work. He now finds it difficult to remember some of the commands when he uses his word processor at home. This is an example of:
    a. work-induced interference.
    b. retroactive interference.
    c. proactive interference.
    d. spontaneous interference.

41. A sales clerk forgets a customer's transaction because twenty other persons' transactions have been completed during the intervening hour. The reduced recall of that customer's purchase reflects:
    a. Alzheimer's disease.
    b. decay.
    c. proactive interference.
    d. retroactive interference.

42. Alzheimer's disease is associated with deterioration of:
    a. the neurological connection between the spinal cord and muscles.
    b. the connection between the hemispheres.
    c. the manufacture of beta amyloid.
    d. the basal ganglia and lower brain structures.

43. Which situation below is most characteristic of retrograde amnesia?
    a. A person begins to experience difficulties in remembering appointments and relevant dates such as birthdays.
    b. A person receives a physical trauma to the head and has difficulty remembering things after the accident.
    c. A person forgets simple skills such as how to dial a telephone.
    d. A person has loss of memory for events prior to some critical event.

44. Kevin is preparing a long speech. He associates the main body of the speech with walking into his living room. This technique is called:
    a. the method of loci.
    b. serial production memory.
    c. the keyword technique.
    d. retroactive interference.

45. Stephanie, the star of the soap opera *When Memory Returns* has found herself without any memory of her past life from a point in time only a few episodes ago. Should her memory failure be real, which of the following types of memory loss best describes her condition?
    a. retrograde amnesia
    b. anterograde amnesia
    c. infantile amnesia
    d. Korsakoff's syndrome

Essay Questions

Essay Question 6.1: *Writing about Repressed Memories*

Recite ❑
Review ❑

What role should psychologists play in helping the courts deal with repressed memories of abuse that have been recovered? Consider both the advantages and disadvantages of the answer you give.

Essay Question 6.2: *Laboratory Memory*

Much of our knowledge about memory comes from strictly laboratory studies. Consider how the lack of "real life" memory studies may bias the kinds of results about how memory works in our daily lives. Do you have any suggestions for how psychologists might study memory in daily life?

Activities and Projects

1. If you are currently studying a foreign language, use the keyword technique to memorize ten words in the language. Learn an additional ten words using the methods you normally use. Either test yourself, or try this prior to a vocabulary test in your language class. Which method is more effective? Does the key word make the foreign term easier to recall? Which set of words did you remember better on the test? Remember, in the keyword system, pair the foreign word with a common, similar-sounding English word to enhance your memory of the foreign word.

Recite ❑
Review ❑

2. Try to remember what you were doing one year ago on this date. This task may seem impossible at first, but when you begin thinking about it, you will probably be able to reconstruct the memory. Verbalize out loud the processes that you are using to remember what you were doing that day. This verbalization should help you understand the steps you are taking as you reconstruct the memory. Ask a friend to try the same.

Record here the steps you take in reconstructing the memory:

_____

_____

_____

_____

3. With other members of your psychology class, construct lists of nonsense syllables in order to replicate the research done by Ebbinghaus. The lists should be 14 to 21 "words" long. Now each person should rehearse a list until it is comfortably memorized. Test each other through the day and record the number of forgotten items and how many hours since the list was memorized. Do not review the list. The forgetting curve can be charted based on the gradual decline in the number of "words" remembered correctly. Several variations of this can be attempted—be creative! In the chart provided, indicate in the columns under each time frame whether or not the word was missed in the trial.

MEMORY TEST FOR NONSENSE WORDS					List # ____
Nonsense Word	**1 hour**	**3 hours**	**9 hours**	**24 hours**	**48 hours**

Cultural Idioms

Recite ❑
Review ❑

p. 204
she rallied: she struggled and used all her strength

p. 205
Trivial Pursuit: a board game where winning depends on how many "trivial" facts a person knows

p. 208
snapshot: a quick photograph

p. 210
"Thirty days hath September...": A poem that U. S. children memorize as a way to remember the number of days in each month ("hath" is an old form of the word "has").

p. 212
sketch pad: a notebook for making quick drawings

p. 214
memory research arena: the scientific field that investigates memory

p.217
sheer quantity: the huge amount
card catalog: the use of index cards to help patrons find books in a library; each book is listed on an index card, which are placed alphabetically in long drawers
search engine: a computer program used to find information on the Internet
Yahoo: the name of a popular Internet search engine (see previous entry)

p. 218
Disney: a company that makes entertainment for children

Snow White and the Seven Dwarfs: a childhood fairy tale
flashbulb: the bright, quick light that a camera uses to take pictures
the space shuttle Challenger: a U. S. spacecraft that exploded during its launch, killing all the people on board
President Kennedy: U. S. president (1961–1963), who was assassinated

p. 220
senior prom: a big dance for U. S. high school students (the "seniors") who are about to graduate
migration of the razor: In people's memories the razor "migrates" (travels) from the White person's hand to the African American's.

p. 221
soap opera: a daytime TV drama; the story continues every day with the same characters and an evolving plot
legal realm: in the area of the law
mistaken identity: when you think a person is someone else; here, witnesses mistakenly thought he was the person who had committed a crime
mugging: attacking people on the street or in the subway for their money

p. 222
anatomically explicit doll: a doll that shows the sex organs; for example, a female doll will have a vagina.

p. 223
murder in the first degree: the most serious kind of murder, in which a person has planned in advance to kill someone
playmate: friend
crying his eyes out: weeping uncontrollably
false chronicles: memories that are not true

p. 224
welfare: money that the government gives to poor families

foster care: when children go to live with a different family, not with their own mother or father

home for delinquents: a school or institution for children who have been in trouble with the police

p. 225
Elvis: Elvis Presley, famous deceased rock star

p. 226
legion: many

p. 230
futuristic scenario: an imaginary scene from the future

p. 231
Oklahoma City bombing: In Oklahoma City, Oklahoma, U. S. terrorists bombed a government building, causing many deaths.

p. 233
The Divine Comedy: An epic poem by the Italian poet Dante, written in Italian in 1321

p. 234
end table: a small table placed next to, or at the end of, a couch

"Less is more": This phrase means that sometimes it's more important to write down less.

7 Cognition and Language

Detailed Chapter Outline

This detailed outline contains all the headings in Chapter 7: Cognition and Language. If you are using the SQ3R method, then an examination of the outline is the best way to begin your survey of the chapter.

Survey ❑
Question ❑

Prologue: One Man's Mousetraps
Looking Ahead

Thinking and Reasoning
Thinking
Mental Images: Examining the Mind's Eye
Concepts: Categorizing the World
Reasoning: Making Up Your Mind
 Deductive and Inductive Reasoning

> **Applying Psychology in the 21st Century:** Can Machines Think?

 Algorithms and Heuristics
Recap, Review, and Rethink

Problem Solving
Preparation: Understanding and Diagnosing Problems
 Kinds of Problems
 Representing and Organizing the Problem
Production: Generating Solutions
 Trial and Error
 Means-Ends Analysis
 Subgoals
 Insight
Judgment: Evaluating the Solutions
Impediments to Problem Solving
 Functional Fixedness and Mental Set
 Inaccurate Evaluation of Solutions
 Creativity and Problem Solving

> **The Informed Consumer of Psychology:** Thinking Critically
> and Creatively

Recap, Review, and Rethink

Language
Grammar: Language's Language
Language Development: Developing a Way with Words
Understanding Language Acquisition: Identifying the Roots of Language
The Influence of Language on Thinking
Do Animals Use Language?

> **Pathways Through Psychology:** Rose Sevcik,
> Language Researcher

> **Exploring Diversity:** Linguistic Variety: Spanglish,
> Ebonics, and Bilingual Education

Recap, Review, and Rethink
Looking Back
Key Terms and Concepts

➤ Now that you have surveyed the chapter, read **Looking Ahead**, page 241.
What questions does the Chapter seek to answer?

Question ❑
Read ❑

Concepts and Learning Objectives

These are the concepts and the learning objectives for Chapter 7. Read them
carefully as part of your preliminary survey of the chapter.

Survey ❑

Concept 1: Cognitive psychology is focused on the study of processes we typically identify
with thinking. Central to our ability to think are the processes of mental representation,
forming concepts, and reasoning.

1. Define cognition and the processes of thinking, mental imagery, and conceptualizing.

2. Distinguish between deductive reasoning, syllogistic logic, and inductive reasoning.

3. Discuss how algorithms and heuristics influence our judgments and decision making.

Concept 2: Problem solving is also a central process related to thinking. We have both systematic and nonsystematic ways of approaching and understanding problems.

4. Explain the importance of understanding and diagnosing problems as the first step in effective problem solving.

5. Describe the heuristics used for generating possible solutions to problems, and explain how solutions should be evaluated.

6. Illustrate how efforts to develop solutions can be blocked by functional fixedness, mental set, and confirmation bias.

7. Describe the factors that contribute to creativity, and the role of creativity in problem solving and critical thinking.

Concept 3: Language is the means by which thoughts can be represented to others and by which objects and events in the world around us can be processed mentally and stored for later use. The relationship between thought and language continues to be of concern for psychologists.

8. Define the basic components of language and grammar.

9. Discuss the developmental processes of language and the theories of language acquisition.

10. Identify the issues that arise with animal language, the linguistic-relativity hypothesis, and bilingual education.

Chapter Guided Review

There are several ways you can use this guided review as part of your systematic study plan. Read the corresponding pages of the text and then complete the review by supplying the correct missing key word. Or, you may want to complete the guided review as a means of becoming familiar with the text. Complete the review and then read the section thoroughly. As you finish each section, complete the **Recap and Review** questions that are supplied in the text.

Survey ❏

CONCEPT 1:   Thinking and Reasoning

- *How do we think?*
- *What processes underlie reasoning and decision making?*

Pages 241-248

The branch of psychology that studies problem solving and other aspects of thinking is called

[a]_____. The term **[b]** _____ brings together the

higher mental processes of humans, including understanding the world, processing information,

making judgments and decisions, and describing knowledge.

[c] _____ is the manipulation of mental representations—words,

images, sounds, or data in any other modality—of information. Thinking transforms the

representation in order to achieve some goal or solve some problem. The visual, auditory, and

tactile representations of objects are called **[d]** _____, and these are a key

component of thought. The time required to scan mental images can be measured. Brain scans

taken while people are forming and manipulating mental images are being used to study the

production and use of these images. **[e]** _____ are categorizations of

objects, events, or people that share common properties. Because we have concepts, we are able

to classify newly encountered material on the basis of our past experiences. Ambiguous

concepts are usually represented by **[f]** _____, which are typical, highly

representative examples of concepts. Concepts provide an efficient way of understanding events

and objects as they occur in the complex world.

Formal reasoning procedures have been studied as a way of understanding reasoning in

general. **[g]** _____ involves the application of inferences and implications

from a set of assumptions to specific cases. The *syllogism* presents two assumptions, called

premises, and a conclusion derived from them. If the premises are true, then the conclusion must

be true. It is possible to have logically valid conclusions even if the premises are untrue.

[h] _____ infers general rules from specific cases. The problem with inductive

reasoning is that conclusions may be biased by insufficient or invalid evidence.

An **[i]** _____ is a rule that guarantees a solution if it is properly

followed. Applying mathematical rules to equations will give us the answer even when we do

not know why it works. A **[j]** _____ is a rule of thumb or some other

shortcut that may lead to a solution. Heuristics can help but they often lead to erroneous

solutions. People often use a **[k]** _____ *heuristic* to determine whether

something belongs to a category or not. The decision is based on whether an observed

characteristic belongs in the category. The **[l]** _____ *heuristic* judges the probability of an event on how easily the event can be recalled from memory. We assume that events that are easier to remember must have happened more often and that similar events are more likely to recur.

CONCEPT 2:   Problem Solving

Survey ❏
Read ❏
Recite ❏

- *How do people approach and solve problems?*
- *What are the major obstacles to problem solving?*

Pages 248-260

Problem solving typically involves three major steps: preparation, production of solutions, and evaluation of solutions. Problems are distinguished as either well-defined or ill-defined. In a

[a]_____, the problem itself is clearly understood and the information needed to solve it is clearly understood. The appropriate solution is thus easily identified. In an

[b] _____, both the problem and what information is needed may be unclear.

There are three categories of problem. [c] _____ require the recombination or reorganization of a group of elements in order to solve the problem. Jigsaw puzzles are a common example. With [d] _____, the problem solver must identify a relationship between elements and then construct a new relationship among them. A common example is number sequence problems where a test taker may be asked to supply the next number in the sequence. The third kind of problem is [e] _____. Transformation problems have a desired goal and require a series of steps or changes to take place in order to reach the goal. The Tower of Hanoi problem described in the text (Figure 8–3) is a transformation problem. Once the kind of problem is understood, it is easier to determine how to represent the problem and how to organize it.

The creation of solutions may proceed at the simplest level as trial and error, but this approach may be inadequate for problems that have a large number of possible configurations. The use of heuristics aids in the simplification of problems. Trial-and-error is the simplest approach to finding a solution. The heuristic of [f] _____ proceeds by testing the difference between the current status and the desired outcome, and with each test it tries to reduce the difference. This strategy is effective only if there is a direct solution. In cases where indirect approaches are necessary, the means-ends analysis would require avoiding these indirect paths and so become a hindrance. Another heuristic divides the goal into intermediate steps, or *subgoals*, and works on each one individually. The problem here is that sometimes problems cannot be subdivided, and this approach may make the problem bigger than it was.

The use of [g]_____ takes a slightly different approach to problem solving, requiring a reorganization of the entire problem in order to achieve a solution. The reorganization of existing elements requires prior experience with the elements.

The final step of problem solving is to evaluate the adequacy of a solution. If the solution is not clear, criteria to judge the solution must be made clear.

In the progress toward a solution, there are several obstacles that can be met. **[h]**_____ refers to the tendency to think of an object according to its given function or typical use. Functional fixedness is an example of a broader phenomenon called **[i]**_____, the tendency for old patterns of solutions to persist. The Luchin's jar problem is an example. In the first trials, a set of combinations is required to solve the problem of filling a jar. The final problem is straightforward, but the problem solver usually attempts to use the solutions applied to the previous trials. Sometimes people inaccurately evaluate solutions and act on the wrong solution because they ignore contradictory evidence. This tendency to ignore contradictory evidence is called the *confirmation bias*, where an initial hypothesis is favored and alternatives are ignored.

[j]_____ is usually defined as the combining of responses or ideas in novel ways. **[k]**_____ refers to the ability to generate unusual yet appropriate responses to problems. **[l]**_____ produces responses that are based primarily on knowledge or logic. *Cognitive complexity* is the use of elaborate, intricate, and complex stimuli and thinking patterns. Humor can increase creative output as well. Apparently intelligence is not related to creativity, perhaps because the tests for intelligence test convergent thinking rather than divergent thinking.

Creativity and problem solving can be improved by engaging in one or more of the following: 1) redefine problems; 2) use fractionation; 3) adopt a critical perspective; 4) consider the opposite; 5) use analogies; 6) think divergently; 7) take the perspective of another person; 8) use heuristics; and 9) experiment with different solutions.

CONCEPT 3: Language

Survey ❑
Read ❑
Recite ❑

- *How do people use language?*
- *How does language develop?*

Pages 261-269

[a]_____ is the systematic, meaningful arrangement of symbols. It is important for cognition and for communication with others. The basic structure of language is **[b]**_____, the framework of rules that determine how thoughts are expressed. The three components of grammar are: **[c]**_____, the smallest units of sound, called **[d]**_____, that affect the meaning of speech and how words are formed; [e] _____, the rules that govern how words and phrases are combined to form sentences; and [f] _____, the rules governing meaning of words and sentences.

Language develops through set stages. At first children [g] _____, producing speechlike but meaningless sounds. Babbling gradually sounds like actual speech, and by one year, sounds that are not part of the language disappear. After the first year, children produce short, two-word combinations followed by short sentences.

[h]_____ refers to the short sentences that contain a critical message but sound as if written as a telegram, with noncritical words left out. As children begin to learn speech rules, they will apply them without flexibility, a phenomenon known as

[i]_____, where an "ed" might be applied to every past tense construction. By the age of 5, most children have acquired the rules of language.

The [j] _____ to language acquisition suggests that the reinforcement and conditioning principles are responsible for language development. Praise for saying a word like "mama" reinforces the word and increases the likelihood of its being repeated. Shaping then makes child language become more adultlike. This approach has difficulty explaining the acquisition of language rules, because children are also reinforced when their language is incorrect. An alternative proposed by Noam Chomsky suggests that there exist innate mechanisms responsible for the acquisition of language. All human languages have a similar underlying structure he calls [k] _____, and a neural system in the brain, the [l] _____, is responsible for the development of language.

Psychologists are also concerned whether the structure of language influences the structure of thought or whether thought influences language. The [m] _____ suggests that language shapes thought, determining how people of a particular culture tend to perceive and understand the world. In an alternative view, language may reflect the different ways we have of thinking about the world, essentially that thought produces language. A study by Eleanor Rosch concerning color perception of the Dani of New Guinea found that even though the Dani have only two color words, they could distinguish colors as well as English-speaking people who have hundreds of color words. In this respect, the linguistic-relativity hypothesis is considered to be unsupported. However, language does influence how we store memories and form categories.

Whether animals use language depends on demonstrating whether they can create unique meanings that use a grammar system. Many animals, as well as insects, have communication systems, but they do not qualify as language. Psychologists have taught chimps to use language at the level of 2-year-old humans. Critics suggest that the language is not sophisticated enough to be considered language. In either case, humans are much better equipped for language.

Children who enter school as nonnative speakers of English face a number of hardships. The debate over whether to take a bilingual approach or whether all instruction should be in English is a major controversy. Evidence suggests that bilingual children have cognitive advantages, being more flexible, more aware of the rules of language, and scoring higher on verbal and nonverbal intelligence tests. Bilingual students raise questions of the advantage of

[n]_____, in which a person is a member of two cultures. Some have

argued that society should promote an [o] _____, in which members of minority cultures are encouraged to learn both cultures.

➤ Now that you have surveyed, questioned, and read the chapter and completed the guided review, review **Looking Back**, pages 269-270.

Review ❑

➤ For additional practice through recitation and review, test your knowledge of the chapter material by answering the questions in the *Key Word Drill*, the *Practice Questions*, and the *Essay Questions*.

Key Word Drill

The following **Matching Questions** test the boldfaced and italicized key words from the text. Check your answers with the Answer Key in the back of the *Study Guide*.

Recite ❑

MATCHING QUESTIONS

_____ 1. syllogism

_____ 2. algorithm

_____ 3. heuristic

_____ 4. representativeness heuristic

_____ 5. availability heuristic

a. A rule in which people and things are judged by the degree to which they represent a certain category.

b. A set of rules that, if followed, guarantee a solution, though the reason they work may not be understood by the person using them.

c. A rule for judging the probability that an event will occur by the ease with which it can be recalled from memory.

d. A rule of thumb that may bring about a solution to a problem but is not guaranteed to do so.

e. A major technique for studying deductive reasoning, in which a series of two assumptions are used to derive a conclusion.

_____ 6. arrangement problems

_____ 7. problems of inducing structure

_____ 8. transformation problems

_____ 9. means-ends analysis

_____ 10. subgoals

a. Problems to be solved using a series of methods to change an initial state into a goal state.

b. A commonly used heuristic to divide a problem into intermediate steps and to solve each one of them.

c. Problems requiring the identification of existing relationships among elements presented so as to construct a new relationship among them.

d. Problems requiring the rearrangement of a group of elements in order to satisfy a certain criterion.

e. Repeated testing to determine and reduce the distance between the desired outcome and what currently exists in problem solving.

_____ 11. insight

_____ 12. mental set

_____ 13. confirmation bias

_____ 14. creativity

_____ 15. divergent thinking

_____ 16. convergent thinking

a. The tendency for patterns of problem solving to persist.

b. Sudden awareness of the relationships among various elements that had previously appeared to be independent of one another.

c. A type of thinking that produces responses based on knowledge and logic.

d. The ability to generate unusual but appropriate responses to problems or questions.

e. A bias favoring an initial hypothesis and disregarding contradictory information suggesting alternative solutions.

f. The combining of responses or ideas in novel ways.

_____ 17. grammar

_____ 18. phonology

_____ 19. phonemes

_____ 20. syntax

_____ 21. semantics

a. The framework of rules that determine how our thoughts can be expressed.

b. Rules governing the meaning of words and sentences.

c. The rules governing how words form sentences.

d. The study of how we use units of sound to produce meaning by forming them into words.

e. The smallest units of sound used to form words.

_____ 22. telegraphic speech

_____ 23. overgeneralization

_____ 24. innate mechanism

_____ 25. universal grammar

_____ 26. language-acquisition
device

_____ 27. cognitive psychology

_____ 28. prototypes

a. A neural system of the brain hypothesized to permit understanding of language.

b. Sentences containing only the most essential words.

c. Applying rules of speech inappropriately.

d. An underlying structure shared by all languages.

e. According to Chomsky, the innate linguistic capability in humans that emerges as a function of maturation.

f. Typical, highly representative examples of a concept.

g. The branch of psychology that specializes in the study of cognition.

Practice Questions

Test your knowledge of the chapter material by answering these **Multiple Choice Questions**. These questions have been placed in three Practice Tests. The first two tests are composed of questions that will test your recall of factual knowledge. The third test contains questions that are challenging and primarily test for conceptual knowledge and your ability to apply that knowledge. Check your answers and review the feedback using the Answer Key in the back of the *Study Guide*.

Recite ❑
Review ❑

MULTIPLE CHOICE QUESTIONS

PRACTICE TEST I:

1. Manipulation of mental images is best shown by subjects' abilities to:
   a. use mental images to represent abstract ideas.
   b. anticipate the exit of a toy train from a tunnel.
   c. understand the subtle meanings of sentences.
   d. mentally rotate one image to compare it with another.

2. A concept is defined as:
   a. an idea or thought about a new procedure or product.
   b. a group of attitudes which define an object, event, or person.
   c. a categorization of people, objects, or events that share certain properties.
   d. one of many facts which collectively define the subject matter for a specific area of knowledge (such as psychology).

3. Applying a student honor code to a particular classroom situation requires:
   a. inductive reasoning.
   b. linguistic reasoning.
   c. transductive reasoning.
   d. deductive reasoning.

4. The use of inaccurate premises, coming to erroneous conclusions, and simply failing to use formal reasoning are all errors related specifically to the use of:
   a. deductive reasoning.
   b. inductive reasoning.
   c. availability heuristics.
   d. algorithms.

5. Which alternative below is **not** a major step in problem solving?
   a. evaluation of solutions generated
   b. preparation for the creation of solutions
   c. documentation of all solutions
   d. production of solutions

6. Assembling a jigsaw puzzle is an example of:
   a. an overdefined problem.
   b. a well-defined problem.
   c. an undefined problem.
   d. an ill-defined problem.

7. According to the text, which of the following is perhaps the most frequently used heuristic technique for solving problems?
   a. the availability heuristic
   b. categorical processing
   c. the representativeness heuristic
   d. means-ends analysis

8. According to the text, which of the following is **not** associated with defining and understanding a problem?
   a. discarding inessential information
   b. simplifying essential information
   c. dividing the problem into parts
   d. clarifying the solution

9. Insight is a:
   a. sudden awareness of the relationships among various elements in a problem that previously appeared to be independent of one another.
   b. sudden awareness of the solution to a problem with which one has had no prior involvement or experience.
   c. sudden awareness of a particular algorithm that can be used to solve a problem.
   d. spontaneous procedure for generating a variety of possible solutions to a problem.

10. A simple computer program will include:
    a. trial-and-error solutions.
    b. a syllogism.
    c. a dozen or more heuristics.
    d. an algorithm.

11. Which kind of thinking is exemplified by logic and knowledge?
    a. creative
    b. convergent
    c. divergent
    d. imaginal

12. A person who can think of 75 distinct uses for her psychology textbook in a 5-minute thinking interval:
    a. has an especially strong mental set.
    b. has superior intelligence.
    c. is especially prone to functional fixedness.
    d. is particularly good at divergent thinking.

13. The syntax of a language is the framework of rules that determine:
    a. the meaning of words and phrases.
    b. how words and phrases are combined to form sentences.
    c. the sounds of letters, phrases, and words.
    d. how thoughts can be translated into words.

14. Telegraphic speech in young children refers to the fact that:
    a. speech is very rapid.
    b. seemingly nonessential words are omitted from phrases and sentences.
    c. the tonal quality of speech is limited.
    d. speech may speed up, slow down, or contain pauses.

15. According to the text, a child acquires most of the basic rules of grammar by:
    a. 2 years of age.
    b. 3 years of age.
    c. 4 years of age.
    d. 5 years of age.

16. The ability to understand language develops _____ the ability to speak.
    a. earlier than
    b. at the same time as
    c. usually later than
    d. always later than

17. Learning theorists view the learning of language as a process of:
    a. classical conditioning.
    b. stimulus generalization.
    c. shaping.
    d. chaining.

PRACTICE TEST II:

18. Cognitive psychologists study all of the following **except**:
    a. how the sensory system takes in information.
    b. how people understand the world.
    c. how people process information.
    d. how people make judgments.

19. Prototypes of concepts are:
    a. new concepts to describe newly emerging phenomena.
    b. new concepts that emerge within a language spontaneously and then are retained or discarded.
    c. representative examples of concepts.
    d. concepts from other languages that are incorporated into a native language if they appear useful.

20. A syllogism is defined as:
   a. a reasoning error made when the decision makers fail to use systematic techniques.
   b. any time a representativeness heuristic is used in a humorous manner.
   c. a series of two assumptions that is used to derive a conclusion.
   d. an analogy concerning the relationship between two sets of paired items, like "A is to B as C is to D."

21. If you fail to solve a problem because you misapply a category or set of categories, you have relied on:
   a. an availability heuristic.   c. functional fixedness.
   b. a mental set.   d. a representativeness heuristic.

22. According to your text, problems fall into one of three categories. Which of the following is **not** one of them?
   a. arrangement   c. structure
   b. affability   d. transformation

23. Identifying existing relationships among elements and constructing a new relationship is an example of:
   a. an inducing-structure problem.   c. an arrangement problem.
   b. an organization problem.   d. a transformation problem.

24. Problems that are solved by changing an initial state into a goal state are called:
   a. transformation problems   c. insight problems.
   b. problems of inducing structure.   d. arrangement problems.

25. A student tells her roommate sardonically, "As a student, I measure success one midterm at a time." Her statement implies that her strategy for achieving a college degree is through:
   a. means-ends analysis.   c. trial and error.
   b. achieving subgoals.   d. application of algorithms.

26. Which of the following statements about insight is true?
   a. It is an unexplained discovery of a solution without prior experience with any elements of the problem.
   b. It results from a methodical trial-and-error process.
   c. It is a sudden realization of relationships among seemingly independent elements.
   d. It is a solution that is independent of trial and error and experience.

27. Functional fixedness and mental set show that:
   a. the person's first hunches about the problem are typically correct.
   b. one's initial perceptions about the problem can impede the solution.
   c. convergent thinking is needed when the problem is well defined.
   d. the person who poses the problem is the one who solves it best.

28. Which of the following is characteristic of a creative thinker?
   a. convergent thought   c. high intelligence
   b. divergent thought   d. recurrent thought

29. The order of the words forming a sentence is generated by:
    a. synthetics.
    b. semantics.
    c. syntax.
    d. systematics.

30. It is **not** true that babbling:
    a. occurs from 3 to 6 months of age.
    b. includes words such as "dada" and "mama."
    c. is speechlike.
    d. produces sounds found in all languages.

31. In the English language, the fact that "mama" and "dada" are among the first words spoken:
    a. is unusual, since these words do not contain the first sounds a child can make.
    b. suggests that they are responses the child is born with.
    c. is not surprising, since these words are easy to pronounce, and the sound capabilities of the young child are limited.
    d. demonstrates that the sounds heard most frequently are the sounds spoken first.

32. According to Noam Chomsky, the brain contains a neural system designed for understanding and learning language called the:
    a. linguistic relativity system.
    b. language acquisition device.
    c. limbic system.
    d. phonological linguistic device.

33. Which of the following statements does **not** reflect Chomsky's view of language acquisition?
    a. All languages share universal grammar.
    b. The main determinant of language is reinforcement.
    c. The brain has a language acquisition device.
    d. Language is a uniquely human phenomenon.

34. The linguistic relativity hypothesis might be paraphrased as:
    a. "Without thought there is no language."
    b. "Thought creates language."
    c. "Language and thought are synonymous."
    d. "Language determines thought."

PRACTICE TEST III: Conceptual, Applied, and Challenging Questions

35. Which alternative below does not fit within your text's definition of cognition?
    a. the higher mental processes of humans
    b. how people know and understand the world
    c. how people communicate their knowledge and understanding to others
    d. how people's eyes and ears process the information they receive

36. Concepts are similar to perceptual processes in that:
    a. concepts, like visual illusions, can produce errors in interpretation.
    b. concepts allow us to simplify and manage our world.
    c. concepts are to language what figure-ground relationships are to perception.
    d. some concepts and perceptual processes are innate.

37. You have had a number of troublesome, time-consuming, expensive, and emotionally trying experiences with people who sell used cars. Then you find out that your roommate for next term is a part-time used-car dealer. You are convinced, even without meeting your future roommate, that you should not be paired with this person. You have used the _____ heuristic to arrive at your conclusion.
    a. means-ends
    b. representativeness
    c. availability
    d. personality

38. Thinking of a wrench in conventional terms may handicap your efforts to solve a problem when a possible solution involves using the wrench for a novel use. This phenomenon is called:
    a. functional fixedness.
    b. insight.
    c. awareness.
    d. preparation.

39. The slight difference in meaning between the sentences "The truck hit the pole" and "The pole was hit by the truck" is determined by the rules of:
    a. grammar.
    b. phonology.
    c. syntax.
    d. semantics.

40. Of the following, which is the first refinement in the infant's learning of language?
    a. production of short words that begin with a consonant.
    b. disappearance of sounds that are not in the native language.
    c. emergence of sounds that resemble words.
    d. production of two-word combinations.

41. Generalizing from information presented in the text, which of the following two-word combinations is **least** likely to be spoken by a 2-year-old?
    a. Daddy up.
    b. Mommy cookie.
    c. I'm big.
    d. More, more.

42. A child exhibits a speech pattern characterized by short sentences, with many noncritical words missing. Which of the following is **not** true?
    a. The child is between 2 and 3 years old.
    b. The child is exhibiting telegraphic speech.
    c. The child is building complexity of speech.
    d. The child is using overgeneralization.

43. Psychologists who argue that the language of the child depends on exposure to the language of the parents would say that language is acquired through:
    a. classical conditioning.
    b. shaping.
    c. universal grammar.
    d. biological unfolding.

44. Which statement below is **not** true about the language skills of humans and apes?
    a. Many critics feel that the language skills acquired by chimps and gorillas are no different from a dog learning to sit on command.
    b. The language skills of chimps and gorillas are equal to those of a 5-year-old human child.
    c. Sign language and response panels with different-shaped symbols have been used to teach chimps and gorillas language skills.
    d. Humans are probably better equipped than apes to produce and organize language into meaningful sentences.

45. Navaho have many names for the bluish, aquamarine color of turquoise. Based on how other, similar facts have been understood, this too could be used to support:
    a. the theory that language determines thought.
    b. the theory that thought determines language.
    c. the existence of the language acquisition device.
    d. development of the nativistic position.

46. Rosch's study with the Dani tribe of New Guinea showed that:
    a. English speakers perceived colors differently from the Dani.
    b. the number of categories in a language depends on perception.
    c. language does not limit the way that colors are perceived.
    d. the number of color names available determines the perception of color.

47. The notion that language shapes the way that people of a particular culture perceive and think about the world is called the:
    a. semantic-reasoning theory.   c. prototypical hypothesis.
    b. cultural-language law.   d. linguistic-relativity hypothesis.

48. Latonia participates in a study in which she is asked to imagine a giraffe. After indicating that she has constructed the entire image, she is then asked to focus on the giraffe's tail. What should the experimenter be doing as she completes this task?
    a. observing her reaction   c. recording her respiration
    b. timing each step   d. getting the next subject ready

49. In a study concerned with concept formation and categorization, you are asked to think about a table. Which of the following would be considered a prototype if you were to have imagined it?
    a. your grandmother's dining room table
    b. a four-legged, rectangular table
    c. the coffee table in the student lounge
    d. a round, pedestal-style oak table

50. A mystery novel will often present all the clues necessary to reveal the murderer. The reader then tries to discover the answer to the mystery by using procedures that depend upon the problem being one of:
    a. transformation   c. arrangement
    b. trial and error   d. inducing structure

51. Attempting to solve a complex word problem, Jeff first realizes that it is a problem of inducing structure, and then after a few moments visualizes the solution rather quickly. The solution technique he has just used is called:
a. insight.
b. subgoal analysis.
c. representativeness heuristic.
d. availability heuristic.

52. According to the text, language influences thought, although not in the strict way presumed by the linguistic-relativity hypothesis. Instead, the influence is as follows:
a. storage and retrieval from memory is influenced by the tags provided by language.
b. language itself must be retrieved from memory to formulate thoughts.
c. language guides the control of motor movements, as when athletes do self-talk during an event.
d. language is used in planning and organizing one's daily activities.

Essay Questions

Essay Question 7.1: *Problem Solving*

Recite ❑
Review ❑

Identify a major challenge that you anticipate facing in the next several years. It can involve choosing a career, getting married, selecting a major, choosing a graduate school, or one of many others. Describe the problem or challenge briefly, then describe how you would apply the problem-solving steps presented in the text to the problem to generate solutions that you might try.

Essay Question 7.2: *Is Language Uniquely Human?*

Some consider language to be the capability that uniquely distinguishes us as human. Weigh the arguments for the language skills of specially trained chimpanzees and develop your position on this issue. Is language unique to humans? If so, how would you characterize the communication skills of chimpanzees? If not, then what capability does distinguish us from other animals?

Activities and Projects

1. To counteract functional fixedness and to foster creativity, record as many uses as you can for a paper clip. Limit yourself to three minutes. Repeat the exercise with a brick and a coat hanger. Ask a friend to do the same thing and then compare the number of unique items each of you have. Consider the extent to which this exercise reflects intelligence (and what kind of intelligence) and creativity. Is the exercise dependent on linguistic or cultural skills? (A particularly interesting variation is to ask a friend from another culture or ethnic group to do the exercise and then determine whether some of the uses are unique as a result of cultural experience.)

    Recite ❑
    Review ❑

Paper Clip:

_____

_____

_____

_____

2. Select several common nouns like "house," "tree," and "dog." Then ask people in the following age groups to give you a definition: Child, age 3 to 4 years old; Child, age 9 to 10 years old; Teenager; Adult. Record their responses on the chart provided below.

    To vary the activity, you may ask a young child to describe the size or some other feature of one or more of the common objects. These descriptions will reflect the child's conception of the object ("a star is about twenty feet bigger than a house"). Be sure to ask the adult and teenager for a description of the same object.

COMPARING COMMON OBJECTS ACROSS AGE GROUPS	
Object:	Child, 3 to 4
	Child, 9 to 10

	Teenager	
	Adult	
Object:	Child, 3 to 4	
	Child, 9 to 10	
	Teenager	
	Adult	

3. Observe and record (with a tape recorder or on a note pad) examples of language production in one or more children between the ages of six months and four years. Then compare the examples with those given in the text. Which of the basic concepts of language acquisition were you able to observe?

LANGUAGE PRODUCTION RECORD		
Age of Subject	Phrase or word	Phenomena illustrated

Cultural Idioms

Recite ❏
Review ❏

p. 240
One Man's Mousetraps: the phrase "to invent a better mousetrap" is a phrase that refers to inventors, who are always trying to think of better ways to do things
the bound proceedings from a scientific symposium: a large book
justify both margins: both sides of the type (the writing) in a book are even; in your textbook, the main text is justified, but the text next to the photos is not

p. 242
taking a foul shot: in basketball, a chance to earn an extra point by throwing the ball into the basket

p. 243
Skippy peanut butter: Skippy is a popular brand name for a mixture made from ground peanuts, popular in the U. S. as a sandwich filling.
coffee table: a low table placed in front of a couch

p. 245
Sherlock Holmes: a brilliant detective who is a character in a series of detective stories by Sir Arthur Conan Doyle
Spice Girls: a music group popular in the 1990s

p. 246
You may not have the foggiest notion: you may not understand or know
tic-tac-toe: a traditional two-person game, where the goal is to draw three "Xs" or three "Os" in a row

p. 247
board games: games played on a board, such as chess or checkers.

p. 248
hitting a home run: in baseball, when a batter hits so well that he or she can go around all the bases and back to home plate, scoring a point

p. 249
assembly line: a group of people who work together in a factory

p. 252
Trial and Error: trying different things until one thing works
Thomas Edison: U. S. inventor (1847–1931)

p. 253
chimps: chimpanzees

p. 258
stock market investors: people who buy business shares of a company, hoping that the share price will go up
"buying low and selling high": in the stock market, it is wise to buy a share of a company when it's not expensive and then sell it when it is worth more, thus making a profit. The author here is comparing creative people with investors,

people who can see in advance that something will be needed, or will become more valuable

p. 259
unique packaging of Pringle's potato chips: a snack food that, instead of being packaged in a bag (like most potato chips) is packaged in a tube-shaped box.

p. 261
" 'Twas brillig, and the slithy toves...": This poem, "Jabberwocky," is a nonsense poem, with most of the words invented by Lewis Carroll.

p. 262
music to their ears: wonderful to hear

p. 263
ground-breaking: original, new

p. 266
great apes: primates such as chimpanzees, gorillas, orangutans

p. 267
Spanglish: a combination of Spanish and English
Ebonics: also called "Black English," the language that many African Americans grow up learning
"Oye, oye": a Spanish expression of surprise
school board: an elected group of people who make decisions about the public schools in an area
standard English: the variety of English that is accepted as standard for writing and public communication (this text is written in standard English; the news on TV is in standard English)

p. 268
political undercurrents: it has become a political issue, not merely an educational one

Detailed Chapter Outline

This detailed outline contains all the headings in Chapter 8: Intelligence. If you are using the SQ3R method, then an examination of the outline is the best way to begin your survey of the chapter.

Survey ❑
Question ❑

Prologue: Mindie Crutcher and Lenny Ng
Looking Ahead

Defining Intelligent Behavior
Measuring Intelligence
   Tests of IQ
   Achievement and Aptitude Tests
   Reliability and Validity

> **Applying Psychology in the 21st Century:** Take-at-Home IQ Tests and Take-at-Home Computer SATs: Becoming a Nation of Test Takers

Alternative Formulations of Intelligence
Is Information Processing Intelligence?   Contemporary Approaches
Practical Intelligence: Measuring Common Sense

> **The Informed Consumer of Psychology:** Can You Do Better on Standardized Tests?

Recap, Review, and Rethink

Variations in Intellectual Ability
Mental Retardation

> **Pathways Through Psychology:** Rob Davies, Advocate for the Mentally Retarded

The Intellectually Gifted

Recap, Review, and Rethink

Individual Differences in Intelligence: Hereditary and Environmental Determinants

Exploring Diversity: The Relative Influence of Heredity and of Environment

Placing the Heredity-Environment Question in Perspective

Recap, Review, and Rethink
Looking Back
Key Terms and Concepts

➤ Now that you have surveyed the chapter, read **Looking Ahead**, page 274. What questions does the Chapter seek to answer?

Question ❑
Read ❑

Concepts and Learning Objectives

These are the concepts and the learning objectives for Chapter 8. Read them carefully as part of your preliminary survey of the chapter.

Survey ❑

Concept 1: Intelligence is understood as a predictor of school success, and it is also viewed as a limited expression of the cognitive capacity of individuals. Alternative views of intelligence include the view that there exist many intelligences, including practical intelligence, which is made up of the skills needed to survive in cultural and social settings.

1. Define intelligence and the issues related to its definition.

2. Discuss how intelligence is measured, the definition of intelligence quotient, and how achievement and aptitude tests differ from intelligence tests.

3. Distinguish between reliability and validity with regard to psychological and intelligence testing.

4. Describe the alternative views of intelligence, including the g factor, fluid and crystallized intelligence, and Gardner's model of multiple intelligences.

5. Explain how cognitive psychologists use information processing to describe intelligence.

6. Describe the concept of practical intelligence, and discuss whether performance on achievement tests can be improved with training.

Concept 2: The extremes in intellectual functioning lead to distinctions of mental retardation and giftedness. The basic challenge for identifying these two groups is to identify and utilize educational resources in order to best serve the two populations.

7. Define mental retardation, and describe its various classifications.

8. Discuss the causes of mental retardation and the care and treatment of retarded individuals.

9. Define and describe intellectual giftedness, and identify some programs for the intellectually gifted.

Concept 3: The major debate in intelligence is over the relative influence on intelligence of heredity and environment, and the extent to which these two influences can be understood in order to improve intellectual potential.

10. Discuss the problem of cultural bias in intelligence tests and the attempts to produce a culture-fair IQ test.

11. Analyze the issues related to the heredity versus environment debate in the study of intelligence.

Chapter Guided Review

Survey ❑

There are several ways you can use this guided review as part of your systematic study plan. Read the corresponding pages of the text and then complete the review by supplying the correct missing key word. Or, you may want to complete the guided review as a means of becoming familiar with the text. Complete the review and then read the section thoroughly. As you finish each section, complete the **Recap and Review** questions that are supplied in the text.

CONCEPT 1: Defining Intelligent Behavior

Survey ❑
Read ❑
Recite ❑

- *How do psychologists conceptualize and define intelligence?*
- *What are the major approaches to measuring intelligence?*

Pages 274-290

Intelligence has many different meanings, depending upon whether it is applied to behavior in a Pacific culture like that of the Trukese, who can navigate in open sea without any equipment, to an African with exceptional hunting skills, or to someone who can get around the Miami transit system. In the examples in the text, the common theme is that intelligent people can use their resources more effectively than others in accomplishing whatever task is at hand. In a survey of lay persons, three major components of intelligence were identified: (1) problem-solving ability, (2) verbal ability, and (3) social competence. **[a]** _____ has been defined by psychologists as the capacity to understand the world, think rationally, and use resources effectively. Intelligence remains difficult to determine, though **[b]** _____ have been successful in identifying individuals who need help in school, who have cognitive difficulties, and who need help making choices about school.

Alfred Binet developed the first formal intelligence test to identify the "dullest" students in the Parisian school system. His test was able to distinguish the "bright" from the "dull" and eventually made distinctions between age groups. The tests helped to assign children a

[c]_____, the average age of children who achieved the same score. In order to compare individuals with different *chronological ages*, the **[d]**_____score, was determined by dividing the mental age by the chronological age and multiplying by a factor of 100. Thus an IQ score is determined by the level at which a person performs on the test in relation to others of the same age.

The Binet's original test became the *Stanford-Binet Test*, and it is based on items that vary according to the age of the subject. Other IQ tests given in America are the *Weschler Adult Intelligence Scale—III*, or *WAIS-III*, and the *Weschler Intelligence Scale for Children—III*, or *WISC-III*. The WAIS-III and the WISC-III have verbal and performance scales. The two scales allow a more accurate picture of the person's abilities. The *Stanford-Binet*, the *WAIS-III*, and *WISC-III* require individual administration. A number of "paper and pencil" tests have been developed, but they sacrifice flexibility and fail to motivate the test taker. Also, they are not easily given to children or to people with low IQs.

The **[e]** _____ is a test meant to determine the level of achievement of an individual, that is, what the person has actually learned. An **[f]** _____ measures and predicts an individual's ability in a particular area. The SAT is an exam that predicts how well a student will do in college. There is quite a bit of overlap among the IQ, achievement, and aptitude tests.

Psychological tests must have **[g]** _____, that is, they must measure something consistently from time to time. The question of whether or not a test measures the characteristic it is supposed to measure is called **[h]** _____. If a test is reliable, that does not mean that is valid. However, if a test is unreliable, it cannot be valid. A reliable test will produce similar outcomes in similar conditions. All types of tests in psychology, including intelligence tests, assessments of psychological disorders, and the measurement of attitudes, must meet tests of validity and reliability. **[i]** _____ are the standards of test performance that allow comparison of the scores of one test-taker to others who have taken it. This standard for a test is determined by calculating the average score for a particular group of people for whom the test is designed to be given.
Then, the extent to which each person's score differs from the others can be calculated. The selection of the subjects who will be used to establish a norm for a test is critical.

In the two dominant tests, the score is considered to be a reflection of the intelligence of the person. It remains unclear whether intelligence is a single factor or a combination of factors. The single-factor view suggests that there is a general factor for mental ability called

[j]_____. Recently, two factors have been accepted by most. They are

[k]_____, the ability to deal with new problems and situations, and

[l]_____, the store of information, skills, and strategies acquired through experience.

In an alternate formulation, Howard Gardner has proposed the existence of seven multiple intelligences: 1) musical intelligence; 2) bodily-kinesthetic intelligence; 3) logical-mathematical intelligence; 4) linguistic intelligence; 5) spatial intelligence; 6) interpersonal intelligence; and 7) intrapersonal intelligence. Gardner suggests that these separate intelligences do not operate in isolation. Results from Gardner's work include the acceptance of more than one answer as correct on a test.

The information processing approach to intelligence views intelligence as the ability to process information. Effective problem solvers have traditionally been those who also score high on intelligence tests. In solving an analogy problem, a bright student will go through a series of steps, first *encoding* the information in a useful way, then *making inferences* about the analogy relationship, then *mapping* the relationship from the first half of the analogy to the second half, then *applying the relationship* to test answers, then *responding* with a solution. People with higher intelligence levels tend to get the right answer and to have qualitatively different methods for solving problems. High scorers spend more of their time on the initial stage of encoding, identifying parts of the problems, and retrieval from memory.

Robert Sternberg has proposed a [m] _____. The three components are: the [n] _____ aspect that focuses on rational behavior, the

[o]_____ aspect that focuses on how prior experience is applied, and the

[p]_____ aspect that focuses on how successful people respond to the demands of the everyday environment.

[q] _____ grows from Sternberg's attention to the practical demands of everyday life. One of the problems is that though IQ tests predict performance in school, they do not correlate with career success. Several tests have been designed that measure practical intelligence in the business world.

There are many coaching services that claim to help students improve their scores on the Scholastic Assessment Test (SAT). Though the service that produces the test originally argued that these were not helpful, it now has accepted that some coaching may help. One must determine what is sought from the coaching in selecting a type of coaching. Hints for improving testing include: 1) previewing each section; 2) timing yourself carefully; 3) checking the test-scoring policy to determine whether guessing is appropriate; and 4) completing the answer sheets accurately.

CONCEPT 2:   Variations in Intellectual Ability

- • *How can the extremes of intelligence be differentiated?*
- • *How can we help people to maximize their full potential?*

Pages 290-294

More than 7 million people in the United States are classified as mentally retarded, and the populations that comprise the mentally retarded and the exceptionally gifted require special attention in order to reach their potential.

[a] _____ is defined by the American Association on Mental Deficiency (1992) as when there is "significantly subaverage general intellectual functioning existing concurrently with deficits in adaptive behavior and manifested during the developmental period." This definition includes mild to severe retardation. [b] _____ includes individuals whose IQ scores fall in the 55 to 69 range. This comprises about 90 percent of the people with mental retardation. [c] _____, with scores ranging from 40 to 54, [d] _____, with scores from 25 to 39, and

[e]_____, with scores below 25, present difficulties that become more pronounced the lower the IQ score. The moderately retarded require some supervision during their entire lives, and the severe and profound groups require institutionalization. One-third of the people classified as retarded suffer from biological causes of retardation, mostly from [f]

_____, a genetic disorder caused by an extra chromosome. [g]

_____ occurs in cases when there is no biological cause but instead may be linked with a family history of retardation. This may be caused by environmental factors like severe poverty, malnutrition, and possibly a genetic factor that cannot be determined. In 1975, Congress passed a law (Public Law 94–142) that entitles mentally retarded individuals to a full education and to education and training in the [h]_____. This law leads to

a process of returning individuals to regular classrooms, a process called [i] _____. The view is that by placing retarded individuals in typical environments, they interact with non-retarded individuals and benefit from the interaction.

The [j] _____ comprise about 2 to 4 percent of the population. This group is generally identified as those individuals with IQ scores higher than 130. Contrary to the stereotype, these individuals are usually outgoing, well-adjusted, popular people who do most things better than the average person. Lewis Terman conducted a well-known longitudinal study following 1,500 gifted children (with IQs above 140). They have an impressive record of accomplishments, though being gifted does not guarantee success.

CONCEPT 3: Individual Differences in Intelligence: Heredity and Environmental Determinants

Survey ❑
Read ❑
Recite ❑

- Are traditional IQ tests culturally biased?
- Are there racial differences in intelligence?
- To what degree is intelligence influenced by the environment and to what degree by heredity?

Pages 295-300

In the determination of the causes of individual differences, cultural differences in the framing of questions on the test can play an important role. Adrian Dove has developed a test that illustrates how foreign culture-specific tests can be by asking questions drawn from the experience of inner-city African-American populations. On standard intelligence tests, some culture and ethnic groups score lower than others, as with African-Americans, who tend to score 15 points lower than Whites. One view suggests that the tests are biased toward Western individualism and against African communalism. Because of the possibility of bias and discrimination, some jurisdictions have banned the use of traditional intelligence tests.

Attempts to develop a **[a]** _____ that does not discriminate have led in some cases to even greater disparities in scores. The controversy based on ethnic and minority differences in intelligence tests reflects a greater concern of whether intelligence is predominantly a result of heredity or of environmental forces. On the heredity side, the explanation for lower performance by a population would be that they are less intelligent as a result of genetics. The debate recently reached a major peak with the publication of Murray and Herrnstein's *The Bell Curve* which argues that the difference between White and African-American IQ scores could not be explained by environmental differences because even when socioeconomic factors were considered, the difference did not disappear. Intelligence does show

a high degree of **[b]**_____, the measure of the extent to which a characteristic is related to genetic, inherited factors. The closer two people are linked genetically, the closer their IQ scores are likely to be. Critics of *The Bell Curve* have argued, with the support of many psychologists, that such a factor as socioeconomic status is itself a highly variable factor, with wide variations from one household to another. Other research has demonstrated that African-Americans raised in enriched environments similar to Whites do not have lower IQ scores. The real differences between IQ scores cannot be between the means of groups but must be understood as the differences between individuals.

The issue of heredity and environment is one in which experimental research that might establish causal relationships cannot be devised because of ethical issues. A question that should be of concern is how can we maximize the potential intellectual development of individuals.

➤ Now that you have surveyed, questioned, and read the chapter and completed the guided review, review **Looking Back**, page 300.

Review ❑

➤ For additional practice through recitation and review, test your knowledge of the chapter material by answering the questions in the *Key Word Drill*, the *Practice Questions*, and the *Essay Questions*.

Key Word Drill

The following **Matching Questions** test the boldfaced and italicized key words from the text. Check your answers with the Answer Key in the back of the *Study Guide*.

Recite ❑
_____

MATCHING QUESTIONS

_____ 1. intelligence tests

_____ 2. Stanford-Binet Test

_____ 3. Wechsler Adult Intelligence Scale—III (WAIS-III)

_____ 4. Wechsler Intelligence Scale for Children—III (WISC-III)

a. A test of intelligence consisting of verbal and nonverbal performance sections, providing a relatively precise picture of a person's specific abilities.

b. A test of intelligence that includes a series of items varying in nature according to the age of the person being tested.

c. A battery of measures to determine a person's level of intelligence.

d. An intelligence test for children consisting of verbal and nonverbal performance sections, providing a relatively precise picture of a child's specific abilities.

_____ 5. mild retardation

_____ 6. moderate retardation

_____ 7. severe retardation

_____ 8. profound retardation

_____ 9. Down syndrome

_____ 10. familial retardation

_____ 11. intellectually gifted

a. Characterized by an IQ between 25 and 39 and difficulty in functioning independently.

b. Mental retardation in which there is a history of retardation in a family but no evidence of biological causes.

c. Characterized by higher-than-average intelligence, with IQ scores above 130.

d. A common cause of mental retardation, brought about by the presence of an extra chromosome.

e. Characterized by an IQ below 25 and an inability to function independently.

f. Characterized by an IQ between 55 and 69 and the ability to function independently.

g. Characterized by an IQ between 40 and 54.

_____ 12. mental age

_____ 13. chronological age

_____ 14. intelligence quotient (IQ) score

_____ 15. fluid intelligence

_____ 16. crystallized intelligence

_____ 17. practical intelligence

a. Intelligence related to overall success in living, rather than to intellectual and academic performance.

b. A measure of intelligence that takes into account an individual's mental and chronological ages.

c. The store of specific information, skills, and strategies that people have acquired through experience.

d. The typical intelligence level found for people at a given chronological age.

e. The ability to deal with new problems and encounters.

f. A person's physical age.

Practice Questions

Test your knowledge of the chapter material by answering these **Multiple Choice Questions**. These questions have been placed in three Practice Tests. The first two tests are composed of questions that will test your recall of factual knowledge. The third test contains questions that are challenging and primarily test for conceptual knowledge and your ability to apply that knowledge. Check your answers and review the feedback using the Answer Key in the back of the *Study Guide*.

Recite ❑
Review ❑

MULTIPLE CHOICE QUESTIONS

PRACTICE TEST I:

1. The basic elements of intelligence agreed upon by most laypersons include:
    a. social competence, assertiveness, and innate knowledge.
    b. algorithmic skill, verbal ability, and thrift.
    c. perceptual speed, focal attention, and problem-solving skill.
    d. verbal skill, problem-solving ability, and social competence.

2. In order to distinguish more intelligent from less intelligent people, psychologists generally have relied on:
    a. intelligence tests.
    b. genealogy.
    c. achievement tests.
    d. projective tests.

3. The measure of intelligence that takes into consideration both mental and chronological age is called the:
    a. achievement scale.
    b. aptitude level.
    c. intelligence quotient.
    d. g-factor.

4. On Alfred Binet's IQ test, suppose that an 8-year-old child can solve the problems that an average 10-year-old can solve. Her chronological age would be:
   a. 8.
   b. 10.
   c. 12.
   d. impossible to judge from these data.

5. The two major categories of the Wechsler intelligence tests are:
   a. visual and conceptual.
   b. spatial and verbal.
   c. performance and verbal.
   d. performance and spatial.

6. Which of the following types of tests were designed to measure a person's level of knowledge in a given subject area?
   a. motor skills tests
   b. personality tests
   c. aptitude tests
   d. achievement tests

7. A student says, "I retook that last test three times, and my score was incredibly different each time." The test she describes is:
   a. invalid.
   b. unreliable.
   c. culturally biased.
   d. subscaled.

8. Crystallized intelligence appears to be dependent on _____ for its development.
   a. heredity
   b. nutrition and diet
   c. fluid intelligence
   d. native intelligence

9. Gardner asserts that there are seven types of intelligence. Which alternative below is **not** one of them?
   a. technical
   b. interpersonal
   c. linguistic
   d. logical-mathematical

10. Cognitive psychologists use the _____ approach to understand intelligence.
    a. structure-of-intellect
    b. deviation IQ
    c. aptitude-testing
    d. information-processing

11. According to Sternberg, general intelligence and success in business:
    a. are strongly correlated.
    b. are minimally correlated.
    c. cannot be correlated.
    d. are inversely correlated.

12. A significantly subaverage level of intellectual functioning accompanied by deficits in adaptive behavior defines:
    a. savant syndrome.
    b. profound retardation.
    c. mental retardation.
    d. severe retardation.

13. The biological cause of Down syndrome is:
    a.   physical trauma to the fetus during pregnancy.
    b.   poisoning of the mother by toxins during particular intervals of the pregnancy when the fetus is very sensitive to those chemicals.
    c.   poisoning of the fetus by alcohol consumed by the pregnant mother.
    d.   an extra chromosome segment in each cell of the body.

14. Familial retardation:
    a.   results from hereditary factors.
    b.   results from environmental factors.
    c.   is a paradox, since there are no known hereditary or environmental causes.
    d.   may result from either hereditary or environmental factors, although there are no known biological causes.

15. For the retarded youngster, mainstreaming means:
    a.   more opportunities to relate to other retarded students.
    b.   increased opportunities for education and socialization.
    c.   the exclusion of other retarded students from the classroom.
    d.   separating retarded and other students.

16. An intellectually gifted person:
    a.   has an IQ higher than 130.
    b.   is very shy.
    c.   is antisocial.
    d.   is successful in everything.

17. A culture-fair intelligence test is one that:
    a.   does not discriminate unfairly against any minority group.
    b.   focuses on technological items and ignores all aspects of culture.
    c.   tests knowledge of diverse cultures sampled from regions worldwide.
    d.   is written in a universal language.

PRACTICE TEST II:

18. Your textbook defines intelligence as:
    a.   the ability to understand subject matters from different disciplines in an academic setting.
    b.   a complex capability in humans and animals that allows them to think, act, and function adaptively.
    c.   the capacity to understand the world, think rationally, and use resources effectively when faced with challenges.
    d.   a multidimensional human capability which is determined by a person's heredity and environment.

19. The first IQ test was devised for the purpose of:
    a.   diagnosing brain damage.
    b.   identifying slow learners for remedial teaching.
    c.   screening applicants for medical school.
    d.   selecting candidates for a school for the intellectually gifted.

20. The intelligence quotient was developed to:
    a. increase the reliability of the early intelligence tests.
    b. provide a way to compare the performance of French and American children on intelligence tests.
    c. permit meaningful comparisons of intelligence among people of different ages.
    d. correct a systematic scoring error in the first American intelligence tests.

21. Spearman's theoretical component that underlies mental ability is called:
    a. the g-factor.
    b. fluid intelligence.
    c. the X-file.
    d. crystallized intelligence.

22. On standardized IQ tests, the full range of scores ascribed to normal intelligence is from:
    a. 50 to 150.
    b. 85 to 115.
    c. 0 to 100.
    d. 70 to 130.

23. Aptitude tests are designed to:
    a. predict future performance.
    b. measure achievement in a certain area.
    c. measure intelligence.
    d. calculate the g-factor.

24. If an individual's test scores vary greatly from one session to the next, it is likely that the test itself is:
    a. invalid but reliable.
    b. unreliable.
    c. nomothetic.
    d. ideographic.

25. Gardner suggested that we have seven types of intelligence. Which of the following is **not** among them?
    a. general information intelligence
    b. musical intelligence
    c. spatial intelligence
    d. interpersonal intelligence

26. Among Gardner's suggested intelligences, which intelligence is described as "skill in interacting with others such as sensitivity to moods"?
    a. linguistic
    b. bodily-kinesthetic
    c. interpersonal
    d. intrapersonal

27. The _____ approach to understanding intelligence emphasizes processes.
    a. cognitive
    b. learning
    c. environmental
    d. physiological

28. Mental retardation is primarily defined by:
    a. ability to get along in the world and with other people.
    b. deficits in intellectual functioning and adaptive behavior.
    c. ability to perform in school.
    d. ability to perform on intelligence tests.

29. IQ scores falling below _____ fit the criterion for mental retardation.
    a. 80
    b. 70
    c. 60
    d. 50

30. Most cases of mental retardation are classified as being caused by:
    a. Down syndrome.
    b. familial retardation.
    c. Kleinfelter's syndrome.
    d. traumatic injury.

31. Mentally retarded individuals who are classified as _____ retarded have the best prospects for successful mainstreaming.
    a. mildly
    b. moderately
    c. severely
    d. profoundly

32. Legislation designed to protect the rights of the mentally retarded, including providing a "least restrictive environment," has led to:
    a. mainstreaming.
    b. special-education classrooms.
    c. resource classrooms.
    d. mandatory IQ testing for all students with suspected deficits.

33. Youngsters with very high IQs:
    a. are gifted in every academic subject.
    b. have adjustment problems later in life.
    c. should not be mainstreamed.
    d. show better social adjustment in school than others.

34. The "heredity vs. environment" debate concerns the issue of:
    a. how varied environmental influences can alter prenatal development.
    b. how experience and heredity influence the expression of traits.
    c. whether there are IQ differences among different racial groups.
    d. whether deprived or enriched early environments can change IQ scores.

―――――――――

PRACTICE TEST III: Conceptual, Applied, and Challenging Questions

35. If an 8-year-old child receives a score on an IQ test that is usually achieved by a typical 10-year-old, the child's IQ is:
    a. 80.
    b. 100.
    c. 125.
    d. 180.

36. Using standard testing procedures and the IQ formula, which of the following will have the highest IQ?
    a. a 12-year-old with a mental age of 10
    b. a 10-year-old with a mental age of 12
    c. a 25-year-old with a mental age of 23
    d. a 23-year-old with a mental age of 25

37. The formula _____ is used to calculate ratio IQ.
    a. $CA \div MA \times 100 = IQ$.
    b. $CA \div MA \times .01 = IQ$.
    c. $MA \div CA \times 100 = IQ$.
    d. $(MA - CA) \div 100 = IQ$.

38. Which statement about the first intelligence test is **not** correct?
    a. It was designed to identify the "gifted" children in the school system.
    b. It was developed by Alfred Binet in France.
    c. It assumed that performance on certain items and tasks improved with age.
    d. Many items were selected for the test when "bright" and "dull" students scored differently on them.

39. About two-thirds of all people have IQ scores of:
    a. 95-105.
    b. 90-110.
    c. 85-115.
    d. 70-110.

40. The administration of the Stanford-Binet test is ended when:
    a. all items have been administered.
    b. the person misses a total of five items.
    c. the person misses a total of ten items.
    d. the person cannot answer any more questions.

41. Which of the following is **not** one of the verbal subtests on the Wechsler intelligence scale?
    a. information
    b. similarities
    c. block design
    d. vocabulary

42. Which of the following is **not** one of the performance subtests on the Wechsler intelligence scale?
    a. comprehension
    b. picture completion
    c. object assembly
    d. digit symbol

43. If you were asked to solve a problem using your own experience as a basis for the solution, you would be using:
    a. availability heuristics.
    b. crystallized intelligence.
    c. fluid intelligence.
    d. g-factors.

44. Seymour Epstein claims that his scale of constructive thinking:
    a. predicts general life success better than is done by IQ tests.
    b. applies mainly to predicting success in the academic world.
    c. identifies which brain regions execute one's intelligent thoughts.
    d. generates results that correlate strongly with those of the Stanford-Binet IQ test.

45. Robert Sternberg's triarchic theory of intelligence:
    a. has three aspects: contextual, componential, and experiential.
    b. proposes that a brain organ, the triarch, is the central processor of intelligence.
    c. emphasizes the importance of divergent reasoning in creativity.
    d. was first developed from animal research and then applied to humans.

46. Which of the following situations best illustrates reliability as a quality of psychological tests?
    a. A prospective Air Force pilot takes a test, passes it, and becomes an excellent pilot.
    b. A college student studies diligently for an important exam and makes an A on it.
    c. A psychiatric patient takes a psychological test which yields the diagnosis that had been suspected.
    d. A mentally retarded patient takes an intelligent test on Monday and again on Tuesday, getting the same result on each administration.

47. Clinton, who is an expert mason, takes a test that has been designed to assess brick-laying skills. He scores very poorly on the test. Since others have observed that he is an expert mason, the test he took could be said to have:
    a. good validity.
    b. poor validity.
    c. poor reliability.
    d. good reliability.

48. Erik enjoys hiking with his parents. On trails, he will often climb trees, find his way to difficult-to-reach locations, and cross bridges by walking on the hand-rail rather than the path. In Gardner's view, his physical competence would be considered most like that of which of the following?
    a. a surgeon
    b. a scientist
    c. a musician
    d. Anne Sullivan

49. Astrid likes to organize activities for her brothers and her dolls. She often takes charge of playtime with other children her age. In Gardner's view, her social competence would be considered most like that of which of the following?
    a. a surgeon
    b. a scientist
    c. a musician
    d. Anne Sullivan

50. Professor Greenland has been developing a test that will predict how well his twenty-year-old students will do in their intended careers. He has been attempting to correlate factors related to social relationships, emotional health, and initiative with later work success. His views are most compatible with which of the following concepts?
    a. multiple intelligences
    b. practical intelligence
    c. information processing
    d. constructive thinking

51. When solving problems, Nels spends most of his time identifying each item and relating it to other relevant information in the problem. After completing this task, he very quickly solves the problem. According to the information processing conception of intelligence, Nels has spent his time _____ and he is most likely _____.
    a. mapping information; of moderate intelligence
    b. applying solutions; high in intelligence
    c. encoding information; high in intelligence
    d. inferring relationships; of moderate intelligence

Essay Questions

Essay Question 8.1: *Defining Intelligence*

Recite ❑
Review ❑

Describe and outline the definitions of intelligence offered in the text. Which of these do you find most acceptable? Support your view with examples or other evidence. What additional evidence would be required to strengthen the validity of the definition you have chosen?

Essay Question 8.2: *The Heredity/Environment Question*

Outline the basic issues involved in the heredity versus environment debate. The text suggests that the more important concern is how to maximize intelligence. Considering the concepts introduced so far in the text, what methods ought to be considered in our efforts to reach our fullest intelligence potential?

Activities and Projects

1. Survey your friends and classmates regarding their views of what makes a person intelligent. Your questions may include items regarding whether intelligence necessarily correlates with success in school or work, items concerning practical intelligence, as well as the

Recite ❑
Review ❑

seven types of intelligence defined by Howard Gardner (page 300 in the text). Your objective should be to determine the preconceived, commonly held attitudes about intelligence. For instance, you may also include questions regarding the social skills of very bright and gifted people, and the view that many intelligent people lack common sense.

2. Explore the views and attitudes concerning the role of genetic inheritance on intelligence and related factors like personality. Do intelligent people view themselves as having their intelligence as a result of their genetic makeup? Do they expect their children to be as intelligent as they are? (This could be a sign of their tacitly holding the view that intelligence is inherited to a large extent.)

Cultural Idioms

Recite ❏
Review ❏

p. 274
a perfect 800 on the math SAT: This is the highest score possible on an SAT (college admission test)
UNC: University of North Carolina
the gifted: people with much higher than average intelligence
open ocean waters: being in a boat in the ocean so far out that you can't see the land
dot of land: small island

p. 275
prevailing winds: the direction that the wind usually blows
coming to grips with: understanding
the heart of urban Miami: downtown Miami
"streetwise": having the experience to deal with the dangers of a big city
hustled: taken advantage of

p. 276
batteries of tests: many different tests
"dullest": least intelligent
"bright": very smart

p. 277
your academic career: your life as a student

p. 278
severe environmental deprivation: a family life with no books or toys and very little exposure to games and stories
ease of administration: they are easy to use

p. 280
home pregnancy testing: In the U. S. a woman can buy a test in a pharmacy and, in private, determine whether or not she is pregnant.
placing a label on a child: putting a child into a category

following suit: doing the same thing; this means that SATs will also be given on the computer
scored a 400: this is not a very high SAT score
scored a 700: this is a high SAT score

p. 283
Trivial Pursuit: a board game where wining depends on how many "trivial" facts a person knows

p. 284
Babe Ruth: famous early baseball player (1895–1948)
T.S. Eliot: poet and critic (1888–1965)
Caroline Islands: islands in the South Pacific Ocean
Anne Sullivan: famous for being Helen Keller's teacher (see below)
Helen Keller: Born blind and deaf, she learned how to talk, read and write; she wrote several books and became an advocate for the blind (1880–1968)
Virginia Woolf: British novelist and essayist (1882–1941)

p. 285
Supreme Court: The U. S. Supreme Court is the highest court in the United States
Law and Order: a TV show; "law and order" is a phrase that refers to the legal system

p. 287
modeling: imitating what someone else does

p. 289
coaching services: businesses that prepare students to take tests
take a deep breath: relax

p. 290

job interviews: In U. S. culture, an employer must meet and ask you questions you before you get a job; this interview is very important.

Fact Track: the name of a computer game

80 sec: 80 seconds

Lakers and the 76ers: two professional basketball games

NBA: National Basketball Association; the best basketball teams in the U. S. are members of the NBA

p. 293

group homes: A house where a group of people live together; here, it is a group of mentally retarded people who live together in a house, instead of being in an institution

juvenile delinquents: teenagers who have been in trouble with the police

sheltered workshop: a special workplace for people with mental or physical disabilities

civil rights: the idea that all people should be treated equally

p. 295

kwang: This and the other words in this example are all nonsense words

splib: This is a vocabulary word that only those familiar with African-American culture and its dialect would know; it is not part of standard English, nor is it found in a standard English dictionary

p. 296

"rugged individualism": U. S. culture values individuals who achieve goals on their own, not as members of a group

p. 298

fanned the flames of the debate: turned the discussion into a big fight

living conditions: all the factors that make up your environment

enriched environments: exposure to books, toys, ideas, art, games, computers, etc.

Motivation and Emotion

Detailed Chapter Outline

This detailed outline contains all the headings in Chapter 9: Motivation and Emotion. If you are using the SQ3R method, then an examination of the outline is the best way to begin your survey of the chapter.

Survey ❑
Question ❑

Prologue: Leap of Faith

Looking Ahead

Explaining Motivation

Instinct Approaches: Born to Be Motivated

Drive-Reduction Approaches: Satisfying Our Needs

Arousal Approaches: Beyond Drive Reduction

Incentive Approaches: Motivation's Pull

Cognitive Approaches: The Thoughts Behind Motivation

Maslow's Hierarchy: Ordering Motivational Needs

Reconciling the Different Approaches to Motivation

Recap, Review, and Rethink

Human Needs and Motivation: Eat, Drink, and Be Daring

The Motivation Behind Hunger and Eating

Eating Disorders

Applying Psychology in the 21st Century:
Shedding Obesity's Secrets

The Facts of Life: Human Sexual Motivation

The Varieties of Sexual Experiences
Masturbation: Solitary Sex
Heterosexuality
Homosexuality and Bisexuality

Exploring Diversity: Female Circumcision: A Celebration of Culture—or Genital Mutilation?

The Need for Achievement: Striving for Success
The Need for Affiliation: Striving for Friendship
The Need for Power: Striving for Impact on Others

Pathways Through Psychology: Thomas Tutko, Sports Psychologist

Recap, Review, and Rethink

Understanding Emotional Experiences
The Functions of Emotions
Determining the Range of Emotions: Labeling Our Feelings

Deciphering Our Emotions
The James-Lange Theory: Do Gut Reactions Equal Emotions?
The Cannon-Bard Theory: Physiological Reactions as the Result of Emotions
The Schachter-Singer Theory: Emotions as Labels
Contemporary Perspectives on Emotion

Recap, Review, and Rethink

Stress and Coping
Stress: Reacting to Threat and Challenge
Coping with Stress

The Informed Consumer of Psychology: Effective Coping Strategies

Recap, Review, and Rethink
Looking Back
Key Terms and Concepts

▸ Now that you have surveyed the chapter, read **Looking Ahead**, page 307. What questions does the Chapter seek to answer?

Question ❑
Read ❑

Concepts and Learning Objectives

These are the concepts and the learning objectives for Chapter 9. Read them carefully as part of your preliminary survey of the chapter.

Survey ❑

Concept 1: The theories of motivation draw upon basic instincts, drives, levels of arousal, expectations, and self-realization as possible sources for motives. Many of the approaches may actually be complementary—each explaining an aspect of the forces that direct and energize behavior.

1. Define motivation and emotion, and discuss the role of each in human behavior.

2. Describe and distinguish among instinct, drive-reduction, arousal, incentive, and cognitive theories of motivation.

3. Explain Maslow's hierarchy of motivation.

Concept 2: Thirst, hunger, and sex are three motives that have a physiological basis, and the needs for achievement, affiliation, and power are learned motives.

4. Differentiate between biological and social factors associated with hunger.

5. Describe the eating disorders anorexia nervosa and bulimia nervosa, and discuss possible causes for these disorders.

6. Explain how sexual normality is understood and defined by society.

7. Describe patterns of heterosexual behavior, including premarital, marital, and extramarital sex .

8. Define homosexuality and bisexuality, and discuss theories that have been proposed regarding the development of sexual orientation.

9. Discuss the issues related to the cultural practice of female circumcision.

10. Discuss the secondary motivations of achievement, affiliation, and power.

Concept 3: Emotions are a highly complex experience that combine physiological arousal, situational conditions, and cognitive understanding. Emotions also serve a number of functions related to preparing for action, shaping behavior, and regulating interaction. Three major theories of emotion are the James-Lange theory, the Cannon-Bard theory, and the Schachter-Singer theory.

11. Describe the functions of emotions and the range of emotional expression.

12. Identify the key points in the James-Lange, the Cannon-Bard, and the Schachter-Singer theories of emotion, and distinguish each theory from the others.

Concept 4: Stress is a key factor in motivation and emotion.

13. Describe and illustrate Selye's general adaptation syndrome.

14. Identify the major categories of stressors and their consequences, including post-traumatic stress disorder.

15. Discuss the concept of learned helplessness, how it develops, and its effect on behavior.

17. Describe coping strategies, including defense mechanisms, social support, hardiness, and related strategies.

Chapter Guided Review

There are several ways you can use this guided review as part of your systematic study plan. Read the corresponding pages of the text and then complete the review by supplying the correct missing key word. Or, you may want to complete the guided review as a means of becoming familiar with the text. Complete the review and then read the section thoroughly. As you finish each section, complete the **Recap and Review** questions that are supplied in the text.

Survey ❏

_____

CONCEPT 1: Explaining Motivation

Survey ❏
Read ❏
Recite ❏

_____

● *How does motivation direct and energize behavior?*

Pages 306-313

The factors that direct and energize behavior comprise the major focus of the study of

[a] _____ . **[b]** _____ are the desired goals that underlie behavior. Psychologists who study motivation seek to understand why people do the things they do. The study of emotions includes the internal experience at any given moment.

There are a number of approaches to understanding motivation. An early approach focused

on **[c]** _____ as inborn, biologically determined patterns of behavior. Proponents of this view argue that there exist preprogrammed patterns of behavior. The problems with these theories include the difficulty in determining a set of instincts and the fact that instinct theories do not explain why a behavior occurs. Also, they are unable to account for the variety of behavior.

[d] _____ focus on behavior as an attempt to remedy the shortage of

some basic biological requirement. In this view, a **[e]**_____ is a

motivational tension, or arousal, that energizes a behavior to fulfill a need. **[f]** _____

meet biological requirements, while **[g]**_____ have no obvious biological

basis. Primary drives are resolved by reducing the need that underlies it. Primary drives are also

governed by a basic motivational phenomenon of **[h]** _____, the goal of

maintaining optimal biological functioning. Drive-reduction theories have difficulty explaining behavior that is not directed at reducing a drive but may be directed instead at maintaining or increasing arousal. Also, behavior appears to be motivated occasionally by curiosity as well.

The theory that explains motivation as being directed toward maintaining or increasing excitement is the **[i]** _____ . If the levels of stimulation are too low, arousal theory says that we will try to increase the levels. Some people intentionally seek high levels of arousal (Table 9–1 on page 310 of the text provides a means for students to assess their level of sensation seeking).

In motivational terms, the reward is the **[j]** _____.

[k]_____ explain why behavior may be motivated by external stimuli. The properties of the incentive direct and energize behavior. External incentives can be powerful enough to overcome the lack of internal stimuli drives. This view is compatible with the drive-reduction theory, as incentives work to "pull" and drives work to "push" behavior.

[l] _____ focus on our thoughts, expectations, and understanding of the world. For instance, **[m]** _____ combines our expectations of reaching a goal with the value we place on it to account for the degree of motivation. **[n]** _____ refers to the value an activity has in the enjoyment of participating in it, and **[o]** _____ refers to behavior that is done for a tangible reward. We work harder for a task that has intrinsic motivation. Also, as tangible rewards become available, intrinsic motivation declines and extrinsic motivation increases.

Abraham Maslow conceptualized motivational needs as fitting in a hierarchy from basic to higher-order. The first level of needs is that of the basic physiological needs of water, food, sleep, and sex. The second level is that of safety, having a secure and safe environment. The third level, the first of the higher-order needs, is that of love and belongingness. The fourth level is that of self-esteem. The final level is that of **[p]** _____, a state of fulfillment where people realize their potential. Research has not validated this view.

CONCEPT 2:   Human Needs and Motivation: Eat, Drink, and Be Daring

Survey ❑
Read ❑
Recite ❑

- _What are the biological and social factors that underlie hunger?_
- _Why, and under what circumstances, do we become sexually aroused?_
- _How do people behave sexually?_
- _How are needs relating to achievement, affiliation, and power motivation exhibited?_

Pages 314-328

One-third of Americans are considered more than 20 percent overweight and thus suffering from

[a] _____ . Most nonhumans will regulate their intake of food even when it is abundant. Hunger is apparently quite complex, consisting of a number of mechanisms that signal changes in the body. One is the level of the sugar glucose in the blood. The higher the

level of glucose, the less hunger is experienced. The **[b]** _____ monitors

the blood chemistry. A rat with its **[c]** _____ damaged will starve itself to

death, and one with the **[d]** _____ damaged will experience extreme overeating.

One theory suggests that the body maintains a **[e]** _____ . This set point controls whether the hypothalamus calls for more or less food intake. Weight set point has been implicated as a cause for obesity. Overweight people may have higher set points than normal-weight people. The size and number of fat cells may account for the high set points. Differences

in people's metabolism may also account for being overweight. **[f]** _____
is the rate at which energy is produced and expended. People with high metabolic rates can eat as much food as they want and not gain weight. People with low metabolism eat little and still gain. There is evidence that people may be born to be fat, that weight is controlled genetically. Children may learn that food is a form of consolation if they are given food after being upset, thus food becomes a treatment for emotional difficulties.

Internal biological factors do not explain our eating behavior fully. For instance, we eat meals on a customary schedule and thus feel hungry on that schedule. We eat about the same amount even if our exercise has changed, and we prefer certain types of food. Oversensitivity to external cues and insensitivity to internal cues is related to obesity. Also, reports of hunger in obese people do not correspond with the period of time deprived of food. As an alternative to the

set-point explanation, the **[g]** _____ proposes a combination of genetic and environmental factors.

[h] _____ is a disease that afflicts primarily females. Sufferers refuse

to eat and may actually starve themselves to death. **[i]** _____ is a condition in which individuals will binge on large quantities of food and then purge themselves with vomiting or laxatives. People suffering from bulimia are treated by being taught to eat foods they enjoy and to have control over their eating. Anorexia is treated by reinforcing weight gain, that is, giving privileges for success. The causes of these eating disorders are thought by some to be a chemical imbalance and by others to be the societal expectations placed on the sufferers of the disorders.

Sexual behavior in humans is filled with meaning, values, and feelings. The basic biology of the sexual response helps us understand the importance of sexual behavior. Human sexual behavior is not governed by the genetic control that other animals experience. In males, the

testes, part of the male **[j]** _____, secrete **[k]** _____, beginning at puberty. Androgens increase the sex drive and produce secondary sex characteristics like body hair and voice change. When women reach puberty, the *ovaries*, the

female reproductive organs produce **[l]** _____ and **[m]** _____, the female sex hormones. Estrogen reaches its highest levels during **[n]** _____, the release of eggs from the ovaries. In many animals, the period of ovulation is the only time they are receptive to sex. Women remain receptive throughout their cycles. Though biological factors are important, we are also conditioned to respond to a wide range of stimuli that lead to arousal.

Until Albert Kinsey undertook his study of sexual behavior, little was known about the sexual behavior of typical Americans. Kinsey collected a large number of sexual histories. One criticism of his approach is with regard to his sampling techniques, which led him to interview a large proportion of college students and well-educated individuals. Also, since the surveys were based on volunteers, it is uncertain whether the attitudes of individuals willing to share sensitive information are different from those who did not volunteer. Kinsey's work has led to a number of other national surveys.

[o] _____ is sexual self-stimulation, and its practice is quite common. Males masturbate more often than females, with males beginning in early teens, while females start later and reach a maximum frequency later. Though thought of as an activity to be done when other sexual partners are unavailable, almost three-quarters of married men masturbate. Negative attitudes about masturbation continue, though it is perfectly healthy and harmless.

[p] _____ refers to sexual behavior between men and women. It includes all aspects of sexual contact—kissing, caressing, sex play, and intercourse. Premarital

sex continues to be viewed through a **[q]** _____, as something acceptable for males but unacceptable for females. However, sexual activity among unmarried women is high, according to several surveys. When younger and older females are compared, there appears to be an increase in premarital sexual activity. Males have shown a similar increase in activity, though it is not as dramatic. The double standard appears to be changing to an attitude

of **[r]** _____, meaning that premarital intercourse is permissible if affection exists between the two persons. There are major cultural differences.

Among married couples, 43 percent have intercourse a few times a month and 36 percent have intercourse two to three times a week, and the longer a couple is married, the less frequently intercourse occurs. The frequency of sexual intercourse has increased with the availability of contraceptives and of abortion. Sex is more openly discussed in the media, and the notion that female sexuality is acceptable has contributed to the increase in activity. The frequency of sexual intercourse is not a predictor of happiness in the marriage.

Humans are not born with an innate attraction to the opposite sex. [s]_____ are individuals sexually attracted to members of the same sex, while [t] _____ are sexually attracted to both sexes. At least 20 to 25 percent of males and about 15 percent of females have had an adulthood homosexual experience, and between 5 and 10 percent of both males and females are exclusively homosexual. Though people view homosexuality and heterosexuality as distinct orientations, Kinsey places the two orientations on a scale from exclusively heterosexual behavior to exclusively homosexual behavior.

There are a number of theories accounting for sexual orientation, with some focusing on biological factors and others on social factors. Recent evidence suggests that there may be a physical difference in the anterior hypothalamus of heterosexual and homosexual males. Other theories focus on childhood and family background. Psychoanalysts suggest that male homosexuals have overprotective and dominant mothers and passive fathers. Learning theory suggests that sexual orientation is learned through rewards and punishments. Experiences with unpleasant outcomes would lead to linking the unpleasant experience with the opposite sex. Rewarding experiences would be incorporated into sexual fantasies. These fantasies are then positively reinforced by the pleasure of orgasm. The problem with learning theory is that the expected punishments of homosexuality from society should outweigh the rewards and prevent the learning. Most researchers believe that a combination of factors must be at work.

The Exploring Diversity section examines the issue of female circumcision. In many African and Asian cultures, women undergo circumcision of the clitoris, an operation often undertaken in crude conditions. The result is that the women do not experience orgasm during sexual intercourse. In some cases, even more of the female genitals are removed. The issue presents the clash between cultural practices and Western values.

The [u] _____ is a learned characteristic involving the sustained striving for and attainment of a level of excellence. People with high needs for achievement seek out opportunities to compete and succeed. People with low needs for achievement are motivated by the desire to avoid failure.

The [v] _____ is used to test achievement motivation. It requires that the person look at a series of ambiguous pictures and then write a story that tells what is going on and what will happen next. The stories are then scored for the amount of achievement imagery used in the story, the amount of striving to win, or working hard—images that suggest an achievement orientation. The achievement levels of societies have been analyzed by examining the achievement imagery in children's stories.

One view suggests that the differences in scholastic achievement may be due to underlying differences in achievement motivation. Sandra Graham has contradicted this view with research that indicates the achievement motivation for African-Americans is high, and that there is little difference with that of Whites.

The **[w]** _____ refers to the needs we have of establishing and maintaining relationships with others. People high in affiliation needs tend to be more concerned with relationships and to be with their friends more. The **[x]** _____ is a tendency to seek impact, control, or influence over others. People with a strong need for power tend to seek office more often than people with a weak need for power. Men tend to display their need for power through aggression, drinking, sexual exploitation, and competitive sports, while women who have high a need for power are more restrained.

CONCEPT 3:   Understanding Emotional Experiences
Deciphering Our Emotions

Survey ❑
Read ❑
Recite ❑

- *What are emotions, and how do we experience them?*
- *What are the functions of emotions?*

Pages 329-337

Though difficult to define, **[a]** _____ are understood to be the feelings that have both physiological and cognitive aspects and that influence behavior. Physical changes occur whenever we experience an emotion, and we identify these changes as emotions. Some psychologists argue that separate systems account for the cognitive responses and the emotional responses. Finally, some argue that we first have cognitions, and then emotional responses follow.

A number of important functions of emotions have been identified.

- *Preparing us for action.* Emotions prepare us for action by preparing effective responses to a variety of situations.

- *Shaping our future behavior.* Emotions shape our future behavior by promoting learning that will influence making appropriate responses in the future by leading to the repetition of responses that lead to satisfying emotional feelings.

- *Helping us to regulate social interactions.* Emotions also help regulate interactions with others.

Psychologists have been attempting to identify the most important fundamental emotions. Many have suggested that emotions should be understood through their component parts. There may be cultural differences as well, though these differences may reflect different linguistic categories for the emotions.

We have many ways to describe the experiences of emotion that we have. The physiological reactions that accompany fear are associated with the activation of the autonomic nervous system. They include: 1) an increase in breathing rate; 2) an increase in heart rate; 3) a widening of the pupils; 4) a cessation of the functions of the digestive system; and 5) a contraction of the muscles below the surface of your skin.

Though these changes occur without awareness, the emotional experience of fear can be felt intensely. Whether these physiological responses are the cause or the result of the experience of emotion remains unclear.

The **[b]** _____ states that emotions are the perceived physiological reactions that occur in the internal organs. They called this *visceral experience*. One of the problems with this view is that in order for this theory to be valid, the visceral changes would have to be fairly rapid, whereas emotional experiences often occur before visceral changes can take place. Another problem is that physiological arousal does not invariably produce emotional experience. Finally, internal organs produce limited sensations.

The **[c]** _____ rejects the view that physiological arousal alone leads to the perception of emotion. In this theory, the emotion-producing stimulus is first perceived, then the thalamus activates the viscera, and at the same time a message is sent to the cortex. The difference between emotional experiences depends upon the message received by the cortex.

The **[d]** _____ emphasizes that the emotion experienced depends on the environment and on comparing ourselves with others. Schachter and Singer conducted a classic experiment in which subjects were injected with epinephrine to cause physiological arousal. One group was informed about the effects and another was kept uninformed. These two groups were then exposed to either a situation in which a confederate of the experimenter was acting angry and hostile or in which the confederate was acting euphoric. The informed subjects were not affected by the situation because they accounted for their arousal as the effects of the drug, but the uniformed subjects accounted for their physiological arousal according to the situation. The experiment then supports the cognitive view of emotions: that emotions depend on general arousal that is labeled according to cues in the environment. The Schachter-Singer theory of emotions has been applied to other circumstances, one of which involved an attractive female as a subject who asked males a series of questions and then gave them her telephone number so they could get the results of the survey. Two groups of men were involved. One group had just crossed a 450-foot suspension bridge over a deep canyon, and the other crossed a stable bridge over a shallow stream. Those who crossed the canyon reported a stronger attraction to the woman, accounting for their arousal by the presence of the female rather than the fear of the canyon.

For each of the three major theories, there is some contradictory evidence. Emotions are a complex phenomena that no single theory can yet explain adequately.

CONCEPT 4: Stress and Coping

Survey ❑
Read ❑
Recite ❑

- **What is stress, how does it affect us, and how can we best cope with it?**

Pages 337-347

The response to events that threaten or challenge a person is called **[a]** _____, and the events themselves are called *stressors*. Stressors can be both pleasant and unpleasant events, though the negative events can be more detrimental. Some view life as a sequence of stresses, with our responses being minor adaptations. Sometimes, though, adaptation requires a major effort and may have responses that result in health problems.

The most immediate reaction to stress is a biological response, including an increase in release of adrenal hormones, an increase in heart rate and blood pressure, and changes in how the skin conducts electrical charges. This change initially helps the body respond to the stress. Continued stress can result in a decline of the body's ability to cope biologically. Body tissues can actually deteriorate. Minor problems can be made worse. The class of medical problems called **[b]** _____, disorders caused by the interaction of psychological, emotional, and physiological problems, are also related to stress. High levels of stress interfere with people's ability to cope with current and new stressors.

Hans Selye proposed that everyone goes through the same set of physiological responses no matter what the cause is, and he called this the **[c]** _____. The first stage is the **[d]** _____, during which the presence of a stressor is detected and the sympathetic nervous system is energized. The second stage is the **[e]** _____, during which the person attempts to cope with the stressor. If coping is inadequate, the person enters the **[f]** _____. The person's ability to cope with stress declines and the negative consequences appear. These include illness, psychological symptoms like the inability to concentrate, and possibly disorientation and losing touch with reality. People wear out in this stage. In order to escape the problems of this stage, people must often avoid the stressor—essentially, get some rest from the problem. GAS has provided a model that explains how stress leads to illness. The primary criticism has focused on the fact that the model suggests that every stress response is physiologically the same. Also, there is little room for psychological factors in the model.

If people are to consider an event stressful, they must perceive it to be threatening and must lack the ability to cope with it adequately. The same event may not be stressful for everyone. The perception of stress may depend upon how one attributes the causes for events.

There are three classes of events that are considered stressors. The first is [g] _____, strong stressors that affect many people at the same time. The stress of these events is usually dealt with well because so many people experience the event and share the problem. Some people experience prolonged problems due to catastrophic events, and this is called [h] _____. People may experience flashbacks or dreams during which they reexperience the event. The symptoms can include a numbing of emotional experience, sleep difficulties, problems relating to others, and drug problems, among others. The second class of stressor is [i] _____, which include life events that are of a personal or individual nature, like the death of a parent or spouse, the loss of a job, or a major illness. Typically, personal stressors cause an immediate major reaction that tapers off. Sometimes, though, the effects can last for a long time, such as the effects of being raped. The third class of stressors is called [j] _____, and they include standing in long lines, traffic jams, and other [k] _____. Daily hassles can add up, causing unpleasant emotions and moods. A critical factor is the degree of control people have over the daily hassles. When they have control, the stress reactions are less. On the other side of daily hassles are [l] _____, positive events that lead to pleasant feelings.

In an environment in which control is seen as impossible, one can experience [m] _____. Victims of learned helplessness have decided that there is no link between the responses they make and the outcomes that occur. When elderly people in nursing homes were given control over simple aspects of their lives, they were less likely to experience an early death. Not everyone experiences helplessness.

Our efforts to control, reduce, or learn to tolerate stress are known as [n] _____. Many of our responses are habitual. The [o] _____ are unconscious strategies that help control stress by distorting or denying the actual nature of the situation. Denying the significance of a nearby geological fault is an example.

[p] _____ is another example in which a person does not feel emotions at all. Another means of dealing with stress is the use of direct and positive means. These include [q] _____, the conscious regulation of emotions, and

[r] _____, the management of the stressful stimulus. People use both strategies, but they are more likely to use the emotion-focused strategy when they perceive the problem as unchangeable.

People can be described as having coping styles. [s] _____ refers to the style that is associated with a low rate of stress-induced illness. The style consists of three components: commitment, challenge, and control. Commitment is a tendency to be involved in whatever we are doing with a sense that it is important and meaningful. Challenge refers to the view that change is the standard condition of life. Control refers to the sense of being able to influence events. The hardy person is optimistic and approaches the problem directly.

Relationships with others help people cope with stress. The knowledge of a mutual network of concerned, interested people helping individuals experience lower levels of stress is called

[t] _____. Social support demonstrates the value of a person to others and provides a network of information and advice. Also, actual goods and services can be provided through social support networks. Even pets can contribute to this support. Stress can be dealt with through several steps: Turn stress into a challenge, make the threatening situation less threatening by changing attitudes about it, change goals in order to remove oneself from an uncontrollable situation, and take physical action. The most successful approach requires that the person be prepared for stress. One method of preparation is called inoculation. With

[u] _____, stress is dealt with through preparation for both the nature of the possible stressors and developing or learning clear strategies for coping.

▶ Now that you have surveyed, questioned, and read the chapter and completed the guided review, review **Looking Back**, pages 347-348.

▶ For additional practice through recitation and review, test your knowledge of the chapter material by answering the questions in the *Key Word Drill*, the *Practice Questions*, and the *Essay Questions*.

_____
Review ❑
_____

Key Word Drill

The following **Matching Questions** test the boldfaced and italicized key words from the text. Check your answers with the Answer Key in the back of the *Study Guide*.

Recite ❏

_____

MATCHING QUESTIONS

1. motives

2. emotions

3. instinct

4. drive

5. primary drives

6. secondary drives

7. intrinsic motivation

8. extrinsic motivation

a. An inborn pattern of behavior that is biologically determined.

b. Participating in an activity for a tangible reward.

c. Participating in an activity for its own enjoyment, not for a reward.

d. Desired goals that prompt behavior.

e. The internal feelings experienced at any given moment.

f. Biological needs such as hunger, thirst, fatigue, and sex.

g. Drives in which no biological need is fulfilled.

h. A tension or arousal that energizes behavior in order to fulfill a need.

9. drive-reduction theory

10. arousal approach to motivation

11. homeostasis

12. incentive approach to motivation

13. cognitive approaches to motivation

a. Motivation by focusing on the role of an individual's thoughts, expectations, and understanding of the world.

b. The theory that claims that drives are produced to obtain our basic biological requirements.

c. The belief that we try to maintain certain levels of stimulation and activity, changing them as necessary.

d. The theory explaining motivation in terms of external stimuli.

e. The process by which an organism tries to maintain an internal biological balance.

_____

14. expectancy-value theory

15. self-actualization

16. need for achievement

17. need for affiliation

18. need for power

a. A tendency to want to seek impact, control, or influence on others in order to be seen as a powerful individual.

b. A need to establish and maintain relationships with other people.

c. A stable, learned characteristic, in which satisfaction comes from striving for and achieving a level of excellence.

d. A state of self-fulfillment in which people realize their highest potential.

e. A view that suggests that people are motivated by expectations that certain behaviors will accomplish a goal and their understanding of the importance of the goal.

_____

19. hypothalamus

20. lateral hypothalamus

21. ventromedial hypothalamus

22. metabolism

23. weight set point

24. weight settling point

a. The part of the brain that, when damaged, results in an organism's starving to death.

b. The particular level of weight that the body strives to maintain.

c. The part of the brain that, when injured, results in extreme overeating.

d. Weight level determined by a combination of genetic and environmental factors.

e. The structure in the brain that is primarily responsible for regulating food intake.

f. The rate at which energy is produced and expended by the body.

---

25. James-Lange theory of emotion

26. Cannon-Bard theory of emotion

27. Schachter-Singer theory of emotion

a. The belief that emotions are determined jointly by a nonspecific kind of physiological arousal and its interpretation, based on environmental cues.

b. The belief that both physiological and emotional arousal are produced simultaneously by the same nerve impulse.

c. The belief that emotional experience is a reaction to bodily events occurring as a result of an external situation.

---

28. heterosexuality

29. homosexuality

30. bisexuality

a. A sexual attraction to a member of one's own sex.

b. Sexual behavior between a man and a woman.

c. A sexual attraction to members of both sexes.

---

31. cataclysmic events

32. personal stressors

33. background stressors

34. daily hassles

35. uplifts

a. The same as background stressors.

b. Strong stressors that occur suddenly, affecting many people at once (e.g., natural disasters).

c. Events, such as the death of a family member, that have immediate negative consequences that generally fade with time.

d. Minor positive events that make one feel good.

e. Events such as being stuck in traffic that cause minor irritations but have no long-term ill effects unless they continue or are compounded by other stressful events.

---

36. learned helplessness

37. coping

38. defense mechanisms

39. social support

40. inoculation

a. Preparation for stress before it is encountered.

b. The efforts to control, reduce, or learn to tolerate the threats that lead to stress.

c. A learned belief that one has no control over the environment.

d. Unconscious strategies people use to reduce anxiety by concealing its source from themselves and others.

e. Knowledge of being part of a mutual network of caring, interested others.

Practice Questions

Test your knowledge of the chapter material by answering these **Multiple Choice Questions.** These questions have been placed in three Practice Tests. The first two tests are composed of questions that will test your recall of factual knowledge. The third test contains questions that are challenging and primarily test for conceptual knowledge and your ability to apply that knowledge. Check your answers and review the feedback using the Answer Key in the back of the *Study Guide*.

Recite ❑
Review ❑

_____

MULTIPLE CHOICE QUESTIONS

PRACTICE TEST I:

1. _____ activate behavior and orient it toward achieving goals.

   a. Instincts
   b. Motives

   c. Emotions
   d. Homeostatic energizers

2. Primary drives are motives that:

   a. people rate as being most important to them.
   b. seem to motivate an organism the most.
   c. arc least likely to be satisfied before self-actualization can occur.
   d. have a biological basis and are universal.

3. The process by which an organism tries to maintain an optimal level of internal biological functioning is called:

   a. primary drive equilibrium.
   b. homeostasis.

   c. drive reduction.
   d. opponent-process theory.

4. Which of the following statements about masturbation is true?

   a. All of society views masturbation as a healthy, normal activity.
   b. The majority of people surveyed have masturbated at least once.
   c. Males and females begin masturbation at puberty.
   d. Psychologists view people who masturbate as poorly adjusted.

5. The double standard for premarital sex means:

   a. twice as many men have premarital sex as women.

   b. premarital sex is discouraged for both men and women.

   c. even people who are marrying for a second time should refrain from sex before their remarriage.

   d. premarital sex is discouraged for women but not for men.

6. Which statement about marital sexual intercourse is correct?

   a. There are few differences in the frequency of marital sex for younger and older couples.

   b. The average frequency of marital sex is 1.3 times per week.

   c. The frequency of marital sex is closely related to happiness in the marriage.

   d. The frequency of marital sex today is higher than ever before.

7. According to the text, a motivation behind behavior in which no obvious biological need is being fulfilled is the definition of:

   a. a primary drive.   c. a secondary drive.

   b. an achievement.   d. instinct.

8. The incentive theory of motivation focuses on:

   a. instincts.

   b. the characteristics of external stimuli.

   c. drive reduction.

   d. the rewarding quality of various behaviors that are motivated by arousal.

9. The desirable qualities of the external stimulus are the focus of:

   a. the incentive motivational approach.

   b. the drive-reduction motivational approach.

   c. the instinctive motivational approach.

   d. the cognitive motivational approach.

10. According to the expectancy-value theory, the two types of cognitions that control motivation are:

    a. drive-reductions and positive incentives.

    b. rewards and punishments.

    c. intrinsic motivation and extrinsic motivation.

    d. hopes and disappointments.

11. According to Maslow, which of the following must be met before people can fulfill any higher-order motivations?

    a.   extrinsic needs   c.   primary needs

    b.   intrinsic needs   d.   secondary needs

12. According to the text, which of the following is thought to be primarily involved in the physiological regulation of eating behavior?

    a.   cortex   c.   hypothalamus

    b.   amygdala   d.   hippocampus

13. A college woman has experienced a major weight loss and has begun refusing to eat. She denies that she has an eating problem and does not recognize that she suffers from:

    a.   hyperphagia.   c.   rolfing.

    b.   bulimia.   d.   anorexia nervosa.

14. The _____ is used to measure an individual's need for achievement.

    a.   Scholastic Assessment Test

    b.   Intelligence Quotient Test

    c.   Yerkes-Dodson Achievement Analysis

    d.   Thematic Apperception Test

15. William James and Walter Lange suggested that major emotions correlate with particular "gut reactions" of internal organs. They called this internal response:

    a.   a physiological pattern.   c.   an autonomic response.

    b.   a psychological experience.   d.   a visceral experience.

16. Which theory postulates that emotions are identified by observing the environment and comparing ourselves with others?

    a.   Schachter-Singer theory   c.   James-Lange theory

    b.   Cannon-Bard theory   d.   Ekman's theory

17. A circumstance that produces threats to people's well-being is known as:

    a.   a stressor.   c.   a defense mechanism.

    b.   a mobilization state.   d.   an inoculation.

18. Which alternative below is **not** a stage of Selye's general adaptation syndrome?

    a.   resistance   c.   alarm and mobilization

    b.   challenge   d.   exhaustion

19. The alarm and mobilization stage of Selye's general adaptation syndrome is characterized by:
    a. preparing to react to the stressor.
    c. emotional and physical collapse.
    b. increased resistance to disease.
    d. becoming aware of the presence of a stressor.

20. According to the text, events that are strong stressors and that occur suddenly and affect many people simultaneously are called:
    a. cataclysmic stressors.
    c. uplifts.
    b. background stressors.
    d. personal stressors.

21. High blood pressure, ulcers, or eczema are common:
    a. defense mechanism disorders.
    c. hardiness disorders.
    b. life-crisis disorders.
    d. psychophysiological disorders.

22. The textbook defines uplifts to be:
    a. minor irritations of life that are encountered daily.
    b. minor positive events that make a person feel good.
    c. exhilarating experiences that leave a person in a dazed state.
    d. major positive life events.

23. The ability to tolerate, control, or reduce threatening events is called:
    a. defense.
    c. coping.
    b. arousal.
    d. adaptation.

PRACTICE TEST II:

24. According to the text, the main function of motivation is to:
    a. create tension.
    c. promote learning of survival behaviors.
    b. provide feeling.
    d. provide direction to behavior.

25. Which of the following is the best example of a drive that is common to both humans and animals?
    a. power
    c. cognition
    b. hunger
    d. achievement

26. The compensatory activity of the autonomic nervous system, which returns the body to normal levels of functioning after a trauma, is called:

    a. homeostasis.
    b. biorhythmicity.
    c. biofeedback.
    d. transference.

27. In the drive-reduction motivation model, _____ is the drive related to the need for water.

    a. the drinking instinct
    b. thirst
    c. repetitive water-intake behavior
    d. water-balance in body tissues

28. According to the text, some psychologists feel that the incentive theory of motivation is strengthened when combined with complementary concepts drawn from:

    a. instinct theory.
    b. drive-reduction theory.
    c. arousal theory.
    d. cognitive theory.

29. Our hopes that a behavior will cause us to reach a certain goal and our understanding that the goal will be meaningful or important to us are combined in:

    a. the expectancy-value theory of motivation.
    b. the drive-reduction theory of motivation.
    c. Maslow's hierarchy of motivation.
    d. arousal theory of motivation.

30. Which theory is **least** tied to biological mechanisms?

    a. instinct theory
    b. cognitive theory
    c. drive-reduction theory
    d. arousal theory

31. Masturbation is:

    a. always viewed as inappropriate behavior.
    b. practiced more by men than women.
    c. more common in older men than younger men.
    d. commonly regarded by experts as counterproductive to learning about one's sexuality.

32. In Maslow's hierarchal pyramid of motivation, self-actualizers:

    a. are notably self-sufficient at all levels: growing their own food, finding their own friends, creating their own artwork, etc.
    b. are dependent upon others but are inwardly focused.
    c. have achieved their major goals in life.
    d. encourage others to do their best while remaining modest themselves.

33. At which of the following ages does the amount of fat cells in the body usually stop declining?

    a. 24 years of age

    b. 20 years of age

    c. 12 years of age

    d. 2 years of age

34. Which of the following is an eating disorder usually affecting attractive, successful females between the ages of 12 and 40 who refuse to eat and sometimes literally starve themselves to death?

    a. metabolic malfunction

    b. bulimia

    c. anorexia nervosa

    d. obesity

35. Which alternative below is **not** true of the need for achievement?

    a. Individuals with a high need for achievement choose situations in which they are likely to succeed easily.

    b. It is a learned motive.

    c. Satisfaction is obtained by striving for and attaining a level of excellence.

    d. High need for achievement is related to economic and occupational success.

36. According to the text, women, as opposed to men, tend to channel their need for power through:

    a. socially responsible ways

    b. questionable means

    c. quietly aggressive ways

    d. uncharted, high-risk opportunities

37. According to the James-Lange theory of emotion, _____ determines the emotional experience.

    a. physiological change

    b. a cognitive process

    c. an instinctive process

    d. the environment

38. Which of the following individuals developed the general adaptation syndrome model?

    a. Martin Seligman

    b. Hans Selye

    c. B. F. Skinner

    d. Sigmund Freud

39. Hans Selye's general adaptation syndrome states that:

    a. stress generates biological responses in animals that differ from those in humans.

    b. stressful situations produce many different responses in individuals.

    c. the same set of physiological reactions to stress occur regardless of the situation.

    d. immobilization happens when the organism confronts a stressor.

40. Background stressors do not require much coping or response, but continued exposure to them may produce:
    a. an inability to use problem-focused techniques.
    b. as great a toll as a single, more stressful incident.
    c. as great a toll as a cataclysmic event.
    d. psychosomatic illness.

41. According to Seligman, _____ occurs when one concludes that unpleasant or annoying stimuli cannot be controlled.
    a. learned helplessness
    b. hysteria
    c. cataclysmic stress
    d. posttraumatic stress

42. According to the text, what are the two types of strategies people may use when consciously attempting to regulate a stressful situation?
    a. control-oriented or defensive coping strategies
    b. emotion-focused or problem-focused coping strategies
    c. emotional insulation or denial coping strategies
    d. conscious or unconcious coping strategies

43. Someone who is classified as hardy:
    a. is unable to cope with stress at all.
    b. is unlikely to develop stress-related disease.
    c. is unlikely to view stress as a challenge.
    d. is affected mostly by hard emotional choices.

PRACTICE TEST III: Conceptual, Applied, and Challenging Questions

44. Advertisements for a job boast that it offers $4 more than minimum wage, a guaranteed cash bonus after 30 days, and a paid vacation. This advertisement emphasizes the concept of:
    a. opponent-process motivation.
    b. arousal motivation.
    c. drive-reduction motivation.
    d. extrinsic motivation.

45. For the American public, which factor appears to play the **least** significant role in hunger?
    a. blood chemistry
    b. stomach contractions
    c. number and size of fat cells
    d. weight set point

46. A thin man and an obese man had lunch just before boarding their plane. When flight attendants serve lunch, what will the two men be expected to do, according to the external-cue theory?

    a. Neither will eat the lunch on the plane.

    b. The obese man will eat a second lunch, while the thin man may skip it.

    c. The thin man will eat a second lunch, but the obese man will skip it.

    d. Both men will eat a second lunch.

47. Sonya developed a cycle of binge eating, during which she consumed a variety of gourmet foods and wines and then induced vomiting afterward. Her doctor told Sonya that she could do permanent damage to her health if she continued the behavior and that if she continued, she could become:

    a. ischemic.

    b. depressed.

    c. volumetric.

    d. bulimic.

48. Jane finished her college degree with honors and received a variety of excellent job offers. Instead, she decided to enter graduate school to acquire more advanced skills and get even better job offers. Jane is demonstrating her:

    a. need for affiliation.

    b. need for achievement.

    c. fear of failure.

    d. need for power.

49. Seth, a teenage male, has discovered that he is fascinated with the male body and finds it sensual. However, he knows that he still likes girls. Which of the following presents the most accurate descriptions of Seth's orientation?

    a. Kinsey's view that sexual orientation is on a gradient from heterosexuality to homosexuality.

    b. The cultural view that you are either heterosexual or homosexual.

    c. The early view that masturbation is harmful and leads to harmful consequences.

    d. Masters and Johnson's view that sexual response goes through a set pattern no matter what the stimulus.

50. According to the text, emotions play an important role in all of the following **except**:
    a. making life interesting.
    b. helping us to regulate social interaction.
    c. informing us of internal bodily needs.
    d. preparing us for action in response to the external environment.

51. The notion that the same nerve impulse triggers simultaneously the physiological arousal and the emotional experience is a hallmark of:
    a. the Cannon-Bard theory of emotion.   c. the Schachter-Singer theory of emotion.
    b. the facial-affect theory of emotion.   d. the James-Lange theory of emotion.

52. Which of the following is most typical of an individual high in the need for power?
    a. Jennifer, who is aggressive and flamboyant
    b. John, who has joined the local chapter of a political party
    c. Jane, who shows concern for others and is highly nurturant
    d. Jeff, who enjoys competitive sports

53. Which of the following is most typical of an individual high in the need for affiliation?
    a. Marianne, who appears sensitive to others and prefers to spend all her free time with friends
    b. Mark, who joins a local political group
    c. Margaret, who enjoys team sports and likes to attend parties
    d. Michael, who is aggressive and controlling whenever he is in groups

54. At first, Lynne is quite excited about keeping her room neat, and she does it without being asked. Her family then begins a system of rewarding good behavior with an additional allowance. According to the cognitive approach to motivation, what is the most likely response that Lynne will have?
    a. Her tendency to clean her room will be increased.
    b. She will probably be less eager to clean her room.
    c. She will be even more enthusiastic, but she will not clean her room any more frequently.
    d. She will be unwilling to clean her room at all.

55. It was the end of the year, and Max realized that he had failed to reach his sales goals, so he set new goals for the following year. Max's behavior is typical for a person at the _____ stage of the general adaptation syndrome.
    a. resistance   c. alarm and mobilization
    b. exhaustion   d. repression

56. For those involved, the terrorist bombing of an office building is which type of stressor?
    a. personal stressor
    b. background stressor
    c. daily hassle
    d. cataclysmic event

57. A college football coach uses his assistants to regulate players' every activity, using aversive procedures and penalties. By the end of the season, the players take no initiative. This demonstrates:
    a. the general adaptation syndrome.
    b. daily hassles.
    c. the inferiority complex.
    d. learned helplessness.

58. Upon visiting the doctor's office and going through extensive testing, Michael finds out that he has a lung disease. Which type of stress is Michael likely to experience?
    a. cataclysmic stress
    b. personal stress
    c. post-traumatic stress
    d. background stress

59. Social support is an effective means of coping with all of the following types of stress. However, based on the descriptions in the text, in which one of the following is social support most likely to occur as a matter of the nature of the stressor?
    a. personal stressors
    b. events leading to posttraumatic stress disorder
    c. cataclysmic events
    d. uplifts

Essay Questions

Essay Question 9.1: *Theories of Motivation*

Recite ❑
Review ❑

Describe each of the main theories of motivation and attempt to explain a single behavior from the point of view of each theory.

Essay Question 9.2: *Human Needs and Motivation*

What are the biological and social factors that affect eating behavior?

Activities and Projects

1. The next time you experience an emotion that is clear enough for you to give it a label, take time afterward to analyze which theory of emotion best applies to your particular emotional experience. For example, would the James-Lange theory apply? Did your experience follow from physiological cues? Or did these processes happen simultaneously as suggested by the Cannon-Bard theory? Or did cognitive processes and labeling on the basis of context play a major role in your experience of the emotion? Use the following chart to record your experiences.

Recite ❑
Review ❑

EMOTION EVENT RECORDER

Time	Emotion	Circumstances	Which Approach?
			❑ James-Lange ❑ Cannon-Bard ❑ Schachter-Singer
			❑ James-Lange ❑ Cannon-Bard ❑ Schachter-Singer
			❑ James-Lange ❑ Cannon-Bard ❑ Schachter-Singer
			❑ James-Lange ❑ Cannon-Bard ❑ Schachter-Singer
			❑ James-Lange ❑ Cannon-Bard ❑ Schachter-Singer
			❑ James-Lange ❑ Cannon-Bard ❑ Schachter-Singer
			❑ James-Lange ❑ Cannon-Bard ❑ Schachter-Singer

			☐ James-Lange
			☐ Cannon-Bard
			☐ Schachter-Singer

2.   Determine where you believe that you fit on Maslow's hierarchy of needs. How do you know that you are at that particular level? What types of thought patterns and behaviors might you engage in during your striving to the next level in the hierarchy? You may also identify your specific concerns and behaviors as they fit each of the levels of Maslow's hierarchy. What behaviors would you identify with your eventual self-actualization?

**MASLOW'S HIERARCHY
SELF-ASSESSMENT**

Overall Achievement	Examples

1. Physiological Needs
    ☐ Meeting
    ☐ Not Meeting	

2. Safety Needs
    ☐ Meeting
    ☐ Not Meeting	

3. Belongingness Needs
    ☐ Meeting
    ☐ Not Meeting	

4. Self-Esteem Needs
    ☐ Meeting
    ☐ Not Meeting	

5. Self-Actualization
Needs
☐ Meeting
☐ Not Meeting

Cultural Idioms

Recite ❏
Review ❏

p. 306

leap of faith: a philosophical idea, meaning that although no one can prove that God exists, many people believe in God via a "leap of faith"; the author is making a joke here, because this Olympic gymnast literally had to leap into the air, believing that she could win, even though she was injured.

vault: an exercise that a gymnast must perform

abandon the meet: to withdraw from the competition

the horse: a piece of gymnastic equipment

p. 307

safer sexual practices: sexual activities that minimize the risk of exposure to the AIDS virus

p. 308

raid the refrigerator: to open the refrigerator looking for a snack

p. 309

gossip columns: newspaper or magazine stories about celebrities' love lives

roller coaster: a fast and scary ride in an amusement park

the rapids: the part of a river where the water moves downhill very fast

p. 311

bungee jumping: jumping from a great height, while attached to a stretchy cord; the jumper does not hit the ground, but bounces back up

mouth-watering dessert: a dessert that looks so delicious that a person starts to salivate

p. 312

magic markers: brightly colored pens that children use for drawing

Eleanor Roosevelt: the wife of President Franklin Roosevelt; she was the first U. S.

delegate to the United Nations

Abraham Lincoln: sixteenth president of the United States; president during the Civil War, he was assassinated in 1865

Albert Einstein: famous 20th century physicist

p. 314

composing copy: writing advertisements

Eat, Drink, and Be Daring: This is a joke, based on the common phrase "Eat, drink, and be merry." This section of the textbook is about eating and about achievement, thus the substitution of "be daring" (that is, take a risk) instead of "be merry" (that is, be happy).

stepping-stone: an intermediate step

p. 315

well-balanced diet: eating a healthy combination of food

p. 316

force-fed: feeding by a tube, or otherwise making sure that food gets into the stomach

"house specialty": the dessert that he is famous for, that he cooks very well

Heath Bar Crunch: a kind of ice cream made by the ice cream company Ben & Jerry's, which consists of ice cream with pieces of Heath Bar candy bar mixed in

p. 317

rice cake: a small, light cracker with very few calories

melting away: disappearing (like an ice cube on a warm day)

p. 318

New Year's resolutions: promises that people make on January 1, to change something in their life; many people make a New Year's resolution to lose weight, or to quit smoking.

genetic tinkering: changing a person's genes

hot fudge sundae: an ice cream dessert

Big Macs: a kind of hamburger that McDonald's fast food restaurants make

p. 328

correspondence course: a class that you take through the mail; the teacher sends you work to do through the mail and you mail back assignments.

General Motors: one of the top three U. S. car companies

p. 329

to put it bluntly: to be honest

p. 330

downplayed: not as important

giving to a charity: donating either time or money to a group that helps others

p. 332

my stomach is filled with butterflies: I feel very nervous

p. 336

scratched the surface: just begun

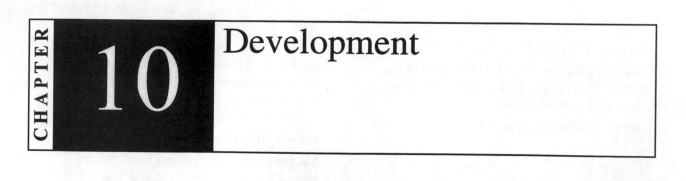

CHAPTER 10 Development

Detailed Chapter Outline

► Now that you have surveyed the chapter, read **Looking Ahead**, pages 354-355. What questions does the Chapter seek to answer?

Question ❑

Read ❑

Concepts and Learning Objectives

These are the concepts and the learning objectives for Chapter 10. Read them carefully as part of your preliminary survey of the chapter.

Survey ❑

Concept 1: The fundamental issue for developmental psychology is the interaction between nature and nurture in human development. Development from conception to birth illustrates the nature-nurture interaction.

1. Define developmental psychology, and discuss various topics of study within the field, especially the influence of nature and nurture on human development.

2. Distinguish among longitudinal, cross-sectional, and cross-sequential research methods.

3. Describe the major events that occur from conception to birth.

4. Discuss genetic abnormalities and environmental influences that affect prenatal development.

Concept 2: Physical and social development are marked by dramatic changes through childhood, from birth to about 12 years of age. Physical and perceptual skills grow rapidly in the early months and years, and attachment is one of the most important social developments in the first years of life. Cognitive development refers to the changes in how the individual understands the world. The period of childhood shows dramatic stages in the process of development.

5. Describe the process of physical development from birth through the end of childhood and discuss the sensory and perceptual capacities of newborn infants and their typical course of development.

6. Describe social influences on development, including the contributions made by the parents, peers, and day care providers.

7. Outline and describe the first four psychosocial stages of development as identified by Erik Erikson.

8. Outline and describe the cognitive developmental stages identified by Jean Piaget.

9. Explain the information-processing approach to cognitive development, as well as Lev Vygotsky's sociocultural approach.

Concept 3: Adolescence begins with the growth spurt and puberty, and it continues until the end of the teenage years. Early and middle adulthood are marked by the formation of a family, the establishment and success (or failure) in work, and the gradual progress toward old age. Old age does not conform to our myths about it, and the elderly often lead active, happy lives.

10. Define adolescence, and describe the physical changes that mark its beginning.

11. Describe the moral and cognitive development that occurs during adolescence.

12. Identify and discuss Erikson's psychosocial stages relevant to adolescence and adulthood.

13. Define adulthood, and describe the physical changes that accompany it, and discuss the concerns of adulthood that result from the demands of society and pressures of work.

14. Describe the roles of males and females in marriage and in the family, specifically as they relate to the course of adult development.

15. Define old age, the physical changes that accompany it, and the theories that attempt to account for it and identify the changes that occur in cognitive ability, intelligence, and memory during old age.

16. Describe the challenges and changes faced by the elderly in regard to their social involvement.

17. List and define Kübler-Ross's five stages of adjustment to death.

Chapter Guided Review

There are several ways you can use this guided review as part of your systematic study plan. Read the corresponding pages of the text, and then complete the review by supplying the correct missing key word. Or, you may want to complete the guided review as a means of becoming familiar with the text. Complete the review and then read the section thoroughly. As you finish each section, complete the **Recap and Review** questions that are supplied in the text.

Survey ❏
_____

CONCEPT 1:   **Nature and Nurture: A Fundamental Developmental Issue**

Survey ❏
Read ❏
Recite ❏
_____

- *How do psychologists study the degree to which development is a joint function of hereditary and environmental factors?*
- *What is the nature of development prior to birth?*
- *What factors affect a child during the mother's pregnancy?*

Pages 355-364

[a] _____ is the branch of psychology focused on explaining the similarities and differences among people that result from the growth and change of individuals throughout life. Developmental psychologists look to both the genetic background that provides built-in biological programming and the environmental influences.

Developmental psychologists are interested in a fundamental question of distinguishing the causes of behavior that are *environmental* from the causes that result from *heredity*. This question is identified as the **[b]** _____. However, both nature and nurture are involved, it is not a question of nature *or* nurture. Both *genetic makeup*, the biological inheritance, and the environment have influence, and the debate is over the extent to which each affects behavior. Some theories focus on learning and the role of the environment, and other theories focus on the role of growth and **[c]** _____, or the development of biologically predetermined patterns, in causing developmental change. The theories agree on some points. Genetics provides for some behaviors and sets limits on some traits and behaviors. Heredity sets limits on intelligence and limits on physical abilities. (Table 10-1 on page 357 lists characteristics with strong genetic components.) Environment plays a role in enabling individuals to reach the potential allowed by both their genetic background. Developmental psychologists take an [d] _____ position, arguing that behavior and development are determined by genetic and environmental influences.

One approach used by developmental psychologists is the study of [e] _____. Different behaviors displayed by identical twins must have some environmental component. Many studies seek to find identical twins who were separated at birth by adoption. Nontwin siblings who are raised apart also make contributions to these kind of studies. The opposite approach takes people of different genetic backgrounds and examines their development and behavior in similar environments. Animals with different genetic backgrounds can be placed in situations where the environments can be experimentally manipulated.

Two categories of research are used by developmental psychologists. [f] _____ refers to the use of a sample of subjects that is based on a selection of groups that represent different ages at the same point in time. The problem with this approach is that different age groups may have had significantly different environmental influences. [g] _____ refers to the selection of a sample from the population and following the sample's development through an extended period of time. The problem with this approach is that many individuals may drop out or they may become familiar with the tests being used to measure their development. An alternative method is called [h] _____. It combines the selection of different age groups with the following of the groups through time. In this approach, age changes can be observed in different age groups without the lengthy longitudinal approach.

Development begins at the point of [i] _____, when the male's sperm penetrates the female's egg. The fertilized egg is at this point called a [j] _____. It contains twenty-three pairs of [k] _____, one-half from the father and the other half from the mother. Each chromosome contains thousands of [l] _____, the individual units that carry genetic information. Genes are responsible for the development of the systems of the body, heart, circulatory, brain, lungs, and so on. And many genes control specific unique characteristics. Sex is determined by a set of chromosomes that combines an X chromosome from the mother and a Y or an X from the father. Girls have an XX combination and boys have an XY combination. At four weeks, the zygote becomes a structure called the [m] _____. It has a rudimentary heart, brain, intestinal tract, and other organs. By the eighth week, the embryo has arms and legs. Beginning at the eighth week, the embryo faces a [n] _____ of development—a period during which specific growth must occur if the individual is to develop normally. Eyes and ears must form, and environmental influences can have significant effects. At the ninth week the individual is called a **[o]** _____. At sixteen to eighteen weeks the movement of the fetus can be felt by the mother. At the twenty-fourth week, the fetus has the characteristics of a newborn, though it cannot survive outside the mother if born prematurely. At twenty-eight weeks, the fetus can survive if born prematurely, and this is called the **[p]** _____. At twenty-eight weeks the fetus will weigh about three pounds.

In 2 to 5 percent of all cases, children have serious birth defects. Common genetic defects include **[q]** _____, a metabolic disorder that can be treated;

[r] _____, a disease afflicting African-Americans, and children with the disease rarely live beyond childhood; **[s]** _____, a disease that results in the inability to break down fat, causing death by age 3 or 4; and **[t]** _____, a problem where an extra chromosome causes an unusual physical appearance and retardation.

Prenatal environmental influences include: the mother's nutritional and emotional state—emotionally anxious mothers tend to have babies that are irritable and who sleep and eat poorly; illness of the mother—diseases like **[u]** _____ (German measles) can cause serious defects in the unborn child and AIDS can be passed from mother to child; the mother's use of drugs can have serious effects on the child, including **[v]** _____, and some babies can be born with their mother's addiction to drugs like cocaine. Sometimes, complications of delivery can cause serious problems, like entanglement of the umbilical cord, which may lead to a loss of oxygen.

CONCEPT 2: Physical, Social, and Cognitive Development

Survey ❑
Read ❑
Recite ❑

- *What are the major milestones of physical, perceptual, and social development after birth?*
- *How can we best describe cognitive development?*
- *What can parents do to promote the competence of their children?*

Pages 365-381

At birth, the newborn baby is called a **[a]** _____. The neonate looks strange because the journey through the birth canal squeezes and shapes the skull. The neonate is covered with **[b]** _____, a white, greasy material that protects the skin prior to birth, and a soft layer of hair called **[c]** _____. The neonate is born with a number of [d] _____, unlearned, involuntary responses. Most are necessary for survival and maturation. The *rooting reflex* causes neonates to turn their head toward anything that touches their cheeks. The *sucking reflex* makes the neonate suck on anything that touches its lips. The *gag reflex* clears the throat, and the *startle reflex* causes a number of movements when a loud noise is sounded. The [e] _____ fans out the toes when the edge of the foot is touched. These reflexes are lost within a few months and replaced by more complex behaviors. Through the first year of life, major changes in physical ability occur, including learning to stand and walk.

In the first year of life, children triple their birth weight and their height increases by 50 percent. From 3 to 13 years of age, the child adds an average of 5 pounds and 3 inches per year. The proportion of body and body parts changes through the time period as well.

At birth, the neonate has a limited capacity to focus vision and can focus only on objects within about 7 to 8 inches. They are also able to follow objects moving in their field of vision. Techniques have been developed to determine the perceptual abilities of neonates that depend upon changes in basic responses and reflexes. Heart rate is closely associated with the reaction to an object being perceived. Changes in heart rate signal [f] _____, or the decrease in responding to the same stimulus. A novel stimulus causes an increase in heart rate. Using this technique, developmental psychologists are able to tell when a baby can detect a stimulus. Other methods include the use of a nipple attached to a computer that measures the rate and force of sucking. Changes in stimuli correlate to changes in sucking. The perceptual abilities of infants have been found to be quite sophisticated. They show preference for certain patterns with contours and edges. They have a sense of size constancy. Neonates can discriminate facial expressions, and they respond to the emotion and mood of caregivers. At the end of the first month, infants can distinguish some colors. By four and five months they can distinguish two- and three-dimensional objects. At the age of three days, newborns can distinguish their mothers' voices. By six months they can discriminate virtually any sound.

In addition to physical and perceptual growth, infants grow socially as well.

[g] _____ refers to the positive emotional bond between a child and a particular individual. Harry Harlow demonstrated the importance of attachment by showing that baby monkeys preferred a terry-cloth "mother" to a wire "mother," even though the wire version provided food and the terry cloth one did not. Others have since suggested that attachment develops from the responsiveness of the caregiver to the signals given by the infant. Full attachment is achieved through a complex sequence of events described by the Attachment Behavioral System. Infants play an active role in the development of the bond.

Attachment has been measured using a procedure developed by Mary Ainsworth, now called the *Ainsworth strange situation*. The measurement involves a series of events during which the mother and child are separated (briefly) in the presence of a stranger. The reactions of the babies are then observed. Ainsworth identified three kinds of attachment: "Securely attached" children use the mother as a home base, "avoidant" children do not cry when the mother leaves but they avoid her on her return, and "ambivalent" children are anxious when the mother leaves and then upset when she returns. Securely attached children tend to have fewer psychological difficulties when older than do ambivalent and avoidant children. They are also more competent socially and more cooperative, capable, and playful. Day care has become a central part of the lives of children in our society. Children in high-quality day care do as well as children who stay at home.

Recently the father's role in children's development has been researched. Fathers spend less time caring for their children, but the attachments can be just as strong. The differences in the attachment result from the fact that the mothers spend more time with care and feeding and the fathers spend more time playing with infants. Fathers play more physical games and mothers play more verbal games. The amount of time spent with children is less important than the quality of that time.

Friendships with peers are crucial for a preschooler's social development. Children become less dependent on their parents from the age of 2 years on. At 2, children pay more attention to toys, and as they get older, they pay more attention to each other. At school age, the interactions become formalized, and children play complex, structured games with rigid rules. Play serves to increase social competence, provides a perspective on the thoughts and feelings of others, and helps to teach children self-control.

Diana Baumrind has proposed that there are three main categories of child-rearing patterns. The [h] _____ are rigid and punitive and expect unquestioning obedience.

[i] _____ are lax and inconsistent though warm. [j] _____ set limits and are firm, but as their children get older, they reason and explain things to them. Children of authoritarian parents tend to be unsociable, unfriendly, and withdrawn. Children of permissive parents are immature, moody, and dependent, with low self-esteem. Children of authoritative parents are likable, self-reliant, independent, and cooperative.

Children are born with [k] _____, or basic, innate dispositions. The temperament can elicit a certain child-rearing style. The child-rearing styles may be applicable to American culture, where independence is highly valued. For instance, Japanese parents encourage dependence to promote values of community and cooperation.

Erik Erikson has proposed an eight-stage theory of social development. Each stage of

[l] _____ involves a basic crisis or conflict. Though each crisis is resolved as we pass through the stages, the basic conflict remains throughout life. First is the

[m] _____ (birth to 18 months), in which feelings of trust are built on basic physiological and psychological needs, especially attachment. The

[n] _____ (18 months to 3 years) is marked by the development of independence if exploration and freedom are encouraged or shame if they are not. The [o] _____ (3 to 6 years) is marked by the conflict between the desire to initiate independent activities and the guilt that arises from the consequences. The last stage of childhood is the [p] _____ (6 to 12 years). On the positive side, development proceeds with the increase in competency, while the opposite is failure and inadequacy.

[q] _____ refers to the developmental changes in the understanding of the world. Theories of cognitive development attempt to explain the intellectual changes that occur throughout life. Jean Piaget proposed that children passed through four distinct stages of cognitive development and that these stages differed in both the quantity of information acquired and the quality of knowledge and understanding. Maturation and relevant experiences are needed for children to pass through the stages.

Piaget's first stage is called the [r] _____ , and it is from birth to 2 years. This stage is marked by the child's lack of ability to use images, language, and symbols. Things not immediately present are not within the child's awareness until the development of [s] _____ , the awareness that objects continue to exist when they are out of sight.

The [t] _____ is from 2 to 7 years of age. Children gain the ability to represent objects internally and can use symbols for objects. Children's thinking has improved over the sensorimotor stage, but it is still inferior to adult thought. This stage is marked by [u] _____ , in which the world is viewed from the child's perspective. The [v] _____ , which states that quantity is unrelated to appearance, is not understood during this period.

The [w] _____ is from 7 to 12 years of age. Its beginning is marked by the mastery of the principle of conservation. Children develop the ability to think in a logical manner. They learn to understand reversibility, or the capacity of things to be reverted to a previous state. They are, however, bound to the concrete, physical world rather than abstract thoughts.

The [x] _____ , from 12 years to adulthood, is marked by the use of abstract, formal, and logical thought. Though it emerges at this time, formal thought is used infrequently. Studies show that only 40 to 60 percent of college students reach this stage and only 25 percent of the general population do so.

Research has shown that Piaget underestimated the abilities of infants and children. Some psychologists suggest that cognitive development is more continuous than Piaget suggested. In this alternative view, the cognitive development is one of quantitative changes. Piaget has had significant influence on educational theory and curricula, even if some of his theory and research has been challenged.

An alternative to Piaget's theory is that of [y] _____, which examines how people take in, use, and store information. According to this theory, cognitive development requires the development of mental programs for approaching problems. The changes that occur relate to speed of processing, attention span, and improvement of memory. The size of chunks of information increases with age. Information processing also points to the changes in

metacognition as a sign of development. [z] _____ refers to the awareness and understanding of one's own cognitive processes.

The Russian developmental psychology Lev Vygotsky suggested that the culture in which we are raised has a strong influence on our cognitive development. According to his view, children's cognitive abilities increase when they are exposed to information that falls into their

[aa] _____, which he describes as the level at which a child can almost, but not fully, comprehend or perform a task on his or her own. Parents, teachers, and peers provide supportive information that serves as [bb] _____ for the child's development.

CONCEPT 3:   Adolescence: Becoming an Adult

Survey ❑
Read ❑
Recite ❑

Early and Middle Adulthood: The Middle Years of Life

The Later Years of Life: Growing Old

- *What major physical, social, and cognitive transitions characterize adolescence?*
- *What are the principal kinds of physical, social, and intellectual changes that occur in early and middle adulthood, and what are their causes?*
- *How does the reality of old age differ from the stereotypes about the period?*
- *How can we adjust to death?*

Pages 382-402

Development continues throughout life, from adolescence to adulthood and old age. The major biological changes that begin with the attainment of physical and sexual maturity and the changes in social, emotional, and cognitive function that lead to adulthood mark the period called

[a] _____ .

The dramatic physical changes of adolescence include a growth in height, the development of breasts in females, the deepening of the male voice, the development of body hair, and intense sexual feelings. The growth spurt begins around age 10 for girls and age 12 for boys. The development of the sexual organs begins about a year later. There are wide individual variations, however. Better nutrition and medical care in western cultures is probably the cause

of the decreasing age of onset of **[b]** _____ . Early-maturing boys have an advantage over later-maturing boys, doing better in athletics and being more popular, though they do have more difficulties in school. Early-maturing girls are more popular and have higher self-concepts than those who mature late, but the obvious changes in breasts can cause separation from peers and ridicule. Late-maturers suffer because of the delay, with boys being ridiculed for their lack of coordination and girls holding lower social status in junior high and high school.

Lawrence Kohlberg has identified a series of stages that people pass through in their moral development. Preadolescent children make moral judgments based on concrete, inflexible rules. Adolescents are able to reason more abstractly and comprehend moral principles. Kohlberg argues that everyone passes through a fixed series of six stages (though not all reach the final stages) that are divided into three levels: (1) preconventional, (2) conventional, and (3) post-conventional. Table 10-5 (page 386 in the text) describes these stages in depth. Kohlberg's ideas are considered to be generally valid, with some criticisms that suggest there is a difference between judgments and actual behavior.

Carol Gilligan has argued that Kohlberg's system is flawed in its application to the moral judgment of women. Different socialization experiences bring about a difference between the moral views of men and of women. Men view morality in terms of justice and fairness, and women view morality in terms of responsibility toward individuals. Compassion is a more important factor for women. Since Kohlberg's views are based on justice, his system cannot adequately describe the moral development of women. Gilligan defines three stages for the moral development of women: The first stage is termed "orientation toward individual survival;" the second is "goodness as self-sacrifice;" the third is "morality of nonviolence."

Erikson's theory of psychosocial development identifies the beginning of adolescence with

his fifth stage, called the **[c]** _____ . During this stage, individuals seek to

discover their abilities, skills, and **[d]** _____ . If one resolves this stage with confusion, then a stable identity will not be formed and the individual may become a social deviant or have trouble with close personal relationships later. The stage is marked by a shift from dependence on adults for information and the turn toward the peer group for support.

During college, the [e] _____ describes the basic conflict. This stage focuses on developing relationships with others. Middle adulthood finds people in the

[f] _____. The contribution to family, community, work, and society comprise generativity; and feelings of triviality about one's activities indicate the difficulties of the stage and lead to stagnation. The final stage is the [g] _____ , and it is marked by a sense of accomplishment if successful in life or a sense of despair if one regrets what might have been.

It was once thought that adolescence was a period of stress and unhappiness, but most adolescents pass through the period without much turmoil. There does exist tension in their lives, and attempts at independence can lead to testing a range of behaviors that parents and society find objectionable. One source of the problems that adolescents have is that in western society they are staying at home much longer than at prior times in history. A large portion of men and women who are unmarried continue to live with their parents into their thirties. There are also many stresses outside the home, including coping with school and dealing with relationships and part-time jobs.

Early adulthood is generally considered to begin at about 20 years of age and to last until about 40 to 45 years, and middle adulthood lasts from 40 to 45 to about 65 years of age. These ages have been studied less than any other. Fewer significant physical changes occur, and the social changes are diverse.

The peak of physical health is reached in early adulthood, and quantitative changes begin at about 25 years as the body becomes less efficient and more prone to disease through time. The

major physical development is the female experience of [h] _____ , the cessation of menstruation and the end of fertility. The loss of estrogen may lead to hot flashes, a condition that is successfully treated with artificial estrogen. Problems that were once blamed on menopause are now seen as resulting from the perceptions of coming old age and society's view of it. Though men remain fertile, the gradual decline of physical abilities has similar effects to menopause, causing the man to focus on the social expectations of youthfulness.

Daniel Levinson's model of adult development identifies six stages from beginning adulthood through the end of middle adulthood. At the beginning, the individual formulates a "dream" that guides career choices and the vision the person has of the future. At about 40 or 45,

people enter a period called the [i] _____ , during which past

accomplishments are assessed, and in some cases, the assessment leads to a [j] _____ , in which the signs of physical aging and a sense that the career will not progress combine to force a reevaluation of and an effort to remedy their dissatisfaction. Most people go through the midlife transition without any difficulties. During their fifties, people become more accepting of others and of their own lives. They realize that death is inevitable and seek to understand their accomplishment in terms of how they understand life. Since Levinson's research was based on males, the difference in roles and socialization has raised questions about whether women go through the same stages.

The most likely pattern today is that a man and woman will first live together, then marry and have children, and then get a divorce. The average age of marriage is higher than at any time since the turn of the century, and about 60 percent of marriages end in divorce. The number of single-parent households has doubled in two decades, with 28 percent of all households having only one parent. Children experience a process of conflict, tension, and breakup, followed by obstacles to establishing relationships with one of the parents. Evidence suggests that children of single-parent households are just as well-adjusted as other children. Close to 95 percent of the population eventually gets married, and people who get divorced tend to get married several more times.

The roles of men and women are changing in marriage, and wives are taking on more responsibilities. Three-quarters of married women with school-aged children work outside the home. The distribution of household chores has not changed substantially. Women still see themselves as responsible for cooking and cleaning, and men see themselves as responsible for fixing things. Working women put in tremendous amounts of time working, doing household chores, and caring for children. Benefits of working appear to outweigh the disadvantages because of the multiple roles that give women a greater sense of mastery, pride, and competence. Success in work increases happiness, the sense of control, and self-esteem in both men and women. Failure can lead to anxiety, depression, impotence, and other psychological symptoms.

[k] _____ study development and the aging process from the age of about 65. Gerontologists are reexamining our understanding of aging, suggesting that the stereotype of aging is inaccurate. Napping, eating, walking, and conversing are the typical activities of both the elderly and college students. The obvious physical changes that appear in old age include thinning and graying hair, wrinkling and folding skin, and a loss of height. Vision and hearing become less sharp, smell and taste are less sensitive, reaction time slows, and oxygen intake and heart-pumping abilities decrease. Two types of theories have been offered to account for these changes. One group includes the [l] _____ , which suggest that there are preset time limits on the reproduction of human cells governed by genetics.

The other group includes the [m] _____ , which suggest that the body simply stops working efficiently. By-products of energy production accumulate, and cells make mistakes in their reproduction. Old age is not a disease, but is instead a natural biological process. Many functions, like sexual behavior, remain pleasurable long into old age. Neither of these theories explain why women live longer than men. At birth there are more males than females; by 65 years of age, 84 percent of women are still alive and 70 percent of men. A consequence of increased health awareness is that the gap is not increasing.

The view that the elderly are forgetful and confused is no longer considered an accurate assessment. IQ tests usually include a physical performance component that measures the reaction time of the elderly, even though reaction time has nothing to do with intelligence. The elderly are often in ill health, and the comparison of healthy young adults with groups of less healthy elderly people exaggerates differences. When healthy elderly are used for comparison, differences are less significant. Also, since more young people attend college, the elderly groups are often less educated. Tests show declines in [n] _____ in old age, but

[o] _____ actually increases. Fluid intelligence may be more sensitive to changes in the nervous system than crystallized intelligence.

One assumption about the elderly is that they are more forgetful. Evidence suggests that forgetfulness is not inevitable. Memory declines tend to be in long-term memory and, specifically, with episodic memories. Life changes may cause a decline in motivation rather than actual memory impairment. Impairments can be compensated by mnemonic strategies. The decline in cognitive function associated with old age is called [p] _____,

but this is now viewed as a symptom caused by other factors, like [q] _____, anxiety, depression, or even overmedication.

Loneliness is a problem for only a small portion of the elderly, though social patterns do change in old age. Two theories account for how people approach old age. The

[r] _____ views aging as a gradual withdrawal from the world on physical, psychological, and social levels. Energy is lower and interaction lessens. This view sees aging

as an automatic process. The [s] _____ suggests that people are happiest who remain active and that people should attempt to maintain the activities and interests they develop during middle age. The nature of the activity is the most important factor, not the quantity. Death requires major adjustments, as the death of those near you causes changes in life and makes you consider the possibility of your own death. Elisabeth Kübler-Ross outlined five

stages of the death process: 1) [t] _____, the person denies the fact that he

or she is dying; 2) [u] _____, the person becomes angry at people who are healthy, angry at the medical profession for not being able to help, and angry at God; 3)

[v] _____, the person may try to postpone death through a bargain in

exchange for extended life; 4) [w] _____, once bargaining fails, the person

experiences depression, realizing that death is inevitable; and 5) [x] _____ signaled by the end of mourning one's own life, and becoming unemotional and noncommunicative as if at peace with oneself.

▸ Now that you have surveyed, questioned, and read the chapter and completed the guided review, review **Looking Back**, pages 403-404.

Review ❑

▸ For additional practice through recitation and review, test your knowledge of the chapter material by answering the questions in the *Key Word Drill*, the *Practice Questions*, and the *Essay Questions*.

Key Word Drill

The following **Matching Questions** test the boldfaced and italicized key words from the text. Check your answers with the Answer Key in the back of the *Study Guide*.

Recite ❏
_____

MATCHING QUESTIONS

1. conception

2. zygote

3. chromosomes

4. genes

5. embryo

6. fetus

a. A zygote that has a heart, a brain, and other organs.

b. The one-celled product of fertilization.

c. A developing child, from nine weeks after conception until birth.

d. Structures that contain basic hereditary information.

e. The parts of a chromosome through which genetic information is transmitted.

f. The process by which an egg cell is fertilized by a sperm.

7. environment

8. heredity

9. genetic makeup

10. maturation

11. interactionist

12. cross-sectional research

13. longitudinal research

14. cross-sequential research

a. The unfolding of biologically predetermined behavior patterns.

b. A research method that investigates behavior through time as subjects age.

c. Influences on behavior that occur in the world around us—in family, friends, school, nutrition, and others.

d. A research method that combines cross-sectional and longitudinal research.

e. Biological factors that transmit hereditary information.

f. Influences on behavior that are transmitted biologically from parents to a child.

g. Someone who believes that a combination of genetic predisposition and environmental influences determines the course of development.

h. A research method in which people of different ages are compared at the same point in time.

15. phenylketonuria (PKU)

16. sickle-cell anemia

17. Tay-Sachs disease

18. Down syndrome

19. rubella

20. fetal alcohol syndrome

a. A disease of the blood that affects about 10 percent of America's African-American population.

b. German measles.

c. A disorder caused by the presence of an extra chromosome, resulting in mental retardation.

d. An inherited disease that prevents its victims from being able to produce an enzyme that resists certain poisons, resulting in profound mental retardation.

e. A genetic defect preventing the body from breaking down fat and typically causing death by the age of 4.

f. An ailment producing mental and physical retardation in a baby as a result of the mother's behavior.

---

21. neonate

22. vernix

23. lanugo

24. reflexes

25. rooting reflex

26. sucking reflex

27. gag reflex

28. startle reflex

29. Babinski reflex

a. A white lubricant that covers a fetus, protecting it during birth.

b. Unlearned, involuntary responses to certain stimuli.

c. The reflex in response to a sudden noise where the infant flings its arms, arches its back, and spreads its fingers.

d. The reflex where an infant's toes fan out in response to a stroke on the outside of its foot.

e. A newborn child.

g. A neonate's tendency to turn its head toward things that touch its cheek.

f. A reflex that prompts an infant to suck at things that touch its lips.

h. A soft fuzz covering the body of a newborn.

i. An infant's reflex to clear its throat.

30. habituation

31. authoritarian parents

32. permissive parents

33. authoritative parents

34. temperament

35. psychosocial development

a. A decrease in responding to repeated presentations of the same stimulus.

b. Development of individuals' interactions and understanding of one another and their knowledge and understanding of themselves as members of society.

c. Basic, innate disposition.

d. Parents who are rigid and punitive and who value unquestioning obedience from their children.

e. Parents who are firm, set clear limits, and reason with and explain things to their children.

f. Parents who are lax, inconsistent, and undemanding, yet warm toward their children.

---

36. trust-versus-mistrust stage

37. autonomy-versus-shame-and-doubt stage

38. initiative-versus-guilt stage

39. industry-versus-inferiority stage

a. The stage of psychosocial development where children can experience self-doubt if they are restricted and overprotected.

b. The first stage of psychosocial development, occurring from birth to 18 months of age.

c. The period during which children may develop positive social interactions with others or may feel inadequate and become less sociable.

d. The period during which children experience conflict between independence of action and the sometimes negative results of that action.

---

40. sensorimotor stage   a. Characterized by abstract thought.

41. object permanence   b. Little competence in representing the environment.

42. preoperational stage   c. Characterized by language development.

43. principle of conservation   d. Characterized by logical thought.

44. concrete operational stage   e. Quantity is unrelated to physical appearance.

45. formal operational stage   f. Awareness that others do not cease to exist when out of sight.

---

46. identity-versus-role-confusion stage   a. A period from late adulthood until death during which we review life's accomplishments and failures.

47. intimacy-versus-isolation stage   b. A period in middle adulthood during which we take stock of our contributions to family and society.

48. generativity-versus-stagnation stage   c. A period during early adulthood that focuses on developing close relationships with others.

49. ego-integrity-versus-despair stage   d. A time in adolescence of testing to determine one's own unique qualities.

50. genetic preprogramming theories of aging

    a. Theories that suggest that the body's mechanical functions cease efficient activity and, in effect, wear out.

51. wear-and-tear theories of aging

    b. A theory that suggests that the elderly who age most successfully are those who maintain the interests and activities they had during middle age.

52. disengagement theory of aging

    c. Theories that suggest a built-in time limit to the reproduction of human cells.

53. activity theory of aging

    d. A theory that suggests that aging is a gradual withdrawal from the world on physical, psychological, and social levels.

---

54. adolescence

    a. The point at which women stop menstruating, generally at around age 45.

55. puberty

    b. The stage between childhood and adulthood.

56. identity

    c. The negative feelings that accompany the realization that we have not accomplished in life all that we had hoped.

57. menopause

58. midlife transition

    d. The distinguishing character of the individual: who each of us is, what our roles are, and what we are capable of.

59. midlife crisis

    e. Beginning around the age of 40, a period during which we come to the realization that life is finite.

    f. The period during which maturation of the sexual organs occurs.

---

60. Erik Erikson   a. Moral development.

61. Lawrence Kohlberg   b. Death and dying.

62. Jean Piaget   c. Psychosocial development.

63. Elisabeth Kübler-Ross   d. Cognitive development.

64. Daniel Levinson   e. Adult social development.

Practice Questions

Test your knowledge of the chapter material by answering these **Multiple Choice Questions**. These questions have been placed in three Practice Tests. The first two tests are composed of questions that will test your recall of factual knowledge. The third test contains questions that are challenging and primarily test for conceptual knowledge and your ability to apply that knowledge. Check your answers and review the feedback using the Answer Key in the back of the *Study Guide*.

Recite ❑
Review ❑

_____

MULTIPLE CHOICE QUESTIONS

PRACTICE TEST I:

1. When theories stress the role of heredity in their explanations of change in individual development, the focus of their accounts would be on:
   a. maturation.
   b. nurture.
   c. environmental factors.
   d. social growth.

2. Which set of subjects would provide the least information for a study regarding the nature-nurture question in humans?
   a. identical twins reared apart
   b. children adopted from different families reared together
   c. siblings reared apart
   d. siblings reared together

3. A study in which several different age groups are examined over different points in time is called:

    a. cross-sectional.   c. longitudinal.
    b. maturational.   d. cross-sequential.

4. Certain events must take place in a specific time frame; otherwise, the entire sequence of fetal growth is thrown off and the result will be either no development or abnormal development. This time frame is called:

    a. longitudinal development.   c. the resolution phase.
    b. cross-section maturation.   d. the critical period.

5. In prenatal development, the age of viability is a developmental stage in which:

    a. the eyes and other sense organs are functional.
    b. the fetus can survive if born prematurely.
    c. development has advanced sufficiently so that the fetus is capable of learning from environmental cues.
    d. the sexual organs of the fetus are differentiated.

6. The infant's later temperament is known to be affected by the mother's:

    a. consumption of "junk foods" during pregnancy.
    b. sleep patterns during early fetal development.
    c. attitude about whether the baby is wanted or unwanted.
    d. emotional state during the late fetal period.

7. Which reflex below helps the newborn infant position its mouth onto its mother's breast when it feeds?

    a. rooting reflex   c. gag reflex
    b. startle reflex   d. surprise reflex

8. The most dramatic changes that occur during the first year after birth have to do with:

    a. speech development.
    b. overall growth.
    c. increase in head size relative to the rest of the body.
    d. the disappearance of reflexes.

9.   Erikson's theory of development:
      a.   was based on experiences of psychotic women.
      b.   covers an entire lifetime.
      c.   takes a behaviorist approach.
      d.   was derived from Piaget's cognitive approach to development.

10.   In order to proceed from one of Piaget's stages of cognitive development to another, it is necessary for children to achieve:
      a.   a certain level of perceptual and cognitive development.
      b.   a certain level of maturation and experience.
      c.   a certain level of memory capacity and physical development.
      d.   a certain level of social and cognitive development.

11.   According to Piaget, a child who exhibits logical and abstract thought has achieved the:
      a.   sensorimotor stage.   c.   concrete operational stage.
      b.   preoperational stage.   d.   formal operational stage.

12.   Metacognition is:
      a.   a flaw in one's perception of one's own knowledge.
      b.   a phase of thinking that occurs in the preoperational stage of cognitive development.
      c.   an alteration in thinking that results from brain damage.
      d.   an awareness and a knowledge of one's own cognitive processes.

13.   The period during development that is marked by dramatic physical and psychological change and attainment of sexual maturity is called:
      a.   adulthood.   c.   puberty.
      b.   adolescence.   d.   childhood.

14.   If a person's behavior reflected the desire to please other members of society, he or she would be considered to be at Kohlberg's:
      a.   preconventional level of moral reasoning.
      b.   conventional level of moral reasoning.
      c.   postconventional level of moral reasoning.
      d.   nonconventional level of moral reasoning.

15. Developmentalist Lawrence Kohlberg's approach to the study of moral reasoning is:
    a. to check the person's criminal record to see whether he or she is a convict.
    b. to collect survey data in which subjects rate their own moral reasoning.
    c. to ask spouses to talk freely and confidentially about their partners.
    d. to study the person's thinking in response to moral dilemma.

16. Which of these is typical of adolescent development?
    a. preconventional morality   c. ego-integrity verus despair
    b. infertility   d. striving for identity

17. According to the text, the most noteworthy feature of Erikson's theory of psychosocial development is that:
    a. both men and women are included in its descriptions of developmental changes.
    b. it accurately describes developmental changes that people in other cultures also experience.
    c. it has greatly increased understanding of infant development.
    d. it suggests that development is a lifelong process.

18. The primary cause of a midlife crisis tends to be:
    a. an awareness of the detrimental physical changes associated with aging.
    b. a series of disappointments and shortcomings in a person's children.
    c. a recognition that a person's reproductive capabilities are decreasing or will soon end.
    d. a failure to achieve desired career goals and objectives.

19. Which of the following has doubled since 1970?
    a. the number of married couples who get divorced within the first ten years of marriage
    b. the number of children under the age of 5
    c. the number of single-parent households
    d. the number of women who stay at home to raise children

20. Interest in gerontology will increase during coming decades because:
    a. the numbers of elderly will increase substantially.
    b. medical research will enable the aging process to be halted.
    c. stereotypical beliefs about the elderly are being dispelled.
    d. crystallized intelligence remains high even into old age.

21. What do the genetic preprogramming theories suggest about physical decline of aging?
   a. Women live four to ten years longer than men.
   b. The body, like a machine, eventually wears out.
   c. There is a built-in time limit to the ability of human cells to reproduce.
   d. Physical aging is a biological process in which all physical functions decline.

22. Fluid intelligence provides the capabilities for many adaptive and functional human behaviors. Which alternative below correctly describes a person's fluid-intelligence capabilities?
   a. Fluid intelligence increases after birth until early adulthood.
   b. Fluid intelligence is high all through a person's lifetime.
   c. Fluid intelligence increases more slowly during late adulthood and old age.
   d. Fluid intelligence remains fairly constant until a person's death.

23. A pattern of reduced social and physical activity as well as a shift toward the self rather than a focus on others characterizes the:
   a. deactivation theory of aging.
   b. activity theory of aging.
   c. withdrawal theory of aging.
   d. disengagement theory of aging.

24. Which of the following is the correct sequence for Kübler-Ross's five stages of facing death?
   a. bargaining, depression, acceptance, anger, denial
   b. denial, depression, anger, bargaining, acceptance
   c. depression, anger, denial, bargaining, acceptance
   d. denial, anger, bargaining, depression, acceptance

PRACTICE TEST II:

25. The philosophical view that infants are born with a blank slate favors which of the following as a dominant influence upon development?
   a. interactionism
   b. nature
   c. nurture
   d. dualism

26. Identical twins are especially interesting subjects for developmental studies because they:
    a. communicate via telepathy, i.e., direct mental transfer of ideas.
    b. have typically shared their lives together in their parents' home.
    c. have identical genetic makeup since they developed from one zygote.
    d. are very highly cooperative in their dealings with psychologists.

27. The units that produce particular characteristics in an individual are called:
    a. chromosomes.
    b. genes.
    c. spores.
    d. somes.

28. The unborn fetus has many of the features and characteristics of a newborn as early as:
    a. 8 weeks.
    b. 12 weeks.
    c. 16 weeks.
    d. 24 weeks.

29. A genetic defect that leads to a very short life due to a breakdown in strategic metabolic processes and occurs most frequently among Jews of Eastern European descent is called:
    a. Tay-Sachs disease.
    b. Down syndrome.
    c. meningitis.
    d. phenylketonuria.

30. Which developmental disorder results from the presence of an extra chromosome?
    a. Down syndrome
    b. sickle-cell anemia
    c. Tay-Sachs disease
    d. phenylketonuria (PKU)

31. Rubella is also known as:
    a. Down syndrome.
    b. German measles.
    c. phenylketonuria.
    d. sickle-cell anemia.

32. A neonate is:
    a. a prenatal infant in its thirtieth to thirty-eighth week of development.
    b. a newborn infant.
    c. an infant born with deformities because of chromosomal abnormalities.
    d. a premature baby up to the time at which the normal due date passes.

33. A researcher compares visual abilities in four groups of infants of ages 1 month, 3 months, 5 months, and 7 months. This is an application of:
    a. the longitudinal research method.
    c. the cross-sectional research method.
    b. the critical period research method.
    d. the cross-sequential research method.

34. According to research findings reported in the text, what is the earliest stage at which a child can imitate adult facial expressions?
    a. At the neonatal stage.
    c. At the toddler stage.
    b. At the infant stage.
    d. At the preschooler stage.

35. From Diana Baumrind's categories of parental styles, _____ parents are those who are firm and set limits and goals, reasoning with their children and encouraging their independence.
    a. temperative
    c. authoritative
    b. permissive
    d. authoritarian

36. In Erik Erikson's psychosocial model, toddlers strive to achieve:
    a. nurturance from an adult.
    c. trust of significant adults.
    b. competence in play activities.
    d. autonomy and independence.

37. The goal of Swiss child psychologist Jean Piaget's research was to identify how the child changes in her abilities to _____ during childhood.
    a. refine movement skills
    c. understand reality
    b. make rapid perceptual decisions
    d. respond socially

38.   Which of the following is **not** one of Kohlberg's stages of moral reasoning?

a.   preconventional

c.   postconventional

b.   conventional

d.   nonconventional

39.   For Carol Gilligan, the beginning level of moral reasoning for women is the stage of:

a.   goodness equated with self-sacrifice.

c.   orientation toward individual survival.

b.   self-worth and self-respect.

d.   morality of nonviolence.

40.   According to Erikson, college-age people typically contend with the conflicts found in the:

a.   intimacy-versus-isolation stage.

c.   ego-integrity-versus-despair stage.

b.   generativity-versus-stagnation stage.

d.   identity-versus-role-confusion stage.

41.   Which of the following represents a major biological change in the life of a female during middle adulthood?

a.   puberty

c.   menarche

b.   menopause

d.   tumescence

42.   According to the text, a major developmental task for people 40 to 50 years old who are experiencing the initial stages of middle adulthood is to:

a.   maintain harmonious relationships with their children.

b.   accept that the die has been cast, and that they must come to terms with their circumstances.

c.   carefully choose goals so that all the major career advances can still be realized before old age.

d.   adjust to changes brought about by menopause and physical deterioration.

43.   A 46-year-old professor reviews her past actions and failed personal goals. She devoted her efforts to her academic career rather than to marriage or children, yet she now realizes that her colleagues regard her research as trivial and uninspired. She feels old and knows that she has accomplished little in her life. She is experiencing:

a.   menopause.

c.   midlife transition.

b.   delayed identity crisis.

d.   midlife crisis.

44.   According to the text, one way that the developmental stages of adult women differ from those of men is that:

    a.   women have more difficulties developing a vision of what their future life will include.

    b.   women's midlife crises are more likely to occur later in their lives.

    c.   women's midlife crises are usually precipitated by their children leaving home, causing the "empty nest syndrome."

    d.   women's developmental stages are more influenced by hormonal and physical changes.

45.   Which theory suggests that some cells may become harmful to the body after a certain amount of time?

    a.   opponent-process   c.   wear-and-tear

    b.   genetic preprogramming   d.   gerontological

46.   The theory of aging that is based on the notion that mechanical functions of the body stop working efficiently is called:

    a.   genetic preprogramming.   c.   wear-and-tear.

    b.   genetic breakdown.   d.   failure of function.

47.   Which type of intelligence actually increases with age?

    a.   fluid intelligence   c.   basic intelligence

    b.   verbal intelligence   d.   crystallized intelligence

48.   The _____ theory of aging states that aging involves a gradual withdrawal from the world on multiple levels.

    a.   wear-and-tear   c.   disengagement

    b.   genetic preprogramming   d.   activity

PracticeTest III: Conceptual, Applied and Challenging Questions

49. The view of developmental psychologists today is that:

 a. environmental stimulation is necessary to achieve full genetic potential.

 b. genetic factors are most important in individual development.

 c. environmental influences are most important in individual development.

 d. different factors are important for different individuals.

50. Of the organs listed below, which is **not** yet formed at the embryonic stage?

 a. heart   c. intestinal tract

 b. brain   d. eyes

51. One-tenth of the black population in the United States has the possibility of passing on _____, which leaves the newborn with a variety of health problems and very short life expectancy.

 a. hypertension   c. phenylketonuria

 b. sickle-cell anemia   d. Tay-Sachs disease

52. Which developmental influence below does not belong with the others?

 a. mother's nutrition and stress level   c. mother's drug and medication intake

 b. hereditary defects   d. birth complications

53. Which statement about the sensory and perceptual capabilities of infants is **not** true?

 a. At 4 days of age, they can distinguish between closely related sounds such as "ba" and "pa."

 b. At 60 days of age, they can recognize their mother's voice.

 c. After 6 months of age, they are capable of discriminating virtually any difference in sounds that is relevant to the production of language.

 d. They prefer sweetened liquids to unsweetened liquids.

54. Why are there generally differences in the form of attachment between the baby and its mother and father?

 a. Mothers spend more time directly nurturing their children, whereas fathers spend more time playing with them.

 b. Mother spend more time playing with their children, whereas fathers spend more time nurturing them.

 c. Mothers generally are identified as primary caregivers, so the attachment is stronger.

 d. Fathers spend more time doing things with their children than mothers.

55. According to the text, which statement best represents the father's typical attachment to his children?

    a. It is superior to the mother's attachment in most situations.

    b. It is aloof and detached.

    c. It is generous with affection, especially during verbal interaction.

    d. It is qualitatively different, but comparable to the mother's attachment.

56. Which type of parents would be most likely to explain things to children and try reasoning with them when conflicts or problems arise?

    a. permissive parents

    b. authoritative parents

    c. caretaking parents

    d. authoritarian parents

57. A developmental psychologist is evaluating a young child's cognitive development. The psychologist shows the child two separate arrangements of red disks. Eight disks are laid in a straight line in one arrangement. Another eight disks are arranged in a random "scatter" pattern in the other. The psychologist asks, "Is the amount of disks in each arrangement the same?" The psychologist is testing the child's understanding of:

    a. spatial reversibility.

    b. conservation

    c. spatial inertia.

    d. reorganization.

58. Jess and Luisa were playing with two balls of clay. Luisa was molding a cake and Jess was making a bowl. Jess then suggested they get new balls of clay so that they could make something different. Luisa informed him that no new clay was necessary; the clay could be remolded to make different objects. What principle was Luisa teaching to Jess?

    a. the principle of conservation

    b. the principle of reversibility

    c. the principle of egocentric thought

    d. the principle of logic

59. According to Piaget, _____ is mastered early in the _____ for most children.

    a. reversibility; sensorimotor stage

    b. conservation; concrete operational stage

    c. object permanence; formal operational stage

    d. abstraction; preoperational stage

60.   The last time Sara used her personal computer, she observed that several files were not copied onto the floppy disk as she had expected. She carefully checked her sequence of operations and considered the characteristics of the software. After evaluating alternative explanations for what had happened, she correctly deduced why the files were not copied. Sara is in Piaget's:

    a.   concrete operational stage of cognitive development.

    b.   preoperational stage of cognitive development.

    c.   sensorimotor stage of cognitive development.

    d.   formal operational stage of cognitive development.

61.   If a developmental psychologist were interested in investigating how different age groups responded to the Gulf War, he or she would probably use the research method known as:

    a.   cross-sectional research.

    b.   cross-sequential research.

    c.   longitudinal research.

    d.   archival research.

62.   A child thinks, "If I steal a cookie, I will get spanked." In which level of moral development is this child functioning?

    a.   amorality

    c.   conventional morality

    b.   preconventional morality

    d.   postconventional morality

63.   Mary Margaret leads a group that has as its focus rape prevention and assistance in recovery from rape. The group represents moral development consistent with Gilligan's notion of:

    a.   morality of nonviolence.

    c.   goodness as self-sacrifice.

    b.   orientation to individual survival.

    d.   preconventional morality.

64.   Being active in civic groups, assisting in recreational programs, and having a stable career are indications that one is in the _____ stage of development.

    a.   intimacy-versus-isolation

    c.   generativity-versus-stagnation

    b.   identity-versus-role-confusion

    d.   ego-integrity-versus-despair

65.   Frank and his wife, who are both in their early thirties, want many children. Frank does not know when he will be incapable of fathering children, and he is getting worried that there might not be enough time. What would you say to Frank?

    a.   Men lose their ability to father children in their late forties, just like women.

    b.   Men lose their fertility in their late fifties, so his wife will lose her fertility first.

    c.   Both men and women remain fertile into their sixties, so there is plenty of time left for them to have children.

    d.   Men don't lose their ability to father children until well into old age.

66. When a child's mother and father work, the mother is generally still viewed as holding the main child-rearing responsibility. Yet, there are also great benefits to working. In what way do the benefits outweigh the disadvantages?

    a. Women who work feel a greater sense of mastery and pride, and generally have higher self-esteem.

    b. Women who work play a greater role in the decisions that affect the lives of their families.

    c. Women who work enjoy more responsibility than those who don't work, yet allow their husbands valuable time alone with their children.

    d. Women who work have better-developed social lives.

67. Doris, who is 75 years old, finds that she has a more difficult time hearing than when she was younger. Which theory best supports the conclusion that Doris' poor hearing is due to the fact that mechanical bodily functions stop working efficiently as an individual ages?

    a. genetic preprogramming theory   c. decreased consumption theory

    b. wear-and-tear theory   d. disengagement theory of aging

68. Dr. Beegood is an authority on Egyptian mummies and has been retired for 13 years. He was recently asked to speak at a monthly faculty luncheon. If he gives one of his "canned" presentations on mummies to the faculty, he will be drawing heavily from his:

    a. crystallized intelligence.   c. fluid intelligence.

    b. common sense.   d. practical intelligence.

69. Dan, a college professor, is satisfied with his position, is quite comfortable with his single lifestyle, and has begun to expand his reflections on the subject he has taught and researched to consider its broader implications for society. He hopes to write a book that will have appeal to an audience wider than the typical academic book. Which of the following best describes Dan's situation?

    a. disengagement theory of aging   c. generativity versus stagnation

    b. concrete operations   d. conventional morality

70. Alice has reached a point where she says, "If I can only live to see my Jenny graduate from college, I will devote the rest of my time to the church." Alice is expressing which of the following?

    a. Kübler-Ross's stage of bargaining

    b. the wear-and-tear theory of aging

    c. Erikson's stage of ego-integrity versus despair

    d. Kübler-Ross's stage of acceptance

71. Dave is told a story about a little boy who accidentally breaks some dishes while helping set the family table for supper. When asked what should be done to the boy, Dave answers that he should be sent to his room and not allowed to have supper. Which of the following best expresses the stage of Dave's thinking?

   a. Dave is expressing preconventional morality.

   b. Dave is expressing preoperational thinking.

   c. Dave is expressing conventional morality.

   d. Dave is expressing concrete operational thinking.

72. Erik has developed an idealistic view of the world. He believes that it is possible for him to accomplish something great in life, like a major scientific discovery or a cure for a devastating disease. As he makes plans for the future, he likes to consider those with these kinds of opportunities. Which of the following combinations best fits Erik's developmental status?

   a. Kübler-Ross's stage of generativity and Kolhberg's postconventional morality

   b. Erikson's autonomy versus shame and doubt and Levinson's "Dream"

   c. Levinson's "Dream" and Kolhberg's conventional morality

   d. Erikson's identity versus role confusion and Piaget's formal operations

Essay Questions

Essay Question 10.1: *Nature-Nurture and Child-rearing Practices*

Recite ❑
Review ❑

Considering the discussion of the nature-nurture issue at the beginning of the chapter, what is your assessment of the role of child-rearing practices in the development of the person as a unique individual? Are certain styles more likely to help individuals reach their potential?

Essay Question 10.2: *The Stresses of Adolescence*

Describe the factors that contribute to problems between parents and teenagers, and suggest ways that these may be overcome. Are the recent changes in childhood and adolescence that result in changes in the family to blame for some of these factors?

Activities and Projects

1. Make a two-column list of genetic and environmental factors that might influence the course of physical, social, and intellectual development. Do any of these factors interact; that is, do genetic factors have environmental influences?

Recite ❑
Review ❑

Genetic Factors	Environmental Factors

2. If you have the opportunity, observe a child under one year of age on several occasions for at least five minutes. Prior to the observation, list the activities and abilities you expect to be demonstrated. Include smile, vocalizations, ability to hold and grasp, interaction with others, etc. After making this list, create a tally of the behaviors you actually see in the observation (your list should include a number of specific actions). When your observation is complete, reflect on the types of actions that occurred but which you had not expected. What do your observations suggest concerning the theories described in Chapter 10?

3. Interview one or more people in the middle years of life and find out their views on life-span development. Do they view themselves as continuing through a developmental process physically, socially, cognitively, or in any other way? What are the major issues to be faced during the middle years, and how do these issues differ from ones in earlier years that had to be faced?

Cultural Idioms

Recite ❏
Review ❏

p. 354

Unabomber: the person who sent bombs through the mail to university professors, killing several people. Because it took several years to discover who the person was, he was referred to as the "Unabomber" or "Unibomber" for "university."

Blood Brothers: biological brothers; however, the term "blood brothers" is also used to talk about a very close friendship

serial killer: a murderer who kills again and again, not just one time

p. 355

volunteer firefighters: Some U. S. towns do not have paid fire fighters; rather, local citizens learn how to put out fires. When there is a fire they leave their regular jobs and rush to the fire.

John Wayne movies: cowboy movies (also called Westerns) starring John Wayne, famous for being a strong brave hero

p. 357

Albert Einstein: famous 20th century physicist

Butterball turkeys: a brand of turkey meat

p. 358

foster parents: not a child's own mother or father, but a different family

"testwise": smart about taking a test; at a certain point, the test can no longer measure what it is supposed to, because the person taking the test has begun to "figure it out."

p. 359

tease out: to separate

p. 361

tinkering with: playing with, as with the parts of a machine

skin lesions: skin cancer

mixed blessing: it has both good and bad aspects

Dr. Seuss story *The Cat in the Hat*: a well-known childhood story book for beginning readers

p. 363

under a cloud: This has two meanings: one, under a cloud of smoke (it is an anti-smoking ad); and two, "under a cloud" also means depressed, sad. Thus, the idea is that smoking while pregnant will harm the baby in several ways.

p. 367

vision chart: a display of letters that eye doctors use to check a patient's vision; the doctor asks the patient to read from the chart, and can then measure how accurately a person can see.

p. 368

sweet tooth: delight in sweet tastes

to nurse: to drink milk as a baby does, from a breast or from a bottle

p. 370

home base: safe, well-known place

exhibit distress: show unhappiness

the father stood in the shadows behind the mother: the father wasn't as important the mother

rough-and-tumble: physical playful games; for example, some fathers throw a child into the air and then catch the child, or "wrestle" with their kids

peekaboo: traditional baby game, involving hiding your face and then reappearing

p. 372

day-care centers: places where parents bring their young children during the day, while the parents are at work

sitter: a person who goes to a family's house to take care of their children while the parents are out (used to be called "baby sitter")

home day care providers: people who take care of children in a home, either the family's home or the day-care provider's home

p. 373

child-rearing patterns: the way that parents treat and interact with their children

p. 376

maddeningly: frustratingly

p. 378

for the record: for your information

p. 380

Success Story: when someone does really well

p. 406

encountered anew: found again

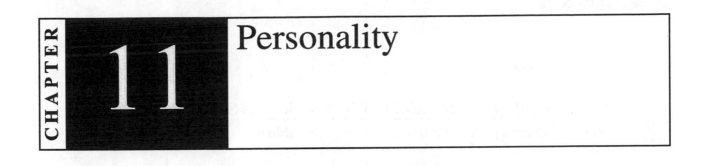

CHAPTER 11

Personality

Recap, Review, and Rethink

Assessing Personality: Determining What Makes Us Special

Exploring Diversity: Should Race Be Used to Establish Norms?

Self-Report Measures of Personality

Pathways Through Psychology: Patricia Dyer, Job Selection Specialist

Projective Methods
Behavioral Assessment

The Informed Consumer of Psychology: Assessing Personality Assessments

Recap, Review, and Rethink
Looking Back
Key Terms and Concepts

➤ Now that you have surveyed the chapter, read **Looking Ahead**, page 410. What questions does the Chapter seek to answer?

Question ❑
Read ❑

Concepts and Learning Objectives

These are the concepts and the learning objectives for Chapter 11. Read them carefully as part of your preliminary survey of the chapter.

Survey ❑

Concept 1: Personality is the sum of the characteristics that differentiate individuals and provide the stability in a person's behavior across situations and time. Psychoanalysis understands personality in terms of how a person manages the unconscious that seeks to dominate behavior.

1. Define personality, and describe the basic structure of personality according to Sigmund Freud.

2. Outline the five stages of personality development according to Freud.

3. Define and describe the defense mechanisms and their role in psychoanalytic theory.

4. Discuss the contribution made by Freud, the criticisms of the psychoanalytic theory of personality, and the contributions made by the neo-Freudians.

Concept 2: Four major alternatives to the psychoanalytic approach are: 1) trait approaches, which focus on basic traits that describe universal characteristics; 2) learning approaches, especially social learning theory, which focus on personality as a set of learned behaviors; 3) biological approaches, which draw upon twin evidence for a genetically based view of personality; and 4) humanistic approaches, which focus on the uniqueness of the individual and the striving toward self-actualization.

5. Describe and evaluate the trait theory approaches to personality development.

6. Describe and evaluate the learning theory approaches to personality development.

7. Describe and evaluate the biological and evolutionary approaches to personality development.

8. Describe and evaluate the humanistic approaches to personality development.

Concept 3: Personality can be assessed several ways. Psychological tests must prove reliable and valid, and they must have standardized norms. The most frequently given assessments include the MMPI, the Rorschach test, and the TAT.

9. Discuss personality assessment, and define the concepts of validity, reliability, and norms.

10. Differentiate among and cite examples of the following methods of personality assessment: self-report, projective, and behavioral assessment.

11. Evaluate the various personality assessment methods.

Chapter Guided Review

There are several ways you can use this guided review as part of your systematic study plan. Read the corresponding pages of the text and then complete the review by supplying the correct missing key word. Or, you may want to complete the guided review as a means of becoming familiar with the text. Complete the review and then read the section thoroughly. As you finish each section, complete the **Recap and Review** questions that are supplied in the text.

Survey ❑

CONCEPT 1: Psychoanalytic Approaches to Personality

- *How do psychologists define and use the concept of personality?*
- *What do the theories of Freud and his successors tell us about the structure and development of personality?*

Pages 410-417

The field of psychology known as [a] _____ studies the characteristics that make a person unique and attempts to explain what makes a person act the same in different situations and through time.

[b] _____ are concerned with understanding the hidden forces that govern people's behavior and remain outside of awareness. These forces have their roots in childhood experiences. This theory, called [c] _____, was developed by Sigmund Freud. Slips of the tongue are examples of how thoughts and emotions are held in the

[d] _____, the part of the personality that remains beyond the person's awareness. Slips reflect these hidden concerns. The unconscious also contains *instinctual drives*, which include infantile wishes, desires, demands, and needs that remain hidden because of the conflicts they can cause. Freud described conscious experience as the top of an iceberg, suggesting that the larger part of our personality was unconscious. In order to understand personality, these unconscious elements must be illuminated. The contents of the unconscious are disguised, thus requiring that slips of the tongue, fantasies, and dreams be interpreted in order to understand how unconscious processes direct behavior.

Freud described a general model of the personality that contains three interacting structures. The [e] _____ is the raw, unorganized, inherited part of the personality aimed at reducing the tension caused by basic drives of hunger, sex, aggression, and irrational impulses. The drives are powered by [f] _____, or "psychic energy," and the id operates according to the [g] _____, or the desire for immediate gratification of all needs. Reality limits the expression of these id impulses. The

[h] _____ is responsible for constraining the id. It serves as a buffer between reality and the pleasure-seeking demands of the id. The ego operates on the

[i] _____, in which restraint is based on the safety of the individual and an effort to integrate into society. The ego is the seat of the higher cognitive functions. The

[j] _____ represents the rights and wrongs of society as represented by the parents and is composed of two parts. The [k] _____ prevents us from

behaving immorally and the [l] _____ motivates us to do the morally correct thing. Both the superego and the id make unrealistic demands. The ego must compromise between the moral-perfectionist demands of the superego and the pleasure-seeking gratification sought by the id.

Freud proposed a theory of development that accounted for how the adult personality comes into existence. Difficulties and experiences from a childhood stage may predict adult behaviors, and each stage focuses on a biological function. The first period of development is the

[m] _____ during which the baby's mouth is the focus of pleasure. This suggested to Freud that the mouth is the primary sight of sexual pleasure.

[n] _____ means that an adult shows personality characteristics that are related to that stage. At about 12 to 18 months until the age of 3, the child is in the

[o] _____ . The major source of pleasure moves to the anal region, and the child derives pleasure from the retention and expulsion of feces. If toilet training is particularly demanding, fixation can occur. Fixation can lead to unusual rigidity and orderliness or the

extreme opposite of disorder or sloppiness. At the age of 3, the [p] _____

begins and the source of pleasure moves to the genitals. The [q] _____ develops at this time. The differences between males and females becomes a concern, and the male begins to see his father as a rival for his mother, thus developing fantasies that parallel the Greek tragedy about Oedipus. The fear of retaliation causes the development of a "castration anxiety." In the end, the child represses his desires for his mother and chooses an *identification* with his father. For girls , the pattern is different. Girls develop desires for father and develop *penis envy*, a wish that they had the anatomical part, the penis, that is clearly missing. According to Freud, they blame their mothers for their "castration." In the end, girls identify with their

mothers and repress these feelings. The next period is called the [r] _____ , beginning around 5 or 6 and lasting to puberty. Sexual concerns become latent. The final

period, the [s] _____ , begins at puberty. Mature adult sexuality emerges during this period.

Anxiety, an intense, negative emotional experience, arises as a signal of danger to the ego. Though anxiety may arise from realistic fears, the *neurotic anxiety* arises because of the irrational impulses from the id that threaten to break into consciousness. The ego has developed

unconscious strategies to control the impulses called [t] _____ . The primary mechanism is *repression*. In repression, unacceptable or unpleasant id impulses are pushed back into the unconscious. In repression, the anxiety-producing impulse is ignored, but it finds ways to be revealed, either through slips of the tongue, dreams or other symbolic ways. When repression does not work, other mechanisms are used. *Regression* involves using behavior from earlier stages of development to deal with the anxiety. *Displacement* is the process of redirecting the unwanted feeling onto a less threatening person. *Rationalization* occurs when reality is distorted by justifying events with explanations that protect our self-esteem. *Denial* occurs when a person simply refuses to acknowledge the existence of an anxiety-producing piece of information. *Projection* involves protecting oneself by attributing unwanted impulses and feelings to someone else. *Sublimation* is the diversion of unwanted impulses to socially acceptable behaviors. According to Freud, these mechanisms are used to some degree by everyone, though some people devote a large amount of energy to dealing with unacceptable impulses to the extent that daily life becomes hampered. He identified this tendency as neurosis.

Freud's theory is an elaborate and complex set of propositions. However, Freud is criticized for the lack of scientific data supporting his theory. Freud's theory is employed in after-the-fact explanations rather than predictive statements. Also, his observations were made with a limited population of upper-middle-class Austrian women living in a puritanical era of the early 1900s. Freud's theory has had a major impact on psychology and many other fields. Freud's emphasis on the unconscious has been partially supported by current research by cognitive psychologists. Experimental techniques have been developed that allow the study of the unconscious in a more sophisticated manner.

The followers of Freud are known as [u] _____. They tend to place greater emphasis on the role of the ego. Carl Jung rejected the primary importance of unconscious sexual urges in favor of viewing the primitive urges of the unconscious more

positively. He suggested that people have a [v] _____, a set of influences that are inherited from our ancestors. The collective unconscious is shared by everyone and

appears in behavior across cultures. Jung also proposed the idea of [w] _____, or universal symbolic representations of particular persons, objects, or experiences. Alfred Adler focused on the human motivation for striving for superiority as a quest for self-

improvement and perfection. His concept of [x] _____ describes situations in which an adult attempts to overcome feelings of inferiority that have persisted since childhood. Other neo-Freudians include Erik Erikson (discussed in Chapters 10 and 11) and Karen Horney. Horney focused on the social and cultural factors in personality, particularly the relationship between parents and the child and how well the child's needs are met, and women's issues.

CONCEPT 2:   Other Major Approaches to Personality: In Search of Human Uniqueness

Survey ❑
Read ❑
Recite ❑

- *What are the major aspects of trait, learning, biological and evolutionary, and humanistic approaches to personality?*

Pages 418-430

A number of theories take a different approach than that of psychoanalysis. These include

[a] _____, which assumes that individuals respond to different situations in

a fairly consistent manner. [b] _____ are the enduring dimensions of personality characteristics along which people differ. Trait theories assume that all people have certain traits, and the degree to which a trait applies to a specific person varies. The approach taken has been to determine the basic traits necessary to describe personality.

Gordon Allport identified 18,000 separate terms that could be used to describe personality, which he then reduced to 4,500 descriptors. In order to make sense of this number, he defined

three basic categories of traits. A [c] _____ is a single characteristic that directs most of a person's activities. Most people do not have cardinal traits; instead, they have five to ten **[d]** _____ that define major characteristics.

[e] _____ are characteristics that affect fewer situations and are less influential than cardinal or central traits. Preferences would be secondary traits.

The statistical technique called **[f]** _____, in which relationships among a large number of variables are summarized into smaller, more general patterns, has been used to identify fundamental patterns or combinations of traits. Raymond Cattell suggested that there are forty-six _surface traits_, or clusters of related behaviors. Cattell then reduced this number to sixteen _source traits_ that represent the basic dimensions of personality. He then developed the Sixteen Personality Factor Questionnaire (16 PF). Hans Eysenck used factor analysis to identify three major dimensions. **[g]** _____ is the dimension marked by quiet and restrained individuals on one end, and outgoing and sociable ones on the other.

[h] _____ is the dimension marked by moody and sensitive behavior (neuroticism) on the one hand, and calm, reliable, and even-tempered behavior (stability) on the other. **[i]** _____ refers to the degree to which reality is distorted. Recent research has suggested that there are five traits: _surgency, neuroticism, intellect, agreeableness,_ and _conscientiousness._

Trait theories have an advantage of being straightforward and easy to apply to practical situations. However, a determination of which traits are fundamental is difficult to make. The traits offer little more than a basic description of the person, and they do not explain behavior.

According to B. F. Skinner, personality is a collection of learned behavior patterns. Similarities across situations are caused by a similarity of reinforcements. Strict learning theorists are less interested in the consistency issue than they are in finding ways to modify behavior. In their view, humans are quite changeable.

[j] _____ emphasizes the role of a person's cognitions in determining personality. According to Albert Bandura, people are able to foresee the outcomes of behaviors prior to carrying them out by using the mechanism of **[k]** _____. We observe a model that displays a behavior and then relate the consequences that result from the behavior to determining whether or not to attempt the behavior. Bandura considers

[l] _____, the expectations of success, to be an important factor in determining the behaviors a person will display. The cognitive-social approach places an emphasis on the reciprocity between individuals and the environment, viewing the interaction as one in which a feedback flows both ways. The key to understanding behavior,

[m] _____ refers to the interaction between environment, behavior, and the individual.

Traditional learning theories have been criticized for ignoring internal processes and reducing behavior to stimuli and responses. Traditional theories and social learning theory have been criticized for their highly _deterministic_ view that maintains that behavior is controlled by forces outside the control of the person. The positive contribution has been to make the study of personality an objective and scientific venture.

[n] _____ to personality suggest that important components of personality are inherited. The study of [o] _____, the basic innate disposition that emerges early in life, is studied through the biological approach. Jerome Kagan's study of inhibited and uninhibited children suggests that *inhibited children* have an inborn characteristic of greater physiological reactivity. However, the stress experienced through childhood is a major factor in the appearance of shyness later.

[p] _____ emphasize the basic goodness of people and their tendency to grow to higher levels of functioning. Carl Rogers is a major representative of this approach. The positive regard others have for us makes us see and judge ourselves through the eyes of other people. The views others have of us may not match our own *self-concept*. If the difference is great, we may have problems with daily functioning. The discrepancy is overcome by support from another person in the form of [q] _____, defined as an attitude of acceptance and respect no matter what the person says or does. Rogers and Maslow (Chapter 10) view the ultimate goal of personality growth to be [r] _____.

The criticisms of humanistic theory are centered on the difficulty of verifying the basic assumptions of the theory. The assumption that all people are basically "good" is unverifiable and injects nonscientific values into scientific theories.

CONCEPT 3: Assessing Personality: Determining What Makes Us Special

Survey ❑
Read ❑
Recite ❑

- *How can we most accurately assess personality?*
- *What are the major types of personality measures?*

Pages 431-437

The intentionally vague statements that introduce the topic of assessment suggest that measuring different aspects of personality may require great care and precision. The assessment of personality requires discriminating the behavior of one person from that of another.

[a] _____ are standard measures that measure aspects of behavior objectively.

Psychological tests must have [b] _____, that is, they must measure something consistently from time to time. A reliable test will produce similar outcomes in similar conditions. The question of whether or not a test measures the characteristic it is supposed to measure is called [c] _____. If a test is reliable, that does not mean that is valid. [d] _____ are the standards of test performance that allow comparison of the scores of one testtaker to others who have taken it. The norm for a test is determined by calculating the average score for a particular group of people for whom the test is designed to be given. Then, the extent to which each person's score differs from the others can be calculated.

The issue of different norms for different racial and ethnic groups is discussed in Exploring Diversity. The selection of the subjects who will be used to establish a norm for a test are critical. A contemporary problem faces test creators in the development of a different set of norms for minorities. Critics of such an approach suggest that this is both unfair and contributes to bigotry. Supporters argue that it is an affirmative action tool that helps minorities.

Instead of conducting a comprehensive interview to determine aspects of childhood, social relationships, and successes and failures, the use of **[e]** _____ allows individuals to respond to a small sample of questions. The most frequently used self-report measure is the **[f]** _____. Originally developed to distinguish people with psychological disturbances from people without disturbances, the MMPI scores have been shown to be good predictors of such things as whether college students will marry within ten years and whether they will get an advanced degree. The test has 567 true-false items, covering areas like mood, opinions, and physical and psychological health. The interpretation of the responses is important-there are no right or wrong answers. The test is scored on ten scales and includes a lie scale for people trying to falsify their answers. The MMPI has undergone a procedure called

[g] _____, by which the test authors have determined which items best differentiate among groups of people, like differentiating those suffering depression from normal subjects. This procedure has produced a number of subscales helpful in diagnosis. When the MMPI is used for proper reasons, it does a good job. However, some employers have used it as a screening tool and have applied the test improperly.

[h] _____ require the subject to describe an ambiguous stimulus. The responses are considered to be projections of what the person is like. The best known is the

[i] _____ , which consists of symmetrical stimuli. The

[j] _____ consists of a series of pictures about which the person is asked to write a story. Inferences about the subject are then based on these stories. These tests are criticized because too much inference depends upon the scorer.

In order to obtain an objective test based on observable behavior, a **[k]** _____ may be conducted either in a natural setting or in a laboratory under controlled conditions. The behavioral assessment requires quantifying behavior as much as possible. For instance, recording the number of social contacts or the number of aggressive acts would quantify the assessment. Behavioral assessment is appropriate for observing and remedying behavioral difficulties.

▶ Now that you have surveyed, questioned, and read the chapter and completed the guided review, review **Looking Back**, pages 438-439.

Review ❑

▶ For additional practice through recitation and review, test your knowledge of the chapter material by answering the questions in the *Key Word Drill*, the *Practice Questions*, and the *Essay Questions*.

Key Word Drill

The following **Matching Questions** test the boldfaced and italicized key words from the text. Check your answers with the Answer Key in the back of the *Study Guide*.

Recite ❑

MATCHING QUESTIONS

_____ 1. unconscious

_____ 2. instinctual drives

_____ 3. id

_____ 4. libido

_____ 5. fixation

a. Behavior reflecting an earlier stage of development.

b. Infantile wishes, desires, demands, and needs hidden from conscious awareness.

c. A person is unaware of this determinant of behavior.

d. The raw, unorganized, inherited part of personality created by biological drives and irrational impulses.

e. The sexual energy underlying biological urges.

_____ 6. pleasure principle

_____ 7. ego

_____ 8. reality principle

_____ 9. superego

_____ 10. conscience

_____ 11. ego-ideal

a. Provides a buffer between the id and the outside world.

b. Motivates us to do what is morally proper.

c. Prevents us from doing what is morally wrong.

d. Represents the morality of society as presented by parents, teachers, and others.

e. The principle by which the ego operates.

f. The principle by which the id operates.

_____ 12. oral stage

_____ 13. anal stage

_____ 14. phallic stage

_____ 15. identification

_____ 16. penis envy

_____ 17. latency period

_____ 18. genital stage

a. A child's attempt to be similar to the same-sex parent.

b. An infant's center of pleasure is the mouth.

c. Children's sexual concerns are temporarily put aside.

d. Marked by mature sexual behavior.

e. A child's interest focuses on the genitals.

f. A child's pleasure is centered on the anus.

g. A girl's wish that she had a penis.

_____ 19. anxiety

_____ 20. neurotic anxiety

_____ 21. defense mechanisms

_____ 22. collective unconscious

_____ 23. archetypes

_____ 24. inferiority complex

a. The concept that we inherit certain personality characteristics from our ancestors and the human race.

b. Anxiety caused when irrational impulses from the id threaten to become uncontrollable.

c. Universal, symbolic representations of a particular person, object, or experience.

d. A feeling of apprehension or tension.

e. A phenomenon whereby adults have continuing feelings of weakness and insecurity.

f. Unconscious strategies used to reduce anxiety by concealing its source from oneself and others.

_____ 25. repression

_____ 26. regression

_____ 27. displacement

_____ 28. rationalization

_____ 29. denial

_____ 30. projection

_____ 31. sublimation

a. An unwanted feeling directed toward a weaker object.

b. Justify a negative situation to protect self-esteem.

c. Unpleasant id impulses are pushed back into the unconscious.

d. Attribute inadequacies or faults to someone else.

e. Behavior reminiscent of an earlier stage of development.

f. The refusal to accept anxiety-producing information.

g. The diversion of unwanted impulses into acceptable thoughts, feelings, or behaviors.

_____ 32. observational learning

_____ 33. self-efficacy

_____ 34. reciprocal determinism

_____ 35. self-concept

_____ 36. unconditional positive regard

_____ 37. self-actualization

a. The realization of one's highest potential.

b. The impression one holds of oneself.

c. Learned expectations about success determines behavior.

d. Supportive behavior for another individual.

e. The interaction of environment, behavior, and the individual causes people to behave the way that they do.

f. Learning by viewing the actions of others.

_____ 38. cardinal trait

_____ 39. central traits

_____ 40. secondary traits

_____ 41. surface traits

_____ 42. source traits

_____ 43. introversion-extroversion

_____ 44. neuroticism-stability

_____ 45. psychoticism

a. A single trait that directs most of a person's activities.

b. The dimension encompassing shyness to sociability.

c. Clusters of a person's related behaviors that can be observed in a given situation.

d. Traits less important than central and cardinal traits.

e. Encompasses moodiness to even-temperedness.

f. The sixteen basic dimensions of personality.

g. A set of major characteristics that compose the core of a person's personality.

h. The dimension that refers to the degree to which reality is distorted.

_____ 46. psychological tests

_____ 47. self-report measures

_____ 48. Minnesota Multiphasic Personality Inventory-2 (MMPI-2)

_____ 49. test standardization

_____ 50. projective personality test

_____ 51. Rorschach test

_____ 52. Thematic Apperception Test (TAT)

a. Used to identify people with psychological difficulties.

b. Consists of a series of ambiguous pictures about which a person is asked to write a story.

c. Uses inkblots of indefinite shapes.

d. Gathering data by asking people about their behavior.

e. Validates questions in personality tests by studying the responses of people with known diagnoses.

f. Standard measures devised to objectively assess behavior.

g. Uses ambiguous stimuli to determine personality.

_____ 53. psychoanalytic theory

_____ 54. trait theory

_____ 55. cognitive-social approaches to personality

_____ 56. biological approaches to personality

_____ 57. humanistic approaches to personality

a. The theory that suggests that personality develops through observational learning.

b. A model that seeks to identify the basic traits necessary to describe personality.

c. The approach that emphasizes people's basic goodness and their natural tendency to rise to higher levels of functioning.

d. The view that unconscious forces act as determinants of personality.

e. The approach that considers important components of personality to be due to heredity.

Practice Questions

Test your knowledge of the chapter material by answering these **Multiple Choice Questions**. These questions have been placed in three Practice Tests. The first two tests are composed of questions that will test your recall of factual knowledge. The third test contains questions that are challenging and primarily test for conceptual knowledge and your ability to apply that knowledge. Check your answers and review the feedback using the Answer Key in the back of the *Study Guide*.

Recite ❏
Review ❏

MULTIPLE CHOICE QUESTIONS

PRACTICE TEST I:

1. According to Sigmund Freud, the _____ harbors repressed emotions and thoughts as well as instinctual drives.
    a. unconscious
    b. collective unconscious
    c. conscience
    d. conscious

2. In Freud's psychoanalytic theory, the most important mental factors were:
    a. those which the person consciously controls or manipulates.
    b. associated with the latency developmental stage.
    c. those about which the person is unaware.
    d. based on social learning and influence.

3. Which of the following is **least** likely to involve making unrealistic demands on the person?
    a. the id
    b. the ego
    c. the superego
    d. the pleasure principle

4. According to the text, Freud's concept of the ego-ideal refers to:
    a. infantile wishes, desires, demands, and needs hidden from conscious awareness.
    b. the part of the superego that motivates us to do what is morally proper.
    c. the part of personality that provides a buffer between the id and the outside world.
    d. the part of the id that prevents us from doing what is ethically correct.

5. A child who is in the midst of toilet training is probably in the:
    a. genital psychosexual stage.
    b. anal psychosexual stage.
    c. phallic psychosexual stage.
    d. oral psychosexual stage.

6. Defense mechanisms are unconscious strategies that people use to:
    a. decrease their reliance on the reality principle.
    b. reduce anxiety.
    c. increase the superego's power to regulate behavior.
    d. prevent Freudian slips.

7. Which of the following defense mechanisms did Freud find most socially acceptable?
    a. repression
    b. sublimation
    c. rationalization
    d. projection

8. According to trait theorists:
    a. everyone has the same traits, but in different amounts.
    b. everyone has different traits that do not change with time.
    c. everyone has different traits, and they change with time.
    d. everyone has different traits, but they cannot be measured.

9. Which of the psychologists listed below is **not** a trait theorist?
    a. Albert Bandura
    b. Gordon Allport
    c. Raymond B. Cattell
    d. Hans Eysenck

10. Factor analysis is:
    a. a method of recording data that requires sophisticated equipment.
    b. a method of understanding how the unconscious works.
    c. a statistical method of finding common traits.
    d. a sociometric method of determining personality traits in a group.

11. From the perspective of learning theorists such as B. F. Skinner, consistencies of behavior across situations relate to:
    a. stable individual characteristics called personality traits.
    b. the dynamics of unconscious forces.
    c. the rewards or punishments received by the person previously.
    d. any conflict between one's experiences and his or her self-concept.

12. Humanistic theories of personality assume that:
    a. the basic goodness of humans is contrasted with an evil unconscious.
    b. humans are self-sufficient and that society corrupts the individual.
    c. humans are basically good and desire to improve.
    d. the fundamental depravity of humans is offset through education.

13. The conscious, self-motivated personal ability to improve is the core of:
    a. the learning theory of personality.
    b. the neo-Freudian psychoanalytic theory of personality.
    c. the humanistic theory of personality.
    d. the trait theory of personality.

14. A student retakes the Graduate Record Exam. Despite her claim that she did badly the first time because she was very sleepy that day, her score is within 2 percent of her first score. This outcome supports the notion that the GRE test is:
    a. a standardized type of assessment tool.   c. a reliable assessment tool.
    b. an academic ability assessment tool.   d. a valid assessment tool.

15. Which one of the following tests is designed to uncover unconscious content?
    a. MMPI   c. California Psychological Inventory
    b. TAT   d. Edwards Personal Preference Schedule

16. Which of the following tests are considered projective instruments?
    a. MMPI and TAT   c. Rorschach and MMPI
    b. TAT and 16 PF   d. Rorschach and TAT

PRACTICE TEST II:

17. Which of the following theories suggests that behavior is triggered largely by powerful forces found in the unconscious?
    a. humanistic theory   c. psychoanalytic theory
    b. learning theory   d. trait theory

18.   Freud's structure of personality has three major parts. Which alternative below is **not** one of
      them?
      a.   libido   c.   superego
      b.   id   d.   ego

19.   Which of the following controls thought, solves problems, and makes decisions?
      a.   id   c.   superego
      b.   ego   d.   conscience

20.   According to Freud's theory of psychosexual development, a child who is constantly putting things
      in its mouth is most likely at the:
      a.   genital stage.   c.   phallic stage.
      b.   anal stage.   d.   oral stage.

21.   According to the text, mature sexual relationships begin to occur at which psychosexual stage?
      a.   phallic   c.   genital
      b.   oral   d.   anal

22.   According to Sigmund Freud, defense mechanisms are:
      a.   unconscious.   c.   learned.
      b.   instinctive.   d.   reflexive.

23.   Victims of child abuse, rape, or incest attacks might not recall the incident or may remember only
      scanty details. Freud suggested that the reason for this is that the defense mechanism of
      _____ was applied.
      a.   sublimation   c.   denial
      b.   repression   d.   projection

24.   For Gordon Allport, _____ traits were so distinct that having only one of these traits will
      define a person's personality.
      a.   general   c.   central
      b.   secondary   d.   cardinal

25.   What are the three important categories of personality dimensions, according to Gordon Allport?
      a.   primary, secondary, and tertiary
      b.   factors, traits, and features
      c.   source, surface, and circumscript
      d.   cardinal, central, and secondary

26.   The basic assumption shared by trait personality theorists is that:
      a.   the traits are consistent across situations.
      b.   the unconscious mind is the underlying source of the traits we have.
      c.   traits are learned habits that are modified by reinforcers.
      d.   people possess the traits to the same degree but differ in how they choose to apply them.

27. According to Bandura, we can modify our own personalities through the use of:
    a. defense mechanisms.
    b. drive reduction.
    c. psychoanalysis.
    d. self-reinforcement.

28. Temperament is presumed to originate from the child's:
    a. personally chosen interests and ideas.
    b. source traits.
    c. early learning experiences with the primary caregiver or mother.
    d. genetic predisposition.

29. If a test provides a consistent score for a particular individual over repeated administrations, the test is said to be:
    a. accurate.
    b. valid.
    c. reliable.
    d. statistical.

30. The MMPI was originally developed to:
    a. identify personality disorders.
    b. uncover unconscious thoughts.
    c. locate traits.
    d. conduct behavioral assessments.

31. Test stimuli are the most ambiguous on the:
    a. 16PF.
    b. California Psychological Inventory.
    c. Rorschach.
    d. MMPI.

32. Which of these tests consists of a series of "inkblot" cards?
    a. Rorschach test
    b. Cattell's 16 Personality Factor Questionnaire
    c. Thematic Apperception Test
    d. Minnesota Multiphasic Personality Inventory

PRACTICE TEST III: Conceptual, Applied, and Challenging Questions

33. Listed below are four alternatives. Three of the four give pairs of items that are related. Which alternative below contains items that are **not** related?
    a. ego; reality principle
    b. Sigmund Freud; Viennese physician
    c. superego; "executive" of personality
    d. id; pleasure principle

34. From the psychoanalytic perspective, a rapist would be considered to have:
    a. unconditioned positive regard for his victim.
    b. a well-developed ego-ideal.
    c. a deficient superego.
    d. brain damage.

35. Of the following, a psychoanalyst most likely would view a thumbsucking 7-year-old as:
    a. a normal youngster.
    b. fixated at the oral stage of development.
    c. having been breastfed as an infant.
    d. ready to enter the phallic stage of development.

36. Tim kept his clothes hung up and neatly pressed, while his roommate Jack rarely laundered or hung up his clothes. Freud might have suggested that both men were fixated at the:
    a. anal stage.
    b. oral stage.
    c. phallic stage.
    d. genital stage.

37. A female college student accepts a date from a young man she greatly admires. At the time of the date, however, the man doesn't show up. In response she exclaims, "I didn't want to go out with him anyway!" This illustrates:
    a. rationalization.
    b. denial.
    c. regression.
    d. repression.

38. The _____ approach emphasizes voluntary conscious aspects of personality, while the _____ approach emphasizes unconscious aspects.
    a. biological; learning
    b. trait; humanistic
    c. humanistic; psychoanalytic
    d. trait; humanistic

39. Freud's stages of psychosexual development:
    a. emphasize adolescence as the key interval in personality development.
    b. designate the oral stage as the highest in the sequence.
    c. identify parts of the body which are biological pleasure zones toward which gratification is focused.
    d. relate to the same behaviors described in Piaget's theory.

40. Listed below are four alternatives. Three of the four list pairs of items that are related. Which alternative below contains items that are **not** related?
    a. Jung; collective unconscious
    b. Horney; women do not have penis envy
    c. Adler; inferiority complex
    d. Cattell; striving for superiority

41. Which of the following statements is most likely to be made by a trait theorist?
    a. He really hurt her feelings, but he's rationalizing it away.
    b. He really could have gone a long way, but his inferiority complex destroyed any confidence.
    c. There are five stages in the process of his development toward fulfilling his highest potential.
    d. He is a sensitive, warm, and considerate person.

42. Stephanie loves art and wants to study it in college. Her parents want her to be a nurse and criticize her for her love of art. According to Carl Rogers, this conflict will lead to:
    a. Stephanie learning to love being a nurse.
    b. anxiety on the part of Stephanie.
    c. Stephanie becoming a fully functioning person.
    d. unconditional positive regard.

43. Various approaches to personality have names and concepts uniquely associated with them. Three of the four alternatives below list pairs of items that are related. Which alternative below contains items that are **not** related?
    a. trait theory; assessment of traits that comprise personality
    b. learning theory; experiences with situations in the environment
    c. learning theory; Skinner
    d. psychoanalytic theory; consistency of behavior across situations

44. Which of the following situations best illustrates reliability as a quality of psychological tests?
    a. A prospective Air Force pilot takes a test, passes it, and becomes an excellent pilot.
    b. A college student studies diligently for an important exam and receives an A on it.
    c. A psychiatric patient takes a psychological test that yields the diagnosis the patient had suspected.
    d. A mentally retarded patient takes an intelligence test on Monday and again on Tuesday, getting the same result on each administration.

45. According to data presented in the text, which of the following statements about the heritability of traits is most accurate?
    a. The degree of heritability of traits is compromised by the important role of parents in shaping the environment.
    b. Traditionalism and stress reaction were highly heritable, while achievement and social closeness were somewhat lower.
    c. Alienation and absorption were low in heritability and social control was high.
    d. Heritability plays about a 50 percent role in important traits and is lower in less important traits.

46. Which of the following would be a confounding variable for studies that are attempting to demonstrate which traits parents pass on to their children genetically?
    a. The fact that social traits like religiosity rate high in twin studies, even when this trait is entirely dependent upon traditional cultural practices.
    b. When twins are separated at birth, they always express similar traits.
    c. The role of parents in shaping the environment.
    d. Evidence that some traits appear more heritable than others.

47. According to Kagan, inhibited children differ from uninhibited children:
    a. because inhibited children are biologically disposed to have higher physiological reactivity.
    b. because uninhibited children are biologically disposed to have higher physiological reactivity.
    c. because inhibited children are genetically disposed to greater social closeness.
    d. because uninhibited children are genetically disposed to greater social closeness.

48. Based on views about personality discussed in the text, which of the following is most accurate?
   a. Studies of twins reared apart is conclusive evidence of the inheritability of most of our important personality traits.
   b. Our ability to make choices and to be responsible for our own destinies suggests that genetic dispositions are far less important influences than personal decisions.
   c. Inhibited children are genetically disposed to greater social closeness.
   d. Some basic aspects of our personalities are so fundamental that they remain fairly unchanged throughout adulthood.

Essay Questions

Essay Question 11.1: *Freud and Female Psychology*

Recite ❑
Review ❑

Given that Freud's theory appears to be primarily focused on male development and thus on a male personality, identify the areas of Freud's theory that are the weakest with regard to female psychological issues. Defend your response with other points of view presented in the text.

Essay Question 11.2: *Diversity and Norming*

A major issue that will affect virtually everyone is the creation of norms for different minority and ethnic groups. Describe the issues involved and discuss whether or not the use of different norms will be helpful, harmful, or a mixture of both.

Activities and Projects

Write four descriptions of someone's personality, each based on a different theory of personality: (a) trait theory; (b) psychoanalytic theory; (c) social-cognitive approach; and (d) humanistic approach. You may choose yourself, a friend, a family member, or a fictional character. With friends and family members, it is not a good idea to share the information with the subjects described. In your trait description, make a list of central and secondary traits; include situational variables if you like. In your psychoanalytic description, include hypotheses about unconscious conflicts and motivations and the use of defense mechanisms. With the social-cognitive approach, include the role of early experiences and reinforcement. Your humanistic description might include the person's strivings, level of self-actualization obtained, and self-concept. Which theoretical framework did you find the most useful to work with? Explain.

Recite ❑
Review ❑

Trait Theory:

Psychoanalytic Theory:

Social-Cognitive Approach:

Humanistic Approach:

Which seems best?

Cultural Idioms

p. 410

Odyssey: long adventurous journey; this is the title of a well-known epic poem by Homer, from Ancient Greece

downtrodden: poor and unfortunate people

soup kitchens: places where hungry and homeless people can get free meals

blood banks: places, like the American red Cross, where people donate their blood so that sick and injured people will be able to obtain blood if they need it

drop out of college: leave college before graduating

floor plan: an architectural drawing showing the exact location of doors, windows, stairs, etc.

web of terrorism: a secret network of terrorists

innocent do-gooder: a person who just wants to help others

The Odd Couple: TV show and play featuring the roommates Oscar Madison and Felix Unger

p. 411

sounding smooth: acting and talking in a sophisticated manner

mulled over: thought about

slip of the tongue: When you say one word, but mean to say another word. Here, the young man said "seduced" when he meant to say "introduced."

tip of the psychological iceberg: The common phrase "the tip of the iceberg" means a small, visible part of something that is much bigger. (According to scientists, most of an iceberg is actually below the surface of the water.) Thus, the author is saying that what a person is aware of is only a small part of what is really there

p. 412

A Stage Approach: looking at personality in terms of different periods of time where different developments occur.

p. 413

toilet training: teaching a child to use the bathroom instead of diapers

"bitingly" sarcastic: cruelly sarcastic; the author is using a "mouth" word to emphasize the oral stage

"swallowing" anything: believing anything; again, as above, the author is using a mouth word

p. 414
temper tantrum: an episode of out-of-control anger, typical of very young children

p. 415
throwing tantrums: having an episode of intense, out-of-control anger, typical of very young children
a classic case: a typical example
lay people: people who are not professional psychologists

p. 416
Puritanical era: a time of great seriousness; fun and pleasure were viewed as bad

p. 417
Batman; the Joker: two characters from the comic book, and later movie, *Batman*
Virgin Mary: in the Christian tradition, the mother of Jesus
Earth Mother: the planet Earth as a mother; in addition, generous, earthy women are sometimes called "earth mothers."
wicked stepmothers: In fairy tales, a stepmother is often cruel to her stepchildren
Mother's Day: a U. S. holiday (the second Sunday in May) when people honor their mothers

p. 419
Mother Teresa: a Roman Catholic nun who abandoned a comfortable life to help poor and sick people in India

p. 421
"Big Five": the five most important factors

p. 422
the stormy fury: wild chaos

p. 423
model: person
"feed back": act in an interactive way

p. 425
"the world is out to get me": life, and everyone, is my enemy

"out to get the world": life is an enemy to be defeated

p. 426
Born to be Mild: Based on the song "Born to be Wild," the author is making a joke. "Mild," or shy, is the opposite of "wild," but the question is the same: are these traits inherited, that is, is someone "born to be" a certain way?
bubbly: outgoing, happy
novel environment: a new situation
marital strife: conflict between spouses
thrill seekers: people who like scary, risky, or dangerous activities
on the prowl: looking for

p. 428
Michelangelo: famous painter and sculptor of the Italian Renaissance
Einstein: Albert Einstein, 20th century physicist

p. 429
Mob: another word for "Mafia," a criminal group known for murder and illegal business activities; this cartoon is making a joke about psychologists

p. 430
hang gliding: a dangerous sport, where people jump off of cliffs while attached to big kites

p. 432
riddled with: full of
fans the flames of racial bigotry: increases racism
affirmative action: a government policy that tries to make up for past discrimination by offering members of groups who have been discriminated against (African Americans, for example) increased opportunities.

p. 434
comes into play: is useful
paper-and-pencil tests: traditional written tests; not tests that people take on a computer

p. 436
temper tantrum: an episode of out-of-control anger

"kinetic energy": lots of physical and emotional enthusiasm

***Wheel of Fortune*:** a TV game show

General Motors: one of the three largest U. S. car manufacturers

J. C. Penney: a large group of stores that sell many different products—for example, clothes, appliances, furniture, jewelry, toys

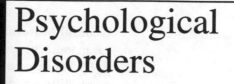

Psychological Disorders

CHAPTER 12

Detailed Chapter Outline

This detailed outline contains all the headings in Chapter 12: Psychological Disorders. If you are using the SQ3R method, then an examination of the outline is the best way to begin your survey of the chapter.

Survey ❏
Question ❏

Prologue: Lori Schiller
Looking Ahead

Normal Versus Abnormal: Making the Distinction

Defining Abnormality
Gradations of Abnormal and Normal Behavior: Drawing the Line on Abnormality
Models of Abnormality: From Superstition to Science
The Medical Model
The Psychoanalytic Model
The Behavioral Model
The Cognitive Model
The Humanistic Model
The Sociocultural Model
Classifying Abnormal Behavior: The ABCs of *DSM*
DSM-IV: Determining Diagnostic Distinctions

Pathways Through Psychology: Meryl Langbort, Homeless Advocate

Classification Concerns

Recap, Review, and Rethink

Major Disorders

Anxiety Disorders
Phobic Disorder
Panic Disorder
Generalized Anxiety Disorder
Obsessive-Compulsive Disorder

➤ Now that you have surveyed the chapter, read **Looking Ahead**, pages
442-443. What questions does the Chapter seek to answer?

Question ❑
Read ❑

Concepts and Learning Objectives

These are the concepts and the learning objectives for Chapter 12. Read them carefully as part of your preliminary survey of the chapter.

Survey ❏

Concept 1: Abnormality is difficult to define, and it is best to consider behavior as on a continuum from normal to abnormal. The contemporary models that attempt to explain abnormal behavior are the medical model, the psychoanalytic model, the behavioral model, the cognitive model, the humanistic model, and the sociocultural model. The *DSM-IV* is the system used by most professionals to classify mental disorders.

1. Discuss the various approaches to defining abnormal behavior.

2. Describe and distinguish the various models of abnormality, and apply those models to specific mental disorders.

3. Describe the *DSM-IV* and its use in diagnosing and classifying mental disorders.

Concept 2: Anxiety disorders, somatoform disorders, and dissociative disorders are three major classes of disorders.

4. Describe the anxiety disorders and their causes.

5. Describe the somatoform disorders and their causes.

6. Describe the dissociative disorders and their causes.

Concept 3: Mood disorders, schizophrenia, and personality disorders are three major disorders in the *DSM-IV*.

7. Describe the mood disorders and their causes.

8. Describe the types of schizophrenia, its main symptoms, and the theories that account for its causes.

9. Describe the personality disorders and their causes.

10. Discuss the other forms of abnormal behavior described in the *DSM-IV*, the prevalence of psychological disorders, and issues related to seeking help.

Chapter Guided Review

There are several ways you can use this guided review as part of your   *Survey* ❑
systematic study plan. Read the corresponding pages of the text and then
complete the review by supplying the correct missing key word. Or, you may
want to complete the guided review as a means of becoming familiar with the text. Complete the review
and then read the section thoroughly. As you finish each section, complete the **Recap and Review**
questions that are supplied in the text.

Concept 1: Normal Versus Abnormal: Making the
Distinction

Survey ❑
Read ❑
Recite ❑

● *How can we distinguish normal from abnormal behavior?*
● *What are the major models of abnormal behavior used by
   mental health professionals?*
● *What classification system is used to categorize abnormal behavior?*

Pages 443-451

A passage from James Joyce's *Ulysses* suggests that madness cannot be determined by a small
sample of a person's behavior. The text examines the following approaches to the definition of
abnormal behavior. They are:

● *Abnormality as deviation from the average.* This definition uses the statistical definition of
   behavior to define abnormal as behavior that is statistically unusual or rare. The problem
   with this approach is that simply being unusual or rare does not define abnormal: Individuals
   with high IQs are rare, but they are not considered abnormal.
● *Abnormality as deviation from the ideal.* This definition classifies behavior as abnormal if it
   deviates from the ideal or standard behavior. However, society has very few standards on
   which everyone agrees.
● *Abnormality as a sense of subjective discomfort.* This approach focuses on the consequences
   of behavior that make a person experience discomfort. However, some people who engage in
   what others would consider abnormal behavior do not experience discomfort.
● *Abnormality as the inability to function effectively.* People who are unable to adjust to the
   demands of society and unable to function in daily life are considered abnormal in this view.
   Judy Smith would be classified as abnormal in this view even if the choice to live on the
   streets were her own.
● *Legal definitions of abnormality.* The legal system uses the concept of insanity to distinguish
   normal from abnormal behavior. Insanity refers generally to whether the defendant could
   understand the difference between right and wrong when the act was committed. The precise
   definition and how it is used varies from one jurisdiction to another.

None of the five approaches is broad enough to include all possibilities of abnormal behavior,
and the line between normal and abnormal remains unclear. The best way to solve the problem
is to consider normal and abnormal as on a continuum, or scale, of behavior rather than to

consider them to be absolute states. In the past, abnormal behavior has been attributed to superstition, to witchcraft, or to demonic possession. The contemporary approach includes six major perspectives on abnormal behavior:

- The [a] _____ views the cause of abnormal behavior to have a physical origin such as a hormonal or chemical imbalance or a physical injury. Many abnormal behaviors have been linked to physical causes, though this view has been criticized because there are many instances in which no physical cause is known.

- The [b] _____ maintains that abnormal behavior comes from childhood. The conflicts of childhood that remain unresolved can cause abnormal behavior in adulthood. One problem with this approach is the difficulty of linking childhood problems with adult behaviors. On the other hand, this approach does suggest that individuals have a rich inner life and that prior experiences do have a profound effect on the present.

- The [c] _____ views the behavior itself as the problem, understanding that behavior is a response to stimuli that one finds in one's environment. In order to understand the behavior, one must examine the circumstances in which it occurs. The strength of this approach is its emphasis on the present and on dealing with observable problems.

- The [d] _____ assumes that *cognitions* are central to a person's abnormal behavior, which can then be changed by learning new cognitions. This model is derived from the behavioral model and sometimes called the *cognitive behavioral approach*.

- The [e] _____ emphasizes the control and responsibility people have for their own behavior. This model considers people to be basically rational, oriented to the social world, and motivated to get along with others. Abnormal behaviors are signs of the person's inability to fulfill basic human needs. This model has been criticized for its reliance on unscientific and unverifiable information.

- The [f] _____ assumes that behavior is shaped by the family group, society, and culture. The stresses and conflicts people experience promote and maintain abnormal behavior. An extreme position suggests that there is no abnormal behavior and that, instead, society is intolerant of deviant behavior. The evidence for the view comes from the link between sociocultural factors and abnormal behavior.

One standard classification system has been accepted by most professionals for classifying mental disorders. Devised by the American Psychiatric Association, the system is known as the

[g] _____ . The manual has more than 200 diagnostic categories. It evaluates behavior according to five dimensions called *axes*. The first three axes address the primary disorder exhibited, the nature of any personality disorders or developmental problems, and any physical disorders. The fourth and fifth axes address the severity of stressors and the

general level of functioning. The *DSM-IV* attempts to be descriptive and to avoid suggestions of cause. The objective is to provide precise description and classification. Criticisms include the fact that it reflects categories that assume a physiological view of causes (arising from the fact that it was developed by physicians) and that the categories are inflexible. In other views, the labeling of an individual as deviant is seen as a lifelong, dehumanizing stigma. A classic study by Rosenhan illustrated how the stigma of being labeled mentally ill can linger. Eight people, including Rosenhan, presented themselves to mental hospitals complaining of only one symptom, hearing voices. Though they did not complain of the symptom again, they stayed for an average of 19 days and were released with labels like "schizophrenia in remission." None of the impostors was detected by the staff. Despite its drawbacks, the *DSM-IV* does provide a reliable and valid way to classify psychological disorders.

Concept 2: Major Disorders

Survey ❑
Read ❑
Recite ❑

- ● *What are the major psychological disorders?*

Pages 452-458

Everyone experiences *anxiety*, a feeling of apprehension or tension, at some time. When anxiety occurs without external reason and interferes with daily functioning, the problem is known as **[a]** _____. **[b]** _____ refers to the disorder in which an individual experiences long-term consistent anxiety without knowing why. The anxiety makes the person unable to concentrate, and life becomes centered on the anxiety. **[c]** _____ is distinguished by **[d]** _____ that may last a few seconds or several hours. In a panic attack, the individual feels anxiety rise to a peak and gets a sense of impending doom. Physical symptoms of increased heart rate, shortness of breath, sweating, faintness, and dizziness may be experienced. **[e]** _____ has as its primary symptom a **[f]** _____, an irrational fear of specific objects or situations. Exposure to the stimulus may cause a full-blown panic attack. (A list of common phobias is given in Table 12-3) Phobias may be minor, or they may cause extreme suffering. **[g]** _____ is characterized by unwanted thoughts and the impulse to carry out a certain action. **[h]** _____ are thoughts or ideas that keep recurring. Though everyone has some obsessions, when they continue for days and months and include bizarre images, they make it difficult for the individual to function. **[i]** _____ are urges to repeat behaviors that seem strange and unreasonable even to the person who feels compelled to act. If they cannot carry out the action, extreme anxiety can be experienced. The cleaning ritual described in the text is a good example of a compulsion. Carrying out the action usually does not reduce the anxiety.

The causes of anxiety disorders are not fully understood. A tendency for both identical twins to have an anxiety disorder if one of them has the disorder suggests that there may be a biological cause. Some chemical deficiencies in the brain have also been linked to the disorder. The behavioral approach suggests that anxiety is a learned response to stress and that the anxiety is reinforced by subsequent encounters with the stressor. The cognitive approach suggests that anxiety grows out of inappropriate and inaccurate cognitions.

[j] _____ involves a constant fear of illness, and physical sensations are misinterpreted as disease symptoms. The symptoms are not faked—hypochondriacs actually experience the symptoms. Hypochondriasis belongs to a class of diseases known as

[k] _____, which are psychological difficulties that take physical form. There are no underlying physical problems to account for the symptoms, or if one does exist, the

person's reaction exaggerates it. A major somatoform disorder is [l] _____, in which actual physical symptoms are caused by psychological problems. These disorders usually have a rapid onset—a person may awaken one morning totally blind or with a numb hand (called "glove anesthesia"). One characteristic is that individuals with conversion disorders seem relatively unconcerned with the symptoms. Conversion disorders have occurred on a large scale. One example is the inexplicable symptoms experienced by student aviators who, rather than quit, developed problems that would otherwise require them to quit, thus allowing a face-saving way to leave the program. Generally, conversion disorders occur when an emotional stress can be reduced by having a physical symptom.

[m] _____ have been the most dramatized disorders, including the multiple-personality stories of *The Three Faces of Eve* and *Sybil*. The central factor is the dissociation, or splitting apart, of critical parts of the personality. There are three major

dissociative disorders. [n] _____, or multiple personality, occurs when two or more distinct personalities are present in the same individual. Each personality is a separate person with desires and reactions to situations. Even vision can change when the personality changes. Since they reside in only one body, they must take turns, causing what appears to be

quite inconsistent behavior. [o] _____ is a failure or inability to remember past experiences. In psychogenic amnesia, information has not been forgotten, it simply cannot be recalled. In some cases memory loss can be quite total, as illustrated in the case of Jane Doe,

who had to go on television to have her identity discovered. [p] _____ is a state in which people take an impulsive, sudden trip and assume a new identity. After a period of time, they realize that they are in a strange place. They often do not recall what they did while wandering.

Concept 3: Major Disorders (Continued)

- *What are the most severe forms of psychological disorders?*

and Beyond the Major Disorders: Abnormal Behavior in Perspective

- *What indicators signal a need for the help of a mental-health practitioner?*

Pages 459-475

Changes in mood are a part of everyday life. However, mood changes can be extreme enough to cause life-threatening problems and to cause an individual to lose touch with reality. These situations result from [a] _____, disturbances in mood severe enough to interfere with daily life. [b] _____ is one of the more common mood disorders. As many as 14 to 15 million people are experiencing major depression at any time. Twice as many women as men experience major depression, and one in four females will encounter it at some time. Depression is not merely sadness, but involves feelings of uselessness, worthlessness, loneliness, and despair. Major depression is distinguished by the severity of the symptoms.

[c] _____ refers to an extended state of intense euphoria and elation. Also, people experience a sense of happiness, power, invulnerability, and energy. They may be involved with wild schemes. When mania is paired with bouts of depression, it is called a [d] _____. The swings between highs and low can occur every several days or can be over a period of years. Typically, the depression lasts longer than the mania.

The psychoanalytic view holds that depression is anger at oneself. Major depression and bipolar disorder may have a biological cause, and heredity may play a role in bipolar disorder.

The cognitive approach draws on the experience of [e]_____, a state in which people perceive that they cannot escape from or cope with stress. According to this view, depression is a response brought on by helplessness. Aaron Beck has suggested that depression involves faulty cognitions held by the sufferers about themselves. Theories about the cause of depression have not explained why twice as many women get it as men. One theory suggests that the stress for women is higher at certain times of life. Women are also more subject to physical and sexual abuse, earn less money than men, and report greater unhappiness with marriage.

[f] _____ refers to the class of disorders in which severe distortion of reality occurs. Thinking, perception, and emotion deteriorate, there is a withdrawal from social interaction, and there may be bizarre behavior. (Classes of schizophrenia are listed in Table 12–5.) The characteristics of schizophrenia include:

- *Decline from a previous level of functioning.*

- *Disturbances of thought and language*, in which logic is peculiar, thoughts do not make sense, and linguistic rules are not followed.
- *Delusions* are unshakable beliefs that have no basis in reality, involving thoughts of control by others, persecution, or the belief that thoughts are being broadcast to others.
- *Perceptual disorders* occur in which schizophrenics do not perceive the world as everyone else does, and they may have **[g]**_____, the experience of perceiving things that do not actually exist.
- *Emotional disturbances* include a lack of emotion or highly inappropriate emotional responses.
- Schizophrenics tend to *withdraw* from contact with others.

The symptoms follow two courses: **[h]** _____ develops symptoms early in life, with a gradual withdrawal from the world; and **[i]** _____ has a sudden and conspicuous onset of symptoms. Reactive schizophrenia responds well to treatment; process schizophrenia is more difficult to treat. Another distinction has been drawn between *positive-symptom schizophrenia* and *negative-symptom schizophrenia*. **[j]** _____ refers to symptoms like withdrawal or loss of ability to function, and **[k]** _____ refers to disordered behavior like hallucinations, delusions, and extremes of emotionality.

Schizophrenia is recognized to have both biological and psychological components at its root. The biological components are suggested by the fact that schizophrenia is more common in some families than others. This suggests a genetic link to the disease. Another biological explanation suggests the presence of a chemical imbalance or a structural defect. The

[l] _____ suggests that schizophrenia occurs when there is excess activity in the areas of the brain that use dopamine to transmit signals across nerve cells. Drugs that block dopamine action are effective in reducing symptoms. These drugs take effect immediately, but the symptoms linger for several weeks, suggesting that there must be other factors at work. Structural differences in the brains of schizophrenics have also been found.

The predominant approach to explaining schizophrenia that combines both biological and psychological factors is the *predisposition model of schizophrenia*. This model says that individuals inherit a predisposition to schizophrenia that makes them vulnerable to stress, and the effect of the stressors occurs when they are coupled with the genetic predisposition.

[m] _____ are characterized by inflexible, maladaptive personality traits. People with personality disorders tend not to be distressed by them. The best known personality disorder is the **[n]** _____. People with this disorder have no regard for moral or ethical rules or for the rights of others. The characteristics of the disorder include: a lack of conscience, guilt, or anxiety over transgressions; impulsive behavior and inability to withstand frustration; and manipulation of others. Explanations include a neglecting or rejecting family, coming from a social group where the societal rules have broken down, and severe socioeconomic deprivation. The **[o]** _____ results in people having difficulty developing a sense of who they are. The **[p]** _____ is characterized by an exaggerated sense of self-importance in which the person with the disorder expects special treatment and disregards the feelings of others.

Other forms of abnormal behavior described by *DSM-IV* include *psychoactive substance-use disorder*, *sexual disorders*, and *organic mental disorders*. The disorders in *DSM-IV* do reflect late-twentieth-century thinking. There was also significant controversy during its development. One controversial disorder was "self-defeating personality disorder," which referred to people in abusive relationships. This disorder was not placed in *DSM-IV*. The other disorder was "premenstrual dysphoric disorder," or premenstrual syndrome. This disorder was included. The Exploring Diversity section discusses the differences between cultures in the nature of abnormal behavior.

Determining the number of people with signs of psychological disorders is a difficult task. A survey of 8,000 Americans found that 30 percent currently had a mental disorder and a total of 48 percent had experienced a disorder at some time in their lives.

The decision concerning if and when to seek help for psychological disorders is difficult, but several guidelines should help. If the following signals are present, help should be considered: long-term feelings of distress that interfere with functioning, occasions when stress is overwhelming, prolonged depression, withdrawal from others, chronic physical problems, a fear or phobia that prevents normal functioning, feelings that other people are talking about the person or are out to get the person, or the inability to interact effectively with others.

➤ Now that you have surveyed, questioned, and read the chapter and completed the guided review, review **Looking Back**, pages 475-476.

Review ❑

➤ For additional practice through recitation and review, test your knowledge of the chapter material by answering the questions in the *Key Word Drill*, the *Practice Questions*, and the *Essay Questions*.

Key Word Drill

The following **Matching Questions** test the boldfaced and italicized key words from the text. Check your answers with the Answer Key in the back of the *Study Guide*.

Recite ❑

MATCHING QUESTIONS

_____ 1. medical model

_____ 2. psychoanalytic model

_____ 3. behavioral model

_____ 4. cognitive model

_____ 5. humanistic model

_____ 6. sociocultural model

a. Suggests that abnormality stems from childhood conflicts over opposing desires regarding sex and aggression.

b. Suggests that people's behavior, both normal and abnormal, is shaped by family, society, and cultural influences.

c. Suggests that people's thoughts and beliefs are a central component to abnormal behavior.

d. Suggests that when an individual displays symptoms of abnormal behavior, the cause is physiological.

e. Suggests that abnormal behavior itself is the problem to be treated, rather than viewing behavior as a symptom of some underlying medical or psychological problem.

f. Suggests that abnormal behavior results from an inability to fulfill human needs and capabilities.

_____ 7. generalized anxiety disorder

_____ 8. panic disorder

_____ 9. panic attack

_____ 10. phobic disorder

_____ 11. dissociative disorder

a. Characterized by the splitting apart of critical personality facets that are normally integrated.

b. Sudden anxiety characterized by heart palpitations, shortness of breath, sweating, faintness, and great fear.

c. The experience of long-term anxiety with no explanation.

d. Characterized by unrealistic fears that may keep people from carrying out routine daily behaviors.

e. Anxiety that manifests itself in the form of panic attacks.

_____ 12. hypochondriasis

_____ 13. somatoform disorder

_____ 14. conversion disorder

_____ 15. dissociative identity
disorder

_____ 16. dissociative amnesia

_____ 17. dissociative fugue

a. Characterized by actual physical disturbances.

b. A condition in which people take sudden, impulsive trips, sometimes assuming a new identity.

c. Characteristics of two or more distinct personalities.

d. A misinterpretation of normal aches and pains.

e. Psychological difficulties that take on physical form.

f. A failure to remember past experience.

_____ 18. anxiety

_____ 19. mood disorder

_____ 20. mania

_____ 21. bipolar disorder

_____ 22. learned helplessness

a. A disorder in which a person alternates between euphoric feelings of mania and bouts of depression.

b. Affective disturbance severe enough to interfere with normal living.

c. A state in which people give up fighting stress, believing it to be inescapable, leading to depression.

d. An extended state of intense euphoria and elation.

e. A feeling of apprehension or tension.

_____ 23. process schizophrenia

_____ 24. reactive schizophrenia

_____ 25. dopamine hypothesis

_____ 26. predisposition model of schizophrenia

a. Suggests that individuals may inherit tendencies that make them particularly vulnerable to stressful factors in the environment.

b. Onset of symptoms is sudden and conspicuous.

c. Symptoms begin early in life and develop slowly.

d. Suggests that schizophrenia occurs when there is excess activity in certain areas of the brain.

_____ 27. personality disorder

a. Characterized by a set of inflexible, maladaptive traits that keep a person from functioning properly in society.

_____ 28. antisocial or sociopathic personality disorder

b. Inability to develop a secure sense of self.

_____ 29. narcissistic personality disorder

c. Characterized by an exaggerated sense of self and an inability to experience empathy for others.

_____ 30. borderline personality disorder

d. Individuals display no regard for moral and ethical rules or for the rights of others.

Practice Questions

Test your knowledge of the chapter material by answering these **Multiple Choice Questions**. These questions have been placed in three Practice Tests. The first two tests are composed of questions that will test your recall of factual knowledge. The third test contains questions that are challenging and primarily test for conceptual knowledge and your ability to apply that knowledge. Check your answers and review the feedback using the Answer Key in the back of the *Study Guide*.

Recite ❏
Review ❏

MULTIPLE CHOICE QUESTIONS

PRACTICE TEST I:

1. When the Titanic sank in 1912, some male passengers saved themselves at the expense of women and children, contrary to the Victorian standard of manly heroism. This behavior was abnormal because it was:
   a. very different from average.
   b. insane.
   c. opposed to an ideal.
   d. severely uncomfortable.

2. The prologue about Lori Schiller illustrates that:
   a. there are unusual treatments for psychological disorders.
   b. women are more prone to certain disorders.
   c. psychological disorders are not necessarily obvious.
   d. when people are denied medication for the medical disorders, they are likely to have serious relapses.

3. If someone's abnormal behavior is related to an endocrine system malfunction, their problem best fits the:
   a. medical model of abnormality.
   b. psychoanalytic model of abnormality.
   c. behavioral model of abnormality.
   d. sociocultural model of abnormality.

4. The _____ model of abnormality suggests that when an individual displays the symptoms of abnormal behavior, the diagnosed causes are physiological.
    a. humanistic
    b. medical
    c. psychoanalytic
    d. sociocultural

5. The sources of one's strange beliefs or actions are hidden conflicts that are carried over from childhood, according to:
    a. the psychoanalytic model.
    b. the humanistic model.
    c. the cognitive model.
    d. the behavioral model.

6. Which of the following models of abnormality is least likely to see the therapist as the expert who cures the patient?
    a. the behavioral model
    b. the humanistic model
    c. the medical model
    d. the psychoanalytic model

7. Many people with psychological disorders come from broken homes and low-income backgrounds. To understand the effects of these and similar conditions on abnormal behavior, a comprehensive diagnosis must include insights from the:
    a. behavioral model.
    b. psychoanalytic model.
    c. humanistic model.
    d. sociocultural model.

8. In the *DSM-IV* there are approximately _____ different diagnostic categories.
    a. 50
    b. 100
    c. 200
    d. 500

9. _____ is a constant fear of illness and the misinterpretation of normal aches and pains.
    a. Phobic disorder
    b. Somatoform disorder
    c. Hypochondriasis
    d. Conversion disorder

10. The term used to describe nervousness and fear that has no apparent justification and impairs normal daily functioning is:
    a. psychosomatic disorder.
    b. personality disorder.
    c. anxiety disorder.
    d. neurotic disorder.

11. Feelings of impending doom or even death paired with sudden and overwhelming bodily reactions are typical symptoms of:
    a. obsessive-compulsive disorder.
    b. panic attack.
    c. personality disorder.
    d. generalized anxiety disorder.

12. The main character in the book *Sybil* suffered from:
    a. schizophrenia.
    b. psychogenic personality.
    c. disordered personality.
    d. dissociative identity disorder.

13. Unable to account for the past three weeks, Portland native Tony X could recall memories prior to his amnesia, but could not relate how he arrived in Tucson. The above description exemplifies:
    a. dissociative identity disorder.
    b. dissociative fugue.
    c. hypochondriasis.
    d. panic attack.

14. A bipolar disorder is one in which an individual has:
    a. opposing phobias.
    b. alternation of mania and depression.
    c. a split personality.
    d. alternation of phobia and panic.

15. The belief that Bigfoot lurks in closets and comes out at night to hide the TV remote would be regarded as a:
    a. compulsion.
    b. hallucination.
    c. delusion.
    d. early sign of narcissism.

16. _____ schizophrenia is characterized by gradual onset, general withdrawal from the world, blunted emotions, and poor prognosis.
    a. Paranoid
    b. Catatonic
    c. Process
    d. Reactive

_____

PRACTICE TEST II:

17. Use of the expression "mental illness" implies that:
    a. demons and devils exert their evil influence on the body through medical ailments, especially ailments of the nervous system.
    b. the target person suffers a lack of unconditional positive regard.
    c. the person has bizarre thoughts but not bizarre behavior.
    d. the speaker or writer accepts the medical model.

18. The main difference between panic disorder and generalized anxiety disorder is that generalized anxiety is:
    a. more intense than panic.
    b. continuous, while panic is short-term.
    c. triggered by alcohol, while panic is triggered by social events.
    d. dissociative, while panic is schizophrenic.

19. Which of the following models of abnormality is likely to hold most strongly to the concept that the patient has little control over his or her actions?
    a. the medical model
    b. the sociocultural model
    c. the behavioral model
    d. the humanistic model

20. The psychoanalytic model of abnormality suggests that abnormal behavior derives from:
    a. failure to develop logical thought processes.
    b. physiological malfunctions.
    c. unresolved childhood conflicts.
    d. confusion in the collective unconscious.

21. Which of the following models of abnormality is most likely to emphasize the patient's responsibility and participation in the treatment?
    a. the medical model
    b. the psychoanalytic model
    c. the behavioral model
    d. the humanistic model

22. According to the text, proponents of which model are most likely to take the position that there is no such thing as abnormal behavior?
   a. the sociocultural model
   b. the psychoanalytic model
   c. the behavioral model
   d. the medical model

23. The *DSM-IV* is used primarily to:
   a. show the causes of and to treat abnormality.
   b. classify and identify causes of abnormality.
   c. classify and describe abnormality.
   d. describe and treat abnormality.

24. The Rosenhan (1973) study in which normal individuals were admitted to mental hospitals showed that:
   a. therapeutic techniques that improve disordered patients can be applied by normal people to make them even better adjusted than they were at first.
   b. mental patients served as models for each others' strange behaviors.
   c. the "mental patient" label affects how ordinary acts are perceived.
   d. the *DSM-IV* categories are prone both to stability and change.

25. According to the text, which of the following is **not** a reasonable criticism of the *DSM-IV*?
   a. Mental disorders are classified into a "category" rather than along a continuum.
   b. The *DSM-IV* materials usually do not reflect changing views in society about mental disorders, since the manual is updated only every 15 years.
   c. The *DSM-IV* system of classification may be too heavily influenced by the medical model.
   d. A diagnosis may become an explanation for a problem.

26. A feature that is shared by dissociative disorders is that:
   a. their hereditary basis is well known and documented.
   b. an obsessive-compulsive disorder usually precedes the onset of any dissociative disorder.
   c. they tend to occur in persons who are poor and have large families.
   d. they allow the person to escape from anxiety-producing situations.

27. Psychological difficulties that take on a physical form but have no actual physical or physiological abnormality are called:
   a. somatoform disorders.
   b. psychological disorders.
   c. psychophysical disorders.
   d. freeform disorders.

28. Together, dissociative identity disorder, amnesia, and dissociative fugue are called:
   a. depressive disorders.
   b. schizophrenic disorders.
   c. somatoform disorders.
   d. dissociative disorders.

29. Mania and bipolar disorder differ mainly in:
   a. the sense that mania applies to both genders but bipolar applies to men.
   b. the fact that mania has a psychological origin but bipolar is biological.
   c. the stability of the emotional state.
   d. the sense that one is a personality disorder while the other is a mood disorder.

30. Sociopaths can fool the lie detector test because they:
    a. feel stress or anxiety more or less continuously.
    b. are psychologically sophisticated; many have studied *DSM-IV*.
    c. feel no guilt or remorse.
    d. have lost touch with reality.

31. Which mental disturbance is most likely to result in the afflicted person's using language in ways that do **not** follow conventional linguistic rules?
    a. schizophrenia
    b. dissociative identity disorder
    c. dissociative fugue
    d. depressive disorder

32. Schizophrenia produces many dramatic and debilitating changes in a person affected with this disorder. Which alternative below is **not** one of them?
    a. delusions
    b. dissociative identity disorder
    c. decline from an earlier level of functioning
    d. withdrawal

PRACTICE TEST III: Conceptual, Applied, and Challenging Questions

33. Which statement below is **not** consistent with the sociocultural model of abnormality?
    a. Behavior is shaped by our family, by society, and by the culture in which we live.
    b. There is something wrong with a society that is unwilling to tolerate deviant behavior.
    c. Competing psychic forces within the troubled individual erode personal standards and values.
    d. Abnormal behaviors are more prevalent among some social classes than others.

34. "The kinds of stresses and conflicts that people experience in their daily interactions with others can promote and maintain abnormal behavior." This statement is consistent with the _____ model of abnormality.
    a. sociocultural
    b. behavioral
    c. humanistic
    d. psychoanalytic

35. Sue was having a disagreement with her fiancé when she suddenly became extremely anxious and felt a sense of impending, unavoidable doom. Her heart beat rapidly, she was short of breath, became faint and dizzy, and felt as if she might die. Sue was experiencing:
    a. phobic disorder.
    b. panic disorder.
    c. generalized anxiety disorder.
    d. obsessive-compulsive disorder.

36. The psychiatrist listened patiently as his client revealed a series of episodes involving irrational fears of water. The psychiatrist probably labeled the client's symptoms as:
    a. schizophrenic reactions.
    b. phobic reactions.
    c. organic reactions.
    d. obsessive-compulsive reactions.

37. Sarah is terrified to ride in an elevator in any building. She is especially bothered by the small, confined space and the fact that she is "trapped" until the elevator doors open. Usually, she avoids this unpleasantness by refusing to ride in elevators. Sarah is experiencing:
    a. phobic disorder.
    b. panic disorder.
    c. obsessive-compulsive disorder.
    d. tension disorder.

38. Sandra has been having a difficult time at college, since she has been very tense and anxious during her professors' lectures. She has been much better lately because she distracts herself by counting the number of times her professors say "the" during their lectures. Sandra's "counting" suggests she is experiencing:
    a. panic disorder
    b. phobic disorder.
    c. obsessive-compulsive disorder.
    d. generalized anxiety disorder.

39. The lead singer for a heavy metal group finds that, two or three hours before an important concert, he cannot talk or sing. The group's doctor cannot find any medical reason for the singer's problem. The doctor is also surprised that the singer seems unconcerned. If the singer's symptoms are the result of a psychological disorder, it would most likely be diagnosed as:
    a. somatoform disorder.
    b. conversion disorder.
    c. panic disorder.
    d. obsessive-compulsive disorder.

40. After depression, what is the most frequent mental disorder in America?
    a. bipolar disorder
    b. obsessive-compulsive disorder
    c. paranoid schizophrenia
    d. alcohol dependence

41. What is one difference between dissociative fugue and dissociative amnesia?
    a. In fugue, memory can be restored with drugs.
    b. In amnesia, the memory loss is temporary.
    c. In fugue, past memory is eventually regained.
    d. In amnesia, the memories are physically lost.

42. When minor symptoms of schizophrenia follow a severe case or episode, the disorder is called:
    a. disorganized schizophrenia.
    b. catatonic schizophrenia.
    c. paranoid schizophrenia.
    d. residual schizophrenia.

43. According to your text, process schizophrenia is different from reactive schizophrenia because with reactive schizophrenia, the patient:
    a. experiences a sudden and conspicuous onset of symptoms.
    b. is less withdrawn.
    c. may be dangerously aggressive and abusive to others.
    d. is less likely to have a hereditary basis for the disorder.

44. Which of the following accounts of schizophrenia assumes that inappropriate behavior is learned by attending to stimuli that are not related to normal social interaction?
    a. learned helplessness hypothesis
    b. dopamine hypothesis
    c. predisposition model
    d. learned-inattention theory

45. According to the text, personality disorder is best characterized by:
    a. firmly held beliefs with little basis in reality.
    b. a mixture of symptoms of schizophrenia.
    c. a set of inflexible, maladaptive traits.
    d. an extended sense of euphoria and elation.

46. A recently admitted patient to a hospital psychiatric ward has complained of hearing voices. In addition, he claims to have direct communication links with the Bosnian-Serb leadership and that it is unfortunate that no one in our government will talk with him. If asked, he is sure that something could be done. The voices, by the way, warn him not to talk with the CIA—they are not to be trusted any more than the ATF. Which of the following best describes this patient?
    a. negative-symptom schizophrenia
    b. positive-symptom schizophrenia
    c. process schizophrenia
    d. reactive schizophrenia

47. Pat is uncooperative, refuses to speak to her coworkers, and frequently disrupts meetings with distracting questions and irrelevant challenges. However, she is fully capable of doing all her work assignments and maintains a reasonable family life. She will use her status as a female to threaten her superiors with "harassment" if they question what she is doing, and she will exploit anyone who is unwitting enough to be caught in one of her self-promotion schemes. Since she believes that she can do whatever she can get away with doing, which of the following categories best fits her?
    a. sociopathic personality disorder
    b. self-defeating personality disorder
    c. premenstrual dysphoric disorder
    d. dissociative identity disorder

48. Which of the following disorders does not share a common quality that the others share?
    a. koro   c. amok
    b. anorexia nervosa   d. phobic disorder

Essay Questions

Essay Question 12.1: *Defining Mental Illness*

Recite ❏
Review ❏

Discuss the implications of Rosenhan's study, in which he and seven other individuals faked mental illness in order to test the ability of mental hospitals to distinguish abnormal behavior from normal, and the effects of labeling. What are the scientific issues related to his study? Are there any ethical issues?

Essay Question 12.2: *Schizophrenia*

Describe the types of schizophrenia, its symptoms, and its causes. Compare the differing theories concerning the cause of schizophrenia.

Activities and Projects

Review the models of abnormality described in the text: medical, psychoanalytic, behavioral, cognitive, humanistic, and sociocultural. Which of these models appeals to you the most? Which the least? Next, find the key issues in Chapter 1. Does the way these models answer these key issues affect their appeal or lack of appeal to you? What measure would you use to test the usefulness or value of each of these models? Can your measure be supported? Use the two charts provided to answer these questions.

Recite ❑
Review ❑

Key Issues	Medical model	Psychoanalytic model	Behavioral model
Nature (heredity) versus nurture (environment)			
Conscious versus unconscious determinants of behavior			
Observable behavior versus internal mental processes			
Freedom of choice versus determinism			
Individual differences versus universal principles			

Key Issues	Cognitive model	Humanistic model	Sociocultural model
Nature (heredity) versus nurture (environment)			
Conscious versus unconscious determinants of behavior			
Observable behavior versus internal mental processes			
Freedom of choice versus determinism			
Individual differences versus universal principles			

Which appeals to you the most?

Cultural Idioms

Recite ❑
Review ❑

p. 442
summer camp: During summer vacation from school, it is common for middle-class children to go away from home (and their parents) to a camp
On a whim: spontaneously
skydiving: jumping out of a plane with a parachute

p. 443
Corn flakes; Raisin Bran: two cold breakfast cereals popular in the U. S.

p. 444
hold a job: keep the same job for a long time

p. 445
Drawing the Line on Abnormality: Deciding how to define "abnormal"
possessed by the devil or some sort of demonic god: People used to think that a devil had entered a person's body and it was this devil inside a person who was acting abnormally

p. 448
Nutty as a fruitcake; Loony; Psycho; Demented: negative slang terms to describe someone who has severe psychological disorders

p. 449
to unravel: to lose touch with reality

p. 452
out of the blue: with no advance warning; suddenly
wreak considerable havoc on: cause disruption to
Greek tragedy: plays written in fourth century B.C., Greece, involving humans, gods, and goddesses

p. 453
tightrope walker: an acrobat who walks across a rope, high above the ground

p. 454
Face flushed: when your face turns red and feels hot
Mind blurred: when you can't think clearly

p. 456
air disaster: plane crash
face-saving: a way to keep your dignity and your self-esteem; by developing a physical problem, these student pilots could leave the program without having to admit that they wanted to quit.

p. 458
Jane Doe: a woman's name that is an often used when no real name can be used; for men, the "universal" name is John Doe.
park ranger: a person who works in a state park or in a U. S. national Park
Good Morning America: a popular morning TV news show

p. 459
New York Mets: a baseball team
mood swings: when a person goes from being happy to being sad

p. 460
uncontrollable crying jags: when a person can't stop crying
wild schemes: unrealistic plans
leave of absence: a few or more months away from a job; you can go back to the job later.
cuckoo clocks: clocks that announce the time with a small mechanical bird that makes the sound "cuckoo"
"tear around town": drive fast around the city
"wheeling and dealing": making business deals
"on top of the world": euphoric

p. 463
Cover Girl: a brand of makeup
Oral Roberts: a religious minister who has a TV show
Mad Magazine: a humor magazine popular with teens
Abbott and Costello: a comedy team that made movies in the early twentieth century
Mick Jagger: rock star, member of the Rolling Stones
Casper the Friendly Ghost: cartoon character
the Union: the United States

p. 466
offspring of dual matings: children of two schizophrenic parents

p. 468
bitched about: a slang expression that means "complained about"
'em: them
doctored ones: the ones that he had changed

p. 469
con men: people who use elaborate plans to cheat and rob other people by tricking them
Glenn Close: U. S. movie actress
Fatal Attraction: a film starring Glenn Close, who plays a woman who becomes angry and violent after a relationship doesn't work out well
on the fringes of society: not in the mainstream, on the edges

p. 471
U. S. Surgeon General: Appointed by the president, the Surgeon General is the most important doctor in the U. S., in charge of public health issues

p. 472
The Mental State of the Union: Every January, the president of the United States makes a speech to Congress, called the State of the Union, in which the president talks about the country's "health." Thus, the author is making a joke here, about the mental health of the United States.
face-to-face: in person, not over the phone or by mail

p. 473
in the closet: secretive, not openly admitting something
Zoloft: a drug used to treat depression
Academy-Award winner: a person who has won an Academy award (also called an "Oscar"), the most prestigious movie award in the U. S.
Baywatch: TV drama
Heisman trophy: an important football award
CNN: Cable News Network, a cable TV station available around the world
General Colin Powell: Former top military person in the United States
Equal Employment Opportunity Commission: government agency that makes sure that no unlawful discrimination takes place
Americans with Disabilities Act: a federal law that ensures that people with physical and mental disabilities will have equal access to goods and services
Woody Allen: a writer/director/movie actor whose humor reflects a "neurotic" outlook
Marcus Welby: a TV character who is uncomplicated and never has any psychological problems

13 Treatment of Psychological Disorders

Detailed Chapter Outline

Which Kind of Therapy Works Best?

Exploring Diversity: Racial and Ethnic Factors in
Treatment: Should Therapists Be Color-Blind?

Recap, Review, and Rethink

Biomedical Therapy: Biological Approaches to Treatment
Drug Therapy
>*Antipsychotic Drugs*
>*Antidepressant Drugs*
>*Lithium*
>*Antianxiety Drugs*

Electroconvulsive Therapy
Psychosurgery
Biomedical Therapies in Perspective: Can Abnormal Behavior Be Cured?
Community Psychology: Focus on Prevention

Pathways Through Psychology: Richard M. Greer,
College Counselor

The Informed Consumer of Psychology:
Choosing the Right Therapist

Recap, Review, and Rethink
Looking Back
Key Terms and Concepts

➤ Now that you have surveyed the chapter, read **Looking Ahead**, pages
480-481. What questions does the Chapter seek to answer?

Question ❑
Read ❑

Concepts and Learning Objectives

These are the concepts and the learning objectives for Chapter 13. Read
them carefully as part of your preliminary survey of the chapter.

Survey ❑

Concept 1: Psychotherapy seeks to remedy psychological difficulties. Psychodynamic
approaches attempt to resolve unconscious conflicts, and behavioral approaches apply
learning theory to therapy.

1. Define psychotherapy, and identify the main approaches/types.

2. Describe the psychodynamic approach to the treatment of abnormal behavior, including the major techniques and concepts employed by psychodynamic therapists.

3. Describe the behavioral approaches to the treatment of abnormal behavior, including aversive conditioning, systematic desensitization, observational learning, and the use of operant conditioning principles.

4. Discuss the cognitive-behavioral therapy approaches of rational-emotive and cognitive therapy.

Concept 2: Humanistic psychotherapy focuses on issues related to the person's taking responsibility for his or her own actions and solving issues regarding the meaning of life. Psychotherapy is considered to be effective, but some therapies are more appropriate for certain disorders than are others.

5. Describe the application of humanistic therapy in the approaches of Rogers's client-centered therapy, existential therapy, and gestalt therapy.

6. Describe group therapy, including family therapy, and explain the eclectic approach to psychotherapy.

7. Discuss the methods used to evaluate psychotherapy and the arguments proposed to support and dispute the effectiveness of psychotherapies.

Concept 3: Drug therapy has made psychotic patients calmer, alleviated depression, and calmed anxiety. Electroconvulsive therapy and psychosurgery are controversial treatments of last resort. The community health movement now must cope with deinstitutionalized patients and has also led to the development of hotlines and campus crisis centers.

8. Name and describe drugs used in the treatment of abnormal behavior, and discuss the problems and controversies surrounding their use.

9. Describe electroconvulsive therapy and psychosurgery, and discuss the effectiveness of biomedical therapies.

10. Explain the concepts of community psychology and deinstitutionalization, and identify recommended guidelines for selecting a psychotherapist.

Chapter Guided Review

There are several ways you can use this guided review as part of your systematic study plan. Read the corresponding pages of the text and then complete the review by supplying the correct missing key word. Or, you may want to complete the guided review as a means of becoming familiar with the text. Complete the review and then read the section thoroughly. As you finish each section, complete the **Recap and Review** questions that are supplied in the text.

Survey ❑
_____

CONCEPT 1: **Psychotherapy: Psychological Approaches to Treatment**

Survey ❑
Read ❑
Recite ❑
_____

- *What are the goals of psychological and biomedical treatment approaches?*
- *What are the basic kinds of psychotherapies?*

Pages 482-491

The common goal of therapy is relief of the psychological disorder and enabling individuals to achieve richer, more meaningful lives. Psychologically based therapy is called

[a] _____, a process in which a patient (client) and a professional work together to deal with psychological difficulties. **[b]** _____ depends on drugs and other medical procedures. Many therapists today draw upon the large number of therapies for the approach most suited to the client, and this is considered an **[c]** _____.

[d] _____ assumes that the primary causes of abnormal behavior are unresolved conflicts from the past and anxiety over unconscious impulses. The **[e]** _____ that individuals use to guard against anxiety do not bury these anxieties completely, and they emerge in the form of *neurotic symptoms*. Freud said that the way to deal with the unwanted desires and past conflicts was to confront them, to make them conscious. The role of the psychodynamic therapist is then to explore the unconscious conflicts and help the patient understand them.

Freudian therapy is called **[f]** _____, and it tends to be lengthy and expensive. Patients meet with their therapists four to six times a week for several years. The technique often used is called **[g]** _____, during which the patient will say anything that comes to mind no matter how insignificant. The ramblings are assumed to be clues from the unconscious, and the therapist looks for connections in the patient's words. Another method is **[h]** _____; again the therapist looks for clues to the unconscious in the dream. People censor thoughts when they dream, so there is a distinction between the **[i]** _____ of dreams, or the description of the dream, and the **[j]** _____ of dreams, or the message of the dreams. Sometimes the patient will unconsciously resist the probing. **[k]** _____ refers to an inability to discuss or reveal particular memories or thoughts. The patient finds it difficult to talk about these particular issues. **[l]** _____ is a phenomenon in which the relationship between the analyst and the patient becomes emotionally charged, and the analyst symbolically takes on the role of significant others from the patient's past. Transference is used to help the patient re-create the past and work through it more positively.

Today, psychodynamic psychotherapy is shorter, and the therapist takes a more active role, controlling the course of therapy and emphasizing the present more than the past. It is still criticized for being time-consuming and expensive, and only certain kinds of patients are well-suited for this kind of therapy. It is difficult to prove that psychodynamic therapies are successful, and some critics challenge the entire theoretical basis for the approach.

The principles of reinforcement are central to **[m]** _____, which suggest that both abnormal and normal behavior is learned. To modify abnormal behavior, new behaviors must be learned. Behavioral psychologists are not interested in the past history of the individual, focusing instead on the current behavior.

Classical conditioning principles are applied to behaviors like alcoholism, smoking, and drug abuse, with a technique known as aversive conditioning. In **[n]** _____, the unwanted behavior is linked with a stimulus that produces an unpleasant response, like a drug that produces vomiting when mixed with alcohol. The long-term effectiveness of the approach is questionable. The most successful classical conditioning technique is called

[o] _____, in which a person is taught to relax and is then gradually exposed to an anxiety-provoking stimulus. One approach involves the development of a

[p] _____ that the patient can use to become exposed to less threatening stimuli at first. The patient relaxes and then imagines the first stimulus on the list for as long as he or she can remain relaxed. The patient then progresses through the hierarchy, eventually actually being placed in the situation or exposed to the stimulus that causes anxiety. Systematic desensitization has been used successfully with phobias, anxiety disorders, and impotence.

[q] _____ is used in therapy by **[r]** _____ appropriate behaviors. People can be taught skills and ways of handling anxiety by observing a model cope with the same situation. The "Fearless Peer" approach helps children overcome their fear of dogs by having another child pet and play with a dog.

Operant conditioning techniques are used in settings where rewards and punishments can be controlled. One example is that of the **[s]** _____, in which individuals are rewarded with tokens that can be exchanged for desired objects or opportunities. *Contingency contracting* requires a written agreement between the therapist and the client. The contract sets behavioral goals to be reached and specifies the consequences of reaching the goals. Behavior therapy works well for phobias and compulsions; however, it is not very effective for deep depression or personality disorders.

Cognitive approaches to therapy attempt to change faulty cognitions held by patients about themselves and the world. The therapies are typically based on learning principles and thus are often called **[t]** _____. **[u]** _____ is one of the best examples of the cognitive approach. The therapist attempts to restructure the person's belief system into a more realistic, rational, and logical set of views. Therapists take an active and directive role in therapy, directly challenging patterns of thought that appear to be irrational.

Another form of therapy is Aaron Beck's [v] _____. The therapist is less confrontive and more like a teacher. Clients are given assignments to help them uncover information that will lead them to think more appropriately.

CONCEPT 2: Psychotherapy: Psychological Approaches to Treatment (Continued)

Survey ❑
Read ❑
Recite ❑

- *What are humanistic approaches to treatment?*
- *How does group therapy differ from individual types of therapy?*
- *How effective is therapy, and which kind of therapy works best in a given situation?*

Pages 492-498

[a] _____ depends upon the perspective of self-responsibility as the basis for treatment. The view is that we control our own behavior and make choices about how to live, and it is up to us to solve our problems. Humanistic therapists see themselves as guides or facilitators.

[b] _____ refers to approaches that do not offer interpretations or answers to problems. First practiced by Carl Rogers, [c] _____ was founded on the nondirective approach. Rogers attempted to establish a warm and accepting environment in order to enable the client to make realistic and constructive choices about life.

The therapist must provide a sense of [d] _____, an acceptance of the individual without conditions no matter what attitude is expressed by the client. It is rare to find client-centered therapy practiced in its pure form because therapies usually now include some directive aspects.

Concern with the meaning and uniqueness of life has given rise to [e] _____, an approach based on the problem of dealing with personal freedom and the anguish, fear, and concern that accompanies such fear. The goal of existential therapy is to help the client come to grips with freedom, to find his or her place in the world, and to develop a system of values that gives meaning to life. The therapist is more directive and probes and challenges the client's views.

[f] _____ has the goal of integrating the client's thoughts and feelings into a whole. The approach was developed by Fritz Perls. He asked the client to go back and work on unfinished business, playing the part of the angry father and taking other roles in a conflict. This leads the client to increase perspectives on a situation.

Humanistic approaches lack specificity, and the form of treatment is most appropriate for the same type of person treated by psychoanalysis. However, the emphasis on human responsibility and uniqueness and on creating an environment that is supportive can help clients find solutions to psychological difficulties.

[g] _____ is a form of treatment that has several unrelated people meet with a therapist at the same time. Problems, usually one held in common with all group members, are discussed with the group. Members of the group provide social support and share how they may have dealt with similar situations. Groups vary according to therapeutic approach and degree of guidance offered by the therapist. Groups are economical, but critics argue that they do not replace the one-on-one aspect of individual therapy.

[h] _____ is a specialized form of group therapy that involves two or more members of a family. Therapists focus on the entire family system rather than only on the family member with the problem, and each family member is expected to contribute to the solution. Family therapists assume that family members engage in set patterns of behavior, and the goal of therapy is to get the family to adopt more constructive behaviors.

Deciding which therapy is appropriate for which kind of problem is a difficult task, but a more critical question is whether any psychotherapy is effective. Hans Eysenck published an article in 1952 that challenged whether psychodynamic therapy was effective. He compared a group receiving treatment with one composed of people on a waiting list for treatment. The group that received no therapy had done just as well as the group that received therapy. The symptoms went away due to [i] _____, or recovery without treatment. Eysenck's study was challenged on the basis of the data he used. Eysenck's early work led to a number of studies, most of which conclude that therapy does work.

The question of which therapy is the best still remains. One study comparing the cure rates for treatment groups found that therapies were 70 to 85 percent more successful than nontreated individuals. Other studies relying on the *meta-analytic* procedure have supported this data. For most people, therapy is effective. In a small number of cases, people may actually deteriorate during therapy. It is also clear that particular kinds of therapy are also more appropriate for some than for others. Most therapists utilize the [j] _____ to therapy, which provides a number of treatment techniques from which to select.

Therapists must take into account how the factors of race, ethnicity, cultural heritage, and social class affect the nature of psychological problems and the course of treatment.

CONCEPT 3: **Biological Therapy: Biological Approaches to Treatment**

Survey ❑
Read ❑
Recite ❑

- *How are drug, electroconvulsive, and psychosurgical techniques used today in the treatment of psychological disorders?*

Pages 499-507
Biomedical treatments that treat brain chemical imbalances and other neurological factors directly are regularly used for some problems. In [a] _____, drugs are

given that alleviate symptoms for a number of psychological disturbances. In the mid 1950s,

[b] _____ were introduced, causing a major change in the treatment of patients in mental hospitals. These drugs alleviate symptoms related to the patient's loss of touch with reality, agitation, and overactivity. Antipsychotic drugs greatly improved the atmosphere in the hospital by calming patients. The drug introduced was *chlorpromazine*, and it proved successful in treating the symptoms of schizophrenia. *Clozapine* and *haloperidol* are the current generation of antipsychotic drugs. Antipsychotic drugs work by blocking dopamine production at sites where the electrical impulses travel across nerve receptors. The drugs do not cure, and they have severe side effects, including dryness of mouth, dizziness, and tremors. A condition known as *tardive dyskinesia* may also result. They also have a numbing effect on the emotional responses of patients.

[c] _____ are used to improve the moods of severely depressed patients. Antidepressant drugs work by increasing the concentration of certain neurotransmitters. Tricyclic drugs increase the concentration of norepinephrine and serotonin; bupropion drugs increase dopamine. Antidepressant drugs can produce long-term recoveries from depression. One antidepressant, *fluoxetine*—also known as *Prozac*—has been the center of recent controversy. Prozac blocks the reabsorption of the neurotransmitter serotonin. One fear is that because of its popularity, people with minor depression will seek prescriptions of the drug rather than seek more suitable treatment.

[d] _____, a form of simple mineral salt, has been used to treat bipolar disorders. It ends manic episodes 70 percent of the time; its success with depression is not as good. Unlike other treatments, lithium is seen as a *preventive* treatment. People who have had manic-depressive episodes in the past take small doses as a means of preventing the return of the symptoms.

[e] _____—Valium and Xanax—are the drugs most prescribed by physicians. Antianxiety drugs reduce the anxiety level experienced by reducing excitability and increasing drowsiness. They have side effects that include fatigue and dependence. When combined with alcohol, some are lethal. The drugs also mask the source of the anxiety and allow the person simply to ignore the cause of the problem.

On the mistaken notion that epileptics—who experience convulsions—do not have schizophrenia, physicians in the 1930s found a way to induce convulsions using electric shocks.

[f] _____ is administered by passing an electric current of 70 to 150 volts through the head of a patient. The patient is usually sedated and given muscle relaxants to prevent violent contractions. ECT is controversial because of its side effects, which include disorientation, confusion, and memory loss. Many patients fear ECT, and some people believe that it may cause permanent neurological damage. It continues to be used because it does help severely depressed patients when other treatments are ineffective.

[g] _____ is brain surgery used to alleviate psychological symptoms.

An early procedure was [h] _____, in which parts of the frontal lobes are removed or destroyed. The patients are then less subject to emotional impulses. Patients also suffered personality changes, becoming bland and unemotional. Patients can also die from the treatment. Drug therapies ended the frequent use of psychosurgery, and today it is used to alleviate problems like severe and uncontrollable pain. Biological therapies have made it possible for many patients to live relatively symptom-free lives. However, the treatments do not remove the cause of the symptoms, and when therapy stops, the symptoms will return.

Psychotherapy and medical therapy are intended to restore the patient to a previous state of health; **[i]** _____ is intended to help prevent or minimize psychological disorders. In the 1960s, plans were made for a nationwide network of community mental-health centers that could provide inexpensive mental-health services, short-term therapy, and educational programs. Former mental patients were returning to the community in a process known as **[j]** _____. The community centers were expected to ensure that the deinstitutionalized patients continued to get proper treatment and that their civil rights were maintained. The original goals were not met, and mental disorders have not declined. Many people who need treatment do not get it. Positive results include the development of "hotlines," where people can call for help and talk to a trained person immediately. The college crisis center also grew out of this movement. The volunteers on hot lines receive careful training for telephone counseling and are prepared to respond to a variety of situations and to make referrals for additional treatment.

Whether one has chosen the right therapist can be determined by considering the following: the relationship between client and therapist should be comfortable, the therapist and the client should agree on the goals for treatment, the therapist should have appropriate credentials and training, clients should feel that they are making progress, and clients should be aware that they must contribute effort to the therapy.

➤ Now that you have surveyed, questioned, and read the chapter and completed the guided review, review **Looking Back**, pages 508-509.

Review ❑

➤ For additional practice through recitation and review, test your knowledge of the chapter material by answering the questions in the *Key Word Drill*, the *Practice Questions*, and the *Essay Questions*.

Key Word Drill

The following **Matching Questions** test the boldfaced and italicized key words from the text. Check your answers with the Answer Key in the back of the *Study Guide*.

Recite ❑

MATCHING QUESTIONS

_____ 1. biomedical therapy

_____ 2. psychodynamic therapy

_____ 3. psychoanalysis

_____ 4. behavioral treatment approaches

_____ 5. cognitive approaches to therapy

_____ 6. rational-emotive therapy

_____ 7. cognitive therapy

a. Basic sources of abnormal behavior are unresolved past conflicts and anxiety.

b. Attempts to restructure one's belief into a more realistic, rational, and logical system.

c. Appropriate treatment consists of learning new behavior or unlearning maladaptive behavior.

d. A form of psychodynamic therapy that often lasts for many years.

e. Uses drugs and other medical procedures to improve psychological functioning.

f. People's faulty cognitions about themselves and the world are changed to more accurate ones.

g. People are taught to change illogical thoughts about themselves and the world.

_____ 8. free association

_____ 9. manifest content

_____ 10. latent content

_____ 11. resistance

_____ 12. transference

a. A patient's transfer of certain strong feelings for others to the analyst.

b. The "true" message hidden within dreams.

c. The patient says everything that comes to mind, providing insights into the patient's unconscious.

d. An inability or unwillingness to discuss or reveal particular memories, thoughts, or motivations.

e. The surface description and interpretation of dreams.

_____ 13. aversive conditioning

_____ 14. systematic desensitization

_____ 15. token system

_____ 16. contingency contracting

a. A person is rewarded for performing desired behaviors.

b. Breaks unwanted habits by associating the habits with very unpleasant stimuli.

c. Requires a written contract between a therapist and a client that sets behavioral goals and rewards.

d. A stimulus that evokes pleasant feelings is repeatedly paired with a stimulus that evokes anxiety.

_____ 17. client-centered therapy

_____ 18. humanistic therapy

_____ 19. existential therapy

_____ 20. gestalt therapy

_____ 21. group therapy

_____ 22. family therapy

_____ 23. community psychology

a. People discuss problems with others who have similar problems.

b. The therapist reflects back the patient's statements in a way that helps the patient to find solutions.

c. People have control of their behavior and are essentially responsible for solving their own problems.

d. Movement aimed at preventing psychological disorders.

e. Addresses the meaning of life, allowing a client to devise a system of values that gives purpose to his or her life.

f. Attempts to integrate a client's thoughts, feelings, and behavior into a whole.

g. Meeting with the family as a unit to which each member contributes.

_____ 24. antipsychotic drugs

_____ 25. antidepressant drugs

_____ 26. antianxiety drugs

_____ 27. chlorpromazine

_____ 28. lithium

_____ 29. fluoxetine

a. Prozac, a widely used antidepressant drug.

b. Used in the treatment of schizophrenia.

c. Improve a patient's mood and feeling of well-being.

d. Used in the treatment of bipolar disorders.

e. Alleviate stress and feelings of apprehension.

f. Temporarily alleviate symptoms such as agitation and overactivity.

Practice Questions

Test your knowledge of the chapter material by answering these **Multiple Choice Questions**. These questions have been placed in three Practice Tests. The first two tests are composed of questions that will test your recall of factual knowledge. The third test contains questions that are challenging and primarily test for conceptual knowledge and your ability to apply that knowledge. Check your answers and review the feedback using the Answer Key in the back of the *Study Guide*.

Recite ❑
Review ❑

MULTIPLE CHOICE QUESTIONS

PRACTICE TEST I:

1. According to the text, what is the common goal of all types of therapy?
   a. integrating the individual into society
   b. relieving psychological disorders
   c. relieving fears and anxiety
   d. reassembling the parts of the personality

2. According to the text, the category of therapy in which change is brought about through discussions and interactions between client and professional is called:
   a. eclectic therapy.
   b. semantic therapy
   c. psychotherapy.
   d. interpersonal therapy.

3. Clients requiring some form of medical treatment are typically treated by a:
   a. psychiatric nurse.
   b. counseling psychologist.
   c. psychiatrist.
   d. clinical psychologist.

4. According to Freud, in order to protect our egos from the unwanted entry of unacceptable unconscious thoughts and desires, we all use:
   a. transference.
   b. aversive conditioning.
   c. systematic desensitization.
   d. defense mechanisms.

5. Listed below are terms associated with psychodynamic therapy. Which alternative below does **not** belong?
   a. hierarchy of fears
   b. neurotic symptoms
   c. defense mechanisms
   d. transference

6. Which of the following approaches to therapy would be **least** concerned with the underlying causes of abnormal behavior?
   a. psychoanalytic
   b. behavioral
   c. eclectic
   d. humanistic

7. A technique used to reduce anxiety or eliminate phobias that is based on classical conditioning is called:
    a. biofeedback.
    b. behavior modification.
    c. systematic desensitization.
    d. aversive conditioning.

8. The behavioral-treatment approach uses all of the following techniques **except**:
    a. aversive conditioning.
    b. systematic desensitization.
    c. modeling.
    d. symptom substitution.

9. In rational-emotive therapy, the goal of therapy is to restructure one's beliefs about oneself and the world into:
    a. a view that focuses on problems that arise only when events fail to turn out as expected.
    b. a realization that it is necessary for one to love and be approved of by each significant person in one's life.
    c. a rational, realistic, and logical system.
    d. an understanding of the role of emotion in behavior.

10. The approach that is the best known of the humanistic therapies and assumes at the outset that a person's troubles reflect unfulfilled potential is called:
    a. rational-emotive therapy.
    b. gestalt therapy.
    c. systematic desensitization.
    d. client-centered therapy.

11. According to the text, the goal of client-centered therapy is to enable people to reach the potential for:
    a. getting in touch with reality.
    b. understanding the unconscious.
    c. taking control of their thoughts.
    d. self-actualization.

12. According to the text, which therapies emphasize establishing inner rather than outer control of behavior?
    a. psychodynamic and humanistic
    b. psychodynamic and behavioral
    c. rational-emotive and behavioral
    d. behavioral and humanistic

13. What is spontaneous remission?
    a. An attack, either verbal or physical, by the therapist against the client when provoked repeatedly.
    b. Disappearance of psychological symptoms even without therapy.
    c. An emotional outburst by the client during the therapy session.
    d. Behavior by a family member (especially one's spouse) that worsens one's psychological symptoms.

14. According to the text, antipsychotic drugs alleviate psychotic symptoms by:
    a. increasing neurotransmitter function.
    b. blocking the production of dopamine.
    c. slowing down the autonomic nervous system.
    d. sedating the patients.

15. According to the text, which medication would most likely be given to someone experiencing a manic episode?
   a. lithium
   b. Valium
   c. chlorpromazine
   d. Librium

16. The most widely applied biological approach to treatment is:
   a. psychosurgery.
   b. electroconvulsive therapy.
   c. genetic engineering.
   d. drug therapy.

17. A procedure by which areas of the brain are removed or destroyed in order to control severe abnormal behaviors is called:
   a. psychosurgery.
   b. shock therapy.
   c. electroconvulsive therapy.
   d. personality therapy.

PRACTICE TEST II:

18. Biomedical therapies:
   a. are the most common therapies used by clinical psychologists.
   b. are reserved for the less severe types of behavioral disorders.
   c. presume that many disorders result from improper nutrition, food additives, or exposure to toxic environmental chemicals.
   d. use drugs, shocks, or surgery to improve the client's functions.

19. The eclectic approach to therapy:
   a. first fragments the personality and then reconstructs it.
   b. is controversial because of its connection to the paranormal world of psychic phenomena.
   c. mixes techniques of various theoretical perspectives.
   d. is based on the teachings of Horatio Eclectic, a Danish therapist who promoted meditation as a therapeutic technique.

20. The basic premise of psychodynamic therapy is the notion that abnormal behavior is:
   a. repressing normal behaviors that need to be uncovered.
   b. the result of the ego repressing the superego.
   c. rooted in unresolved past conflicts, buried in the unconscious.
   d. the result of the ego failing to gain access to consciousness.

21. According to Freud, neurotic symptoms are caused by:
   a. defense mechanisms.
   b. anxiety.
   c. inappropriate choices.
   d. contingency contracting.

22. What technique is used in psychoanalysis to help the patient remember the experiences of a past relationship?
     a. transcendence
     b. transference
     c. translation
     d. transrotation

23. What happens to the reaction to alcohol following aversive conditioning for alcoholism?
     a. The reaction takes on the response associated with the aversion.
     b. There is no longer a craving for the alcohol.
     c. There is a fear of the alcohol.
     d. The alcohol becomes a source of anxiety.

24. The emphasis in humanistic approaches to therapy is on:
     a. environmental control over actions.
     b. probing for unresolved hidden conflicts that arose long ago.
     c. discovering the unreasonableness of one's thoughts.
     d. personal choice and responsibility.

25. According to the text, in rational-emotive therapy, the therapist challenges the client's:
     a. defensive views of the world.
     b. self-centered views of the world.
     c. paranoid views of the world.
     d. irrational views of the world.

26. Which of the following approaches to treatment takes the view that it is primarily the responsibility of the client to make needed changes?
     a. behavioral therapy
     b. rational-emotive therapy
     c. humanistic therapy
     d. psychoanalytic therapy

27. In humanistic therapy, unconditional positive regard is provided to the client:
     a. as a reinforcement when goals have been met.
     b. as part of the contingency contract.
     c. no matter what the client says or does.
     d. to help resolve inner conflicts.

28. According to the text, which of the following therapies is most closely associated with the concepts of freedom, values, and the meaning of human existence?
     a. behavioral therapy
     b. rational-emotive therapy
     c. humanistic therapy
     d. existential therapy

29. As compared with individual therapy, group therapy gives the client:
     a. insight into his or her unconscious ideas.
     b. automatically performed fresh new habits.
     c. impressionistic feedback from others.
     d. logically correct thinking, free from delusions.

30. According to the text, chlorpromazine is most commonly used in the treatment of:
     a. mood disorders.
     b. anxiety disorders.
     c. schizophrenia.
     d. bipolar disorder.

31. According to the text, which drug is used to help prevent future occurrences of the behavioral disorder that it is used to treat?
    a. Valium
    b. lithium
    c. chlorpromazine
    d. Librium

32. Antidepressant drugs improve the mood of depressed patients by:
    a. increasing the activity of the autonomic nervous system.
    b. suppressing the function of certain neurotransmitters.
    c. increasing the speed of neural transmission.
    d. increasing the concentration of certain neurotransmitters.

33. According to the text, which of the following types of treatment is rarely, if ever, still used?
    a. electroconvulsive shock therapy
    b. antipsychotic drugs
    c. psychotherapy
    d. psychosurgery

34. According to the text, which of the following would suggest that you had chosen a good therapist or style of therapy?
    a. You feel somewhat afraid of the therapist.
    b. You don't need to put effort into the therapy.
    c. You feel no particular sense of progress.
    d. You are involved in the therapy.

─────────

PRACTICE TEST III: Conceptual, Applied, and Challenging Questions

35. Based on the descriptions in the text, if you were having trouble adjusting to the death of a friend, who would you be most likely to see?
    a. psychiatrist
    b. psychoanalyst
    c. psychiatric social worker
    d. counseling psychologist

36. Charles is the director of guidance at a student mental-health clinic. He holds a degree appropriate to his position, so he must hold a doctorate or masters degree in:
    a. psychiatric social work.
    b. counseling psychology.
    c. clinical psychology.
    d. educational psychology.

37. Dr. Prober has clients explore their past by delving into the unconscious using dream interpretation and free association. Dr. Prober practices:
    a. existential therapy.
    b. cognitive therapy.
    c. behavioral therapy.
    d. psychodynamic therapy.

38. Which problem below is least likely to be treated with aversive conditioning?
    a. substance (drug) abuse
    b. depression
    c. smoking
    d. alcoholism

39. _____ is the basis for behavioral approaches to therapy.
   a. Removing negative self-perception
   b. Emphasizing personal responsibilities
   c. Understanding the unconscious mind
   d. Training new habits

40. Peggy, a 17-year-old client of Dr. Ertle, explains, "I answered a question wrong in history class and made a perfect fool of myself." In response, Dr. Ertle says "Is it important for you to be perfectly competent in every area of your life?" Dr. Ertle is using:
   a. behavioral therapy.
   b. rational-emotive therapy.
   c. humanistic therapy.
   d. existential therapy.

41. If a therapist asks you to act out some past conflict or difficulty in order to complete unfinished business, he or she most likely is using:
   a. behavior therapy.
   b. existential therapy.
   c. rational-emotive therapy.
   d. gestalt therapy.

42. Helen is in therapy with a psychotherapist to work through her feelings about her recent broken engagement. She is telling her therapist that she really didn't love her fiancé, and that she realized how different she and her fiancé are. Suddenly, her therapist says, "Helen, I heard the words that you just said, but they don't tell the same message that your facial expression and other nonverbal cues do. See if you can sense the differences." Helen's therapist is most likely:
   a. a gestalt therapist.
   b. a psychoanalytic therapist.
   c. a client-centered therapist.
   d. a behavioral therapist.

43. Generalizing from the discussion in the text, both humanistic and psychoanalytic approaches to therapy are more appropriate for clients who are:
   a. highly verbal.
   b. severely disordered.
   c. experiencing sexually related disorders.
   d. reluctant to converse with someone else.

44. Recently a student was assaulted. Since then, she is nervous, overreacts to ordinary stimuli, and has trouble getting to sleep. Her psychiatrist prescribes a drug for her, which most likely is:
   a. an antianxiety drug.
   b. an antidepressant drug.
   c. an antipsychotic drug.
   d. an analgesic drug.

45. Which of the following types of treatment appears actually to *cure* the disorder, so that when the treatment is discontinued the symptoms tend not to recur?
   a. antipsychotic drugs
   b. antidepressant drugs
   c. antianxiety drugs
   d. chlorpromazine

46. Today, electroconvulsive shock treatment (ECT) is usually reserved for severe cases of:
   a. mania.
   b. schizophrenia.
   c. depression.
   d. panic attack.

47. Electroconvulsive therapy (ECT):
   a. relieves the patient from severe depression.
   b. has been used since about 1910.
   c. is used in preference to drug therapy.
   d. can be administered by clinical psychologists.

48. During a therapy session, Richard explores an image of his home that he had in a dream. The therapist asks him to say what the house feels, to express the unfinished business of the house. Richard's therapist is most likely:
   a. a psychoanalyst.
   b. a group therapist.
   c. an existential therapist.
   d. a gestalt therapist.

49. Carlos and his therapist spend much of their time discussing issues arising from deep religious and philosophical questions. Often the question of the meaning of life comes up, and other concerns about the real meaning of human self-determination are discussed. Carlos is working with:
   a. a behavioral therapist.
   b. a psychoanalyst.
   c. an existential therapist.
   d. a group therapist.

50. Sally has prepared a list of experiences that run from the most frightening to the least frightening. She has prepared a _____, and her therapist is probably a _____.
   a. systematic desensitization; behavioral therapist
   b. hierarchy of fears; behavioral therapist
   c. systematic desensitization; humanistic therapist
   d. hierarchy of fears; humanistic therapist

51. Which of the following statements about the effectiveness of psychotherapy is most accurate?
   a. Research has been unable to determine conclusively which of the many forms of therapy is most beneficial.
   b. Behavioral therapy is more effective because it works with the most serious of problems.
   c. Humanistic and psychoanalytic approaches work only when the client is highly verbal and economically well-off.
   d. Psychotherapy is no more effective than the passage of time in the treatment of psychological problems.

Essay Questions

Essay Question 13.1: *The Effectiveness of Psychotherapy*

Recite ❑
Review ❑

Describe the reasons why you think that psychotherapy works. Draw upon the principles of psychology that have been discussed in previous chapters, such as learning principles, theories of development, and theories of personality, to explain why you think it is effective.

Essay Question 13.2: *Should Electroconvulsive Therapy Be Banned?*

Describe the advantages and disadvantages of electroconvulsive therapy. Do you think that it should be banned from use? Explain your answer.

Cultural Idioms

Recite ❑
Review ❑

p. 480

prom: a big formal dance for U. S. high school students who are about to graduate

formals: fancy evening dresses (formal gowns) that girls wear to proms

ear-to-ear grin: huge smile

shimmied: danced enthusiastically

high-stepping: elegant

cut in: in formal dances, a way of politely changing partners in the middle of a song

flat-out boogied: danced to rock and roll

long nightmare of insanity: they had suffered for a long time from serious psychological disorders

long-term drug therapy: taking a drug for a long time

p. 482

Samaritan: a person who helps others

knock that out of your head: change that thought

rest her soul: "God rest her soul," a common expression that people say when talking about someone who is dead

this rotten therapy: Sandy is saying that her therapy is worthless

p. 485

no pat answer: no easy or predictable answer

p. 487

Psalm 23: a familiar passage from the Old Testament portion of the Bible

Shalom: the Hebrew word for "peace"

underpopulation problem: There would not be enough people in the world (because so many people would die); the author is making a joke, because in reality the world has an overpopulation problem

p. 488

Virtual Therapy: therapy that seems real, but is, in fact, on a computer screen

virtual reality: A reality that seems "real" but is not; "virtual reality" is computer reality; By wearing special helmets with small TV screens inside them, people feel, for example, that they are experiencing being up high, when in fact they are sitting in a chair at ground level.

Vietnam veterans: soldiers who fought in the Vietnam War (1954–1975); these soldiers often returned home with many psychological problems because of the horrors that they witnessed and participated in

World Wide Web sites: places on the Internet

online chats with a service provider: interactive discussions on the Internet

p. 489

poker chip: In the card game of poker, money is often bet using flat round tokens, called poker chips

play money: fake money, used by children

National Rifle Association: a group of people who believe that there should be very little governmental control over access to guns

gun control: the political movement that aims to limit access to guns

p. 491

"Lost your mittens? You naughty kittens! Then you shall have no pie!": These are lines from a familiar children's story, called the "Three Little Kittens."

p. 493

to act out that rage: to express your anger

ganging up on him: acting against him

mumbo-jumbo: nonsense

p. 498
Color-Blind: a term for people who have trouble distinguishing different colors; in addition, it has come to mean someone who relates to people as individuals, not as members of certain races or ethnic groups
passive aggressive: indirect ways of expressing hostility; for example, instead of telling a friend that you are mad, you "forget" to return his library book for him

p. 500
insane asylum: old term for a mental hospital

p. 501
Kurt Vonnegut: author who is well-known for his descriptions of the craziness of war
Newsweek: popular weekly news magazine
Prozac; Zoloft; Paxil: controversial new drugs used to treat depression and other disorders
all-purpose mood booster: a drug that will make anyone feel happier, whether or not they have a problem
Washington State Board of Psychology: the professional group that oversees psychologists in the state of Washington

wonder drugs: drugs that act miraculously, such as antibiotics

p. 503
One Flew Over the Cuckoo's Nest: a novel by Ken Kesey, made into a movie, which contains a frightening scene of electroshock therapy

capital punishment: the death penalty; putting someone to death for his or her crime
questionable procedure: an activity that seems wrong

p. 504
cure-all: something that will fix all problems
civil rights: the idea that all people should be treated equally and with respect and dignity
National Institute of Mental Health (NIMH): the U. S. government agency that studies psychological disorders
telephone "hotlines": a phone number that you can call to talk about your problems; there is always someone who will answer the phone; you don't have to give your name and the help is free. For example, if a woman has a boyfriend who hits her, she can call a special number for help.
college crisis center: a place where students can telephone for help in emergencies

p. 505
nontraditional students: college students who are older than 25

p. 506
no breach of etiquette: not rude

p. 507
self-help shelves of bookstores: the area of a bookstore that has books for people who want to learn more about how to fix their personal problems

p. 509
prom-goers: people who attend a formal dance called a prom

Detailed Chapter Outline

This detailed outline contains all the headings in Chapter 14: Social Psychology. If you are using the SQ3R method, then an examination of the outline is the best way to begin your survey of the chapter.

Survey ❏
Question ❏

Prologue: The Death of a Princess
Looking Ahead

Attitudes and Social Cognition
Forming and Maintaining Attitudes
    Classical Conditioning and Attitudes
    Operant Conditioning Approaches to Attitude Acquisition
Persuasion: Changing Attitudes
    Message Source
    Characteristics of the Message
    Characteristics of the Target
The Link Between Attitudes and Behavior

> **Pathways Through Psychology:** Ann Altman,
> Advertising Executive

Social Cognition: Understanding Others
    Understanding What Others Are Like
    Impression Formation
Attribution Processes: Understanding the Causes of Behavior
Biases in Attribution: To Err Is Human

> **Exploring Diversity:** Attributions in a Cultural Context: How
> Fundamental Is the Fundamental Attribution Error?

Recap, Review, and Rethink

Social Influence
Conformity: Following What Others Do
    Groupthink: Caving in to Conformity
Compliance: Submitting to Direct Social Pressure

Applying Psychology in the 21st Century:
Producing Good Decisions in the Air: Helping People to Work Together More Effectively

Obedience: Obeying Direct Orders

Recap, Review, and Rethink

Prejudice and Discrimination
The Foundations of Prejudice
Working to End Prejudice and Discrimination

Recap, Review, and Rethink

Positive and Negative Social Behavior
Liking and Loving: Interpersonal Attraction and the Development of Relationships
> *How Do I Like Thee? Let Me Count the Ways*
> *How Do I Love Thee? Let Me Count the Ways*
> *Tracing the Course of Relationships: The Rise and Fall of Liking and Loving*
> *The Decline of a Relationship*

Aggression and Prosocial Behavior: Hurting and Helping Others
> *Hurting Others: Aggression*
> *Instinct Approaches: Aggression as a Release*
> *Frustration-Aggression Approaches: Aggression as a Reaction to Frustration*
> *Observational Learning Approaches: Learning to Hurt Others*
> *Helping Others: The Brighter Side of Human Nature*

The Informed Consumer of Psychology: Dealing with Anger Effectively

Recap, Review, and Rethink
Looking Back
Key Terms and Concepts

➤ Now that you have surveyed the chapter, read **Looking Ahead**, pages 608–609. What questions does the Chapter seek to answer?

Question ❏
Read ❏

Concepts and Learning Objectives

These are the concepts and the learning objectives for Chapter 14. Read them carefully as part of your preliminary survey of the chapter.

Survey ❑

Concept 1: Attitudes are composed of affective, behavioral, and cognitive components. People attempt to maintain a consistency between their attitudes and behavior. We form schemas to help us categorize people and events in the world around us and to help predict the actions of others.

1. Define attitudes, and describe how they develop and are maintained.

2. Explain how attitudes are changed through persuasion, and describe how attitudes and behavior influence one another.

3. Describe the main principles of social cognition, including schemas, impression formation, attribution, and biases.

Concept 2: Social influence includes behaviors that result from the actions of others, as found in conformity, compliance, and obedience.

4. Define social influence and conformity, and describe the factors that influence conformity.

5. Define compliance, and describe how the foot-in-the-door technique, the door-in-the-face technique, and other sales tactics lead to compliance.

6. Describe Milgram's study of obedience to authority and its results.

Concept 3: Prejudice is a consequence of stereotyping, and both create challenges for people living in a diverse society.

7. Define prejudice, and describe its relationship to stereotyping and discrimination.

8. Explain how prejudice originates and what can be done to minimize its impact.

Concept 4: The study of liking and loving has revealed a number of factors that influence the degree of friendship between people. Aggression involves the intention to hurt another. Prosocial behavior involves helping others.

9. Define interpersonal attraction, and describe the factors that contribute to friendship and liking.

10. Describe the efforts that have been made to understand love, and outline the stage sequence for the development and decline of relationships.

11. Define aggression, and compare the instinct, frustration-aggression, and observational-learning theories of aggression.

12. Define prosocial behavior and altruism, and describe the factors that encourage or hinder bystanders from helping during emergencies.

Chapter Guided Review

There are several ways you can use this guided review as part of your systematic study plan. Read the corresponding pages of the text and then complete the review by supplying the correct missing key word. Or, you may want to complete the guided review as a means of becoming familiar with the text. Complete the review and then read the section thoroughly. As you finish each section, complete the **Recap and Review** questions that are supplied in the text.

Survey ❑
_____

Concept 1: Attitudes and Social Cognition

Survey ❑
Read ❑
Recite ❑
_____

- *What are attitudes, and how are they formed, maintained, and changed?*
- *How do we form impressions of what others are like and of the causes of their behavior?*
- *What are the biases that influence the ways in which we view others' behavior?*

Pages 513-524

[a] _____ is the study of how people's thoughts, feelings, and actions are affected by others. Attempts to persuade people to purchase specific products involves principles derived from the study of attitudes. [b]_____ are learned predispositions to respond in a favorable or unfavorable manner to a particular person, behavior, belief, or object. According to the [c] _____, attitudes have three components. The

[d] _____ component includes emotions about something, the

[e] _____ component consists of a predisposition or intention to act in a

certain way, and the [f] _____ component refers to the beliefs and thoughts we have about a person or object.

The formation of attitudes follows classical and operant learning principles. Attitudes can be formed by association, as soldiers who had been stationed in the Persian Gulf may develop negative attitudes about sand. Advertisers link products with a positive feeling or event so that the product will evoke the positive feeling in consumers. Attitudes can be reinforced positively or punished by the responses others may have to them, and a person may develop an attitude through **[g]** _____. This type of learning occurs when a person learns something through observation of others. Children learn prejudices through others by hearing or seeing others express prejudicial attitudes. Television, films, and other media also are means by which we develop attitudes vicariously.

Celebrity endorsements are meant to match the product with a particular type of person, and the celebrity must be believable and trustworthy, and must represent qualities that the advertisers want to project. Changing attitudes depends on these factors in persuasion. The source of the message can have major impact when the communicator is attractive and believable and has the appropriate expertise. In addition, the communicator must not appear to have an ulterior motive. The character of the message is also important, and when an unpopular message is presented, it will be more effective if both sides are presented. Fear-producing messages are also effective unless the fear is too strong and the message is ignored as a defense mechanism.

Another important component consists of the characteristics of the recipient. The intelligence of the recipient influences the ability to remember and recall the message, yet intelligent people are more certain of their opinions. Highly intelligent people tend to be more difficult to persuade. A small difference in persuadability exists between men and women, with women being slightly easier to persuade. The means by which the information is processed also has influence on the persuasion. **[h]** _____ occurs when the recipient considers the arguments involved. **[i]** _____ occurs when the recipient uses information that requires less thought. Central-route processing produces more long-lasting change. In some cases, a celebrity may detract from a central-route message by causing the recipient to focus on information other than the message. People high in the need for cognition employ central-route processing more than peripheral-route processing Advertisers are using demographic information about people to help target their advertisements. **[j]** _____ is a technique for dividing people into lifestyle profiles that are related to purchasing patterns.

Attitudes influence behavior, but the strength of the relationship varies. People do try to keep behavior and attitudes consistent. Sometimes, in order to maintain the consistency, behavior can influence attitudes. **[k]** _____ occurs when a person holds two *cognitions* (attitudes or thoughts) that are contradictory. In a classic experiment, participants were offered $1 to convince others that a boring task was interesting. Others were paid $20. Those paid a small amount actually changed their attitudes about the task because the small amount caused dissonance where the large amount did not. The individual is motivated to reduce the dissonance by (1) modifying one or both of the cognitions, (2) changing the perceived importance of one cognition, (3) adding cognitions, or (4) denying that the two cognitions are related. In cases where dissonance is aroused, the prediction is that behavior or attitudes will change in order to reduce the dissonance.

The area of social psychology called **[l]** _____ is focused on understanding how we develop our understanding of others and how we explain the behavior of others. Social cognition refers to the processes that underlie our understanding of the world. Individuals have highly developed schemas, or sets of cognitions, about people and experiences.

[m] _____ are important because they organize how we recall, recognize, and categorize information about others. They also help us make predictions about others.

[n]_____ refers to the process by which an individual organizes information about another person, forming an overall impression of that person. Information given to people prior to meeting them can have dramatic effects on how the person is perceived. Research has focused on how people pay attention to unusually important traits, called [o] _____, as they form impressions of others. Information-processing approaches have been used to develop mathematical models of how personality traits are combined to form impressions. Research suggests that we form a psychological average of the individual traits. As we experience people, our impressions become more complex. Schemas are susceptible to a variety of factors—like mood—that can influence the accuracy of our impressions.

[p] _____ attempts to explain how we take instances of behavior and decide the specific causes of a person's behavior. The first determination is whether the cause is situational or dispositional. [q] _____ result from the environment. A

[r] _____ is the person's internal traits or personality characteristics.

Since people do not always possess knowledge sufficient to make logical attributions, there are several biases in the way they are made. People tend to attribute other people's behavior to dispositional causes and their own behavior to situational causes. This bias is known as the

[s] _____. This bias is common because people tend to focus on the behaving person rather than the more stable situation, and when they consider their own

behavior, the changes in the environment are more noticeable. The [t] _____refers to our tendency to assume that if a person has some positive characteristics, then other positive traits are inferred, and if there are negative traits, other negative traits are inferred. The halo effect reflects *implicit personality theories*, theories that indicate how we think traits are grouped

together in individuals. The [u] _____ is the assumption that other people think just like you. The Exploring Diversity discussion examines whether the fundamental attribution error is the same across cultures. Because people account for behavior differently in different cultures, the error is not common in other cultures.

CONCEPT 2:   Social Influence

Survey ❏
Read ❏
Recite ❏

- **What are the major sources and tactics of social influence?**

Pages 525-532

The area called [a] _____ is concerned with how the actions of an individual affect the behavior of others.

In uncertain situations, we tend to look to the behavior of others to guide our own behavior.

[b] _____ is the change in behavior or attitudes that results from a desire to

follow the beliefs or standards of other people. An experiment by Solomon Asch demonstrated the power of the judgments of others on the perceptual judgments of an individual participant. The participant would hear the judgments about which one of three lines was identical to a fourth "standard" line, and even though the judgments were quite visibly wrong, the participant would conform to the judgments of the group (which were always uniformly the same). About 75 percent of the participants conformed to the group judgment at least once. Research since the time of Asch's experiment has found several variables that produce conformity:

- *The characteristics of the group* influence the judgment more if the group is attractive to the group members. Individuals that have a low social rank, or [c] _____, in the group are more likely to conform to the group.
- *The nature of the individual's response* conforms more when it must be made publicly.
- *The kind of task* influences conformity. The more ambiguous the task, the higher the conformity. If the individual is less competent, conformity is also higher.
- If *the group is unanimous*, pressures to conform are greatest. If people with dissenting views have a supporter, called a [d] _____, then conformity is reduced.

[e] _____ is a type of thinking in which group members share strong motivation to achieve consensus that leads them to lose the ability to critically evaluate alternatives. The group overrates its ability to solve problems and underrates contradictory information. The consequences of uncritical acceptance of a group decision are often negative.

The behavior that occurs in response to direct, explicit pressure to endorse a particular view or to behave in a certain way is called [f] _____. Several techniques are used by salespersons to get customers to comply with purchase requests. Several techniques have been described. One technique is called the [g] _____, in which a person agrees to a small request and is then asked to comply with a bigger request. Compliance increases when the person first agrees to the smaller request. The technique works because compliance to the small request increases interest. Another explanation suggests that self-perceptions are formed based on compliance to the initial request, and compliance to the larger request is a result of a desire to be consistent. The [h] _____ is the opposite of the foot-in-the-door technique. The door-in-the-face technique follows a large request with a smaller one, making the second request appear more reasonable. In a study, half the participants were willing to take on a small obligation after being asked to make a major commitment where only 17 percent of the control group agreed. The [i] _____, presents a deal at an inflated price, then a number of incentives are added. The [j] _____ is another method that creates a psychic cost by giving "free" samples. These samples instigate a *norm of reciprocity*, leading people to buy as a matter of reciprocation.

Compliance follows a request, but obedience follows direct orders. [k] _____ is defined as a change in behavior due to the commands of others. Obedience occurs in situations involving a boss, teacher, parent, or someone who has power over us. The classic study by Stanley Milgram involved participants administering shocks to people they thought to be other participants, supposedly testing to see if shocks would improve memory. The other participants were actually confederates of the experimenter. Researchers predicted that no more than 2 percent of the participants would administer the strongest shocks, but almost two-thirds of the participants gave the highest level of shock. Participants reported their reasons for giving the level of shock to be their belief that the experimenter was responsible for the ill effects of the shocks. The experiment has been criticized for establishing extreme conditions and for methodological reasons.

Concept 3: Prejudice and Discrimination

Survey ❑
Read ❑
Recite ❑

- *What is the distinction between stereotypes, prejudice, and discrimination?*
- *How can we reduce prejudice and discrimination?*

Pages 532-535

[a] _____ are the beliefs and expectations about members of groups held simply because of membership in the group. Stereotypes can lead to

[b] _____, the negative evaluation of members of a group that are based primarily on membership in the group rather than on the behavior of a particular individual. Common stereotypes are maintained concerning racial, religious, and ethnic categories. When negative stereotypes lead to negative action against a group or members of a group, the behavior

is called [c] _____. Stereotypes can actually cause members of stereotyped groups to behave according to the stereotype, a phenomenon known as [d] _____. Expectations about a future event increase the likelihood that the event will occur. People are also primed to interpret behaviors according to stereotypes.

The [e]_____ say that people's feelings about various groups are shaped by the behavior of parents, other adults, and peers. The mass media also provide a major source of information about stereotypes for both children and adults. According to

[f] _____, we use membership in groups as a source of pride and self-worth. We then inflate the positive aspects of our own group and devalue groups to which we do not belong. Other views suggest that prejudice arises from competition for scarce resources and that we categorize people on the basis of physical characteristics.

Psychologists have developed a number of techniques for reducing the negative effects of stereotyping. These include:

- *Increasing contact between the target of stereotyping and the holder of the stereotype.* The evidence shows that when people come into contact, they develop more accurate schemas. The contact must be intimate: individuals must be on an equal status, or there must be mutual dependence.
- *Making positive values more conspicuous* involves showing people the inconsistencies between the values they hold and the negative stereotypes. Values of equality and freedom are inconsistent with negative perceptions of minority group members.

- *Providing information about the objects of stereotyping.* This can be achieved through education and can increase the positive perceptions of people and explain puzzling behavior that may lead to stereotypes.
- *Reducing stereotype vulnerability.* Claude Steele suggests that African Americans suffer from stereotype vulnerability. This results when people accept society's stereotypes.

Concept 4: Positive and Negative Social Behavior

Survey ❑
Read ❑
Recite ❑

- **Why are we attracted to certain people, and what is the progression that social relationships follow?**
- **What factors underlie aggression and prosocial behavior?**

Pages 536-547

Another area of social influence is called **[a]** _____, which encompasses the factors that lead to positive feelings about others. Research on liking has identified the following factors as important in the development of attraction between people.

[b] _____ refers to the physical nearness or geographical closeness as a factor in development of friendship. Proximity leads to liking. **[c]** _____ also leads to liking. The more often one is exposed to any stimulus, the more the stimulus is liked. Familiarity with a stimulus can evoke positive feelings. **[d]** _____ influences attraction because we assume that people with similar backgrounds will evaluate us positively. This is called the **[e]** _____. We also assume that when we like someone, that person likes us in return. *Need complimentarity* refers to attraction that is based on the needs that the partner can fulfill. We may then be attracted to the person that fulfills the greatest number of needs. The **[f]** _____ was first proposed in the 1950s, and the evidence in support of it has been inconsistent. It does appear that people with complimentary abilities are attracted to one another. **[g]** _____ is a key factor if all other factors are equal. More attractive people tend to be more popular. Physical attractiveness may be the single most important factor in college dating.

For a long time, social psychologists considered research into love too difficult to conduct scientifically. Love is not merely a more intense liking, but differs from liking on qualitative grounds. An early effort by Zick Rubin involved a scale that was able to distinguish those who scored high on love from those who did not. High scorers were found to gaze at each other more and to have intact relationships six months after the test. Physiological arousal was hypothesized to characterize loving, and arousal for whatever reason was found to be attributed as a feeling of love for a person present at the time of arousal. This theory does explain that when someone is rejected or hurt by another, they may still feel themselves in love as a consequence of arousal.

Several kinds of love have been hypothesized, one being **[h]** _____ , which is an intense state of absorption in another person. Another is **[i]** _____ , which is strong affection that we have for someone with whom our lives are deeply involved.

Robert Sternberg has proposed that love is made of three components. The
[j] _____ includes feelings of closeness and connectedness; the
[k] _____ is made of the motivational drives related to sex, physical closeness, and
romance; and the [l] _____ encompasses the initial cognition that one loves
someone, and the long-term feelings of commitment to maintain love.

Relationships deteriorate for a number of reasons. One factor is the change in the judgments
about the partner's behavior. Forgetfulness that is initially charming may become "boorish
indifference." Communication may become disrupted. Decline follows a common pattern. The
first phase occurs when a person decides that the relationship cannot be tolerated. In the second
phase, the person confronts the partner and tries to determine if repair is possible. The next
phase is marked by a public acknowledgment that the relationship is being dissolved, and an
accounting is made to others. The fourth and last phase is "grave dressing," which is the major
activity of ending the physical and psychological relationship. The degree of distress
experienced depends upon what the relationship was like prior to the breakup. The number of
activities that were mutually shared and the expectation of the difficulty of entering a new
relationship influence the amount of distress experienced.

Drive-by shootings, carjackings, and abductions give a pessimistic impression of human
behavior. The helping behavior of many, however, counteracts the impression. Social
psychology seeks to explain these extremes.

Aggression occurs at societal and individual levels, and the basic questions concern whether
aggression is inevitable or whether it results from particular circumstances.

[m] _____ is defined as the intentional injury of or harm to another person.

Instinct theories explain aggression as the result of innate urges. Konrad Lorenz suggested
that aggressive energy is built up through the instinct of aggression and that its release is

necessary. The discharge of this energy is called [n] _____. Lorenz
suggested that society should provide an acceptable means of achieving catharsis, like sports.
There is no way to test this theory experimentally.

The frustration-aggression theory says that the frustration of a goal *always* leads to

aggression. [o] _____ is defined as the thwarting of a goal-directed
behavior. More recently the theory has been modified to suggest that frustration creates a
readiness to act aggressively. Actual aggression depends upon the presence of *aggressive cues*,
stimuli that have been associated in the past with aggression. In one experiment, the presence of
a rifle and a revolver increased the amount of aggression. Participants who had viewed a violent
movie were also more aggressive.

The observational learning view suggests that we learn to act aggressively by observing
others. Aggression is not inevitable and can be seen in terms of the rewards and punishments it
involves. In the example of a girl hitting a younger brother for damaging her toy, the instinct
theory would suggest that the act results from pent-up aggression; the frustration-aggression
theory would say that the frustration of not being able to play with the toy led to aggression; and
the observational theory would say that aggression had been previously reinforced.
Observational learning theory also suggests that the rewards and punishments received by a
model are important in the learning of aggression. This formulation has wide support.

[p] _____ refers to helping behavior. The prosocial behavior studied most by psychologists is bystander intervention. When more than one person witnesses an emergency, [q] _____, the tendency for people to feel that responsibility is shared among those present, increases. Latané and Darley developed a four-step model describing the process of helping others: The first step is the awareness that someone requires help. In the second step, the individual may look to the behavior of others and interpret their inaction as an indication that help is not needed. The third step involves assuming responsibility for taking action. If people with life-saving training are present, then those that have no training are less likely to help because they do not have expertise. The fourth step is deciding and implementing some form of help. Helping may be indirect, in the form of calling the police, or direct, in the form of giving first aid or driving the person to the hospital. A *rewards-costs approach* helps predict the nature of help given. The rewards of helping must outweigh the costs. Once the decision to help has been made, one actual step remains, that of giving help. In some cases people act altruistically. [r] _____ is helping behavior that is beneficial to others but may require self-sacrifice. Some people who intervene in situations and offer help may have personality characteristics that differentiate them from others. People high in *empathy* may be more likely to respond than others. Situational factors and mood may also affect helping behavior. Both good and bad moods appear to increase helping behavior.

➤ Now that you have surveyed, questioned, and read the chapter and completed the guided review, review **Looking Back**, pages 644–645.

Review ❑

➤ For additional practice through recitation and review, test your knowledge of the chapter material by answering the questions in the *Key Word Drill*, the *Practice Questions*, and the *Essay Questions*.

Key Word Drill

The following **Matching Questions** test the boldfaced and italicized key words from the text. Check your answers with the Answer Key in the back of the *Study Guide*.

Recite ❑

MATCHING QUESTIONS

_____ 1. attitudes

_____ 2. affect component

_____ 3. behavior component

_____ 4. cognition component

_____ 5. central route processing

_____ 6. peripheral route processing

_____ 7. cognitive dissonance

a. A predisposition to act in a way that is relevant to one's attitude.

b. Learned predispositions to respond in a favorable or unfavorable manner to a particular object.

c. That part of an attitude encompassing how one feels about the object of one's attitude.

d. Characterized by thoughtful consideration of the issues.

e. Characterized by consideration of the source and related general information rather than of the message itself.

f. The beliefs and thoughts held about the object of one's attitude.

g. The conflict resulting from contrasting cognitions.

_____ 8. impression formation

_____ 9. central traits

_____ 10. fundamental attribution error

_____ 11. halo effect

_____ 12. assumed-similarity bias

a. Tendency to think of people as being similar to oneself.

b. Major traits considered in forming impressions of others.

c. Organizing information about another individual to form an overall impression of that person.

d. A tendency to attribute others' behavior to dispositional causes but to attribute one's own behavior to situational causes.

e. An initial understanding that a person has positive traits is used to infer other uniformly positive characteristics.

_____ 13. foot-in-the-door technique

_____ 14. door-in-the-face technique

_____ 15. obedience

_____ 16. compliance

a. Behavior that occurs in response to direct social pressure.

b. Going along with an important request is more likely if it follows compliance with a smaller previous request.

c. A change in behavior due to the commands of others.

d. A large request, refusal of which is expected, is followed by a smaller request.

_____ 17. self-fulfilling prophecy

_____ 18. prejudice

_____ 19. stereotype

_____ 20. social identity theory

_____ 21. discrimination

a. Negative behavior toward members of a particular group.

b. Negative or positive judgments of members of a group that are based on membership in the group.

c. The expectation of an event or behavior results in the event or behavior actually occurring.

d. Beliefs and expectations about members of a group are held simply on the basis of membership in that group.

e. The view that people use group membership as a source of pride and self-worth.

_____ 22. passionate (or romantic) love

_____ 23. companionate love

_____ 24. intimacy component

_____ 25. passion component

_____ 26. decision/commitment component

a. The motivational drives relating to sex, physical closeness, and romance.

b. Feelings of closeness and connectedness.

c. The initial cognition that one loves someone, and the longer-term feelings of commitment.

d. The strong affection we have for those with whom our lives are deeply involved.

e. A state of intense absorption in someone that is characterized by physiological arousal, psychological interest, and caring for another's needs.

_____ 27. proximity

_____ 28. reciprocity-of-liking effect

_____ 29. need-complementarity hypothesis

_____ 30. prosocial behavior

_____ 31. diffusion of responsibility

_____ 32. rewards-costs approach

_____ 33. altruism

_____ 34. empathy

a. Helping behavior that is beneficial to others while requiring sacrifice on the part of the helper.

b. The hypothesis that people are attracted to others who fulfill their needs.

c. One person's experiencing of another's emotions, in turn increasing the likelihood of responding to the other's needs.

d. The tendency to like those who like us.

e. The tendency for people to feel that responsibility for helping is shared among those present.

f. Any helping behavior.

g. Nearness to another, one cause for liking.

h. The notion that, in a situation requiring help, a bystander's perceived rewards must outweigh the costs if helping is to occur.

Practice Questions

Test your knowledge of the chapter material by answering these **Multiple Choice Questions**. These questions have been placed in three Practice Tests. The first two tests are composed of questions that will test your recall of factual knowledge. The third test contains questions that are challenging and primarily test for conceptual knowledge and your ability to apply that knowledge. Check your answers and review the feedback using the Answer Key in the back of the *Study Guide*.

Recite ❑
Review ❑
_____

MULTIPLE CHOICE QUESTIONS

PRACTICE TEST I:

1. In the ABC model of attitudes, that part of an attitude encompassing how the person feels about the object of the attitude is:
    a. the behavior component.
    b. the cognition component.
    c. the affect component.
    d. the anxiety component.

2. The component of an attitude that refers to the beliefs and thoughts we hold about a particular object is called:
    a. affect component.
    b. manner component.
    c. behavioral component.
    d. cognitive component.

3.   Advertisers often try to link a product they want consumers to buy to a:
      a.   positive feeling or event.   c.   peripheral route.
      b.   cognition.   d.   dissonant stimulus.

4.   Fear-evoking advertising messages are most effective when:
      a.   they include advice for steps to avoid the described danger.
      b.   viewers' cognitive defense mechanisms are activated.
      c.   they reach a small and indifferent audience.
      d.   they frighten people into buying the product.

5.   Schemas serve as _____ for social cognitions.
      a.   organizing frameworks   c.   feeling-communicators
      b.   defenses against stereotypes   d.   insincerity whistle-blowers

6.   According to the text, when forming an impression of another person, people rely heavily on:
      a.   central tendencies.   c.   primary traits.
      b.   central traits.   d.   schematic tendencies.

7.   In Asch's classic (1951) conformity experiment, what was the bogus psychological task that
      subjects thought was the purpose of the study?
      a.   Measurement of males' arousal while they viewed photos of attractive nude women.
      b.   Taste quality judgments of several brands of peanut butter.
      c.   Estimation of time-interval durations.
      d.   Visual matching of lines to a standard-length line.

8.   The tendency for people to attribute others' behavior to dispositional causes and their own
      behavior to situational causes is known as:
      a.   ingroup versus outgroup error.   c.   dispositional attribution error.
      b.   fundamental attribution error.   d.   stereotypic attribution error.

9.   The classic demonstration of pressure to conform comes from a series of studies carried out in the
      1950s by:
      a.   B. F. Skinner.   c.   Philip Zimbardo.
      b.   Solomon Asch.   d.   Stanley Milgram.

10.   People working on tasks and questions that are ambiguous are more susceptible to:
      a.   inoculation.   c.   forewarning.
      b.   obedience.   d.   social pressure.

11.   A mail-order music sales "club" offers five CDs for one cent each (wow!), but the fine print of the
      agreement requires that you must later buy ten other CDs at full price. This sales tactic is called:
      a.   the foot-in-the-door technique.   c.   the Dutch auction technique.
      b.   the that's-not-all technique.   d.   the door-in-the-face technique.

12. The classic experiment demonstrating the power of authority to produce obedience was performed by:
   a. Albert Bandura.   c. Stanley Milgram.
   b. Solomon Asch.   d. B. F. Skinner.

13. Obedience becomes relatively more important than compliance or conformity in situations in which:
   a. the behavior is highly profitable.
   b. participants are all of relatively equal status.
   c. the requester has authority over the person receiving the request.
   d. social desirability is important to the participants.

14. When stereotypes are attributed to a particular group, the stereotype may induce members of that group to act in ways that confirm the stereotype. This is known as:
   a. the interdependent view of self.
   b. a self-fulfilling prophecy.
   c. reverse discrimination.
   d. the ingroup-outgroup bias.

15. The Bosnian concept of "ethnic cleansing" that results in genocide of unwanted groups reflects:
   a. reverse discrimination.   c. prejudice and discrimination.
   b. individualism.   d. deterrence.

16. Beliefs and expectations about members of groups held simply on the basis of their group membership are called:
   a. self-fulfilling prophecies.   c. stereotypes.
   b. culture.   d. contingencies.

17. Prejudices are typically based on:
   a. economic class.
   b. jealousy for the superior qualities of the other group.
   c. interdependent qualities.
   d. racial, ethnic, and religious categories.

18. All of the following are strong influences on the formation of friendships **except**:
   a. others who are like them.   c. others whom they see frequently.
   b. others who live nearby.   d. others who are exceptionally attractive.

19. According to many social psychologists, love represents:
   a. a greater quantity than liking.
   b. a different physiological state than liking.
   c. an emotion, unlike liking.
   d. essentially the same state as liking.

20. Which of the following elements does love have that liking does not?
   a. proximity   c. similarity
   b. complementarity   d. physical arousal

21. According to Sternberg, different types of love are made up of different quantities of:
    a. liking, loving, and commitment.
    c. emotion, motivation, and attraction.
    b. passion, compassion, and attraction.
    d. intimacy, passion, and commitment.

22. During _____ of a relationship on the decline, more and more friends and acquaintances of the affected couple are made aware of the demise of the relationship and the reasons for it.
    a. phase 1
    c. phase 3
    b. phase 2
    d. phase 4

23. The most recent formulation of the frustration-aggression theory states that frustration:
    a. always leads to aggression.
    b. arouses an innate need for catharsis.
    c. leads to aggression only when others are present.
    d. produces anger, leading to a readiness to act.

24. Prosocial is a more formal way of describing behavior that is:
    a. helping.
    c. innate.
    b. cathartic.
    d. aggressive.

PRACTICE TEST II:

25. Our negative and positive feelings about other people, objects, and concepts reveal which component of our attitude?
    a. cognitive
    c. affective
    b. intentional
    d. behavioral

26. One of the basic processes that underlies the formation and development of attitudes relates to learning principles. Which of the following learning methods best explains how attitudes are acquired?
    a. peripheral-route processing
    c. central-route processing
    b. classical and operant conditioning
    d. punishment

27. The advertising industry draws upon findings from _____ regarding persuasion.
    a. experimental psychology
    c. abnormal psychology
    b. psychometrics
    d. social psychology

28. Richard is on a diet. When he sees a piece of cake, Richard wants to eat it but knows that he shouldn't. Festinger called this:
    a. cognitive dissonance.
    c. tension reduction.
    b. cathartic interference.
    d. frustration-aggression.

29. The processes that underlie our understanding of the social world are called:
    a. social cognitions.
    c. central traits.
    b. schemas.
    d. stereotypes.

30. Impression formation is the process by which:
    a. an individual exaggerates the good personality traits of a stranger.
    b. drastic differences in people are determined by contrasting certain important traits.
    c. experiences create an overall picture of an individual and place him or her in a stereotypical ingroup.
    d. an individual organizes information about another individual to form an overall impression of that person.

31. Warm and cold are considered:
    a. attributions that have little impact on first impressions.
    b. central traits.
    c. stereotyped descriptions of men and women.
    d. the basis for ingroup-outgroup bias.

32. The task of _____ is to explain how people understand the causes of behavior.
    a. discrimination theory   c. attribution theory
    b. social cognition   d. directive-behavior theory

33. Conformity is a change in behavior or attitude brought about by:
    a. an increase of knowledge.
    b. a desire to follow the beliefs or standards of others.
    c. intense pressure to be a distinct individual.
    d. an insecure self-image.

34. Considering the discussion of gender differences in conformity, which of these individuals would be most likely to conform?
    a. a man
    b. a woman
    c. an individual who is familiar with the task at hand
    d. an individual who is unfamiliar with the task at hand

35. According to the text, a change in behavior that results from direct, explicit social pressure to behave in a certain way is called:
    a. conformity.   c. commission.
    b. congruence.   d. compliance.

36. What is the correct term for the technique in which a large request is asked, followed by expected refusal and later a smaller request?
    a. obedience   c. door-in-the-face technique
    b. social compliance   d. foot-in-the-door technique

37. The social influence technique of the not-so-free sample given in grocery stores involves:
    a. actually paying for the sample in the price of the groceries.
    b. being told that you are allowed a certain number of free samples before you must make a purchase.
    c. creating psychic costs that bring you around to purchasing a product because you feel you owe it to the store, even though you may not need the product.
    d. a cost of resisting the sample that is higher than giving in and buying the product.

38. In the Milgram study on obedience, those who were willing to "electrocute" the learner did so because:
    a. they thought the learner would not be hurt.
    b. they thought they would not be held responsible for injury.
    c. they thought the learner deserved the shocks.
    d. they thought they would be punished for noncompliance.

39. Stereotypes are:
    a. concepts that define the characteristics of an individual.
    b. actions taken against members of a group.
    c. judgmental attitudes about a person.
    d. beliefs about a person based on group membership.

40. The negative behavior toward an individual because of his or her membership in a particular group is known as:
    a. stereotyping.
    b. discrimination.
    c. prejudice.
    d. self-fulfilling prophecy.

41. Social identity theory claims that:
    a. we learn prejudices from observing others.
    b. we use group membership as a source of pride.
    c. outgroup biases determine how we think about the identity of others.
    d. we are likely to fulfill the expectation that others have of us.

42. Proximity is defined as:
    a. nearness to another person.
    b. a tendency to like those who like us.
    c. a tendency of those whom we like to like us.
    d. distance from another.

43. The text describes a popular questionnaire used by some social psychologists that contains items such as "I would do almost anything for (person's name to whom the individual completing the questionnaire is attracted)." "I think that (person's name) is unusually well adjusted." The questionnaire is designed to measure:
    a. proximity.
    b. companionate love.
    c. love and liking.
    d. need complementarity.

44. _____ love is a state of intense absorption in someone, with bodily arousal, mental interest, and care for the other's needs.
    a. The intimacy component of
    b. The decision/commitment component of
    c. Companionate
    d. Passionate (romantic)

45. During _____ of a relationship on the decline, one partner would be most likely to say, "How do you think we should reshape our relationship?"
    a. phase 1
    b. phase 2
    c. phase 3
    d. phase 4

46. The phase of a relationship on the decline, in which each partner copes with the demise of the relationship so that events associated with it appear reasonable and acceptable, is called:
    a. dyadic.
    b. ambivalent.
    c. grave-dressing.
    d. social.

47. Frustration is most likely to lead to aggression:
    a. in the presence of aggressive cues.
    b. immediately after being frustrated.
    c. during late adolescence.
    d. several hours after being frustrated.

48. Diffusion of responsibility can occur when:
    a. aggressive cues are present.
    b. the catharsis hypothesis is in effect.
    c. there is more than one bystander to an incident.
    d. innate behaviors are operative.

PRACTICE TEST III: Conceptual, Applied, and Challenging Questions

49. Which of the following statements represents a positive cognitive component of an attitude about green beans?
    a. I like green beans better than any other vegetable.
    b. Green beans are a tasty source of vitamins.
    c. Green beans grow on vines.
    d. I eat green beans regularly.

50. Many corporations link their products with beautiful women or strong, handsome men. Which of the following suggests that classical conditioning is being used to sell the product?
    a. They feel that the product will "sell itself" with this method.
    b. Companies believe that individuals will buy their product since only beautiful people will buy such good quality.
    c. The positive feelings associated with good-looking people will be paired with their products.
    d. They feel that beautiful men and women usually make the best salespeople.

51. A 5-year-old boy who overhears his father tell his mother that "Southerners are ignorant" may grow up to believe this opinion and adopt it as an attitude as a result of the process of:
    a. direct reinforcement.
    b. vicarious learning.
    c. cognitive dissonance.
    d. persuasive communication.

52. For a message that presents an unpopular viewpoint, if it presents both the communicator's point of view and an opponent's point of view, it is most likely to be:
    a. dangerous because it may cause people to disagree with the communicator.
    b. a one-sided message, because the communicator cannot possibly be fair.
    c. difficult for most audiences to grasp due to the need to present simple messages.
    d. more effective for the communicator because it appears to be more precise and thoughtful.

53. According to the text, if a target audience pays more attention to the celebrity doing the commercial than to the advertisement message, which processing route is being used the most by the audience?
    a. central-route processing
    b. circumference-route processing
    c. peripheral-route processing
    d. The message is not being processed.

54. Many variables influence the effectiveness of communication to create attitude change. In which of the following situations will the impact be the greatest?
    a. The recipient appraises the message with central route processing.
    b. The recipient of the message is male.
    c. The recipient appraises the message with peripheral route processing.
    d. The recipient is very intelligent.

55. According to Festinger's theory of cognitive dissonance, if a smoker holds the cognitions "I smoke" and "Smoking causes cancer," he or she should be motivated to do all of the following *except*:
    a. modify one or both cognitions.
    b. enter a stop-smoking program.
    c. make the attitudes consistent.
    d. change the importance of one cognition.

56. Of the following, the best example of cognitive dissonance is:
    a. stating that women should earn less money than men for doing the same job.
    b. exaggerating the merits of a product in order to promote sales.
    c. knowing that cigarette smoking is harmful, but doing it anyway.
    d. believing that handicapped people cannot hold good jobs and therefore not recommending them.

57. Which one of the following statements is the best example of dispositional-attribution bias?
    a. John is being good because the teacher is watching.
    b. Even though I am not feeling sociable, I will go to the party if you do.
    c. I become very anxious when criticized.
    d. Sue is staying up all night to study because she is a conscientious student.

58. Which of the following situations best describes a situational cause for the described behavior?
    a. Barbara straightens the guest room, which is normally a messy sewing room, because relatives will be staying at her house for a week.
    b. Chris helps an old lady across the street because he is always thoughtful.
    c. John, who is normally grumpy, frowns about an exam as he walks down the hall.
    d. Mindy is a punctual person who is on time for school every morning.

59. According to the text, the tendency to attribute others' behavior to dispositional causes but one's own behavior to situational causes is best illustrated by which of the following?
    a. The tendency toward this bias is infrequently expressed.
    b. This tendency is often reflected in newspaper columns such as "Dear Abby" and "Ann Landers."
    c. The tendency is rarely found in psychiatric patients who have been diagnosed with schizophrenia.
    d. This tendency applies to close friends, not to casual acquaintances.

60. An important concept that the fundamental-attribution bias illustrates about attributional processes is that:
   a. people make explanations about others that tend to be less flattering than the explanations they make about themselves.
   b. people sometimes observe their own behavior and make judgments about others on the basis of their own behavior.
   c. people tend to overrate the effect of situation on others.
   d. people tend to underrate the effect of situation on themselves.

61. Considering that Asch's experiment involved a perceptual judgment that was fairly obvious, what variable related to conformity does the experiment appear to contradict?
   a. The task variable—if an individual feels competent in a task, conformity is less likely.
   b. The characteristics of the group—the group members were completely unknown to the participants because the experiment was done blindly.
   c. The nature of the response—since the participants were allowed to write down an answer, there should have been little pressure.
   d. The nature of the group—since the group could not agree, the participant should have been freer to respond without pressure.

62. What measure may be most effective for reducing the tendency of people to conform in a group situation?
   a. Make sure all members value the group highly.
   b. Include lots of members in the group.
   c. Use a show of hands when voting.
   d. Use a secret ballot when voting.

63. According to the text, which of the following has been shown to affect the amount of conformity displayed by members of a group?
   a. obedience of each member of the group to the legal authority
   b. the kind of task the group is assigned
   c. the amount of individuality expressed by each person in the group, as measured by how they are dressed
   d. the consistency of the group's leader

64. Stereotypes differ from prejudices in that:
   a. stereotypes are beliefs that lead to prejudices, which are judgments.
   b. stereotypes must involve action against a group.
   c. prejudices must involve action against a group.
   d. prejudices are beliefs that lead to stereotypes, which are judgments.

65. Of the following, which factor is the best predictor of whether two people will be initially attracted to each other?
   a. similarity   c. proximity
   b. mere exposure   d. complementarity

66. According to Sternberg's theory of love, each of the following is a component of love except:
   a. intimacy.   c. decision/commitment.
   b. passion.   d. individuation/separation.

67. Instinct theorist Konrad Lorenz would argue that opportunities to exercise and play sports ought to be given to prisoners because they:
  a. provide models of prosocial behavior.
  b. present violent models to be seen and imitated by prisoners.
  c. enable natural aggressive energy to be released harmlessly.
  d. reduce the frustration that causes aggression.

68. According to Levinger, which of the following events seems to be an important reason for the decline of a relationship?
  a. a change in judgments about the meaning of the partner's behavior
  b. an increase in punishment of the partner
  c. turning to others for the needs that the partner used to fulfill
  d. an increase in discussions that are critical of the partner

69. Following the Oklahoma City bombing in April 1995, thousands of unpaid volunteers assisted at the site, thereby demonstrating:
  a. the fundamental attribution error.   c. altruism.
  b. diffusion of responsibility.   d. the halo effect.

Essay Questions

Essay Question 14.1: *The Consistency Between Attitudes and Behavior*

Recite ❏
Review ❏

  Much has been made of attitudes and behavior and how they may or may not be consistent. Describe a situation in which your attitudes and behavior may not have been consistent, and then compare the cognitive-dissonance explanation and the self-perception explanation of the situation.

Essay Question 14.2: *Conformity and Violence*

  What factors would be at work when prejudices erupt into violence against racial groups? Analyze the factors of conformity, obedience, and stereotyping, including ingroup and outgroup biases.

Activities and Projects

1. Think about how you became friends or acquaintances with the people you currently know. What roles were played by the following factors in the formation and maintenance of your relationships: proximity, mere exposure, similarity, physical attraction, the reciprocity-of-liking effect?

Recite ❏
Review ❏

2. Watch some prime-time television and keep a log of violent incidents. How many violent incidents can you count in one hour? What is the nature of the violence? Do you believe that television violence leads to real violence? Explain.

Cultural Idioms

Recite ❑
Review ❑

p. 512
cyberspace chat rooms: interactive discussions on the Internet

p. 513
Bill Cosby: comedian and star of a TV show called *The Cosby Show*
Rosie O'Donnell: TV talk show host and comedienne
Tiger Woods: professional golf player
Mariah Carey: popular singer

p. 514
legalized abortion: a controversial issue in the United States; one side says that all abortion is murder, and the other side says that women should be allowed to have safe and legal abortions

p. 515
Reeboks: a brand of athletic shoe
Shaquille O'Neal: a basketball superstar

p. 612
safer sex: sexual activities that minimize the risk of getting the AIDS virus

p. 516
Peter Pan peanut butter: a popular brand of peanut butter
theme parks: large amusement parks, such as Disneyland, popular as family vacation spots

p. 517
they would never touch it again: they would never use it again
to turn that around: change that result

p. 518
"Teflon president": Teflon is a coating that is used to make nonstick pans; thus, he was the Teflon president because no trouble "stuck" to him, no matter how many inappropriate things he said.

p. 521
student judiciary board: a group of students who make decisions about other students who have broken college rules; a student jury

p. 523
To Err Is Human: To make a mistake is something that all humans do; this is part of an expression: "to err is human, to forgive, divine," meaning that everyone makes mistakes, but only really extraordinary people can forgive other people
less attention-grabbing: less obvious

p. 525
confederates: people who are actually part of the experiment, not innocent participants

p. 526
founding fathers: A group of men who wrote the U. S. Constitution and designed the government
Caving in: giving in; being defeated by

p. 527
sales tactics: strategies that people use to try to sell things

p. 528
the approach: when a plane is getting near the airport, getting ready to land

cockpit decisions: decisions that the pilots make (pilots sit in the cockpit part of the plane)

p. 529
flight crews: the people who work together during an airplane's flight
voice recorder: Every plane has a tape recorder that records all the conversation in the cockpit; after a crash, workers find the recorder and listen to it, to help them discover why the plane crashed
rugged individualism: the idea that people have to act alone; pilots have traditionally had total power and control
out of your league: more than you can afford
field experiment: an experiment that is not done in a laboratory, but out in the world
allowance: in U. S. families, a certain amount of money that parents often give their children each week

p. 531
fraternity; sorority: organized groups of men (fraternities) and women (sororities) who live together or socialize together on college campuses
school segregation: school systems where African American students could not go to school with White students
Mafia-like mobsters: criminals
jive: the dialect of English spoken by some African Americans
"gay pride": slogan created by homosexuals to increase their visibility and self-esteem
"black is beautiful": slogan created by the Black Power movement to increase positive awareness about African Americans and their heritage

p. 534
Like father, like son: This common phrase means that a son will often be very similar to his father
school integration: fixing schools so that African Americans and Whites go to school together

p. 535
"disidentify" with academic success: stop trying to succeed academically

p.536
thee: an old form of the pronoun "you"

p. 537
birds of a feather flock together: a proverb that means that people who are similar are attracted to each other

p. 538
keep confidences: when someone tells you a secret, you don't tell anyone else
willing to make time: if a friend wants to spend time with you, you won't say no
full-blown love: genuine love; the author is making a joke here, because the phrase "full-blown" usually applies to a disease

p. 542
"grave-dressing" phase: literally, putting flowers on the grave of a dead person; here, it means thinking back over the relationship that has ended
Drive-by shootings: when someone in a moving car shoots someone who is standing on the street
carjackings: a violent way of stealing someone's car

p. 543
mounts it as a trophy: to have a dead animal embalmed in order to display it on a wall
Girl Scout: an organization for girls that emphasizes helping others
weeded out: eliminated

p. 545
bystander intervention: the help a stranger offers in a public emergency
an intern: a doctor

p. 547
boxing equipment: special stuffed balls and bags that boxers can hit as practice
Terminator 3: a violent movie

Timothy McVeigh: U. S. terrorist who hated the government and bombed a government building

p. 549

land mines: bombs that are buried in the ground that explode when a person walks on them

p. 550

tabloid press: newspapers that primarily report gossip; these newspapers are often sold in supermarkets near the cash registers.

ANSWER KEYS

■ CHAPTER 1: ANSWER KEY

GUIDED REVIEW		MATCHING		
Concept 1: [a] Psychology [b] Biopsychology [c] Experimental [d] Cognitive [e] Developmental [f] personality [g] Health [h] Clinical [i] Counseling [j] Educational [k] School [l] Social [m] Industrial-organizational [n] Consumer [o] cross-cultural [p] evolutionary psychology [q] clinical neuropsychology [r] environmental [s] forensic [t] sport and exercise [u] program	**Concept 2:** [a] models [b] structuralism [c] introspection [d] functionalism [e] Gestalt psychology [f] biological [g] psychodynamic [h] cognitive [i] behavioral [j] humanistic [k] free will. **Concept 3:** [a] scientific method [b] Theories [c] hypothesis [d] Operationalization [e] Archival research [f] Naturalistic observation [g] survey research [h] case study [i] Correlational research [j] experiment	[k] experimental manipulation [l] variables [m] treatment [n] experimental group [o] control group [p] independent variable [q] dependent variable [r] random assignment to condition [s] replication. **Concept 4:** [a] informed consent [b] experimental bias [c] Experimenter [d] Participant [c] placebo [f] significant outcome	1. c 2. a 3. e 4. d 5. b 6. a 7. d 8. c 9. e 10. b 11. e 12. d 13. a 14. c 15. b 16. d 17. c 18. e 19. a 20. f 21. b	22. b 23. c 24. e 25. a 26. d 27. e 28. f 29. c 30. a 31. d 32. b 33. d 34. c 35. e 36. b 37. g 38. a 39. f 40. c 41. b 42. f 43. d 44. e 45. a

Essay Question 1.1: Conceptual Perspectives

■ Identify the key principle of the perspectives you have chosen. For instance, in the psychodynamic perspective, one of the key principles is unconscious motivation. For the biological perspective, the focus is on the physiological and organic basis of behavior.

■ Offer a reason, perhaps an example, that illustrates why you like this perspective. Asserting that you just "liked it" or that "it makes the most sense" is not a sufficient answer.

■ Identify one or two perspectives that you clearly reject. Again, your response must be reasoned rather that asserted.

Essay Question 1.2: Deceptive Practices

■ Try to imagine yourself in this kind of situation—if you have had a similar experience (where you were deceptively manipulated) an example of your reactions would be appropriate.

■ Psychologists are now expected to avoid harm, which can include undue stress, and to inform subjects to the extent possible. Also, informed consent suggests that a subject may discontinue at any point.

■ In some cases there do exist alternatives, but in others, the only alternative is naturalistic observation, and the desired qualities of experimental research, such as establishing cause and effect relationships, are likely to be lost.

Multiple Choice Feedback:

Practice Test I:

1. b obj. 8 p. 4
a. Incorrect. Intuitive thought describes something other than an approach to collecting data, referring perhaps to thinking about intuitions.
*b. Correct. Scientists refer to their systematic methods for collecting and analyzing data as the scientific method.
c. Incorrect. Common sense is an approach available to all, and does not necessarily have the qualities of systematic and rigorous data collection and analysis associated with science.
d. Incorrect. Literature, art, and philosophy often construct theories of interpretation or truth, or may utilize theories to account for evil, and so on.

2. a obj. 2 p. 7
*a. Correct. Biopsychology is indeed specifically focused upon the biological basis of behavior, though it may make contributions to all the other alternatives.
b. Incorrect. This describes the focus of developmental psychology.
c. Incorrect. This describes the interests and research focus of social psychology.
d. Incorrect. This describes the work of clinical psychology.

3. a obj. 2 p. 16
*a. Correct. Psychodynamic psychology follows a coherent conceptual perspective.
b. Incorrect. Cross-cultural psychology involves a collection of approaches.
c. Incorrect. Experimental psychology involves a collection of theoretical approaches, though all utilize experimental methods.
d. Incorrect. Counseling psychology involves a wide range of approaches.

4. d obj. 2 p. 8
a. Incorrect. Counseling psychology is dedicated to providing counseling to clients in need.
b. Incorrect. Health psychology may utilize such tests, but its focus is upon the understanding of healthy lifestyles and the promotion of health.
c. Incorrect. Personality psychologists do utilize testing and evaluation processes, but in the service of their research on personality structure and theory.
*d. Correct. The clinical psychologist is predominantly focused upon testing and evaluation as a basis for diagnosis and treatment of psychological disorders.

5. b obj. 2 p. 8
a. Incorrect. Parenting skills comprise only a minor interest of developmental psychology.
*b. Correct. "Development" refers to growth, maturation, and change through life.
c. Incorrect. Peer relationships and marriage comprise only a minor interest of developmental psychology.
d. Incorrect. This too may be considered only a minor interest of developmental psychology.

6. b obj. 2 p. 10
a. Incorrect. Experimental psychologists, among other activities, conduct controlled experiments, typically in laboratory settings.
*b. Correct. Program evaluation is a major interest to psychologists involved in school settings.
c. Incorrect. Forensic psychologists are involved primarily in evaluating jury processes and utilizing that evaluation for making recommendations to attorneys.
d. Incorrect. Cognitive psychologists research how people think and solve problems.

7. d obj. 5 p. 14
a. Incorrect. Freud did not have a laboratory, and his work began in the 1880s.
b. Incorrect. The APA was founded long after the beginning of psychology.
c. Incorrect. James established a lab in 1875 and some students conducted research in it.
*d. Correct. Wundt is given this credit because of his 1879 laboratory, complete with funding and graduate students.

8. d obj. 4 p. 12
a. Incorrect. The effort must involve more than social psychologists.
b. Incorrect. Studies demonstrating the importance of cultural diversity may help, but they will not remedy the situation.
c. Incorrect. Being sensitive to ethnic origins of one's clients is important, but it will not remedy the problem.
*d. Correct. The only way to solve the problem of too little diversity is to recruit more individuals from diverse backgrounds.

9. c obj. 6 p. 15
a. Incorrect. This statement is completely associated with Gestalt psychology.
b. Incorrect. This statement is completely associated with Gestalt psychology.
*c. Correct. This statement reflects the Gestalt view that the mind organizes perceptions as it adds information to them.
d. Incorrect. This statement is completely associated with Gestalt psychology.

10. b obj. 6 p. 15
a. Incorrect. This was an import from Germany.
*b. Correct. She coined the term "gifted" and also studied many women's issues.
c. Incorrect. Freud recognized this, as has everyone since.
d. Incorrect. This was pioneered by June Etta Downey.

11. d   obj. 7   p. 16
a.   Incorrect. The cognitive model is focused on understanding thought processes.
b.   Incorrect. The psychodynamic model is focused upon understanding the role of unconscious motivation and primitive forces in behavior.
c.   Incorrect. The behavioral model is focused upon understanding how behavior is conditioned and modified by stimuli and reinforcements.
*d.   Correct. The biological model does examine the role of genetics in all aspects of human behavior.

12. a   obj. 8   p. 22
*a.   Correct. And of all these people, not one called the police.
b.   Incorrect. Wrong number.
c.   Incorrect. Wrong number.
d.   Incorrect. Wrong number.

13. d   obj. 8   p. 23
a.   Incorrect. Naturalistic observation (not explanation) does not have a prescribed step of formulating an explanation.
b.   Incorrect. Experimenter bias is a phenomena related to unintended effects of the experimenter's expectations.
c.   Incorrect. The ethics review panel reviews proposed studies to ensure that they do not violate the rights of animal or human subjects.
*d.   Correct. The scientific method follows three steps, according to the text, and the formulation of an explanation is the second step.

14. a   obj. 8   p. 24
*a.   Correct. Typically, theories are general statements about the relationships among the phenomena of interest, while hypotheses are specific statements about those relationships.
b.   Incorrect. This is opposite the general trend.
c.   Incorrect. All theories are potentially provable, but hypotheses can be disproved.
d.   Incorrect. If it were a fact, it would not be a theory.

15. c   obj. 8   p. 23
a.   Incorrect. This would come second.
b.   Incorrect. This would follow formulating an explanation.
*c.   Correct. First, one must identify what shall be studied.
d.   Incorrect. The hypothesis can only be confirmed after data are collected.

16. d   obj. 9   p. 25
a.   Incorrect. Many data collected by science are not useful to anyone.
b.   Incorrect. Good scientific practice suggests that procedures be followed exactly, but this is not what is meant by operationalization.
c.   Incorrect. Good scientific practice suggests that variables be correctly manipulated, but this is not what is meant by operationalization.
*d.   Correct. Operationalization means that the hypothesis and its prediction have been put in a form that can be tested.

17. c   obj. 9   p. 27
a.   Incorrect. This is not a term in psychology, except as it may refer to the way students should study for exams.
b.   Incorrect. Perhaps a learning theorist may conduct a study to test the generalization of stimuli or responses, but such would not fit the definition given.
*c.   Correct. This definition describes a case study.
d.   Incorrect. This is not a term in psychology.

18. c   obj. 9   p. 28
a.   Incorrect. A dependent variable is that variable that changes as a result of changes in the independent variable.
b.   Incorrect. The experimenter manipulates variables during an experiment.
*c.   Correct. This defines a correlation.
d.   Incorrect. The manipulation of variables is sometimes called a treatment.

19. b   obj. 9   p. 29
a.   Incorrect. The public is unlikely to be impressed by such a move.
*b.   Correct. Experiments are the only procedures that provide a definitive account of causal relationships.
c.   Incorrect. Statistical methods can be applied to non-experimental procedures.
d.   Incorrect. Government funding is not contingent upon experiments, only sound research practices.

20. a   obj. 10   p. 29
*a.   Correct. The experiment must compare the behavior of one group to that of another in order to demonstrate that a specific variable caused the difference. The group receiving no treatment is one in which the variable should not change.
b.   Incorrect. A case may refer to one instance of the event.
c.   Incorrect. An independent variable is the variable that is changed in order to be "treated."
d.   Incorrect. All variables should be measured, even those in the "no treatment" group.

21. a   obj. 10   p. 30
*a. Correct. The dependent variable changes as a result of a change in the independent variable.
b.   Incorrect. The independent variable is manipulated by the experimenter, and it causes the change in the dependent variables.
c.   Incorrect. The control involves a group that does not receive the treatment, and the dependent variable is not expected to change.
d.   Incorrect. A confounding variable is a variable that causes change in the dependent variable unexpectedly.

22. c   obj. 7   p. 35
a.   Incorrect. This refers to someone who legally serves as a parent in absence of an actual parent.
b.   Incorrect. Subject expectations may result in the subjects behaving as they think the experimenter wants them to behave, thus spoiling the experiment.
*c. Correct. The subject signs the informed consent to indicate that he or she has been fully informed about the experiment, what to expect, and that he or she can withdraw at any time.
d.   Incorrect. This refers to when an experimenter accidentally reveals his or her expectations, thus gaining the compliance of the subjects and invalidating the outcome.

23. c   obj. 11   p. 37
a.   Incorrect. The placebo effect occurs whenever the subject responds to a non-existent independent variable (a sugar pill rather than medicine).
b.   Incorrect. When an experimenter accidentally reveals his or her expectations, thus gaining the compliance of the subjects and invalidating the outcome.
*c. Correct. Whenever the subject interprets expectations of the experimenter and behaves accordingly.
d.   Incorrect. The treatment condition is the group that is exposed to the independent variable.

24. b   obj. 11   p. 38
a.   Incorrect. The control is the group that does not receive the treatment.
*b. Correct. This is the term for a pill or any other event that has an effect only because the recipient thinks it should.
c.   Incorrect. The dependent variable changes as a result of a change in the independent variable.
d.   Incorrect. The independent variable is manipulated by the experimenter, and it causes the change in the dependent variable.

25. a   obj. 12   p. 34
*a. Correct. The ability of others to repeat a study is critical to its conclusions being accepted by the scientific community.
b.   Incorrect. Cheating is rare in the scientific community precisely because of the need to be able to replicate results.
c.   Incorrect. Not in this lifetime.
d.   Incorrect. The data are themselves probably suspect.

Practice Test II:
26. b   obj. 1   p. 4
a.   Incorrect. Not all psychologists seek to apply their knowledge to social situations.
*b. Correct. Mental processes and behavior constitute the area of study of psychology.
c.   Incorrect. Few psychologists appear to respect the ideas of Freud.
d.   Incorrect. Only special areas of psychology are interested in animal behavior.

27. c   obj. 3   p. 7
a.   Incorrect. Experiments are conducted by almost every major specialty of psychology.
b.   Incorrect. Cognitive psychology is very interested in studying learning and any other process related to mental life.
*c. Correct. Cognitive psychology began as a subspecialty of experimental psychology, though it is now a specialty in its own right.
d.   Incorrect. It is the other way around.

28. d   obj. 3   p. 8
a.   Incorrect. Forensic psychologists study legal issues.
b.   Incorrect. Social psychologists study social behavior.
c.   Incorrect. Cognitive psychologists study how we understand the world and solve problems.
*d. Correct. Health psychologists are focused on health issues such as obesity.

29. b   obj. 3   p. 9
a.   Incorrect. Relationships with others and the influence of others does influence the scope of therapy, but researching these questions is not a concern of counseling psychologists.
*b. Correct. Social psychologists are quite interested in exploring topics of the influence of others on individuals and the way relationships affect our behavior.
c.   Incorrect. Relationships with others and the influence of others does have a role in understanding abnormal behavior, but researching these questions is not a concern of clinical psychologists.
d.   Incorrect. Relationships with others and the influence of others does influence health and wellness, but researching these questions is not a focal concern of health psychologists.

30. d   obj. 4   p. 10
a.   Incorrect. Social psychologists are not interested in the insanity laws of the state.
b.   Incorrect. Counseling psychologists are not interested in the insanity laws of the state.
c.   Incorrect. Clinical psychologists are not interested in the insanity laws of the state.
*d. Correct. Forensic psychologists study legal issues and behavior.

31. c   obj. 3   p. 10
a.   Incorrect. This is of interest to physiological and health psychology.
b.   Incorrect. The ethics involved in experimentation affect every psychologist and would be of interest to all, though primarily to experimental psychologists.
*c. Correct. Environmental psychologists claim the study of crowding as their domain.
d.   Incorrect. The determination of program effectiveness is the domain of psychologists concerned with program evaluation.

32. c   obj. 2   p. 11
a.   Incorrect. Figure 1–2 shows 22% self-employed.
b.   Incorrect. Figure 1–2 shows 9% in private not-for-profit institutions.
*c. Correct. Figure 1–2 shows 33% in colleges or universities.
d.   Incorrect. Figure 1–2 shows 19% in private for-profit institutions.

33. d   obj. 5   p. 15
a.   Incorrect. This is probably an issue for existential and humanistic psychology.
b.   Incorrect. This was structuralism's concern.
c.   Incorrect. The neurological psychologist would be more interested in neuron function.
*d. Correct. The functionalists were primarily interested in the adaptive work of the mind.

34. c   obj. 6   p. 15
a.   Incorrect. Much too early.
b.   Incorrect. This is the date for Wundt's laboratory.
*c. Correct. Gestalt psychology has maintained a steady, though small, interest in perceptual processes since its founding in the early 1900s.
d.   Incorrect. The 1950s is more likely to be associated with the peak of behaviorism and the early beginnings of cognitive psychology.

35. a   obj. 7   p. 17
*a. Correct. Not only was he the first, but he was the founder of the perspective called behaviorism.
b.   Incorrect. Abraham Maslow and Carl Rogers share this honor.
c.   Incorrect. Since this has to do with the mind, Watson probably would reject such an association.
d.   Incorrect. Not only does it have to do with the mind, psychoanalysis attends to the unconscious mind, a double error for Watson.

36. b   obj. 7   p. 16
a.   Incorrect. Cognitive psychologists would view these as information-processing errors.
*b. Correct. Psychodynamic psychologists are interested in issues of the unconscious.
c.   Incorrect. Biological psychologists would be more interested in the tongue itself.
d.   Incorrect. Humanistic psychologists would want the person to accept the conscious intent of the slip of the tongue.

37. a   obj. 7   p. 16
*a. Correct. Dreams provide important insight into these subconscious forces because the powers that inhibit their expression are weakest during sleep.
b.   Incorrect. This reflects the interests of humanistic psychology more than psychoanalysis.
c.   Incorrect. This is an area of study of cognitive psychology.
d.   Incorrect. Biopsychology is concerned with inherited characteristics and their role in behavior.

38. c   obj. 8   p. 23
a.   Incorrect. True, this is done in survey research, but it happens elsewhere too, making another alternative better.
b.   Incorrect. True, this is done in case study research, but it happens elsewhere too, making another alternative better.
*c. Correct. The scientific method incorporates the other methods listed in the alternatives, and identifying questions of interest is recognized as one of the key steps of the method.

d.   Incorrect. True, this is done in experimental design, but it happens elsewhere too, making another alternative better.

39.   b   obj. 9   p. 24
a.   Incorrect. This is the answer in reverse.
*b.   Correct. Hypotheses are testable versions of theories, and predictions are testable versions of explanations.
c.   Incorrect. Both hypothesis and prediction are operationalizations of broader concepts of theory and explanation.
d.   Incorrect. Both hypothesis and prediction are operationalizations of broader concepts of theory and explanation.

40.   b   obj. 2   p. 26
a.   Incorrect. A case study focuses on one or a few individuals to gain an in-depth description of a given phenomena.
*b.   Correct. This is one technique of surveyors.
c.   Incorrect. An experiment utilizes more exacting controls and would probably not use this technique.
d.   Incorrect. Archival research involves the researchers using information that has been stored in a library, in an electronic form, or in some other form of data storage.

41.   c   obj. 2   p. 26
a.   Incorrect. Archival research involves searching records and libraries.
b.   Incorrect. Correlational research involves a statistical analysis of pairs of data sets.
*c.   Correct. One means of naturalistic observation is to blend into the situation and be unnoticed.
d.   Incorrect. An experiment requires careful subject selection and control of variables.

42.   d   obj. 2   p. 29
a.   Incorrect. This statement is true, and it suggests the strongest possible positive correlation.
b.   Incorrect. This statement is true, and it reflects the least amount of relationship whatsoever.
c.   Incorrect. If a correlation is not 0.0, then it tells us about the relationship; if 0.0, then it tells us that there is no relationship.
*d.   Correct. Only experiments can scientifically demonstrate cause and effect relationships.

43.   c   obj. 10   p. 30
a.   Incorrect. This is called the control group, not the variable.
b.   Incorrect. This is the experimental or treatment group.
*c.   Correct. A variable is any behavior or event in an experiment that can be changed, either directly or indirectly.
d.   Incorrect. This is a subject.

44.   b   obj. 10   p. 31
a.   Incorrect. Not knowing the subjects does not mean that potential biases resulting from other factors would not influence the selection.
*b.   Correct. Only a selection by chance will ensure random assignment of subjects.

c.   Incorrect. Knowing the subjects may result in biased assignment to groups.
d.   Incorrect. The factors of the experiment should not influence the assignment of subjects to a condition.

45.   b   obj. 10   p. 30
a.   Incorrect. The dependent variable changes as a result of the independent variable, not the manipulation of the experimenter.
*b.   Correct. The experimenter manipulates levels of the independent variable in order to test its effect on the dependent variable.
c.   Incorrect. The control variable should not be manipulated.
d.   Incorrect. The confounding variable is one that unexpectedly appears and has an effect on the dependent variable.

46.   d   obj. 10   p. 35
a.   Incorrect. Moral refers to "right and wrong" and thus does not quite fit this context.
b.   Incorrect. Behavioral scientists may choose not to undertake a kind of study on personal, religious grounds, but this does not describe the relationship to subjects.
c.   Incorrect. Professional standards refers to a broad category of standards that apply to the conduct of a professional.
*d.   Correct. The American Psychological Association has published a set of ethical guidelines that are meant to ensure the welfare of subjects in research.

47.   a   obj. 11   p. 35
*a.   Correct. Sometimes subjects can determine the expected outcomes from the experimental conditions themselves, so deception is used to disguise the conditions.
b.   Incorrect. Confusing the subject is not usually an intent of the design of research.
c.   Incorrect. Deception may help eliminate the effect of experimenter expectations, but only the double-blind procedure guarantees their elimination.
d.   Incorrect. They are confused enough.

48.   d   obj. 13   p. 38
a.   Incorrect. Often it is the goal of a confederate to influence subjects in an experiment.
b.   Incorrect. An experiment must have dependent variables; otherwise, it would not be an experiment.
c.   Incorrect. The placebo effect can occur under many conditions, even the double-blind procedure.
*d.   Correct. This is the only procedure that will guarantee that both subject and experimenter expectations are eliminated.

Practice Test III:
49.   d   obj. 1   p. 7
a.   Incorrect. A social psychologists would more likely study the prosocial (helping) behaviors exhibited shortly after an earthquake.
b.   Incorrect. A consumer psychologist might be interested in the aspects of consumer behavior that are affected by a natural disaster.
c.   Incorrect. An educational psychologist might have an interest on how information regarding earthquakes could

be transmitted most effectively.

*d. Correct. A cognitive psychologist would be interested in memory phenomena, and an earthquake may have elements of phenomena such as the flashbulb memory.

50. a   obj. 1   p. 9
*a. Correct. The helping behavior studied by social psychologists is called prosocial behavior.

b. Incorrect. An environmental psychologist may be remotely interested in determining whether the climatic conditions influence prosocial behavior.

c. Incorrect. This would not be of interest to a clinical perspective.

d. Incorrect. This would not be of interest to an I/O psychologist.

51. d   obj. 3   p. 8
a. Incorrect. A social psychologist does not study traits directly, but may be interested in the role of groups as they influence such a trait.

b. Incorrect. The only interest that a cross-cultural psychologist may have is whether the trait was common to more than one cultural group.

c. Incorrect. An educational psychologist would probably be interested in whether the trait could be acquired for learning purposes.

*d. Correct. The study of traits is specifically the domain of personality psychologists.

52. d   obj. 3   p. 10
a. Incorrect. A clinical psychologist could not offer this kind of consultation.

b. Incorrect. A school psychologist conducts assessment and recommends corrective measures for students.

c. Incorrect. A forensic psychologist is more interested in the legal system than in the hall system.

*d. Correct. Environmental psychologists examine factors like crowding and architectural design to understand the influences they may have on behaviors like aggression.

53. d   obj. 6   p. 14
a. Incorrect. Cognition is a specialty area of psychology and refers to how we perceive, process, and store information; it is not a method of investigation.

b. Incorrect. Though it may lead to some kind of "mind expansion," such is not the psychological research technique.

c. Incorrect. Perception refers to any processing of sensory stimuli.

*d. Correct. This does define the concept of introspection and the way that Tichener sought to utilize the procedure.

54. d   obj. 3   p. 9
a. Incorrect. This responses has the two types switched.

b. Incorrect. The school psychologist does more than promoting the needs of special students.

c. Incorrect. The difference is not one of a group versus the individual, as this option suggests.

*d. Correct. Both halves of this statement are indeed true, and they reflect the broadest formulation of the goals of the two areas.

55. b   obj. 6   p. 13
a. Incorrect. There is no evidence that the purpose was to enable mind-reading.

*b. Correct. Trephining for the purpose of letting evil spirits out has been the conclusion of most anthropologists, though it has never been shown that having a hole in one's head does not actually let the evil spirits in.

c. Incorrect. There is no evidence that the purpose of these holes was to increase telekinetic powers.

d. Incorrect. Since mental illness was probably viewed as possession by evil spirits, choice "b" is a better answer.

56. c   obj. 6   p. 15
a. Incorrect. These are the two early psychologists who were also female.

b. Incorrect. Freud was associated with psychoanalysis, and Wundt is frequently identified as a major contributor to structuralism.

*c. Correct. Both James and Dewey contributed to the development of functionalism, though James more often thought of himself as a philosopher.

d. Incorrect. These two men hold in common the founding of the earliest psychology laboratories, and both are considered responsible for the early development of the two early schools: James with functionalism, and Wundt with structuralism.

57. c   obj. 7   p. 17
a. Incorrect. The biological perspective is associated with genetic and organic aspects of behavior.

b. Incorrect. The psychodynamic perspective focuses on inner, primitive forces that are hidden in the unconscious and manifest through behavior.

*c. Correct. In the behavioral perspective, the environment plays a critical role as the source of stimuli and reinforcement.

d. Incorrect. The humanistic perspective is focused on the capacity of the individual to direct behavior from within.

58. d   obj. 4   p. 10
a. Incorrect. Should these various research interests lead to programs for change, then program evaluation may be related, but not centrally.

b. Incorrect. Only the aspect of work is relevant to I/O psychology.

c. Incorrect. To the extent that these may also be studied in various cultural contexts, there exists some similarity.

*d. Correct. The focus of Professor Chung is centered on issues that illustrate how genetics influence behavior.

59. b   obj. 6   p. 14
a.   Incorrect. While this may be part of an experiment, the subjects are not "doing" experimental psychology.
*b. Correct. The subjects are each engaging in introspection, that is, examining their own thought processes.
c.   Incorrect. Gestalt psychology may be interested in how these representations are formed, but this example does not support the view that the subjects are somehow engaged in Gestalt psychology.
d.   Incorrect. Functionalism was much more concerned with the processes that lead to adaption than to the internal processes of mental representation.

60. a   obj. 7   p. 16
*a. Correct. Since the biological perspective is interested in the common genetic inheritance that accounts for behavior, then cross-cultural studies would be of least interest except where they may show universal patterns or localized variations.
b.   Incorrect. The psychodynamic perspective is very interested in the cultural issues related to child development, dream symbolism, and other cultural artifacts.
c.   Incorrect. The cognitive perspective examines the different cultural patterns of such things as problem solving, perception, and language, among others.
d.   Incorrect. The behavioral perspective should be interested in the variations from one culture to another of stimuli and reinforcement.

61. c   obj. 7   p. 17
a.   Incorrect. These two perspectives are both highly deterministic.
b.   Incorrect. The behavioral approach is highly deterministic, while the humanistic approach is focused on free choices.
*c. Correct. Both of these approaches would accept self-determination in decision making.
d.   Incorrect. While the cognitive approach would allow for free will, the behavioral approach is highly determined.

62. a   obj. 7   p. 16
*a. Correct. This is one of the ways that a behavior may be determined, that is, by its passage from one generation to the next.
b.   Incorrect. This would suggest that something genetic was at work here, affecting more family members.
c.   Incorrect. If individual differences were key here, then violence would not be passed from one generation to another, instead appearing without regard to family influence.
d.   Incorrect. If conscious control of behavior were at work, then this generational violence would not be as likely.

63. c   obj. 9   p. 26
a.   Incorrect. Situational research is not a formal method of research.

b.   Incorrect. Archival research involves searching through records.
*c. Correct. This example describes a survey.
d.   Incorrect. An experiment requires control over variables.

64. d   obj. 9   p. 25
a.   Incorrect. There is no such thing as "delayed" naturalistic observation.
b.   Incorrect. A case study would involve in-depth analysis of one wedding.
c.   Incorrect. A survey requires living participants.
*d. Correct. The psychologist is searching "archives" and thus conducting archival research.

65. a   obj. 9   p. 27
*a. Correct. Case studies involve in-depth examinations of an individual or a group of individuals.
b.   Incorrect. Correlational data is data used to make comparisons between two variables.
c.   Incorrect. Dependent variables are found in experiments, not case studies.
d.   Incorrect. Since the examinations took place in the setting of therapy, this could not be considered naturalistic observation.

66. d   obj. 9   p. 27
a.   Incorrect. A survey involves many subjects.
b.   Incorrect. An experimental study would require greater controls and randomly selected subjects.
c.   Incorrect. Naturalistic observation would require that the executive be observed in his or her natural setting (perhaps during actual work).
*d. Correct. The collection of in-depth information is most like a case study.

67. c   obj. 9   p. 28
a.   Incorrect. Correlations cannot demonstrate causal relationships.
b.   Incorrect. The factors of additional experiences were not included in the statement of the correlation.
*c. Correct. The presence of one factor predicts the likelihood of the other factor being present too.
d.   Incorrect. This conclusion is beyond the evidence of the correlation.

68. d   obj. 10   p. 34
a.   Incorrect. No statistical test was mentioned or suggested in this scenario.
b.   Incorrect. The amount of light and the levels of stress would need to be operationalized from the very beginning.
c.   Incorrect. A hypothesis would already need to be in place for this series of studies to have any meaning.
*d. Correct. Often researchers will repeat their studies with slight variations as they test the limits of their theories.

69. c   obj. 10   p. 35
a.   Incorrect. This is not the correct phrase.
b.   Incorrect. This is not the correct phrase.
*c. Correct. Without spoiling the research, participants should

be fully aware of what they will encounter during the study.
d. Incorrect. This is not the correct phrase.

70. a obj. 11 p. 38
*a. Correct. The experimenter's anticipation of favorable results can lead to subtle (and not-so-subtle) clues like those just described.
b. Incorrect. In this procedure, she would not know which group of participants was before her.
c. Incorrect. Randomization applies to participant selection.
d. Incorrect. The placebo effect is a participant bias, not an experimenter bias.

71. a obj. 9 p. 23
*a. Correct. The first step after one has formulated a theory is to create a testable hypothesis.
b. Incorrect. One does not define correlation coefficients for specific studies.
c. Incorrect. True, but before collecting the data, it is necessary to define what data needs to be collected.
d. Incorrect. This will come after the data has been defined and collected.

72. d obj. 9 p. 23
a. Incorrect. "Dramatically" is not very well defined.
b. Incorrect. "Disgruntled" needs careful definition.
c. Incorrect. "Happy" is not well defined.
*d. Correct. Both the amount of physical exercise and the decline in heart-related disease can be measured and recorded.

73. b obj. 9 p. 24
a. Incorrect. If colors are a key to problem solving, then they must be very relevant.
*b. Correct. The hypothesis suggest that color-scheme influences tension, so varying the schemes would serve as the independent variable.
c. Incorrect. The level of tension is the dependent variable.
d. Incorrect. A confounding variable would be some factor not found in the design of the experiment.

74. a obj. 9 p. 24
*a. Correct. Tension would depend upon both the color scheme and the challenge of the problem.
b. Incorrect. A confounding variable would be some factor not found in the design of the experiment.
c. Incorrect. The color scheme is the independent variable.
d. Incorrect. Levels of stress are quite relevant to the hypothesis.

■ CHAPTER 2: ANSWER KEY

GUIDED REVIEW			MATCHING	
Concept 1:	Concept 2:	[c] reticular formation	1. a	18. f
[a] biopsychologists	[a] central nervous system	[d] thalamus	2. e	19. d
[b] neurons	(CNS)	[e] hypothalamus	3. c	20. a
[c] Dendrites	[b] spinal cord	[f] limbic system	4. b	21. e
[d] axons	[c] reflexes		5. d	22. g
[e] terminal buttons	[d] Sensory (afferent) neurons	Concept 4:		23. c
[f] myelin sheath	[e] Motor (efferent) neurons	[a] cerebral cortex	6. e	24. h
[g] resting state	[f] Interneurons	[b] lobes	7. a	25. b
[h] action potential	[g] peripheral nervous system	[c] motor	8. d	
[i] all-or-none law	[h] somatic division	[d] sensory	9. f	26. h
[j] synapse	[i] autonomic division	[e] association	10. g	27. e
[k] neurotransmitters	[j] sympathetic division	[f] hemispheres	11. b	28. a
[l] excitatory messages	[k] parasympathetic division	[g] lateralization	12. c	29. f
[m] inhibitory messages	[l] evolutionary psychology	[h] split-brain patients		30. b
[n] reuptake	[m] behavioral genetics	[i] endocrine system	13. b	31. g
		[j] hormones	14. e	32. c
	Concept 3:	[k] pituitary gland	15. c	33. d
	[a] central core	[l] biofeedback	16. d	
	[b] cerebellum		17. a	

Essay Question 2.1: The Benefits of Knowledge about the Brain

■ Knowledge of the brain leads to improved medical and psychological therapies of the injured and of stroke sufferers.

■ Knowledge about brain function should provide greater knowledge about behavior.

■ An understanding of neurotransmitter function can be applied to many phenomena, such as pain, drug abuse, healing processes, and thinking processes.

■ Knowledge of male and female differences will help us understand differences and similarities among individuals as well.

Essay Question 2.2: Ethics and Brain Research

■ Split brain research may actually create the phenomena observed, yet many people wish to use it to substantiate strong differences between left- and right-brain dominant individuals. Also, this research depends upon this operation.

■ The danger of transplanting tissue is not that it will create some monster, but that tissue needed may come from sources that raise questions, like fetal tissue.

■ You should identify moral and ethical reasons both for and against this research and related procedures.

Multiple Choice Feedback:

Practice Test I:

1.　　d　　obj. 2　　p. 48
a.　Incorrect. Cellular predators cannot be frightened.
b.　Incorrect. The only waving done in the body is with the hand.
c.　Incorrect. Indeed, each neuron has a unique number and distribution of dendrites, but this is not the purpose of the dendrites.
*d.　Correct. Dendrites act as the receivers for the neuron.

2.　　d　　obj. 2　　p. 48
a.　Incorrect. Glial cells are the cells that support neurons.
b.　Incorrect. The myelin sheath is the fatty substance that forms an insulating covering around axons.
c.　Incorrect. The soma is the cell body of the neuron.
*d.　Correct. Dendrites receive stimulation and axons convey information to the next neuron.

3.　　c　　obj. 3　　p. 50
a.　Incorrect. This is the end of the axon branches.
b.　Incorrect. This is the part that contains the nucleus and metabolic units of the neuron.
*c.　Correct. The word synapse even means gap.
d.　Incorrect. A refractory period is a period at the conclusion of an action potential during which the neuron cannot fire again.

4.　　b　　obj. 3　　p. 51
a.　Incorrect. Individual neurons do not exhibit the cognitive skill of "expectation."
*b.　Correct. Neurotransmitters lock into specific sites receptive to that type of neurotransmitter.
c.　Incorrect. All nerve impulses act according to the all-or-nothing law, thus this information would be irrelevant to the receiving neuron.
d.　Incorrect. If the neuron has the receptor sites, it always is affected by the neurotransmitter, whether it is firing or not.

5.　　d　　obj. 3　　p. 52
a.　Incorrect. The need for new production is minimized by reuptake.
b.　Incorrect. This is not reuptake.
c.　Incorrect. Some neurotransmitters are metabolized by enzymes in the synaptic cleft–this material may return to the neuron in another manner other than reuptake.
*d.　Correct. Reuptake is the reabsorption of unmetabolized neurotransmitters in the area of the synapse.

6.　　b　　obj. 5　　p. 56
a.　Incorrect. Actually, it could be said that the role of the brain is to override reflexes.
*b.　Correct. Many messages that are processed reflexively simply pass through the spinal cord and are not sent to the brain.

c.　Incorrect. We do indeed sense the stimuli that cause reflexes, but can actually have them without our sensation of them.
d.　Incorrect. However, without a motor system, we would not have reflexes. There is a better alternative.

7.　　d　　obj. 5　　p. 56
a.　Incorrect. Reflexes are inborn and not learned.
b.　Incorrect. They involve the peripheral nervous system and often the central nervous system.
c.　Incorrect. Some reflexes may not involve the central nervous system.
*d.　Correct. Fundamentally, reflexes are processed through the spinal cord or by lower parts of the brain.

8.　　c　　obj. 5　　p. 56
a.　Incorrect. These kinds of processes involve the brain and the voluntary muscles.
b.　Incorrect. The autonomic nervous system is not responsible for spinal cord functions.
*c.　Correct. Of these choices, this is the only one included in the activity controlled by the autonomic system.
d.　Incorrect. The spinal reflexes involve the somatic system and voluntary muscles.

9.　　a　　obj. 5　　p. 57
*a.　Correct. The sympathetic system activates and energizes responses necessary for survival and quick responses, thus it shuts down the digestive processes.
b.　Incorrect. The sympathetic response increases heart rate in order to increase energy availability.
c.　Incorrect. The sympathetic response increases sweating in order to provide for additional cooling.
d.　Incorrect. The sympathetic response increases pupil size, probably to increase the available detail about the visible world.

10.　　b　　obj. 8　　p. 64
a.　Incorrect. Memory is stored here.
*b.　Correct. Most of the structures related to pleasure, especially the hypothalamus and the amygdala, are part of the limbic system.
c.　Incorrect. The medulla controls things like breathing.
d.　Incorrect. The cerebellum controls voluntary muscle movements.

11.　　a　　obj. 8　　p. 62
*a.　Correct. This is the medulla's role.
b.　Incorrect. The cerebellum helps control voluntary muscle and coordinate movement.
c.　Incorrect. The thalamus is responsible for handling incoming and outgoing messages for the cortex.
d.　Incorrect. The hypothalamus is responsible for regulating basic biological needs.

12.   a   obj. 9   p. 66
*a.   Correct. The convolutions increase the surface area of the cortex dramatically.
b.   Incorrect. Mapping helps the neuroscientists, but not the brain itself.
c.   Incorrect. Lateralization arises due to the cerebrum being divided into two hemispheres.
d.   Incorrect. Hemispheric dominance is not related to the amount of surface area of the cortex.

13.   d   obj. 9   p. 70
a.   Incorrect. This area of the cortex is responsible for processing incoming sensory information.
b.   Incorrect. This area of the cortex is responsible for processing sensory information coming from the body areas.
c.   Incorrect. This area of the cortex is responsible for processing outgoing muscle information.
*d.   Correct. Quite a lot of the cortex is devoted to processing thought, once associated with associations, and thus called association area.

14.   c   obj. 9   p. 70
a.   Incorrect. "Lexia" is related to the root of lexicon and refers to words.
b.   Incorrect. Aphasia refer to processing errors, like the inability to process language or the inability to produce speech.
*c.   Correct. The root of *praxia* means "practice" or "action."
d.   Incorrect. Paraplegia refers to paralysis in two limbs.

15.   a   obj. 10   p. 73
*a.   Correct. Logic, sequential, and many language functions are controlled in the left hemisphere.
b.   Incorrect. The right hemisphere has been associated more with spatial relations and emotional expression.
c.   Incorrect. The frontal lobes are more responsible for planning and physical movement.
d.   Incorrect. The occipital lobes are devoted to visual experience.

16.   c   obj. 10   p. 73
a.   Incorrect. This is true of most right-handed people.
b.   Incorrect. This is true of most right-handed people.
*c.   Correct. The left hemisphere is associated with language and reasoning.
d.   Incorrect. This applies to both left- and right-handed people.

17.   a   obj. 12   p. 78
*a.   Correct. Of the four choices, the use of biofeedback to treat impotence has not proven effective.
b.   Incorrect. Biofeedback can be used effectively to treat headaches.
c.   Incorrect. Biofeedback can be used effectively to treat high blood pressure.

d.   Incorrect. Biofeedback can be used effectively to treat skin temperature problems.

Practice Test II:
18.   c   obj. 1   p. 48
a.   Incorrect. Like any other cell, activity requires energy.
b.   Incorrect. Actually, they regenerate only in special circumstances.
*c.   Correct. Many neurons have very long axons, and the axons are attached to specific targets.
d.   Incorrect. Neurons live no longer than any other cells.

19.   a   obj. 3   p. 49
*a.   Correct. During the absolute refractory period prior to returning to the resting state, the neuron cannot fire.
b.   Incorrect. There is no "rising phase."
c.   Incorrect. Reuptake occurs continuously and independently of the firing of the neuron.
d.   Incorrect. The nerve impulse never reverses (though many neurons have feedback loops).

20.   d   obj. 3   p. 50
a.   Incorrect. A chemical process takes place between neurons.
b.   Incorrect. An electrical process carries the message within the neuron.
c.   Incorrect. The parts are reversed, try: chemically between neurons and electrically within each neuron.
*d.   Correct. A neurotransmitter (chemical) passes between neurons, while an electrical charge moves down neurons.

21.   b   obj. 4   p. 52
a.   Incorrect. Acetylcholine is not associated with depression.
*b.   Correct. A deficiency of acetylcholine has been associated with Alzheimer's disease.
c.   Incorrect. Underproduction of dopamine has been associated with Parkinson's disease.
d.   Incorrect. Huntington's chorea is a hereditary disorder of the basal ganglia.

22.   b   obj. 4   p. 54
a.   Incorrect. Endorphins do not have a role in the contraction of muscle tissue.
*b.   Correct. Endorphins are similar in structure to opiates, and have similar pain-relieving properties.
c.   Incorrect. Endorphins do not have a role in smoothing and coordinating muscle movements.
d.   Incorrect. Endorphins do not have a role in alertness and emotional expression.

23.   d   obj. 4   p. 53
a.   Incorrect. The answer is insufficient dopamine.
b.   Incorrect. The answer is insufficient dopamine.
c.   Incorrect. The answer is insufficient dopamine.

*d.   Correct. The answer is insufficient dopamine, and these symptoms are linked to Parkinson's Disease.

24.   c   obj. 5   p. 56
a.   Incorrect. This is the central nervous system.
b.   Incorrect. Neurons with myelin sheath can be found in both the central and peripheral nervous system.
*c.   Correct. The peripheral system consists of the voluntary and involuntary control systems of the body.
d.   Incorrect. It also includes afferent neurons.

25.   c   obj. 5   p. 57
a.   Incorrect. Fight and flight are the options available whenever the sympathetic system is activated.
b.   Incorrect. Both sympathetic and parasympathetic divisions are part of the peripheral system.
*c.   Correct. The sympathetic division arouses and the parasympathetic division calms.
d.   Incorrect. Both divisions are necessary to survival (thus helpful?).

26.   a   obj. 7   p. 60
*a.   Correct. EEG stands for electroencephalograph, or electrical recording of the brain.
b.   Incorrect. MRI scans use the magnetic fields of the object being scanned.
c.   Incorrect. CAT scans use computers and x-ray images.
d.   Incorrect. PET scans utilize recordings of the metabolism of isotopes of a special glucose.

27.   b   obj. 9   p. 62
a.   Incorrect. The cerebellum helps smooth and coordinate muscle movement.
*b.   Correct. The medulla controls unconscious functions like breathing and blood circulation.
c.   Incorrect. The pons helps transmit muscle information.
d.   Incorrect. The spinal cord helps relay muscle information.

28.   a   obj. 9   p. 66
*a.   Correct. The cortex is rich in axons and dendrites that are very close together, thus supporting rapid processing of large amounts of information.
b.   Incorrect. The medulla controls unconscious functions like breathing and blood circulation.
c.   Incorrect. The cerebellum helps smooth and coordinate muscle movement.
d.   Incorrect. The limbic system includes a number of structures related to emotion, motivation, memory, pain, and pleasure.

29.   a   obj. 9   p. 69
*a.   Correct. The parts of the little man are represented in proportion to the amount of surface area devoted to the feature controlled by that area.
b.   Incorrect. Motor functions are controlled by both hemispheres.

c.   Incorrect. The opposite is true.
d.   Incorrect. This is true, but this alternative is referring to the sensory cortex, not the motor cortex.

30.   d   obj. 9   p.70
a.   Incorrect. Compared to the association areas, the motor area is quite small.
b.   Incorrect. Compared to the association areas, the somatosensory area is quite small.
c.   Incorrect. Compared to the association areas, the sensory areas are quite small.
*d.   Correct. All the areas not specifically associated with an identified function, like sensation, motor activity, or language, are called association areas.

31.   a   obj. 10   p. 73
*a.   Correct. The right side of the brain is often associated with more global processing and emotional or expressive information.
b.   Incorrect. The left side of the brain is more often associated with linear and logical processing.
c.   Incorrect. The occipital lobes are necessary for the visual information about art and dance, but their role is more specialized to visual processing.
d.   Incorrect. The temporal lobes are primarily responsible for hearing, and may contribute well to understanding dance and music, but less well to processing other forms of art.

32.   c   obj. 10   p. 73
a.   Incorrect. The frontal lobe is responsible for higher-order thought and planning, among other activities.
b.   Incorrect. The left side of the brain is more often associated with linear and logical processing.
*c.   Correct. The right side of the brain is often associated with more global processing, emotional or expressive information, and pattern recognition and spatial memory.
d.   Incorrect. The temporal lobes are primarily responsible for hearing.

33.   c   obj. 11   p. 77
a.   Incorrect. Injury to these glands seems to affect only sexual performance and reproduction.
b.   Incorrect. The pancreas contributes to insulin production
*c.   Correct. The pituitary is considered the master gland, and it contributes both to growth and to stress responses.
d.   Incorrect. The thyroid influences metabolism, and damage to it has only indirect consequences elsewhere.

34.   d   obj. 12   p.79
a.   Incorrect. In order to begin, one must attend to the directions of then person attaching the machine, but that is the only suggestion required.
b.   Incorrect. This may be part of the process, but it is not the technique.

c.   Incorrect. This may be feedback, but it is not biofeedback.
*d.   Correct. The technique does involve focus upon electronic signals and attention to changes in them.

Practice Test III:

35.   d   obj. 2   p. 48
a.   Incorrect. The myelin sheath deteriorates and the axon is then exposed to stimulation from other axons.
b.   Incorrect. The myelin sheath deteriorates and the axon is then exposed to stimulation from other axons.
c.   Incorrect. The myelin sheath deteriorates and the axon is then exposed to stimulation from other axons.
*d.   Correct. The myelin sheath breaks down and loses its insulating capacity, allowing the short circuits to occur.

36.   c   obj. 2   p. 49
a.   Incorrect. Neurotransmitters are released at the synapse as a result of an action potential.
b.   Incorrect. This is the work of other structures in the cell body.
*c.   Correct. Some nourishment is brought to the cell body through the process of reverse flow.
d.   Incorrect. The action potential is regenerated in the refractory period by the sodium pump.

37.   b   obj. 3   p. 52
a.   Incorrect. Deactivation by enzymes in the receiving cell happens to all neurotransmitters.
*b.   Correct. Most are reabsorbed in the process called reuptake some are broken down by enzymes in the area surrounding the synapse.
c.   Incorrect. Some, but not most, are processed out of the body this way.
d.   Incorrect. None are absorbed by the receiving neuron.

38.   d   obj. 8   p. 64
a.   Incorrect. Thinking is associated with the frontal lobes.
b.   Incorrect. Waking is associated with the pons and the reticular formation.
c.   Incorrect. Emergency is associated with the sympathetic nervous system.
*d.   Correct. The limbic system is associated with emotions, as well as pain, pleasure, motivation, and memory.

39.   c   obj. 8   p. 63
a.   Incorrect. The hippocampus is associated with memory and motivation.
b.   Incorrect. The cerebral cortex is associated with thinking.
*c.   Correct. This describes the primary role of the hypothalamus.

d.   Incorrect. The cerebellum is responsible for smoothing and coordinating voluntary muscle activity.

40.   d   obj. 8   p. 64
a.   Incorrect. Damage here might affect motor behavior but not emotion, and the individual would probably have difficulty waking up from the coma.
b.   Incorrect. Damage here would affect breathing and circulation; however, emotional expression would be limited by the mobility of the heart-lung machine.
c.   Incorrect. The cerebellum is responsible for smoothing and coordinating voluntary muscle activity.
*d.   Correct. The limbic system is associated with emotions, as well as pain and pleasure, motivation, and memory.

41.   b   obj. 9   p.68
a.   Incorrect. Pleasure centers are in the limbic system.
*b.   Correct. The amount of surface area correlates to the sensitivity or refinement of control of the associated function.
c.   Incorrect. This is true only in the motor cortex.
d.   Incorrect. Damage to the somatosensory area may affect all the bodily sensation for the corresponding body area, but it will not affect the motor control.

42.   b   obj. 9   p. 70
a.   Incorrect. The neuromuscular area is not very close to the area affected.
*b.   Correct. The areas affected must have been association areas because they are important for planning.
c.   Incorrect. The damage described does not relate to damage to the somatosensory areas.
d.   Incorrect. The damage described does not relate to damage to the motor areas.

43.   a   obj. 9   p. 70
*a.   Correct. Wernicke's area is associated with the comprehension of speech.
b.   Incorrect. Lou Gehrig's disease does affect speech, but because it affects motor control-not the comprehension of speech.
c.   Incorrect. Broca's aphasia results in difficulty producing speech, while the sufferer may be able to understand the speech of others perfectly well.
d.   Incorrect. Phineas Gage did not have a disease, he had an accident that effectively gave him a frontal lobotomy.

44.   b   obj. 10   p. 73
a.   Incorrect. Successive functioning sounds a lot like sequential functioning.
*b.   Correct. In broad terms, these two choices reflect the description of the styles of activity associated with the hemispheres.
c.   Incorrect. Successive functioning sounds a lot like sequential functioning.

d.   Incorrect. The choices are reversed.

45.   d   obj. 9   p. 70
a.   Incorrect. Probably not, though the terms have a technical ring to them.
b.   Incorrect. Actually, Wernicke's area is closely aligned with the sensory cortex and Broca's area is closely aligned with the motor cortex.
c.   Incorrect. Overeating would be associated with the hypothalamus and other limbic structures, while an irregular gait could be associated with motor cortex damage or damage to the cerebellum.
*d.   Correct. These choices describe the correct aphasias. Both aphasias have an effect on the production of speech.

46.   b   obj. 10   p. 75
a.   Incorrect. Just not true: Logic processing tends to occur in the left side of the brain for males and females.
*b.   Correct. Language is more localized in the left hemisphere in males.
c.   Incorrect. Not true, it may occasionally be dominant in left-handed people.
d.   Incorrect. Just not true: Spatial abilities tend to be processed in the right hemisphere for both males and females.

47.   b   obj. 10   p. 76
a.   Incorrect. The bundle of neural fibers called the corpus callosum has been severed in split-brain patients.
*b.   Correct. The bundle of neural fibers called the corpus callosum has been severed in split-brain patients.
c.   Incorrect. The bundle of neural fibers called the corpus callosum has been severed in split-brain patients, but not all the patients had damage to a hemisphere.
d.   Incorrect. The bundle of neural fibers called the corpus callosum has not been cut in all patients with epilepsy.

48.   d   obj. 2   p. 49
a.   Incorrect. Alzheimer's has been associated with a deficiency of acetylcholine.
b.   Incorrect. Parkinson's has been associated with an underproduction of dopamine.
c.   Incorrect. Multiple sclerosis involves the deterioration of the myelin sheath.
*d.   Correct. Also known as Lou Gehrig's disease.

49.   b   obj. 4   p. 53
a.   Incorrect. Alzheimer's disease does not come and go.
*b.   Correct. Parkinson's disease has been associated with a shortage of dopamine, and one of the symptoms is this on-and-off type of behavior.
c.   Incorrect. Multiple sclerosis involves the deterioration of the myelin sheath.
d.   Incorrect. Lou Gehrig's disease involves the failure of the reverse flow mechanism in the neurons.

50.   c   obj. 3   p. 51
a.   Incorrect. These kinds of reactions do occur in sensory messages, but they do not define the sensory message.
b.   Incorrect. These kinds of reactions do occur in motor messages, but they do not define the motor message.
*c.   Correct. This is what happens in inhibitory messages.
d.   Incorrect. The autonomic system utilizes both inhibitory and excitatory messages.

51.   c   obj. 9   p. 70
a.   Incorrect. Wernicke's aphasia involves inability to comprehend speech and difficulty producing speech.
b.   Incorrect. Lou Gehrig's disease is not associated with stroke.
*c.   Correct. The term for the inability to accomplish simple physical tasks like these is apraxia.
d.   Incorrect. Korsakoff's syndrome results from decades of alcohol abuse.

■ CHAPTER 3: ANSWER KEY

GUIDED REVIEW			MATCHING		
Concept 1:	[i] rhodopsin	[i] frequency theory of hearing	1. c	17. a	29. b
[a] sensation	[j] optic nerve	[j] semicircular canals	2. a	18. e	30. f
[b] perception	[k] optic chiasm	[k] otoliths	3. d	19. c	31. d
[c] stimulus	[l] tunnel vision	[l] Pheromones	4. e	20. b	32. a
[d] Psychophysics	[m] feature detection	[m] skin senses	5. b	21. d	33. c
[e] Absolute threshold	[n] trichromatic	[n] gate-control theory of pain			34. e
[f] Signal detection theory	theory of color vision		6. d	22. d	
[g] difference threshold	[o] Opponent-process	Concept 4:	7. f	23. c	35. d
[h] just noticeable difference	theory	[a] gestalt laws of organization	8. a	24. g	36. a
[i] Weber's law		[b] feature analysis	9. g	25. b	37. f
[j] adaptation	Concept 3:	[c] top-down processing	10. b	26. f	38. e
	[a] Sound	[d] Bottom-up processing	11. e	27. a	39. b
Concept 2:	[b] eardrum	[e] perceptual constancy	12. c	28. e	40. c
[a] visual spectrum	[c] middle ear	[f] depth perception	13. j		41. g
[b] cornea	[d] oval window	[g] binocular disparity	14. h		42. h
[c] pupil	[e] cochlea	[h] monocular cues	15. i		
[d] iris	[f] basilar membrane	[i] Visual illusions	16. k		
[e] retina	[g] hair cells	[j] Müller-Lyer illusion			
[f] rods	[h] place theory of	[k] Subliminal perception			
[g] cones	hearing				
[h] dark adaptation					

Essay Question 3.1 The Problem of Extra Senses

The major points that should be included in your answer:

- Discuss the importance of sensory selectivity—of sense organs being sensitive to limited ranges of physical stimuli.

- Though we would probably adjust to the differences, additional information might create duplications.

- Describe the things we would be able to hear, smell, taste, and feel if our sensory ranges were broader.

- Reflect on the possibility that our ability at sensory adaptation might have to increase.

Essay Question 3.2: Gestalt versus Feature Analysis

- The major point is perception of wholes versus perception of parts. Top-down processing and bottom-up processing may also be used to distinguish the two approaches.

- Phenomena such as perception of objects when parts are hidden from view and the reading of words without having to identify each letter are better explained by the gestalt approach. Identification of unusual objects by identifying and analyzing parts of the object is better accounted for by feature analysis.

Multiple Choice Feedback:

Practice Test I:
1. a   obj. 1   p. 85
*a. Correct. Sensory psychology focuses on sensation.
b. Incorrect. Perceptual psychology focuses on sensation and perception.
c. Incorrect. Gestalt psychology focuses primarily on perception.
d. Incorrect. Do not know of any such field.

2. d   obj. 2   p. 86
a. Incorrect. This defines a difference threshold.
b. Incorrect. This is referred to as the range of stimulation.
c. Incorrect. This would be some kind of maximum threshold.
*d. Correct. The absolute threshold is the smallest magnitude of a physical stimulus detectable by a sensory organ.

3. d   obj. 2   p. 89
a. Incorrect. The difference threshold would account for the initial detection of the new stimulus.
b. Incorrect. Sexual experience may alter his cognitive understanding of the ring, but not his sensory attention to it.
c. Incorrect. Actually, if this applies, it would be the top-down processing of ignoring the stimulus, as described in answer d.
*d. Correct. This phenomenon is called sensory adaptation.

4. a   obj. 3   p. 91
*a. Correct. The larger pupil allows more light to enter the eye.
b. Incorrect. The smaller the pupil, the less light enters the eye.
c. Incorrect. The pupil enlarges in order to allow more light to enter the eye.
d. Incorrect. The wavelength of light is not relevant to the size of the pupil.

5. a   obj. 3   p. 91
*a. Correct. The lens accommodates, or focuses, the image on the retina.
b. Incorrect. The lens may be constricted in some cases in order to focus the image, but this is not the term used to describe the process.
c. Incorrect. All sensory organs adapt to the level of stimulation, but the process of focusing is not known by this name.
d. Incorrect. Muscles contract to cause the lens to change its shape, but the process of focusing an image is not known by this name.

6. d   obj. 3   p. 93
a. Incorrect. Ganglion cells are found throughout the retina.
b. Incorrect. The concentration of rods is greater outside the fovea.
c. Incorrect. Bipolar cells are found throughout the retina.
*d. Correct. The fovea is recognized by its great concentration of cones, and these cones provide fine detail acuity.

7. b   obj. 3   p. 93
a. Incorrect. The cone provides fine detail.
*b. Correct. The periphery of the retina is rich in rods, and this is where peripheral vision occurs.
c. Incorrect. The fovea is used for detailed, focused vision.
d. Incorrect. This is the chemical in the rods that reacts to light photons.

8. d   obj. 4   p. 95
a. Incorrect. This kind of recognition of details occurs in other processing areas.
b. Incorrect. The fovea is responsible for this capability.
c. Incorrect. The discrimination of faces occurs in the association areas of the brain.
*d. Correct. Feature detection is responsible for pattern recognition.

9. b   obj. 5   p. 99
a. Incorrect. Gate control relates to pain perception.
*b. Correct. Trichromatic accounts for the three different color spectra to which the cones are responsive, while the opponent-process theory explains how four colors can be perceived with only three types of cones.
c. Incorrect. Place relates to hearing, and gate control to pain perception.
d. Incorrect. These are reversed.

10. c   obj. 6   p. 101
a. Incorrect. They are not connected to the basilar membrane.
b. Incorrect. Otoliths are found in the semicircular canal, not the middle ear.
*c. Correct. The bones transfer, focus, and amplify mechanical sound from the ear drum to the oval window.
d. Incorrect. Nothing can minimize these effects.

11. b   obj. 6   p. 102
a. Incorrect. This describes high-frequency, not low-frequency sound.
*b. Correct. Our perception of low frequency is low sound.
c. Incorrect. The decibel value applies to all sound, regardless of frequency.
d. Incorrect. Many pets can hear both higher and lower frequencies than their human attendants.

12. b   obj. 8   p. 105
a. Incorrect. Smell does not have four basic qualities of sensation.
*b. Correct. Smell and taste are known as the chemical senses.
c. Incorrect. They do not utilize the same area.
d. Incorrect. These sensations do not have opponent processes.

13. d   obj. 9   p. 108
a. Incorrect. Endorphins are neurotransmitters involved in reduction of the perception of pain.
b. Incorrect. Opiates are like endorphins and have similar effects on the neural pain messages.
c. Incorrect. Opponent processes are related to pain in the release of endorphins, and the persistence of their effects after the pain stimulus has subsided.
*d. Correct. This is the name of the theory of pain.

14. b   obj. 11   p. 111
a. Incorrect. This refers to feature detection.
*b. Correct. The gestalt psychologists suggested that people organize their perceptions according to consistent principles of organization based on figure/ground relationships and simplicity.
c. Incorrect. Though gestalt psychology may work in this fashion, this is not the foundation of gestalt psychology.
d. Incorrect. This shall remain a mystery for some time.

15. c   obj. 11   p. 111
a. Incorrect. In a figure/ground relationship, one instrument would stand out against the others.

b. Incorrect. The law of similarity applies to the similarity of items leading to their being grouped together.
*c. Correct. The fact that the orchestra creates a sound that is more complex than merely the sum of the sounds made by the individual instruments illustrates this concept.
d. Incorrect. Perceptual constancy applies to other phenomena altogether.

16. a   obj. 11   p. 114
*a. Correct. Top-down processing refers to processing that begins with a broad, general perspective and then completes details from this context.
b. Incorrect. Bottom-up processing builds the final picture from the details.
c. Incorrect. Perceptual constancy refers to our tendency to view an object as having a constant size, shape, color, or brightness even when we see it in different environments or from different points of view.
d. Incorrect. Feature analysis refers to detection of patterns in an array of neural activity.

17. d   obj. 14   p. 114
a. Incorrect. See answer d.
b. Incorrect. See answer d.
c. Incorrect. See answer d.
*d. Correct. But this applies more to social perception than sensation and perception.

18. c   obj. 11   p. 116
a. Incorrect. This describes bifocal disparity.
b. Incorrect. This is retinal size.
*c. Correct. Since the eyes are a small distance apart, the images on the eyes vary slightly, and the disparity can be used to determine distance and depth.
d. Incorrect. This is called linear perspective, and it is a monocular cue.

19. a   obj. 11   p. 117
*a. Correct. This is the standard example of linear perspective.
b. Incorrect. The figure/ground relation refers to a figure standing out before a background.
c. Incorrect. Binocular disparity refers to the fact that the visual image on the retina of each eye is slightly different.
d. Incorrect. Motion parallax arises when distant objects appear to move less than close objects when the observer moves by them.

20. b   obj. 14   p. 121
a. Incorrect. ESP typically involves messages about which only the perceiver is aware.
*b. Correct. Perceiving messages below the threshold of awareness is called subliminal perception.
c. Incorrect. Sounds good, but what is it?
d. Incorrect. Being tiny crystals, otoliths do not process anything.

Practice Test II:
21. c   obj. 1   p. 86
a. Incorrect. Introspection refers to observing and describing one's own conscious experiences.
b. Incorrect. Operationalization refers to stating a hypothesis in a manner that can be tested.
*c. Correct. Psychophysicists measure the relationship between the physical world and a person's perception of it.
d. Incorrect. This is the general process of organizing sensations into meaningful events.

22. b   obj. 2   p. 87
a. Incorrect. Absolute threshold could be determined prior to signal detection theory.
*b. Correct. Psychological factors appear to influence the sensitivity of people to certain signals.
c. Incorrect. Magnitude estimation is a procedure that has been available for some time to psychophysicists.
d. Incorrect. The nature of the stimulus is determined by sensory organs.

23. d   obj. 2   p. 86
a. Incorrect. See answer d.
b. Incorrect. See answer d.
c. Incorrect. See answer d.
*d. Correct. Actually, the organ is the nasal epithelium, and the more area it has, the fewer odorant molecules required to detect an odor.

24. d   obj. 3   p. 91
a. Incorrect. The retina helps detect color, but only gives the eye its red glow in photos.
b. Incorrect. The pupil is clear.
c. Incorrect. The cornea is also transparent.
*d. Correct. The iris is the colored muscle that opens and closes the hole known as the pupil.

25. c   obj. 3   p. 92
a. Incorrect. The lens turns the image upside down.
b. Incorrect. The light energy in the image is not redistributed, but it is converted to neural messages.
*c. Correct. This is the role of the retina, and the rods and the cones of the retina initiate the process.
d. Incorrect. The size of the pupil is controlled by the muscles of the iris.

26. d   obj. 3   p. 93
a. Incorrect. Buds occur on branches of dendrites, axons, and trees, and in the tongue, but they are not the name of visual receptors.
b. Incorrect. Cones are more responsive to bright light.
c. Incorrect. Ossicles are another pronunciation of the word "icicles."
*d. Correct. Rods are capable of detecting small amounts of light.

27. d   obj. 4   p. 94
a. Incorrect. Deterioration of the cones would lead to color blindness.

b. Incorrect. Deterioration of the rods would lead to night blindness.

c. Incorrect. Carpel tunnel syndrome of the eye?

*d. Correct. For this reason, glaucoma tests create pressure on the outside of the eye to test the inner pressure.

28. c   obj. 3   p. 93

a. Incorrect. This is due to the low number of rods in the fovea, our typical focal point in the eye in normal light.

b. Incorrect. This results from the low levels of light making the operation of the cones less effective.

*c. Correct. Sensitivity changes in low levels of illumination, and coming into bright light can be painful.

d. Incorrect. These people have what is known as night blindness due to problems related to the rods or to processing information from the rods.

29. a   obj. 5   p. 99

*a. Correct. The opponent color is activated to balance, or adapt to, the intensity of the initial color. When the initial color is removed, the opponent color is seen (the afterimage).

b. Incorrect. Trichromatic theory could not account for negative afterimages.

c. Incorrect. There is not a place theory of color vision, only one for hearing.

d. Incorrect. The receptive-field theory of color vision is yet to be developed.

30. a   obj. 6   p. 102

*a. Correct. The bone conducts sound differently from the air, and the only voice we hear through bone is our own, and no one else hears it through your bone.

b. Incorrect. Everyone hears through tympanic vibrations.

c. Incorrect. Bone conduction is the reason we hear our voices differently from how others hear them.

d. Incorrect. But your voice changes too.

31. a   obj. 8   p. 105

*a. Correct. The primary means of communication they promote is sexual reproduction.

b. Incorrect. Neurotransmitters are within the body not between bodies.

c. Incorrect. Hormones are within-body communicators, not between bodies.

d. Incorrect. Odorants can come from any source and are not restricted to members of a species.

32. d   obj. 8   p. 105

a. Incorrect. Most receptors respond to only one taste.

b. Incorrect. Only four types are known.

c. Incorrect. Taste receptors are only on the tongue.

*d. Correct. The four basic tastes are sweet, sour, bitter, and salty.

33. a   obj. 11   p. 111

*a. Correct. *Gestalt* means "form" or "pattern."

b. Incorrect. See answer a.

c. Incorrect. See answer a.

d. Incorrect. See answer a.

34. b   obj. 11   p. 111

a. Incorrect. The basic element might refer to simplicity.

*b. Correct. In the principle called closure, the perceiver completes a picture by filling in the missing or hidden gaps.

c. Incorrect. Constancy refers to a principle of perception that concerns the tendency to view an object as if it is unchanged even when viewed from different points of view.

d. Incorrect. This is the principle of similarity.

35. b   obj. 11   p. 111

a. Incorrect. Indeed they are similar, but they are not selected from a larger set of dissimilar objects.

*b. Correct. Objects that are close together tend to be grouped together.

c. Incorrect. Closure would lead to filling in the missing "p"s in the sequence.

d. Incorrect. Constancy refers to the fact that we view P and p as the same object.

36. b   obj. 11   p. 111

a. Incorrect. Proximity applies to objects that are close to each other.

*b. Correct. Similar objects do tend to be grouped together.

c. Incorrect. Figure/ground refers to the tendency to see objects in contrast to their background.

d. Incorrect. Closure refers to our tendency to fill in missing or hidden parts of an object.

37. b   obj. 12   p. 115

a. Incorrect. Top-down processing would begin by understanding the sentence and then defining each word.

*b. Correct. Bottom-up processing identifies each part and the builds the larger picture.

c. Incorrect. Selective attention refers to our ability to ignore irrelevant information or sensory inputs and concentrate on a selected set of data.

d. Incorrect. Constancy refers to a principle of perception that concerns the tendency to view an object as if it is unchanged even when viewed from different points of view.

38. d   obj. 13   p. 115

a. Incorrect. This refers to the habituation to a sensory stimulus.

b. Incorrect. In bottom-up processing, each new view would generate a new image and identity.

c. Incorrect. Subliminal perception may occur at the limits of conscious perception, but it does not influence perceptual constancy.

*d. Correct. When an object is perceived as not changing even though its visual image changes, then perceptual constancy is at work.

39. b   obj. 13   p. 116

a. Incorrect. The gestalt principle of figure/ground suggests that we see an object in context of its background.

*b. Correct. Binocular disparity works on the basis of the slight disparity between the two images of the retinas, since they have slightly different points of view.
c. Incorrect. Monocular cues, by definition, come from only one eye.
d. Incorrect. Motion parallax arises when distant objects appear to move less than close objects when the observer moves by them.

40. b   obj. 13   p. 116
a. Incorrect. Unseen bulges in the middle of the columns make it look more perfectly square and taller.
*b. Correct. Unseen bulges in the middle of the columns make it look more perfectly square and taller.
c. Incorrect. Unseen bulges in the middle of the columns make it look more perfectly square and taller.
d. Incorrect. Unseen bulges in the middle of the columns make it look more perfectly square and taller.

Practice Test III:
41. b   obj. 1   p. 85
a. Incorrect. Just noticeable difference is inappropriate here.
*b. Correct. The pinprick is the stimulus and the pain is the sensation.
c. Incorrect. The pinprick does not represent a difference threshold.
d. Incorrect. Quite a few pinpricks would be needed to develop a sensory adaptation, especially if the pain is short in duration.

42. a   obj. 2   p. 87
*a. Correct. This is a situation described by signal detection theory, in which expectations play a role in detection.
b. Incorrect. If it depended upon sensory factors, the frequency of the blips would be irrelevant.
c. Incorrect. If this were true, then they would be more likely to detect an infrequent blip.
d. Incorrect. Past exposure influences our expectations about signals like blips on the radar screen.

43. a   obj. 2   p. 87
*a. Correct. Signal detection theory does account for how we can become inattentive to a stimulus like a siren.
b. Incorrect. Weber's law addresses the change in a stimulus, not the change in our sensitivity to it.
c. Incorrect. If the strength or pitch of the siren changed, then just noticeable difference would be relevant to this example.
d. Incorrect. Absolute thresholds address the minimum level of stimulus needed in order to be detected.

44. b   obj. 3   p. 93
a. Incorrect. This is reversed.
*b. Correct. Rods need little light to be activated, cones require much more.
c. Incorrect. The amount of rhodopsin is the relevant factor in dark adaptation, not the rod and cone differences.
d. Incorrect. This is the opposite as well.

45. b   obj. 4   p. 94
a. Incorrect. The impulses across the optic nerve become restricted.
*b. Correct. There can be a number of causes of this phenomena, including diabetes.
c. Incorrect. This is a consequence of glaucoma, caused by increasing pressure within the eye.
d. Incorrect. This problem is not very common.

46. d   obj. 6   p. 101
a. Incorrect. If you could hear your own voice, then you would be hearing through bone conduction, and the cochlea, basilar membrane, and auditory cortex would be functioning properly.
b. Incorrect. If you could hear your own voice, then you would be hearing through bone conduction, and the cochlea, basilar membrane, and auditory cortex would be functioning properly.
c. Incorrect. If you could hear your own voice, then you would be hearing through bone conduction, and the cochlea, basilar membrane, and auditory cortex would be functioning properly.
*d. Correct. Some blockage would have had to occur in the middle ear because you would be hearing through bone conduction, and the cochlea, basilar membrane, and auditory cortex would be functioning properly.

47. b   obj. 6   p. 102
a. Incorrect. Pitch does not depend on how hard the keys are struck on a piano.
*b. Correct. The keys on the left side would have a lower frequency, and thus lower pitch, than the keys on the right side.
c. Incorrect. The keys on the left side would have a lower frequency, and thus lower pitch, than the keys on the right side.
d. Incorrect. Pitch is a function of frequency.

48. b   obj. 6   p. 102
a. Incorrect. Intensity may affect resonance, but frequency does not relate to loudness.
*b. Correct. The greater the intensity, the louder the sound; and the higher the frequency, the higher the pitch.
c. Incorrect. These do not have a match at all.
d. Incorrect. Intensity will affect all the ear, though the external ear will be affected least, yet consonance will be unaffected by frequency.

49. d   obj. 6   p. 102
a. Incorrect. However, pitch is how we perceive the differences between different frequencies.
b. Incorrect. Intensity refers to loudness, or how tall the crests would be.
c. Incorrect. This is intensity, or how tall the crests would be.
*d. Correct. The count of the number of crests per second is the frequency of the sound.

50. a   obj. 6   p. 103
*a. Correct. Loudness is measured in decibels and frequency is measured in cycles per second.
b.   Incorrect. See answer a.
c.   Incorrect. See answer a.
d.   Incorrect. See answer a.

51. c   obj. 7   p. 104
a.   Incorrect. This symptom is associated with something eaten, not vertigo.
b.   Incorrect. This symptom is more likely to be found in schizophrenia.
*c. Correct. Vertigo is a disorder or disruption of the sense of balance, and it results in motion sickness and dizziness.
d.   Incorrect. This results from too many illegal drugs.

52. a   obj. 13   p. 110
*a. Correct. This principle is central to the gestalt approach.
b.   Incorrect. Only in illusions.
c.   Incorrect. This is the principle of proximity.
d.   Incorrect. That is the physical attraction principle found in later chapters.

53. d   obj. 11   p. 110
a.   Incorrect. The less predominant the ground, the easier it is to alternate figure and ground.
b.   Incorrect. The less predominant the figure, the easier it is to alternate figure and ground.
c.   Incorrect. Often the images are quite different, causing a dramatic effect.
*d. Correct. If they can alternate, then the reversibility is possible.

54. d   obj. 11   p. 111
a.   Incorrect. There is no gestalt principle of "figure/group."
b.   Incorrect. Closure involves completing an incomplete figure by filling in missing components.
c.   Incorrect. Proximity involves grouping elements that are close together.
*d. Correct. This activity involves grouping according to similar features.

55. a   obj. 12   p. 114
*a. Correct. In top-down processing, incomplete information is completed by drawing upon context and memory.
b.   Incorrect. Bottom-up processing would require all the parts of the image.
c.   Incorrect. While selective attention may be involved (the car may have actually been a snowmobile), this example does not illustrate selective attention.
d.   Incorrect. Feature analysis helped you detect the word "mobile," but it was not used in completing the word.

56. a   obj. 13   p. 116
*a. Correct. There are many monocular, or single-eye, cues for depth.
b.   Incorrect. They appear smaller because of the physics involved.

c.   Incorrect. Actually, the greater discrepancy makes the depth determination easier.
d.   Incorrect. This is backward.

57. b   obj. 13   p. 117
a.   Incorrect. Right, and its about to explode.
*b. Correct. Right, so you better take cover–the image is getting larger on your retina.
c.   Incorrect. It would have to be moving toward you.
d.   Incorrect. It could have started out sideways, and if it is then turning sideways, it would be getting smaller.

58. c   obj. 13   p. 117
a.   Incorrect. The ball moves too quickly for the player to track the ball all the way to the plate.
b.   Incorrect. Focusing is less of a problem than tracking, and if the player cannot track the ball, he certainly cannot focus on it.
*c. Correct. The player must anticipate the location of the ball when it reaches the plate because it approaches too quickly to be tracked all the way, and he must begin his swing before the ball reaches the plate.
d.   Incorrect. Eye coordination is critical, but he would not be a major league player if he did not already have good coordination.

59. d   obj. 15   p. 121
a.   Incorrect. Try subliminal perception, and no, it probably will not work.
b.   Incorrect. Try subliminal perception, and no, it probably will not work.
c.   Incorrect. It is called subliminal perception, but it probably will not work.
*d. Correct. There is little evidence supporting the use of subliminal tapes for complex learning.

60. a   obj. 14   p. 120
*a. Correct. Educational level has no impact on the perception of illusions.
b.   Incorrect. Culture does appear to influence the perception of illusions, especially illusions involving objects or situations unfamiliar to members of the culture.
c.   Incorrect. The structure of the eye is one of the factors influencing how illusions work.
d.   Incorrect. Some illusions arise from incorrect interpretations at the level of the brain.

■ CHAPTER 4: ANSWER KEY

GUIDED REVIEW			MATCHING	
Concept 1:	[k] latent content of dreams	**Concept 2:**	1. d	18. e
[a] Consciousness	[l] manifest content of dreams	[a] Hypnosis	2. c	19. a
[b] electroencephalogram (EEG)	[m] reverse learning theory	[b] Meditation	3. e	20. c
[c] stage 1 sleep	[n] dreams-for-survival theory		4. a	21. b
[d] Stage 2 sleep	[o] activation-synthesis theory	**Concept 3:**	5. b	22. d
[e] Stage 3 sleep	[p] daydreams	[a] Psychoactive drugs		23. f
[f] Stage 4 sleep	[q] insomnia	[b] Addictive drugs	6. a	
[g] rapid eye movement (REM)	[r] sleep apnea	[c] stimulant	7. e	24. b
[h] Circadian rhythms	[s] narcolepsy	[d] Cocaine	8. c	25. h
[i] Nightmares		[e] Amphetamines	9. d	26. a
[j] unconscious wish fulfillment theory		[f] depressants	10. b	27. d
		[g] Alcohol		28. f
		[h] Barbiturates	11. e	29. g
		[i] Narcotics	12. c	30. e
		[j] hallucinogens	13. f	31. c
		[k] marijuana	14. a	
			15. g	
			16. b	
			17. d	

Essay Question 4.1: Dreams

The major positions that should be considered in your answer:

■ The psychoanalytic view argues that the symbols of dreams reflect deep meanings, many of which are unfulfilled wishes or repressed conflicts.

■ The opposing views hold that dreaming is a natural process of cleaning excess material from the day, a survival mechanism, or a by-product of random electrical activity in the brain. These views may not necessarily be incompatible.

Essay Question 4.2: Decriminalizing Psychoactive Drugs

The major points that should be included in your answer:

■ Identify the drugs that have been involved in this issue lately. This would include marijuana, but also, some have argued that drug use should be completely legalized and viewed as a medical or psychological problem.

■ State your view, identifying which drug(s) should be decriminalized and which should not. Many people suggest that the medical benefits of some drugs cannot be explored and used because of their status. Other reasons should be offered as well. For instance, the use of some drugs can be considered victimless, though the drug trade has many victims.

■ If you believe that all drugs should remain illegal, than support your reasoning. Harm to society and to individuals is a common argument. Examples could be given.

Multiple Choice Feedback:

Practice Test I:
1. d   obj. 1   p. 130
a. Incorrect. We are not aware of the functioning of our nervous system.

b. Incorrect. Our individual consciousness is not observable by others.

c. Incorrect. These are unconscious forces.

*d. Correct. This is the definition of our personal conscious experience.

2. a obj. 2 p. 132
*a. Correct. The transition to sleep occurs in Stage 1.
b. Incorrect. See answer a.
c. Incorrect. See answer a.
d. Incorrect. The occurrence of REM is associated with dreaming, while the transition to sleep normally occurs in Stage 1.

3. d obj. 2 p. 133
a. Incorrect. REM sleep has very irregular waveforms; this describes Stage 4 sleep.
b. Incorrect. Stage 2 is characterized by electrical signals that are faster than Stage 3 or 4.
c. Incorrect. Stage 3 is characterized by electrical signals that are faster than Stage 4.
*d. Correct. This is an accurate description of Stage 4 sleep.

4. d obj. 2 p. 133
a. Incorrect. Both brain activity and eye movement are high.
b. Incorrect. Brain activity is high, and muscle activity is low.
c. Incorrect. True, but this is not why it is called paradoxical.
*d. Correct. The brain is active, but the body is completely inactive.

5. b obj. 2 p. 134
a. Incorrect. Paradoxical sleep refers to the period of REM during which the brain is active and the body is paralyzed.
*b. Correct. After sleep deprivation, the sleeper recovers lost REM time by having extra REM sleep for several nights.
c. Incorrect. Latent dreaming would be hidden dreaming, and this is not associated with REM rebound.
d. Incorrect. Somnambulism occurs most often in Stage 4 sleep, and it is not a result of sleep deprivation.

6. c obj. 3 p. 135
a. Incorrect. They include daily activities, but this is not what interested Freud.
b. Incorrect. They tend to reflect unconscious activity.
*c. Correct. Unconscious and repressed wishes often find their way into the content of dreams.
d. Incorrect. Freud might accept this view, but he was interested in the content of current dreams.

7. d obj. 3 p. 139
a. Incorrect. This would be a mental house-messing.
b. Incorrect. This view accepts the notion of random activity as the source for dreams.
c. Incorrect. This approach understands dreams as a means of making sense of the information gathered through the day.
*d. Correct. Reverse learning implies undoing, or "cleaning," unnecessary information.

8. a obj. 3 p. 141
*a. Correct. This includes during work, school, and any other activity.
b. Incorrect. People daydream at work, at school, and during any other activity about 10 percent of the time.
c. Incorrect. People daydream at work, at school, and during any other activity about 10 percent of the time.
d. Incorrect. You might want to reappraise what you do with your time. People, on average, daydream at work, at school, and during any other activity about 10 percent of the time.

9. c obj. 4 p. 142
a. Incorrect. Falling asleep uncontrollably is called narcolepsy.
b. Incorrect. This is an unusual amount of sleep for an adult, but infants and small children sleep this much.
*c. Correct. Insomnia simply refers to having difficulty falling asleep or returning to sleep once awakened during the night.
d. Incorrect. This is not a condition associated with insomnia.

10. b obj. 4 p. 142
a. Incorrect. The symptom of narcolepsy is falling into REM sleep uncontrollably.
*b. Correct. Associated with snoring, the gasping for breath often awakens the person suffering from sleep apnea.
c. Incorrect. This refers to excessive sleep.
d. Incorrect. Insomnia is difficulty falling asleep and staying asleep.

11. b obj. 4 p. 142
a. Incorrect. Narcolepsy has not been associated with infant death syndrome.
*b. Correct. Sleep apnea is thought to be the cause of infant death syndrome--in effect, the child forgets to breathe.
c. Incorrect. Somnambulism refers to sleep-walking.
d. Incorrect. Insomnia involves difficulties falling asleep.

12. c obj. 5 p. 147
a. Incorrect. "You will encourage your friends to enroll in this class."
b. Incorrect. Most of us are aware of the outdoors.
*c. Correct. Frequent daydreamers do appear to be more easily hypnotized than infrequent daydreamers.
d. Incorrect. This correlation has not been studied.

13. a obj. 6 p. 148
*a. Correct. The repeated word is called a mantra.

b.   Incorrect. The repeated word is called a mantra.
c.   Incorrect. The repeated word is called a mantra.
d.   Incorrect. The repeated word is called a mantra.

14. c   obj. 7   p. 151
a.   Incorrect. The drug works without regard to the person's willingness to be affected.
b.   Incorrect. Not all psychoactive drugs are addictive.
*c. Correct. Psychoactive drugs affect all three.
d.   Incorrect. Psychoactive drugs affect emotions, perceptions, and behavior.

15. b   obj. 7   p. 157
a.   Incorrect. The barbiturate phenobarbital is not as common as other depressants.
*b. Correct. Alcohol is indeed the most common taken depressant.
c.   Incorrect. Valium is an antianxiety drug that is quite commonly prescribed.
d.   Incorrect. This is a common depressant, but not the most common.

16. d   obj. 8   p. 161
a.   Incorrect. PCP is common, but not the most common.
b.   Incorrect. LSD is common, but not the most common.
c.   Incorrect. Cocaine is a stimulant, not a hallucinogen.
*d. Correct. Marijuana is by far the most commonly used hallucinogen.

Practice Test II:
17. a   obj. 2   p. 133
*a. Correct. Later in the night's sleep cycle, sleep is less deep.
b.   Incorrect. Later in the night's sleep cycle, sleep is less deep.
c.   Incorrect. Later in the night's sleep cycle, sleep is less deep.
d.   Incorrect. Dreams occur at the least deep levels of sleep.

18. d   obj. 2   p. 133
a.   Incorrect. It gets slower and more regular.
b.   Incorrect. It gets slower and more regular.
c.   Incorrect. It gets slower and more regular.
*d. Correct. The waveforms during the slowest phase are called delta waves.

19. c   obj. 2   p. 134
a.   Incorrect. During Stage 1, breathing becomes more regular, blood pressure drops, and respiration slows.
b.   Incorrect. During Stage 2, breathing continues to become more regular, blood pressure continues to drop, and respiration continues to slow.
*c. Correct. And this happens while the voluntary muscles are inhibited to the point of paralysis.
d.   Incorrect. During non-REM sleep, breathing becomes more regular, blood pressure drops, and respiration slows.

20. d   obj. 2   p. 134
a.   Incorrect. Paralysis occurs during REM sleep.
b.   Incorrect. Paralysis occurs during REM sleep.
c.   Incorrect. Paralysis occurs during REM sleep.
*d. Correct. Ironically, REM sleep is also characterized by irregular breathing, increased blood pressure, and increased respiration.

21. c   obj. 3   p. 140
a.   Incorrect. This view sees dreams as a means for repressed desires to be expressed.
b.   Incorrect. This approach understands dreams as a means of making sense of the information gathered through the day.
*c. Correct. This view accepts the notion of random activity as the source for dreams.
d.   Incorrect. Reverse learning implies undoing, or "cleaning," unnecessary information.

22. c   obj. 3   p. 139
a.   Incorrect. Libidinal content would be sexual and may or may not be the obvious story line of the dream.
b.   Incorrect. The unconscious content of dreams is most often the hidden, or latent content.
*c. Correct. This is the term he used for the story line of the dream.
d.   Incorrect. The latent content is the hidden content of the dream.

23. d   obj. 3   p. 141
a.   Incorrect. Daydreams are often a source of creative inspiration for the dreamer.
b.   Incorrect. We often daydream about the most mundane things, like doing laundry or writing answer explanations.
c.   Incorrect. Daydreams are very much a part of our normal conscious experiences.
*d. Correct. Few daydreams are sexual in nature (surprised?).

24. a   obj. 4   p. 142
*a. Correct. A narcoleptic can fall asleep at any time, though stress does seem to contribute to the narcoleptic's symptoms.
b.   Incorrect. Insomnia involves difficulty getting to sleep or staying asleep.
c.   Incorrect. Somnambulism is also known as sleepwalking.
d.   Incorrect. This concept is from some sci-fi movie, no doubt.

25. a   obj. 4   p. 142
*a. Correct. Narcolepsy is uncontrollable.
b.   Incorrect. Sleep apnea will make one tired throughout the next day due to the frequent awakening through the night.
c.   Incorrect. Hypersomnia is excessive sleep at night.
d.   Incorrect. Insomnia involves difficulty getting to sleep or staying asleep.

26. b   obj. 4   p. 142
a. Incorrect. Narcolepsy has not been identified as a cause of sudden infant death syndrome.
*b. Correct. Sleep apnea has been associated with sudden infant death syndrome.
c. Incorrect. Somnambulism is sleepwalking, and the infants tend to die in their cribs (it is also called crib death).
d. Incorrect. Insomnia involves difficulty getting to sleep or staying asleep and is commonly an adult problem.

27. d   obj. 4   p. 144
a. Incorrect. A regular bedtime makes for a habit of falling asleep.
b. Incorrect. Here we apply "reverse" psychology on ourselves.
c. Incorrect. Caffeine contributes to sleeplessness.
*d. Correct. The TV belongs in the den or living room, not in the bed. TV is usually stimulating and not restful.

28. d   obj. 6   p. 148
a. Incorrect. Transactional analysis comes from Berne's *I'm O.K., You're O.K.*
b. Incorrect. Zen Buddhists practice meditation, though.
c. Incorrect. Not quite.
*d. Correct. The name for this process is transcendental meditation, and research has shown that the effects can be achieved through practiced relaxation methods as well.

29. a   obj. 8   p. 161
*a. Correct. Methadone produces an addiction, but it does not have the psychoactive properties of heroin.
b. Incorrect. Methadone does not cause mental retardation.
c. Incorrect. Everyone is at risk, methadone docs not increase the risk.
d. Incorrect. Most drug users find the marijuana high to be appealing; nothing about the methadone causes this.

30. b   obj. 7   p. 153
a. Incorrect. Since they stimulate the nervous system, they do not have an anesthetic effect.
*b. Correct. Each of these is considered a stimulant.
c. Incorrect. In some cases, even small doses of these drugs can cause anxiety.
d. Incorrect. With extreme doses, hallucinations are possible, but they do not occur in typical doses.

31. b   obj. 7   p. 159
a. Incorrect. An opiate is a narcotic.
*b. Correct. These are all classes of the depressant group known as barbiturates.
c. Incorrect. These drugs do not cause hallucinations under normal circumstances.
d. Incorrect. These drugs do not cause hypnosis.

32. b   obj. 7   p. 159
a. Incorrect. These are hallucinogens.
*b. Correct. These are the two primary examples of narcotics given in the text.

c. Incorrect. These are depressants.
d. Incorrect. These are stimulants.

Practice Test III:
33. a   obj. 2   p. 132
*a. Correct. The electrical properties are recorded as waveforms by the EEG, and thus are referred to as brain waves.
b. Incorrect. The time from sleep to stage is not a factor in defining the stages, and people go through several cycles of the stages each night.
c. Incorrect. Stage 4 and REM sleep have specific sleep events associated with them, but these are not used to define the stages.
d. Incorrect. With the exception of REM sleep, when the sleeper is quite still, the body movements are generally the same from one stage to another.

34. d   obj. 2   p. 134
a. Incorrect. There are no long-term effects from sleep deprivation.
b. Incorrect. He is unlikely to get sick, though he might make mistakes at work and be prone to accidents elsewhere.
c. Incorrect. There are no long-term consequences for staying awake 36 hours.
*d. Correct. If he is staying awake to study, then he might be jeopardizing his grade– it would be more effective to break the study into smaller parts and get some rest.

35. d   obj. 3   p. 139
a. Incorrect. Probably more than a friendship.
b. Incorrect. Nothing in the dream suggests any anxiety about talking to Jim.
c. Incorrect. This is a possible reading of the manifest content of the dream, but Freudian approach would not differ from any other approach on this view.
*d. Correct. Climbing stairs is indeed an act symbolic of sexual intercourse.

36. b   obj. 3   p. 139
a. Incorrect. This may be what it means, but it is a strange way of making the image clear, and besides, this is not what a Freudian would see.
*b. Correct. Grapefruits can generally be viewed as feminine bodies, but more specifically as breasts.
c. Incorrect. This is not a likely interpretation.
d. Incorrect. The trip down the tunnel may have a quality of a wish to return to the womb, but the grapefruits do not fit the image.

37. b   obj. 3   p. 139
a. Incorrect. Though the increase in anxiety would lead to additional wish-fulfillment types of dreams.
*b. Correct. The need to make sense of environmental, survival-oriented information makes this choice the better candidate.
c. Incorrect. The random activity would be just as random in either circumstance.

d. Incorrect. Would they not dream less since more of the information form the day was important and relevant?

38. b   obj. 3   p. 141
a. Incorrect. This is not a common fantasy during nervous breakdowns.
*b. Correct. Fantasies about escape are common in daydreams.
c. Incorrect. Since he was in class, and probably not asleep, a nighttime emission is unlikely.
d. Incorrect. A mantra is a word repeated during meditation.

39. a   obj. 4   p. 142
*a. Correct. Sleepwalkers can be awakened, but they will probably be confused and disoriented.
b. Incorrect. Sleepwalking most often occurs in Stage 4.
c. Incorrect. If awakened, sleepwalkers can have a vague sense of where they are and what they were doing.
d. Incorrect. Sleepwalking is common throughout age groups.

40. a   obj. 6   p. 148
*a. Correct. The changes in brain activity can be recorded on an EEG.
b. Incorrect. They both may result in a decrease in blood pressure, but they may not.
c. Incorrect. Hypnosis is an invention of European origin.
d. Incorrect. "Total relaxation" is a bit overstated.

41. b   obj. 7   p. 152
a. Incorrect. Addiction may be either or both biologically and psychologically based.
*b. Correct. This may be true in cases of alcoholism, but other addictions arise from the nature of the body-drug interaction.
c. Incorrect. There simply is no foundation for this statement.
d. Incorrect. Addiction may be either or both biologically and psychologically based.

42. b   obj. 7   p. 153
a. Incorrect. However, that must be some vitamin!
*b. Correct. This is what stimulants do.
c. Incorrect. Depressants slow the heart rate.
d. Incorrect. A hallucinogen could cause these symptoms (among many others), but not necessarily.

43. c   obj. 8   p. 151
a. Incorrect. Heroin is a narcotic.
b. Incorrect. Cocaine is a stimulant.
*c. Correct. Marijuana is a hallucinogen.
d. Incorrect. Morphine is a narcotic.

44. b   obj. 3   p. 138
a. Incorrect. The latent content would be what the jacket and showing off might symbolize.
*b. Correct. This is what she actually did in her dream.
c. Incorrect. The manifest content can be quite relevant to the meaning, as it contains the symbols.

d. Incorrect. These would be day residues only if this is what she did the day before.

45. a   obj. 3   p. 138
*a. Correct. As symbols, they hold keys to the repressed or hidden latent content of the dream.
b. Incorrect. The wearing of the jacket and the parading were the manifest content.
c. Incorrect. Activation process is not relevant to the dream interpretation.
d. Incorrect. He would only need to ask Elizabeth about the daytime activities to make this determination.

46. a   obj. 5   p. 146
*a. Correct. Unless she is an exhibitionist, she would not undress.
b. Incorrect. With slightly lowered inhibitions, she could easily flirt.
c. Incorrect. She is likely to recall a past life, even if she does not have one.
d. Incorrect. Making people do stupid animal tricks is a common hypnotic activity.

■ CHAPTER 5: ANSWER KEY

GUIDED REVIEW		MATCHING		
Concept 1:	[e] primary reinforcer	**Concept 3:**	1. c	13. a · 25. b
[a] Learning	[f] secondary reinforcer	[a] cognitive-social	2. e	14. f · 26. e
[b] classical conditioning	[g] Positive reinforcers	learning theory	3. g	15. b · 27. c
[c] neutral stimulus	[h] Negative reinforcers	[b] Latent learning	4. f	16. d · 28. g
[d] unconditioned stimulus (UCS)	[i] escape conditioning	[c] cognitive map	5. a	17. e · 29. a
[e] unconditioned response (UCR)	[j] avoidance conditioning	[d] observational learning	6. d	18. c · 30. f
[f] conditioned stimulus (CS)	[k] Punishment	[e] model	7. b	19. c · 31. d
[g] conditioned response (CR)	[l] schedules of reinforcement	[f] Behavior modification		
[h] extinction	[m] continuous reinforcement schedule		8. b	20. e · 32. c
[i] systematic desensitization	[n] Partial reinforcement schedule		9. a	21. d · 33. e
[j] spontaneous recovery	[o] fixed-ratio schedule		10. e	22. f · 34. f
[k] Stimulus generalization	[p] variable-ratio schedule		11. c	23. a · 35. d
[l] Stimulus discrimination	[q] Fixed-interval schedules		12. d	24. b · 36. b
[m] higher-order conditioning	[r] Variable-interval schedules			37. a
	[s] stimulus control training			
Concept 2:	[t] Superstitious behavior			
[a] Operant conditioning	[u] shaping			
[b] law of effect				
[c] Reinforcement				
[d] reinforcer				

Essay Question 5.1: Using Physical Punishment

■ Cite examples of the use of physical punishment. Describe alternatives for each use.

■ Identify the conditions under which physical punishment may be necessary. These could include the need for swift and attention-getting action to prevent physical harm. Some parents use corporal punishment when children hit one another; some do so to establish control when alternatives have failed.

■ Indicate your views and explain them.

Essay Question 5.2: Which Approach Is Correct?

■ Describe each of the three approaches in such a way that they are clearly distinguished.

■ Identify points of contradiction with each. In classical conditioning, the stimuli must precede the responses; in operant conditioning, the reinforcing stimuli come after the responses; in observational learning, the behavior does not need to be practiced. Mental processes are also involved in observational learning.

■ Observational learning may actually be reconciled with the other two once mental processes and reinforcement of the model (rather than the learner) are allowed.

Multiple Choice Feedback:

Practice Test I:
1. d   obj. 1   p. 168
a. Incorrect. Learning refers to performance changes as well.
b. Incorrect. Learning refers to permanent changes.
c. Incorrect. Performance changes can result from fatigue.

*d. Correct. Performance is the means of measuring learning.

2. c   obj. 1   p. 168
a. Incorrect. If learning has occurred, then there must be a way to measure it.

b. Incorrect. Learning should result in relatively permanent change.
*c. Correct. Since learning is an internal change, it must be observed indirectly through changes in behavior.
d. Incorrect. Learning differs from maturational changes.

3. a   obj. 1   p. 170
*a. Correct. Meat powder caused salivation to occur without any training and thus is "unconditioned."
b. Incorrect. The conditioned stimulus originally did not cause any salivation.
c. Incorrect. The response was salivation.
d. Incorrect. The response was salivation.

4. d   obj. 2   p. 172
a. Incorrect. Learning has already occurred in this scenario.
b. Incorrect. Perception is a mental event related to understanding sensory stimuli.
c. Incorrect. Systematic desensitization is a specialized technique for eliminating a learned response.
*d. Correct. When the CS is repeatedly presented without the UCS being paired with it, then the CS-CR connection becomes extinguished.

5. d   obj. 2   p. 172
a. Incorrect. Operant conditioning does not engage in systematic desensitization.
b. Incorrect. A token economy is a method that applies operant conditioning to discipline.
c. Incorrect. Spontaneous recovery occurs after extinction and may occur after systematic desensitization has occurred.
*d. Correct. Systematic desensitization is a means of achieving extinction of a CS-CR relationship.

6. b   obj. 2   p. 172
a. Incorrect. This method is unlikely to extinguish the initial response.
*b. Correct. This is the standard method of extinction.
c. Incorrect. This refers to the process of acquiring a UCS-CS connection initially.
d. Incorrect. This will actually strengthen the CS.

7. b   obj. 3   p. 175
a. Incorrect. The principle of classical conditioning are meant to apply uniformly to all organisms with the capacity to learn.
*b. Correct. Garcia found that animals could be conditioned in open trial and that the time between the UCS and the CS could be quite long.
c. Incorrect. This is not quite the point of Garcia's research.
d. Incorrect. The effects can be achieved by spinning the rats, so this claim is not true.

8. c   obj. 4   p. 177
a. Incorrect. The law of frequency suggests that conditioning requires frequent pairings.
b. Incorrect. This is the Gestalt principle of perception, not a rule for classical or operant conditioning.

*c. Correct. The law of effect says that if a behavior has pleasing consequences, then it is more likely to be repeated.
d. Incorrect. The principle of contiguity in classical conditioning suggests that the CS and the UCS should be close together in time and space.

9. a   obj. 4   p. 178
*a. Correct. Indeed, primary reinforcers are items like food and water; secondary are like praise and money.
b. Incorrect. Organisms may differ in their preferences but not in any uniform manner.
c. Incorrect. For organisms that respond to operant conditioning, secondary reinforcers have an effect.
d. Incorrect. This statement is reversed.

10. b   obj. 4   p. 178
a. Incorrect. Punishers decrease the likelihood of a response being repeated.
*b. Correct. This defines reinforcers.
c. Incorrect. A response is the behavior, not the consequence.
d. Incorrect. An operant is a kind of response.

11. c   obj. 4   p. 179
a. Incorrect. It is a form of reinforcement, and it results in the increase of the desired behavior.
b. Incorrect. Rewards are not withheld in negative reinforcement; in fact, the removal of the aversive stimulus is considered to be a reward.
*c. Correct. The removal of the aversive stimulus is a pleasing consequence and will lead to the repetition of the behavior.
d. Incorrect. Only instrumental conditioning utilizes reinforcement.

12. d   obj. 5   p. 182
a. Incorrect. The rate depends upon the schedule of reinforcement that has been chosen.
b. Incorrect. The rate depends upon the schedule of reinforcement that has been chosen.
c. Incorrect. The response is actually difficult to extinguish.
*d. Correct. The variability and the partial nature of the reinforcement results in behaviors that are highly resistant to extinction.

13. a   obj. 5   p. 173
*a. Correct. The ratio of successful sales to attempts made varies from sale to sale.
b. Incorrect. This would mean that the frequency of making a sale would be fixed at every fourth, or every fifth attempt (or some number).
c. Incorrect. A variable interval would mean that another sale would not take place until a set amount of time had passed.
d. Incorrect. A fixed interval would mean that a sale would take place on a time schedule, say every hour or every two hours.

14. d   obj. 5   p. 185

a.   Incorrect. Superstitious behaviors are rarely reinforced.
b.   Incorrect. This results in some other behaviors, not superstitious ones.
c.   Incorrect. This probably arises for other reasons.
*d. Correct. The superstitious behavior of a major-league batter might arise because once he hit a home run after tapping the back of his foot with the bat and then touching his hat. Now he repeats this pattern every time he goes to bat.

15. a   obj. 8   p. 189
*a. Correct. Quicker learning in later trials with reinforcement present suggest that some form of map or learning had developed in the unrewarded exploration.
b.   Incorrect. No aversion would occur unless the maze were filled with traps.
c.   Incorrect. Rat interest cannot yet be judged regarding mazes.
d.   Incorrect. Since rats are very superstitious, the maze would have little effect on their beliefs.

Practice Test II:
16. d   obj. 1   p. 168
a.   Incorrect. This definition fits maturation better.
b.   Incorrect. This definition applies to circumstantial changes.
c.   Incorrect. This definition applies to reflex.
*d. Correct. This is the definition given in the text.

17. c   obj. 2   p. 170
a.   Incorrect. No such term is used in learning theory.
b.   Incorrect. The unconditioned stimulus elicits the unconditioned stimulus without any conditioning.
*c. Correct. The term applied to this stimulus is the conditioned stimulus.
d.   Incorrect. This stimulus helps an organism in instrumental conditioning discriminate between times when a reinforcement would be given and times when a reinforcement is not available.

18. d   obj. 2   p. 170
a.   Incorrect. Since the rat did not give rise to the fear response, then it could not have been considered an unconditioned stimulus for this study.
b.   Incorrect. This has another meaning in some other area of science.
c.   Incorrect. The discriminative stimulus helps an organism in instrumental conditioning discriminate between times when a reinforcement would be given and times when a reinforcement is not available.
*d. Correct. Because it would not give rise to the fear response, it would be considered neutral.

19. b   obj. 2   p. 173
a.   Incorrect. This situation sounds more like extinction or avoidance.
*b. Correct. This hierarchy allows the learner to extinguish the fear gradually.
c.   Incorrect. This sounds like avoidance.

d.   Incorrect. This reverses the graduated approach used in systematic desensitization.

20. b   obj. 2   p. 172
a.   Incorrect. This does not describe escape conditioning.
*b. Correct. The conditioned stimulus loses its value as a predictor of the unconditioned stimulus.
c.   Incorrect. This does not describe stimulus generalization.
d.   Incorrect. Negative reinforcement would is actually intended to increase a desired behavior.

21. a   obj. 3   p. 175
*a. Correct. The cognitive learning theorists have demonstrated that learning can occur as the transformation of mental processes, like the construction of a cognitive map, that later guide behavior.
b.   Incorrect. The Brelands primarily utilized operant conditioning and are concerned with other issues.
c.   Incorrect. Thorndike's law of effect does not repudiate classical ideas so much as add to them.
d.   Incorrect. Operant conditioning does not repudiate the ideas of classical conditioning, and in fact, is subject to the same challenges.

22. c   obj. 5   p. 184
a.   Incorrect. See answer c.
b.   Incorrect. See answer c.
*c. Correct. The period of time (interval) is set (fixed).
d.   Incorrect. See answer c.

23. d   obj. 4   p. 176
a.   Incorrect. The consequence of the behavior is escape.
b.   Incorrect. The consequence of the behavior is the avoided speeding ticket.
c.   Incorrect. The consequence of the behavior is the biscuit reward.
*d. Correct. The chemistry professor is a conditioned stimulus to which high blood pressure is the response.

24. c   obj. 4   p. 176
a.   Incorrect. Pavlov developed classical conditioning.
b.   Incorrect. Skinner developed operant conditioning.
*c. Correct. Wertheimer was one of the Gestalt psychologists.
d.   Incorrect. Thorndike developed the law of effect, a cornerstone of operant conditioning.

25. c   obj. 4   p. 178
a.   Incorrect. Food is not considered to be a discriminative stimulus unless an organism has been trained to view it as such.
b.   Incorrect. Food satisfies a need; but it may also be a motive (as is true with money).
*c. Correct. Since food satisfies a basic need, it is considered primary; since money must be conditioned to have any reinforcing value, it is a secondary reinforcer.
d.   Incorrect. Food may be a drive reducer, but money is not a natural reinforcer.

26. b   obj. 4   p. 178
a.   Incorrect. Money requires conditioning to become a reinforcer.
*b. Correct. Water satisfies a basic need, thus it is a primary reinforcer.
c.   Incorrect. Good grades require conditioning to become reinforcers.
d.   Incorrect. To be a reinforcer, the hammer would require some, though not much, conditioning.

27. d   obj. 4   p. 179
a.   Incorrect. The employee would probably become angry for being punished for such a minor offense.
b.   Incorrect. The physical spanking reinforces the idea that violence is a way to make others cooperate.
c.   Incorrect. Punishment for a teenager can often become an opportunity for reinforcement through attention from friends.
*d. Correct. When self-endangerment occurs, quick and angerless punishment can make the child become attentive to the danger.

28. d   obj. 5   p. 183
a.   Incorrect. The time interval for making each piece can change, but the rate is one payment for every three pieces.
b.   Incorrect. Variable interval would suggest that the worker would not know when payment would come.
c.   Incorrect. In this pattern, the payment would come after five, then three, then four, etc; pieces were made-not every three.
*d. Correct. This is a fixed-ratio schedule.

29. d   obj. 5   p. 184
a.   Incorrect. They may speed up just before the interval end.
b.   Incorrect. They do not become extinguished.
c.   Incorrect. They slow down just after the reinforcement.
*d. Correct. The predictability of the interval leads the organism to pause just after the reinforcement.

30. b   obj. 5   p. 185
a.   Incorrect. Reinforcement does not inhibit the desired behavior.
*b. Correct. Shaping is the technique of rewarding each successive behavior that gets closer to the desired behavior.
c.   Incorrect. Reinforcement would not disrupt the targeted behavior.
d.   Incorrect. Reinforcement would not eliminate the target behavior.

Practice Test III:
31. a   obj. 2   p. 170
*a. Correct. The bell is being used just as the unconditioned stimulus had been in the earlier training.
b.   Incorrect. While the bell is a conditioned stimulus, for the purpose of the second training event, it is unconditioned stimulus.
c.   Incorrect. The bell is not a response.
d.   Incorrect. The bell is not a response.

32. a   obj. 2   p. 170
*a. Correct. The food elicits a response that has not been conditioned.
b.   Incorrect. The juicer is the unconditioned response.
c.   Incorrect. Food is not a response.
d.   Incorrect. Food is not a response.

33. b   obj. 2   p. 170
a.   Incorrect. The food is the unconditioned stimulus.
*b. Correct. The child has become conditioned to the blender as the signal for food.
c.   Incorrect. The blender is not a response.
d.   Incorrect. The blender is not a response.

34. a   obj. 1   p. 170
*a. Correct. The sickness occurs without any training, and should thus be considered the "unconditioned" response.
b.   Incorrect. Sickness is a response, not a stimulus in this scenario.
c.   Incorrect. As a response to the poison, the sickness is unconditioned.
d.   Incorrect. If the response of sickness were to the sight of the bait, then it would be "conditioned."

35. b   obj. 4   p. 177
a.   Incorrect. Generalization would imply the dog barking at any little girl.
*b. Correct. The bark may have occurred freely, without association and without reinforcement, and would thus be "operant."
c.   Incorrect. Typically, a reinforcer follows the reinforced behavior.
d.   Incorrect. Barking may accompany aversive responses, but the pattern requires something to be avoided.

36. c   obj. 2   p. 174
a.   Incorrect. This appears to be a classically conditioned dislike.
b.   Incorrect. In stimulus discrimination, he would probably have learned to dislike only his favorite brand of cigarette.
*c. Correct. This is an example of higher-order conditioning, where the store had once been a signal for buying the cigarettes and is now a signal for the dislike of the cigarette.
d.   Incorrect. Systematic desensitization would have been used to get rid of a fear or other phobia, not a desired habit.

37. a   obj. 2   p. 174
*a. Correct. Of these choices, this best fits: The child learns to discriminate among different qualities of roses.
b.   Incorrect. With generalization, the discrimination of colors would decline.
c.   Incorrect. There is no such concept as spontaneous generalization.
d.   Incorrect. Spontaneous recovery occurs after extinction has been followed by a period of rest.

38. a   obj. 8   p. 174
*a. Correct. This is very discrete training and requires that the dog not respond to similar odors.
b.   Incorrect. If response generalization existed, this would not be it.
c.   Incorrect. Partial reinforcement may have been used in the training, but the ability indicates stimulus generalization.
d.   Incorrect. Spontaneous recovery requires extinction to occur.

39. c   obj. 5   p. 174
a.   Incorrect. See answer c.
b.   Incorrect. See answer c.
*c. Correct. The learner quickly identifies the apparent "wait time" that follows a reinforcement in a fixed-interval training schedule and thus does not respond for a period of time as no reinforcement will be forthcoming.
d.   Incorrect. See answer c.

40. c   obj. 8   p. 189
a.   Incorrect. A personality psychologist would be more interested in traits than learned maps.
b.   Incorrect. A sensory psychologist would measure the sensory responses of the children.
*c. Correct. He was demonstrating how children form cognitive maps and then demonstrate their knowledge at a later point in time.
d.   Incorrect. A biopsychologist might be interested in the underlying processes that account for the learning.

41. d   obj. 8   p. 188
a.   Incorrect. Partial reinforcement supports the idea that not all performance needs to be reinforced.
b.   Incorrect. Classical conditioning depends upon performance for evidence of learning.
c.   Incorrect. Shaping involves the gradual modification of behavior toward a desired form.
*d. Correct. While performance is a measure of learning, the possibility of unmeasured learning is not ruled out.

42. c   obj. 4   p. 180
a.   Incorrect. Playing the music loud in the first place was a form of punishment.
b.   Incorrect. Positive reinforcement refers to pleasant consequences for a target behavior (studying is the target behavior, not finding peace and quiet).
*c. Correct. "Negative" in this case is the removal of an unwanted stimulus in order to increase a desired behavior (studying).
d.   Incorrect. She is being rewarded, not punished by removal.

43. d   obj. 8   p. 191
a.   Incorrect. Some scientists make stronger claims with only twenty or thirty subjects.
b.   Incorrect. This cannot be determined from this statement.
c.   Incorrect. The study does not indicate how the viewing data was gathered.

*d. Correct. This is correct only if the researchers claim or imply a causal relationship.

44. a   obj. 9   p. 195
*a. Correct. This describes the qualities of the relational learning style.
b.   Incorrect. Classical conditioning may help him learn, but the style described is the relational learning style.
c.   Incorrect. However, he could serve as a model, this stem does not answer the question.
d.   Incorrect. The relational style does include explicit learning.

45. b   obj. 9   p. 195
a.   Incorrect. Identifying which area to work on first should precede this step.
*b. Correct. Identifying objective goals is the first step in making a realistic attempt to improve learning.
c.   Incorrect. This is a later step of the program.
d.   Incorrect. After identifying which classes to work on, he could then identify a specific study skill.

■ CHAPTER 6: ANSWER KEY

GUIDED REVIEW			MATCHING		
Concept 1: [a] Encoding [b] Storage [c] Retrieval [d] memory [e] sensory memory [f] Short-term memory [g] Long-term memory [h] iconic memory [i] echoic memory [j] chunks [k] rehearsal [l] Elaborative rehearsal [m] mnemonics [n] Working memory [o] declarative memory [p] procedural memory	[q] episodic memories [r] semantic memories [s] associative models [t] Priming [u] Explicit memory [v] implicit memory [w] levels-of-processing theory **Concept 2:** [a] tip-of-the-tongue phenomenon [b] retrieval cues [c] flashbulb memories [d] constructive processes [e] schemas [f] soap opera effect [g] Autobiographical memories	**Concept 3:** [a] decay [b] memory trace [c] engram [d] interference [e] proactive interference [f] Retroactive interference [g] long-term potentiation [h] consolidation [i] Alzheimer's disease [j] Amnesia [k] Retrograde amnesia [l] Anterograde amnesia [m] encoding specificity	1. d 2. f 3. a 4. c 5. e 6. b 7. e 8. d 9. b 10. c 11. f 12. a	13. e 14. a 15. d 16. c 17. f 18. b 19. b 20. g 21. c 22. a 23. e 24. f 25. d	26. c 27. g 28. a 29. d 30. b 31. e 32. f 33. a 34. c 35. e 36. d 37. b

Essay Question 6.1: Writing about Repressed Memories

■ State the evidence supporting the existence of repressed memories and describe the problems that can arise from mistaken recovered memories.

■ One might argue that psychologists interfere with and compound the problem further by encouraging clients to "recover" memories that they may not have actually had, something like the demand characteristic in research. Consider whether there are ways to reduce false memories.

Essay Question 6.2: Laboratory Memory

■ Give several examples of laboratory research. The advantages include control over the experiment and the ability to document that prior memories do not influence the outcome.

■ Identify experiences that are best examined in an everyday context. Much case study and archival research is based on reports that are made when an event occurs or on reports from several points of view and are thus a form of everyday memory research. Other examples should be given.

■ As stated in the text, both of these techniques are needed to understand memory fully.

Multiple Choice Feedback:

Practice Test I:

1. a obj. 1 p. 205
*a. Correct. Encoding places the information in a manageable form.
b. Incorrect. Storage refers to the retention of the encoded memory.
c. Incorrect. Decoding must mean the removal of the code into which something has been encoded.
d. Incorrect. Retrieval is the recovery of stored, encoded information.

2. b obj. 1 p. 205
a. Incorrect. Storage refers to the retention of the encoded memory.
*b. Correct. Retrieval is the recovery of stored, encoded information so that it can be used.

c.   Incorrect. Recording is the work of committing information to a record, like taking notes, etc.

d.   Incorrect. See Chapter 5.

3.   b   obj. 2   p. 206

a.   Incorrect. Sensory memory has a life of less than a second.

*b.   Correct. Unless material is rehearsed, information is quickly lost from the short-term memory.

c.   Incorrect. Iconic memory refers to visual sensory memory and has a duration of less than a quarter of a second.

d.   Incorrect. The duration of long-term memory is indefinite.

4.   b   obj. 2   p. 208

a.   Incorrect. It can hold up to nine items, but the average would be seven.

*b.   Correct. Psychologists accept the view that we can hold about seven, plus or minus two, items in short-term memory.

c.   Incorrect. Psychologists accept the view that we can hold about seven, plus or minus two, items in short-term memory.

d.   Incorrect. Psychologists accept the view that we can hold about seven, plus or minus two items in short-term memory.

5.   d   obj. 2   p. 209

a.   Incorrect. Rehearsal facilitates all memory.

b.   Incorrect. It does help short-term memory items persist in short-term memory.

c.   Incorrect. It does aid in the transfer of memory to long-tem storage.

*d.   Correct. It helps both short-term duration and long-term consolidation.

6.   b   obj. 3   p. 212

a.   Incorrect. No such memory concept.

*b.   Correct. Memory of life events, or episodes, is one of the types of long-term memory.

c.   Incorrect. Semantic memory is memory for declarative knowledge like words and definitions.

d.   Incorrect. No concept like this has been used in contemporary psychology.

7.   a   obj. 3   p. 212

*a.   Correct. Episodic memory is the storage of stories and details about life - that is, episodes.

b.   Incorrect. Facts like these are considered semantic.

c.   Incorrect. Episodic memory has little to do with speaking.

d.   Incorrect. This would not affect short-term memory.

8.   a   obj. 5   p. 217

*a.   Correct. Retrieval cues are aspects-connections, similarities, etc-of information that help us recall, or retrieve, the information.

b.   Incorrect. Distractors are the stems of multiple choice questions that are designed to distract the test-taker.

c.   Incorrect. This is not the answer.

d.   Incorrect. The sensory code is relevant to short-term memory and our ability to manipulate that memory.

9.   d   obj. 5   p. 217

a.   Incorrect. Difficulties in encoding may make it impossible to retrieve any information.

b.   Incorrect. Decoding is not a memory phenomenon.

c.   Incorrect. A difficulty with storage would appear in the inability to form new memories.

*d.   Correct. We may know that we know something, but not be able to retrieve it.

10.   d   obj. 6   p. 219

a.   Incorrect. See answer d.

b.   Incorrect. See answer d.

c.   Incorrect. See answer d.

*d.   Correct. In terms of memory phenomena, construction processes apply to episodic memory, motivation, and procedural memory.

11.   b   obj. 7   p. 226

a.   Incorrect. After two days, the memory loss had settled down.

*b.   Correct. Within an hour, a significant portion of the list had been forgotten.

c.   Incorrect. Only a supermemory could remember the list ten days later.

d.   Incorrect. The most dramatic loss occurred within the first hour.

12.   c   obj. 8   p. 228

a.   Incorrect. May actually magnify if an error is repeated.

b.   Incorrect. Trace decay may not occur anyway.

*c.   Correct. Different brain areas are at work as the rehearsal begins to influence consolidation.

d.   Incorrect. This is not a symptom of this disease.

13.   c   obj. 8   p. 232

a.   Incorrect. Had they been encoded wrong, they could not be recovered.

b.   Incorrect. Had they not been stored, they could never be recovered.

*c.   Correct. Since they had not been destroyed, they could still be retrieved.

d.   Incorrect. Association is not one of the traditional memory processes.

14.   b   obj. 8   p. 232
a.   Incorrect. This is retrograde amnesia, which covers the period prior to the trauma.
*b.   Correct. This is common for head-injury patients, who lose the time following the accident.
c.   Incorrect. This is an apraxia.
d.   Incorrect. This is another kind of memory difficulty.

15.   b   obj. 9   p. 233
a.   Incorrect. The keyword technique suggests that a similar sounding word would help in memory.
*b.   Correct. In this description, a similar sounding word is used.
c.   Incorrect. One would already need to know the word to make similar imagery.
d.   Incorrect. This is a free association technique.

Practice Test II:
16.   b   obj. 1   p. 205
a.   Incorrect. Encoding involves getting the information into a form that can be stored.
*b.   Correct. Storage refers to the process of retaining the information for later use.
c.   Incorrect. Memory has no decoding process.
d.   Incorrect. Retrieval refers to the recovery of memory from storage.

17.   c   obj. 2   p. 212
a.   Incorrect. This is a form of long-term memory.
b.   Incorrect. Short-term memory can last about 15 to 20 seconds
*c.   Correct. Sensory memory lasts for less than a second.
d.   Incorrect. This is a form of long-term memory.

18.   a   obj. 2   p. 206
*a.   Correct. With meaning, the items in short-term memory have greater duration.
b.   Incorrect. Memory does not have an intensity except in the emotional sense.
c.   Incorrect. Memories can not be measured in terms of length, though their duration can.
d.   Incorrect. Some visual memory will be coded verbally for easier manipulation.

19.   c   obj. 2   p. 208
a.   Incorrect. Similarity is the Gestalt organizational principle.
b.   Incorrect. Priming refers to a cognitive theory that suggest memories, thoughts, and other cognitive material can be primed.
*c.   Correct. The technical term is chunking, and it refers to grouping information together in any way that can be recalled.

d.   Incorrect. Closure is a Gestalt principle of perceptual organization.

20.   b   obj. 2   p. 210
a.   Incorrect. Massed practice is not a very effective approach to enhancing long-term memory consolidation.
*b.   Correct. Elaborative rehearsal strengthens the memory by providing a rich array of retrieval cues.
c.   Incorrect. None of the researchers have suggested a process called interpolation (yet).
d.   Incorrect. Interference will actually make consolidation more difficult.

21.   c   obj. 3   p. 212
a.   Incorrect. There is not a form of memory known as periodic memory.
b.   Incorrect. Episodic memory refers to the personal memories of experiences and life-events.
*c.   Correct. This is a definition of the form of declarative memory known as semantic memory.
d.   Incorrect. None of the researchers have suggested a process called serial production memory (yet).

22.   d   obj. 4   p. 215
a.   Incorrect. The stage of memory?
b.   Incorrect. The meaning can be very important and very significant, but still be forgotten.
c.   Incorrect. Memories do not have qualities in a sense relevant to the levels-of-processing approach.
*d.   Correct. The depth of processing is determined by the extent of elaboration and the kinds of information to which the new information was associated.

23.   d   obj. 5   p. 218
a.   Incorrect. This is a form of guessing, like your selecting this answer.
b.   Incorrect. Recall refers to the free recall of information without any specific cues.
c.   Incorrect. Mnemonics refers to the techniques or memory aids that can be used to improve memory.
*d.   Correct. Since the answer is among the four items presented as alternatives, the test-taker only needs to recognize the right answer.

24.   c   obj. 5   p. 218
a.   Incorrect. A cognitive map is a more mundane memory item created while wandering about.
b.   Incorrect. A schema is an organizational unit that gives structure or organization to a set of information.
*c.   Correct. Significant events are often remembered in great detail and apparent specificity, as if a photograph were taken of the event (thus flashbulb memory).

d.   Incorrect. A seizure is a very traumatic experience, and probably would not have this kind of memory associated with it.

25.   a   obj. 3   p. 212
*a.   Correct. Procedural memories are skill-based memories, like riding a bicycle or skating.
b.   Incorrect. Semantic memory is memory of words, definitions, procedures, grammatical rules, and similarly abstract information.
c.   Incorrect. This is a kind of rehearsal that involves making many connections and relationships for an item being remembered.
d.   Incorrect. Declarative memory combines episodic and semantic memory.

26.   d   obj. 7   p. 226
a.   Incorrect. Decay theory says that we lose memories because they fade away.
b.   Incorrect. Interference accounts for memory loss by the displacement of one memory by another.
c.   Incorrect. We may not have lost the memory, but with inadequate cues, we cannot recall it.
*d.   Correct. This is not a theory of forgetting.

27.   b   obj. 8   p. 228
a.   Incorrect. The hippocampus is thought to play a role in the consolidation of short-term memories into long-term memories.
*b.   Correct. The sucli have yet to be implicated in memory.
c.   Incorrect. Neurotransmitters support the memory consolidation process.
d.   Incorrect. Changes at the synapse that are relatively permanent are called long-term potentiation.

28.   d   obj. 6   p. 220
a.   Incorrect. True only if "other type" refers to fabrication.
b.   Incorrect. Usually they are recovered in therapy, not treated.
c.   Incorrect. They do have a noticeable effect, but this is not an identifying feature.
*d.   Correct. The problem faced by all is the ability to verify the genuineness of the memories.

29.   a   obj. 8   p. 232
*a.   Correct. The loss of all memories prior to an accident is very uncommon, though it is the most popularized form of amnesia.
b.   Incorrect. Retrograde amnesia, the loss of all memories prior to an accident or trauma, is very uncommon, though it is the most popularized form of amnesia.

c.   Incorrect. Retrograde amnesia, the loss of all memories prior to an accident or trauma, is very uncommon, though it is the most popularized form of amnesia.
d.   Incorrect. Retrograde amnesia, the loss of all memories prior to an accident or trauma, is very uncommon, though it is the most popularized form of amnesia.

30.   a   obj. 9   p. 234
*a.   Correct. This is called massed practice, and it is not very effective.
b.   Incorrect. Overlearning is an effective form a study.
c.   Incorrect. Organization helps memory by providing a meaningful scheme for the information.
d.   Incorrect. This helps elaborate the material-putting it in your own words.

Practice Test III:
31.   d   obj. 2   p. 206
a.   Incorrect. Episodic memory would mean that the items had been committed to long-term memory.
b.   Incorrect. This is the sensory memory for hearing, and it only lasts about a second.
c.   Incorrect. This is the sensory memory for vision, and it only lasts about a quarter of a second.
*d.   Correct. Short-term memory would account for most of this ability of recollection. Some, however, think this is a special skill developed by husbands who watch football too much.

32.   b   obj. 2   p. 206
a.   Incorrect. This is difficult to judge, since our sensory receptors are always active.
*b.   Correct. The sensory information in the sensory memory has not been processed any further than the sensory register, thus it represents the information as it was taken in.
c.   Incorrect. The sensory information in the sensory memory has not been processed any further than the sensory register, thus it represents the information as it was taken in, and it is therefore as complete as the sensory system makes it.
d.   Incorrect. The information will be lost if it is not processed, but some information can be processed and be meaningless.

33.   a   obj. 6   p. 220
*a.   Correct. This constructive process helps give the memory its narrative quality.
b.   Incorrect. We tend not to lose the distinctive features.
c.   Incorrect. Engrams are not sheep.
d.   Incorrect. Ambiguous details are not a hallmark of flashbulb memories.

34.   b   obj. 2   p. 206
a.   Incorrect. A flashbulb memory implies a photo-like recollection.
*b.   Correct. The visual echo or afterimage of the screen is much like the sensory activation in iconic memory.
c.   Incorrect. The parallel here would be the persisting buzz of the radio tube for the brief moment following it being turned off.
d.   Incorrect. Declarative memory is very long term and does not appear to fade in this manner.

35.   d   obj. 3   p. 212
a.   Incorrect. Working memory applies to memories that soon become insignificant, like what we ate for lunch yesterday or where we parked our car yesterday (though where we parked it today is very important).
b.   Incorrect. Declarative does not account for physical skills like this.
c.   Incorrect. This contributes to our personal experiences and episodic memory.
*d.   Correct. The tennis stroke is a procedural skill and thus would be stored in procedural memory.

36.   b   obj. 3   p. 212
a.   Incorrect. Working memory is significant for only a few days.
*b.   Correct. Procedural memory is just this kind of skill-based memory.
c.   Incorrect. Only if he had been in a serious bicycle accident could the possibility of a repressed memory play a role.
d.   Incorrect. Although this may be an important moment in the lives of Mark and his son, it is the procedural memory that contributes to Mark's ability to recall this old skill.

37.   c   obj. 6   p. 219
a.   Incorrect. Freud did not introduce this idea.
b.   Incorrect. Piaget used it, but it was introduced by someone else.
*c.   Correct. This was Bartlett's contribution.
d.   Incorrect. This is the author of the textbook.

38.   c   obj. 4   p. 215
a.   Incorrect. If attention means rehearsal, then this would be true.
b.   Incorrect. There is no mental imagery model of memory.
*c.   Correct. "Attention" would have an effect on how the memory was elaborated (thus given depth).
d.   Incorrect. The is no specific cultural diversity model of memory.

39.   d   obj. 7   p. 227
a.   Incorrect. Try the opposite, where the first list influences the later list.
b.   Incorrect. This is a dissociative state similar to amnesia.
c.   Incorrect. This is a type of memory failure.
*d.   Correct. In proactive interference, an earlier list interferes with a later list.

40.   b   obj. 7   p. 227
a.   Incorrect. This is not a recognized form of interference.
*b.   Correct. In retroactive interference, a later list interferes with an earlier list.
c.   Incorrect. In proactive interference, an earlier list interferes with a later list.
d.   Incorrect. This is not a recognized form of interference.

41.   d   obj. 7   p. 227
a.   Incorrect. Alzheimer's disease would affect all the transactions.
b.   Incorrect. Decay is not thought to be a significant factor, especially if the sales clerk would have remembered had the other transactions not intervened.
c.   Incorrect. Proactive means the previous interfere with the current.
*d.   Correct. Retroactive means that the intervening events interfere with the recall of the earlier event.

42.   c   obj. 8   p. 232
a.   Incorrect. Try: the manufacture of beta amyloid.
b.   Incorrect. Try: the manufacture of beta amyloid.
*c.   Correct. Platelets form and constrict brain tissue, causing it to die.
d.   Incorrect. Try: the manufacture of beta amyloid.

43.   d   obj. 8   p. 232
a.   Incorrect. This sounds like Alzheimer's disease.
b.   Incorrect. This is anterograde amnesia.
c.   Incorrect. This sounds like advanced Alzheimer's disease or stroke victim.
*d.   Correct. Memories are lost from prior to the accident.

44.   a   obj. 9   p. 233
*a.   Correct. Placing parts of a speech or something to be remembered on "loci" or place in a room.
b.   Incorrect. Serial production memory is not a type of memory or a memory process.
c.   Incorrect. The keyword technique involves associating new items with familiar items.
d.   Incorrect. In retroactive interference, a later list interferes with an earlier list.

45.   a   obj. 8   p. 232
*a.   Correct. Retrograde amnesia is marked by the loss
        of ability to recall events from prior to an accident
        or trauma.
b.   Incorrect. Anterograde amnesia involves the loss of
        memory from the point of an accident or trauma
        forward.
c.   Incorrect. This is a loss of memory from early
        childhood, usually prior to the development of
        language skills.
d.   Incorrect. This is a memory loss syndrome that
        results from severe, long-term abuse of alcohol.

■ CHAPTER 7: ANSWER KEY

GUIDED REVIEW			MATCHING		
Concept 1:	Concept 2:	Concept 3:	1. e	17. a	
[a] cognitive psychology	[a] well-defined problem	[a] Language	2. b	18. d	
[b] cognition	[b] ill-defined problem	[b] grammar	3. d	19. e	
[c] Thinking	[c] Arrangement problems	[c] phonology	4. a	20. c	
[d] mental images	[d] problems of inducing structure	[d] phonemes	5. c	21. b	
[e] Concepts	[e] transformation problems	[e] syntax	6. d		
[f] prototypes	[f] means-ends analysis	[f] semantics	7. c	22. b	
[g] Deductive reasoning	[g] insight	[g] babble	8. a	23. c	
[h] Inductive reasoning	[h] Functional fixedness	[h] Telegraphic speech	9. e	24. e	
[i] algorithm	[i] mental set	[i] overgeneralization	10. b	25. d	
[j] heuristic	[j] Creativity	[j] learning-theory approach	11. b	26. a	
[k] representativeness heuristic	[k] Divergent thinking	[k] universal grammar	12. a	27. g	
[l] availability heuristic	[l] Convergent thinking	[l] language-acquisition device	13. e	28. f	
		[m] linguistic-relativity hypothesis	14. f		
		[n] biculturalism	15. d		
		[o] alternation model	16. c		

Essay Question 7.1: Problem Solving

■ Describe your problem or challenge. It would be best to identify both the positive and the negative aspects of the challenge, including what is gained and what is given up.

■ Define the problem in terms of the steps that must be taken to achieve the solution.

■ State several possible solution strategies as they apply to your problem.

■ State how you will know when you have effectively solved the problem. Remember, if the problem is long-term, selecting one solution strategy may preclude using another.

Essay Question 7.2: Is Language Uniquely Human?

■ Chimpanzees acquire an ability to speak that is comparable to a two-year-old child.

■ The physical ability in humans to produce language has the greatest production capability.

■ You may be familiar with research in dolphin and whale communication or work with other animals. Examples could be used to support your answer.

■ What is meant by "unique" must be defined to complete this answer. Indeed human language is unique, but other animals do communicate.

Multiple Choice Feedback:

Practice Test I:

1. d   obj. 1   p. 242
a.   Incorrect. This is difficult to document.
b.   Incorrect. This probably relates to spatial-temporal skills.
c.   Incorrect. This has to do with language skills.
*d.   Correct. Mental rotation and comparison is one technique used to study how people manipulate mental images.

2.   c   obj. 1   p. 243
a.   Incorrect. Concepts include more than new procedures and products.
b.   Incorrect. The term attitudes is too restrictive, and this is a definition of a stereotype.
*c.   Correct. Concepts are used to categorize thought.
d.   Incorrect. Concepts can include natural objects as well as scientific knowledge.

3.   d   obj. 2   p. 244
a.   Incorrect. Inductive reasoning works from a series of examples to generate a conclusion.
b.   Incorrect. Not sure what this is.
c.   Incorrect. The term "transductive" has been applied to reasoning during the preoperational period of childhood.
*d.   Correct. Deriving a solution or conclusion from a set of laws or principles describes deductive reasoning.

4.   a   obj. 3   p. 234
*a.   Correct. Deductive reasoning is only as valid as its premises, and the conclusions can be in error because of faulty use of formal reasoning.
b.   Incorrect. Inductive reasoning does not derive from premises, rather from cases and examples.
c.   Incorrect. Availability heuristics draw conclusions from the most apparent (available) evidence and may ignore other evidence.
d.   Incorrect. Algorithms are themselves rules for problem solution and do not have premises.

5.   c   obj. 4   p. 249
a.   Incorrect. This is an important step.
b.   Incorrect. Good preparation is an important step in effective problem solving.
*c.   Correct. To reach a solution, it is not necessary to document all possible solutions.
d.   Incorrect. To solve a problem, one must produce at least one solution.

6.   b   obj. 4   p. 249
a.   Incorrect. Perhaps a problem could be so overdefined that it confused the problem solver.
*b.   Correct. The answer as well as the means of solving the problem are clearly understood.
c.   Incorrect. This is not a traditional way of understanding problem types.

d.   Incorrect. If there were no picture on the puzzle, then it might be considered ill-defined.

7.   d   obj. 5   p. 253
a.   Incorrect. The text names means-ends analysis as the most common.
b.   Incorrect. The text names means-ends analysis as the most common.
c.   Incorrect. The text names means-ends analysis as the most common.
*d.   Correct. Consider how often we turn to the desired outcome and let it shape how we approach the problem.

8.   d   obj. 4   p. 249
a.   Incorrect. Removing the inessential may help make the definition of the problem clearer.
b.   Incorrect. Making the information simpler, even putting it in a graphic form like a chart, helps make the problem easier to understand.
c.   Incorrect. Often, dividing the problem into parts helps define the whole problem more clearly.
*d.   Correct. Clarifying the solution applies more to the later stages of solving the problem.

9.   a   obj. 5   p. 254
*a.   Correct. This is the definition of insight, where one becomes aware of a new or different arrangement of elements.
b.   Incorrect. Insight does not suggest that an individual has no experience with a problem.
c.   Incorrect. While one might discover an algorithm for a problem through insight, it is not a necessary aspect of insight.
d.   Incorrect. This refers more to brainstorming than insight.

10.   d   obj. 3   p. 244
a.   Incorrect. This requires very complex programming.
b.   Incorrect. This is an example of "d," thus not the best answer.
c.   Incorrect. Heuristics require much more complicated programming.
*d.   Correct. An algorithm is a set of rules that guarantee an answer.

11.   b   obj. 7   p. 258
a.   Incorrect. Creativity draws upon knowledge and experience, but not necessarily so.
*b.   Correct. Convergent thinking is defined as thinking exemplified by the use of logical reasoning and knowledge.
c.   Incorrect. Divergent thinking often defies logic and is not dependent upon a knowledge base.
d.   Incorrect. The use of the imagination does not exemplify logical processes and is perhaps the least dependent on knowledge.

12.   d   obj. 7   p. 257
a.   Incorrect. If the mental set is strong, it will have an impeding effect.
b.   Incorrect. Since intelligence and creativity have not been correlated, this is not necessarily true.
c.   Incorrect. Exactly the opposite.
*d.   Correct. Divergent thinking involves recognizing alternatives and optional uses.

13.   b   obj. 8   p. 261
a.   Incorrect. Semantics determines the meaning of words and phrases.
*b.   Correct. Syntax refers to the meaningful structuring of sentences.
c.   Incorrect. Phonology governs the production of sounds.
d.   Incorrect. Somewhat broader than syntax, grammar governs the translation of thoughts into language.

14.   b   obj. 9   p. 262
a.   Incorrect. Speed and rate of speech are not factors in telegraphic speech.
*b.   Correct. Like sending a telegraph, some words may be omitted and the message is still clear.
c.   Incorrect. The sound of the speech is not relevant to telegraphic speech.
d.   Incorrect. Speed and rate of speech are not factors in telegraphic speech.

15.   d   obj. 9   p. 262
a.   Incorrect. At 2 years children are just beginning to utilize speech and build vocabularies.
b.   Incorrect. At 3, vocabulary and grammatical rules are still being acquired.
c.   Incorrect. At 4, vocabulary and grammatical rules are still being acquired.
*d.   Correct. By the age of five, most children can produce grammatically correct speech.

16.   a   obj. 9   p. 262
*a.   Correct. Evidence shows that children can understand far more language than they can produce.
b.   Incorrect. See answer a.
c.   Incorrect. See answer a.
d.   Incorrect. See answer a.

17.   c   obj. 9   p. 263
a.   Incorrect. While classical conditioning has a role for the learning theorists in language, it is not the key process.
b.   Incorrect. While stimulus generalization may have a minor role for the learning theorists in language, it is not the key process.
*c.   Correct. Shaping is the key force for learning theorists because it modifies the many sounds made by infants as the sounds become better approximations of words.
d.   Incorrect. Chaining is an important process in linking words together, but shaping is a more

critical process for the learning theorists in language development.

Practice Test II:

18.   a   obj. 1   p. 241
*a.   Correct. Perceptual psychologists focus on how the sensory system takes in information.
b.   Incorrect. Our understanding of the world is a focal point of study for cognitive psychologists.
c.   Incorrect. How we process information is a focal point of study for cognitive psychologists.
d.   Incorrect. Decision making is a focal point of study for cognitive psychologists.

19.   c   obj. 1   p. 241
a.   Incorrect. While "prototype" may refer to a new or first type, it also refers to the template or standard.
b.   Incorrect. Prototypes are neither spontaneous nor discarded quickly.
*c.   Correct. In this sense, the prototype is the template or standard for a concept.
d.   Incorrect. The concept described here is known as "cognate" or "loan words."

20.   c   obj. 2   p. 243
a.   Incorrect. Syllogism is not an error, but instead is a form of argument.
b.   Incorrect. Nice try, but a syllogism is a form of logical reasoning.
*c.   Correct. The syllogistic form of logical reasoning does derive a conclusion from two premises, or assumptions.
d.   Incorrect. An analogy is similar to a syllogism, as it may show a relationship between several concepts, but a syllogism is a form of logical reasoning.

21.   d   obj. 3   p. 247
a.   Incorrect. In the availability heuristic, one applies the most available category to the situation.
b.   Incorrect. A mental set is a set of expectations and inferences drawn from memory that indeed may cause reasoning errors, but not in this manner.
c.   Incorrect. Functional fixedness refers specifically to applying objects to a problem in the manner of their typical or common function, thus being fixated on a particular approach.
*d.   Correct. The representative heuristic selects a category that may represent the situation but can be erroneously applied (or misapplied).

22.   b   obj. 4   p. 251
a.   Incorrect. Problems of arrangement may include puzzles and similar problems.
*b.   Correct. No such type of problem!
c.   Incorrect. A problem of inducing structure involves finding relationships among existing elements.
d.   Incorrect. Transformation problems involve changing from one state to another (the goal state).

23.   a   obj. 4   p. 251

*a.   Correct. True, this describes a problem of inducing structure.

b.   Incorrect. This is not one of the three types of problems, and thus the definition does not apply.

c.   Incorrect. An arrangement problem is more like a jigsaw puzzle, where elements may be rearranged.

d.   Incorrect. A transformation problem involves moving from one state to another (goal state).

24.   a   obj. 4   p. 251

*a.   Correct. Changing from one state to another is a transformation.

b.   Incorrect. This refers to another kind of problem.

c.   Incorrect. Insight is a means of solving a problem, not a type of problem (unless someone is without any insight).

d.   Incorrect. This refers to another kind of problem.

25.   b   obj. 5   p. 253

a.   Incorrect. A means-ends approach might be more, "I know the steps I need to take, and I am taking them."

*b.   Correct. Each step is a subgoal.

c.   Incorrect. Trial and error might be more: "I think I'll try this major next semester."

d.   Incorrect. Algorithmic approach might be more "I need three courses from this group, two from that, . . ."

26.   c   obj. 5   p. 254

a.   Incorrect. Indeed, insight may be difficult to explain or articulate, and it may occur without prior experience, but these are not the defining elements of insight.

b.   Incorrect. Insight does not result from trial-and-error processes.

*c.   Correct. This sudden realization of relationship or recognition of patterns is key to insight.

d.   Incorrect. Insight may be founded upon trial-and-error and experience, but the restructuring that occurs during insight may be independent, or it may also be a result of experience or creative reorganization.

27.   b   obj. 6   p. 256

a.   Incorrect. These hunches may actually make it hard to see alternatives.

*b.   Correct. Initial perceptions may include more conventional ways of using the elements of the problem and tools at hand to solve it.

c.   Incorrect. While true, it does not apply to these two concepts.

d.   Incorrect. Not really sure what this means.

28.   b   obj. 7   p. 257

a.   Incorrect. Convergent thinking involves logical reasoning and knowledge in the process of thinking.

*b.   Correct. Divergent thinking is the only consistently identified characteristic of creative thinking.

c.   Incorrect. Many creative thinkers are highly intelligent, but this is not a necessary characteristic.

d.   Incorrect. Recurrent thought does not characterize creativity.

29.   c   obj. 8   p. 261

a.   Incorrect. Synthetics is a science fiction word used to describe synthetically produced biological organisms.

b.   Incorrect. Semantics is the study of the meanings of words.

*c.   Correct. Syntax governs the order in of words in a sentence.

d.   Incorrect. Systematics is a neologism (not really a word, but it sounds like one), and is probably used by a lot of people.

30.   b   obj. 9   p. 262

a.   Incorrect. Babbling does occur from 3 to 6 months of age.

*b.   Correct. "Dada" and "mama" are early words formed of babbling sounds.

c.   Incorrect. Babbling has many speechlike patterns.

d.   Incorrect. Indeed, babbling does produce all the sounds that humans make.

31.   c   obj. 9   p. 262

a.   Incorrect. Actually, it is usual because they are among the first sounds made.

b.   Incorrect. We know of no words that are innate.

*c.   Correct. These are easy and composed of sounds commonly heard in the babbling phase.

d.   Incorrect. Babies can even make sounds they have never before heard, especially if the parents' language does not include the sound.

32.   b   obj. 9   p. 263

a.   Incorrect. There is no linguistic relativity system, instead, it is the linguistic relativity hypothesis - a theory about how language and thought interrelate.

*b.   Correct. This is the term used by Noam Chomsky to refer to this neural wiring.

c.   Incorrect. The limbic system is the organization of several parts of the brain that is generally devoted to pleasure, emotion, motivation, and memory.

d.   Incorrect. Sounds good, but this is not the term used, and it does not refer to any actual concept.

33.   b   obj. 9   p. 266
a.   Incorrect. Early in his work on language, Chomsky argued for the existence of a universal grammar.
*b.   Correct. Chomsky is not a behaviorist and even criticizes the learning approach because reinforcement is too slow a process to account for the rapid acquisition of language.
c.   Incorrect. Much of the brain is devoted to the development and production of language, and the brain controls the processes.
d.   Incorrect. Chomsky believes that language is uniquely human, and no other animal is properly "wired" for language.

34.   d   obj. 10   p. 265
a.   Incorrect. While this may be true, it is not the point of the linguistic relativity hypothesis.
b.   Incorrect. Also, however, language may create thought. This is not part of the linguistic relativity hypothesis.
c.   Incorrect. Language and thought are not synonymous, and this is not a paraphrase of the linguistic relativity hypothesis.
*d.   Correct. The linguistic relativity hypothesis claims that language determines thought, and if a specific language cannot formulate a concept, then the speakers of the language do not use the concept in their thinking.

Practice Test III:
35.   d   obj. 1   p. 241
a.   Incorrect. This is one of the components of the text's definition.
b.   Incorrect. Cognition refers to the processes involved in how people come to know their world.
c.   Incorrect. Cognition includes language and the interpretation of language.
*d.   Correct. This statement describes the processes of sensation and perception. While not part of cognition, they are companion processes.

36.   b   obj. 1   p. 243
a.   Incorrect. Concepts may result from errors in some way, but they do not themselves produce errors.
*b.   Correct. Like perception, concepts help make the world understandable by simplifying and organizing it.
c.   Incorrect. Even if this analogy is true, it does not address the similarity between concepts and perception.
d.   Incorrect. We know of no innate concepts.

37.   b   obj. 3   p. 247
a.   Incorrect. The means-ends does not apply here.
*b.   Correct. Since your roommate is a member of the category of car salespersons, the representative heuristic suggests that somehow he might be representative of that group of people.
c.   Incorrect. The availability heuristic would suggest that you utilized only currently available or the most prominent information about car dealers and ignored other more important information that is easily recalled from memory. While true, you had no other information about your roommate.
d.   Incorrect. There is no such heuristic.

38.   a   obj. 6   p. 256
*a.   Correct. Functional fixedness forces us to focus on the wrench's traditional function, ignoring that it could be used as a weight or a clamp, or even an electrical conductor.
b.   Incorrect. Insight is the restructuring of given elements.
c.   Incorrect. Awareness seems to be restricted in this case.
d.   Incorrect. Overpreparation may lead to functional fixedness by encouraging the habitual use of an object, but it is not the name of the phenomena.

39.   d   obj. 8   p. 261
a.   Incorrect. Grammar governs how a thought becomes language in a general sense, and a more precise possibility is given in the options.
b.   Incorrect. Phonology governs the production of sounds.
c.   Incorrect. Syntax refers to the structure of sentences and not their meaning.
*d.   Correct. Semantics governs the use of words and sentences to make specific meanings, and would govern how the same words can be rearranged to make different meanings.

40.   b   obj. 9   p. 262
a.   Incorrect. This occurs shortly after the first major development of dropping sounds that the native language does not contain.
*b.   Correct. The first thing that happens occurs when babbling sounds that are not in the native language disappear.
c.   Incorrect. This can happen at any time but becomes consistent after dropping sounds that the native language does not contain.
d.   Incorrect. This occurs after several other milestones.

41. c   obj. 9   p. 262
a.   Incorrect. This two-word phrase has a telegraphic quality common to the language of 2-year-olds.
b.   Incorrect. This two-word phrase has a telegraphic quality common to the language of 2-year-olds.
*c.   Correct. Contractions will not occur until later.
d.   Incorrect. Here is a holophrase meaning "I want you to get me more food now." It is repeated for emphasis.

42. d   obj. 9   p. 262
a.   Incorrect. This commonly occurs in this age range.
b.   Incorrect. This is a description of telegraphic speech.
c.   Incorrect. The complexity of speech is built slowly, first by combining critical words and succeeding in communicating, and then by building on this foundation.
*d.   Correct. Overgeneralization involves the use of a grammatically correct construction in more than the correct situation, like making the past tense by adding "-ed" to everything, producing the term "goed."

43. b   obj. 9   p. 263
a.   Incorrect. Classical conditioning would be insufficient to account for language, as the language response must be, in effect, combined with new stimuli (and thus the language would need to be a pre-existing response).
*b.   Correct. As babbling may suggest, the language of the infant does progress through a process of successive approximations (shaping).
c.   Incorrect. A universal grammar would not require exposure to the language of the parents.
d.   Incorrect. Biological unfolding suggests an innate, rather than learned, process.

44. b   obj. 10   p. 267
a.   Incorrect. True, critics have compared the language skills of apes to other trained animals.
*b.   Correct. The comparison has been made to a 2-year-old. A 5-year-old has most of the grammar skills of an adult.
c.   Incorrect. This describes one of the more common techniques used on training apes to produce communication.
d.   Incorrect. This reflects the major problem faced by apes: they do not have the correct physical apparatus for speech.

45. a   obj. 10   p. 265
*a.   Correct. By having many names for turquoise, the Navaho may be able to make more refined distinctions about turquoise (thus think about it differently).
b.   Incorrect. This is a reverse statement of the linguistic relativity hypothesis and is the general view of how grammar works.
c.   Incorrect. The language acquisition device does not address how having many words for an object would influence how we think.
d.   Incorrect. While the Navaho are considered native Americans, this example does not support the nativist position.

46. c   obj. 10   p. 265
a.   Incorrect. This was not supported, and the Dani were able to distinguish as many colors as English-speaking individuals.
b.   Incorrect. This was not supported, as the Dani were able to perceive many different colors, but have only two basic color words.
*c.   Correct. This conclusion was supported, because the Dani have only two color names, yet they could distinguish many different colors.
d.   Incorrect. This was not supported, as the Dani were able to perceive many different colors, but have only two basic color words.

47. d   obj. 10   p. 264
a.   Incorrect. If this theory existed, this might be a good definition of it.
b.   Incorrect. No such law has ever been stated.
c.   Incorrect. No such hypothesis has been named.
*d.   Correct. The linguistic-relativity hypothesis states that language determines thought.

48. b   obj. 2   p. 242
a.   Incorrect. Reactions might be possible items to observe, but little about cognition could be gained from them in this study.
*b.   Correct. Timing the process actually provides evidence of how different images can be formed and how people may produce images.
c.   Incorrect. After some study, the experimenter would probably find that respiration does not change much while imagining giraffes.
d.   Incorrect. Someone has been the subject of too many experiments!

49. a   obj. 2   p. 243
*a.   Correct. This example would probably come to mind more readily than the other options.
b.   Incorrect. This is not a specific example, but is instead a definition of one type of table.
c.   Incorrect. This specific table would be less familiar to you, but could serve as a prototype for someone else.
d.   Incorrect. This is not a specific example, but is instead a definition of one type of table.

50.   c   obj. 4   p. 251
a.   Incorrect. While the goal state for the mystery reader may be to succeed and solve the puzzle, the key to the mystery is not a transformation problem.
b.   Incorrect. Trial and error may be the method used, but it is not a type of problem.
*c.   Correct. Here the problem is one of arranging all the pieces of the mystery, much like a jigsaw puzzle.
d.   Incorrect. In the mystery, the relationships already exist, and the mystery is to reveal them by rearranging the elements.

51.   a   obj. 5   p. 254
*a.   Correct. Problems of inducing structure involve recognizing or identifying relationships, and even creating new relationships. Insight works by rearranging elements in a situation.
b.   Incorrect. Subgoal analysis would require that Jeff break the problem into a series of smaller steps.
c.   Incorrect. The representativeness heuristic depends upon categorizing people and things according to the representative features of groups to which they may belong.
d.   Incorrect. The availability heuristic draws upon information that is easily available in memory, not the rearrangement of elements.

52.   a   obj. 10   p. 264
*a.   Correct. Retrieval cues are strongly influenced by language thus influencing thought.
b.   Incorrect. This part of the process is not very well understood.
c.   Incorrect. If athletes used self-talk for performance, it could impede performance.
d.   Incorrect. While the statement is true, it does not appear to apply to the question.

■ CHAPTER 8: ANSWER KEY

GUIDED REVIEW			MATCHING	
Concept 1:	[l] crystallized intelligence	[d] severe retardation	1. c	12. d
[a] Intelligence	[m] triarchic theory of	[e] profound retardation	2. b	13. f
[b] intelligence tests	intelligence	[f] Down syndrome	3. a	14. b
[c] mental age	[n] componential	[g] Familial retardation	4. d	15. e
[d] intelligence quotient	[o] experiential	[h] least restrictive		16. c
[e] achievement test	[p] contextual	environment	5. f	17. a
[f] aptitude test	[q] Practical intelligence	[i] mainstreaming	6. g	
[g] reliability		[j] intellectually gifted	7. a	
[h] validity	**Concept 2:**		8. e	
[i] Norms	[a] Mental retardation	**Concept 3:**	9. d	
[j] g, or g-factor	[b] Mild retardation	[a] culture-fair IQ test	10. b	
[k] fluid intelligence	[c] Moderate retardation	[b] heritability	11. c	

Essay Question 8.1: Defining Intelligence

■   Describe Binet's conception of intelligence, the g-factor view, Gardner's multiple intelligence, the triarchic theory, and the concepts of practical and emotional intelligence. (A good answer would not have to have all of these approaches.)

■   State which you find most acceptable and for what reason. For instance, the concept of practical intelligence may be appealing because it focuses on something other than educational ability.

■   The most important evidence is evidence that predicts, but if a definition appears to agree with commonly held views, then it will also have some validity because people do act upon these kinds of views.

Essay Question 8.2: The Heredity/Environment Question

■   Note that this returns to one of the major issues introduced in the beginning of the text, and that there is no ready answer for the debate.

■   The most fundamental issue is that we have quite a bit of evidence supporting both the role of the environment and the role of genetic factors. Psychologists do not want to select one over the other.

■   Of particular relevance was the discussion of problem solving and creativity.

■   The extent to which intelligence is dependent upon the environment affects the possibility of developing a culture-fair test.

Multiple Choice Feedback:

Practice Test I:
1.   d   obj. 1   p. 275
a.   Incorrect. Few people accept a notion of innate knowledge.
b.   Incorrect. Thrift is not associated with intelligence
c.   Incorrect. These categories may be more acceptable to scientists trying to define intelligence for a scientific study.
*d.   Correct. Most people think of intelligence as an ability to succeed at normal life concerns.

2.   a   obj. 1   p. 276
*a.   Correct. While intelligence tests have many faults, they are successful predictors of performance in

many kinds of activities, and they are standardized for large populations.
b.   Incorrect. Genealogy does suggest family patterns, but familial, genetic traits do not always appear in each family member.
c.   Incorrect. Achievement tests indicate only what an individual has been able to accomplish with his or her intellectual capacity, and they do not indicate what that capacity is.
d.   Incorrect. Projective tests are useful indicators of certain personality traits and do not indicate intelligence levels.

3.   c   obj. 2   p. 277

a.   Incorrect. Achievement scales would show only levels of achievement.

b.   Incorrect. Aptitude indicates areas of interest and inclinations toward certain areas of work.

*c.   Correct. The intelligence quotient is calculated by dividing the mental age (as tested) by the chronological age.

d.   Incorrect. The g-factor refers to the notion that one single factor of intelligence (a general factor) underlies different components of intelligence.

4.   a   obj. 2   p. 276
*a.   Correct. The chronological age is the age in years.
b.   Incorrect. Reread the question, then see answer a.
c.   Incorrect. Reread the question, then see answer a.
d.   Incorrect. Reread the question, then see answer a.

5.   c   obj. 2   p. 277
a.   Incorrect. Neither fit, try another choice.
b.   Incorrect. Spatial belongs to another test, and verbal is correct.
*c.   Correct. The Wechsler tests assess nonverbal performance and verbal skills.
d.   Incorrect. Performance is correct, but spatial belongs to another test.

6.   d   obj. 2   p. 278
a.   Incorrect. Motor skills tests test a level of motor skill, not knowledge.
b.   Incorrect. Personality tests assess personality traits and characteristics.
c.   Incorrect. Aptitude tests predict an individual's interests and abilities in a certain area and line of work.
*d.   Correct. Achievement tests measure the level of performance and knowledge in given areas, usually academic areas.

7.   b   obj. 3   p. 280
a.   Incorrect. The test may have tested what it sought to test, but generated different results on each taking.
*b.   Correct. Typically, if a test produces different results for the same subject in different administrations, the test reliability is low.
c.   Incorrect. Culturally biased tests do not account for variability in the score for the same subject.
d.   Incorrect. Many tests have subscales, but this would not cause unreliability.

8.   c   obj. 3   p. 282
a.   Incorrect. Heredity may influence intelligence generally, but it is the development of fluid intelligence that determines the strength of crystallized intelligence.
b.   Incorrect. Poor nutrition and diet may degrade intelligence, but crystallized intelligence does not depend on them.
*c.   Correct. The development of crystallized intelligence appears to depend upon fluid intelligence, as an individual high in fluid intelligence has a greater likelihood to be high in crystallized intelligence.

d.   Incorrect. Native intelligence is a term used by some to refer to intellectual capacity (possibly genetic endowment).

9.   a   obj. 4   p. 284
*a.   Correct. The list of seven is: musical, bodily kinesthetic, logical-mathematical, linguistic, spatial, interpersonal, and intrapersonal intelligence.
b.   Incorrect. See answer a.
c.   Incorrect. See answer a.
d.   Incorrect. See answer a.

10.   d   obj. 5   p. 283
a.   Incorrect. Structure-of-intellect is associated with another approach.
b.   Incorrect. The deviation IQ is a formula introduced to adjust the conventional way of calculating IQ scores to fit any age.
c.   Incorrect. Aptitude testing is used by school counselors and personnel counselors to guide job selection and placement.
*d.   Correct. Cognitive psychologists use the information-processing approach because it addresses how people store, recall, and utilize information.

11.   b   obj. 5   p. 286
a.   Incorrect. They are only minimally correlated.
*b.   Correct. This minimal correlation suggest that other types of intelligence may be responsible for business success.
c.   Incorrect. They are minimally correlated.
d.   Incorrect. They are minimally, positively correlated.

12.   c   obj. 7   p. 291
a.   Incorrect. This refers to the syndrome in which an individual, usually mentally retarded, has an extraordinary ability in one area, like mathematics, music, or art.
b.   Incorrect. This defines mental retardation, and severe retardation is a category of mental retardation.
*c.   Correct. This is the definition of mental retardation.
d.   Incorrect. This defines mental retardation, and severe retardation is a category of mental retardation.

13.   d   obj. 8   p. 292
a.   Incorrect. This causes other forms of retardation.
b.   Incorrect. Toxins in the environment have detrimental effects on the fetus, but they are not identified with Down syndrome.
c.   Incorrect. Fetal alcohol syndrome has its own special set of symptoms, and is not the same as Down syndrome.
*d.   Correct. The extra chromosome is the definitive marker of Down syndrome.

14.   d   obj. 8   p. 292
a.   Incorrect. It may result from hereditary factors, but these are unknown.

b.   Incorrect. Environmental factors may play a role, but the actual cause is unknown.

c.   Incorrect. It is not a paradox, the causes are simply unknown at this time.

*d. Correct. Familial retardation is characterized by having more than one retarded person in the immediate family group.

15. b   obj. 8   p. 292

a.   Incorrect. Mainstreaming increases the opportunities to interact with non-retarded students.

*b. Correct. These opportunities are intended to improve educational access and remove the stigma of special classes.

c.   Incorrect. The intent of mainstreaming is to include all persons in the classroom.

d.   Incorrect. Mainstreaming is intended to end the separation of retarded and non-retarded students.

16. a   obj. 9   p. 294

*a. Correct. The IQ of 130 is used as a standard to identify intellectually gifted, and about 2 to 4 percent of the population score above 130.

b.   Incorrect. Some are quite outgoing.

c.   Incorrect. There is no higher incidence of antisocial behavior in this group as compared to any other.

d.   Incorrect. Intellectually gifted individuals can be just as great a failure as anyone else.

17. a   obj. 10   p. 297

*a. Correct. But researchers have not been able to create a completely culture-fair test.

b.   Incorrect. This would be very culture-biased in favour of those who were technologically literate.

c.   Incorrect. This would be biased toward those who were broadly knowledgeable of other cultures

d.   Incorrect. There is no universal language.

Practice Test II:

18. c   obj. 1   p. 276

a.   Incorrect. This is not a definition of intelligence, perhaps it defines aptitude.

b.   Incorrect. Though close, this is not the textbook's definition.

*c. Correct. Intelligence is generally accepted to include an individual's ability to utilize resources in the environment.

d.   Incorrect. This sounds good, but it is not the definition given in the text.

19. b   obj. 2   p. 276

a.   Incorrect. No IQ test has been devised for diagnosing brain damage.

*b. Correct. Binet was trying to develop a means of placing slower children in special classes.

c.   Incorrect. This probably would not work anyway.

d.   Incorrect. This is a common use today, but the original use was to identify slow learners.

20. c   obj. 2   p. 277

a.   Incorrect. Other techniques were used to increase the reliability of earlier tests.

b.   Incorrect. It does make this possible, but it was not the purpose of developing the intelligence quotient.

*c. Correct. The IQ is a standardized quotient and it allows for comparisons between chronological ages.

d.   Incorrect. This was not the purpose for developing the intelligence quotient.

21. a   obj. 4   p. 282

*a. Correct. Spearman introduced the g factor to indicate general intelligence.

b.   Incorrect. Others introduced this.

c.   Incorrect. See Mulder and Scully about this one.

d.   Incorrect. Others introduced this.

22. d   obj. 7   p. 291

a.   Incorrect. See answer d.

b.   Incorrect. See answer d.

c.   Incorrect. See answer d.

*d. Correct. These scores represent the range that includes the first two standard deviations from the mean. Above 130 is considered gifted while below 70 is considered retarded.

23. a   obj. 2   p. 278

*a. Correct. Aptitude tests are designed to predict future performance in specific skills and work areas.

b.   Incorrect. Achievement tests measure achievement in a certain subject area.

c.   Incorrect. Intelligence tests measure intelligence, not aptitude.

d.   Incorrect. The g-factor is the general intelligence factor believed by some to underlie intelligence.

24. b   obj. 3   p. 280

a.   Incorrect. This is evidence of unreliability, but not invalidity.

*b. Correct. In taking the same test more than once, a wide variation in scores suggests that the test is inconsistent, or unreliable, unless other factors may account for the score differences.

c.   Incorrect. Nomothetic refers to a type of study that involves many subjects and seeks to identify normative characteristics of a phenomena.

d.   Incorrect. Ideographic refers to a type of research that focuses on a phenomenon in great detail, like a case study.

25. a   obj. 4   p. 284

*a. Correct. The list of seven is: musical, bodily kinesthetic, logical-mathematical, linguistic, spatial, interpersonal, and intrapersonal intelligence.

b.   Incorrect. See answer a.

c.   Incorrect. See answer a.

d.   Incorrect. See answer a.

26. c   obj. 4   p. 284

a.   Incorrect. This refers to linguistic capacity.

b.   Incorrect. This refers to physical control skills, like that dancers may have.

*c. Correct. Interpersonal skill is recognized as the skill of interaction with others.

d. Incorrect. Intrapersonal intelligence refers to the individual's self-awareness.

27. a obj. 5 p. 283
*a. Correct. Cognitive refers to mental processes like thought, memory, and problem solving, among others.
b. Incorrect. Learning approaches emphasize the role of reinforcements and observational learning.
c. Incorrect. An environmental approach would focus on the characteristics of the learning environment.
d. Incorrect. A physiological approach would focus on biological and genetic factors in intelligence.

28. b obj. 7 p. 291
a. Incorrect. Many mentally retarded people are quite capable of getting along in the world and with others.
*b. Correct. Intellectual and adaptive deficits define mental retardation.
c. Incorrect. Sometimes the intellectually gifted cannot perform in school.
d. Incorrect. Everyone (and anyone) can "perform" on an intelligence test.

29. b obj. 7 p. 291
a. Incorrect. Try 70.
*b. Correct. Any score below 70 is considered to indicate mental retardation.
c. Incorrect. Any score below 70 is considered to indicate mental retardation. This answer is incorrect because all scores below 60 are indeed considered, but other scores belong as well.
d. Incorrect. Any score below 70 is considered to indicate mental retardation. This answer is incorrect because all scores below 50 are indeed considered, but other scores belong as well.

30. b obj. 8 p. 292
a. Incorrect. Down syndrome is the major biological cause of mental retardation, but biologically caused mental retardation comprises only about one-third of the cases.
*b. Correct. Familial retardation has no known biological or environmental cause.
c. Incorrect. This is a fairly unusual cause of mental retardation.
d. Incorrect. Traumatic injury may result in retardation, but it is not as common as familial retardation.

31. a obj. 8 p. 291
*a. Correct. Of this list, this group suffers the least impairment and thus has the greatest chance for success in the mainstreamed environment.
b. Incorrect. See answer a.
c. Incorrect. See answer a.
d. Incorrect. See answer a.

32. a obj. 8 p. 293
*a. Correct. The primary result has been an effort to place mentally retarded students into an

environment where they receive the same opportunities as other students.
b. Incorrect. They were in special-education classrooms, and the legislation mandated that at least part of their time be in ordinary classrooms.
c. Incorrect. The resource classroom is often another term for special-education classroom.
d. Incorrect. In fact, some states have outlawed the use of IQ tests for placement.

33. d obj. 9 p. 294
a. Incorrect. They may be gifted in only one subject, and they may not show academic achievement in any subject.
b. Incorrect. They are typically well-adjusted.
c. Incorrect. They are almost always in the mainstream setting.
*d. Correct. Intellectually gifted students have fewer social problems and adjustment problems than their peers.

34. b obj. 11 p. 298
a. Incorrect. It would of great importance to the nature-nurture debate.
*b. Correct. For personality theory.
c. Incorrect. This would be of interest to the nature-nurture debate as well.
d. Incorrect. This would be of interest to the nature-nurture debate as well.

Practice Test III:
35. c obj. 2 p. 277
a. Incorrect. See answer c.
b. Incorrect. See answer c.
*c. Correct. 8 divided by 10 equals 1.25; 1.25 times 100 equals 125, or the intelligence quotient for this individual.
d. Incorrect. See answer c.

36. b obj. 2 p. 277
a. Incorrect. 10 divided by 12 equals .83; .83 times 100 equals 83, or the intelligence quotient for this individual.
*b. Correct. 12 divided by 10 equals 1.2; 1.2 times 100 equals 120, or the intelligence quotient for this individual.
c. Incorrect. 23 divided by 25 equals .92; .92 times 100 equals 92, or the intelligence quotient for this individual.
d. Incorrect. 25 divided by 23 equals 1.09; 1.09 times 100 equals 109, or the intelligence quotient for this individual.

37. c obj. 2 p. 277
a. Incorrect. Try: MA ÷ CA × 100 = IQ.
b. Incorrect. Try: MA ÷ CA × 100 = IQ.
*c. Correct. This calculation is accurate for children, but the deviation IQ was developed to reflect the IQs of adolescents and adults.
d. Incorrect. Try: MA ÷ CA × 100 = IQ.

38. a obj. 2 p. 277
*a. Correct. The original design was to distinguish between "bright" and "dull" students. Binet

developed the test to help place students according to their tested skill level, and students who performed only as well as younger students were considered "dull."
b.   Incorrect. See answer a.
c.   Incorrect. See answer a.
d.   Incorrect. See answer a.

39.   c   obj. 2   p. 276
a.   Incorrect. See answer c.
b.   Incorrect. See answer c.
*c.   Correct. Two-thirds includes the first standard deviation on either side of the average, which for IQ scores is between 85 and 115.
d.   Incorrect. See answer c.

40.   d   obj. 2   p. 278
a.   Incorrect. The administration ends when the test-taker cannot answer any more questions, long before all items have been administered.
b.   Incorrect. See answer d.
c.   Incorrect. See answer d.
*d.   Correct. Some tests end after a set number of questions have been missed in a row. Often, the number is 5, but the Stanford-Binet ends when the person cannot answer any more questions.

41.   b   obj. 2   p. 278
a.   Incorrect. See answer b.
*b.   Correct. The subtests are: information, comprehension, arithmetic, similarities, digit symbol, picture completion, and object assembly.
c.   Incorrect. See answer b.
d.   Incorrect. See answer b.

42.   a   obj. 2   p. 278
*a.   Correct. The subtests are: information, comprehension, arithmetic, similarities, digit symbol, picture completion, and object assembly; comprehension is a verbal subtest.
b.   Incorrect. See answer a.
c.   Incorrect. See answer a.
d.   Incorrect. See answer a.

43.   b   obj. 2   p. 282
a.   Incorrect. You may utilize the availability heuristic, but not necessarily so.
*b.   Correct. Crystallized intelligence comprises the knowledge individuals have acquired through experience.
c.   Incorrect. Fluid intelligence is based on intellectual capacity, not experience.
d.   Incorrect. The g-factor is the term used to represent general intelligence factor that some believe underlies all intelligence.

44.   a   obj. 5   p. 288
*a.   Correct. Epstein was attempting to create a test that predicted life success more effectively than traditional IQ tests.
b.   Incorrect. The traditional IQ test is more likely to make this kind of prediction.

c.   Incorrect. This would be a good find; then we could locate the unintelligent thoughts.
d.   Incorrect. But the results do not appear to correlate with the Standford-Binet.

45.   a   obj. 5   p. 285
*a.   Correct. This is why it is called the "tri-archic" theory.
b.   Incorrect. No such brain organ, though there is a "triune" theory of the brain.
c.   Incorrect. This is someone else's idea.
d.   Incorrect. Few theories of intelligence have begun with animal research.

46.   d   obj. 3   p. 282
a.   Incorrect. See answer d.
b.   Incorrect. See answer d.
c.   Incorrect. See answer d.
*d.   Correct. Each time the test is given, it yields the same scores, suggesting that it is reliable from one situation to another. This example illustrates validity, since this test clearly measured what it was supposed to measure.

47.   b   obj. 3   p. 281
a.   Incorrect. This is an example of poor validity, since the test did not measure what it was intended to measure.
*b.   Correct. This test clearly did not measure what it was supposed to measure.
c.   Incorrect. Reliability cannot be judged with one use of the test.
d.   Incorrect. Reliability cannot be judged with one use of the test.

48.   a   obj. 4   p. 284
*a.   Correct. A surgeon, like Erik, has good bodily kinesthetic intelligence.
b.   Incorrect. A scientist would be high in logical-mathematical intelligence.
c.   Incorrect. A musician would have good musical intelligence.
d.   Incorrect. Anne Sullivan would be recognized for her interpersonal intelligence.

49.   d   obj. 4   p. 284
a.   Incorrect. A surgeon has good bodily kinesthetic intelligence.
b.   Incorrect. A scientist would be high in logical-mathematical intelligence.
c.   Incorrect. A musician would have good musical intelligence.
*d.   Correct. Anne Sullivan, like Astrid, would be recognized for her interpersonal intelligence.

50.   b   obj. 6   p. 286
a.   Incorrect. Though multiple intelligence approaches would be more compatible than some, the concept of practical intelligence is more appropriate.
*b.   Correct. Practical intelligence reflects efforts to measure common sense, and common sense would be more appropriate to career prediction.

c.   Incorrect. The information processing approach does not offer any special view of practical intelligence, which is described here.

d.   Incorrect. The g-factor refers to the general intelligence factors, which some psychologists believe underlies all intelligence; measures of general intelligence have not been very successful at predicting job performance.

51.   c   obj. 5   p. 285

a.   Incorrect. Try encoding information and high intelligence.

b.   Incorrect. High intelligence is correct, but people high in intelligence spend less time applying solutions.

*c.   Correct. How information is encoded governs how difficult the solution will be to find, and people high in intelligence spend more time encoding than others.

d.   Incorrect. See answer c.

■ CHAPTER 9: ANSWER KEY

GUIDED REVIEW			MATCHING	
Concept 1: [a] motivation [b] Motives [c] instincts [d] Drive-reduction approaches to motivation [e] drive [f] Primary drives [g] secondary drives [h] homeostasis [i] arousal approaches to motivation [j] incentive [k] Incentive approaches to motivation [l] Cognitive approaches to motivation [m] expectancy-value theory [n] Intrinsic motivation [o] extrinsic motivation [p] self-actualization Concept 2: [a] obesity [b] hypothalamus [c] lateral hypothalamus [d] ventromedial hypothalamus [e] weight set point [f] Metabolism [g] settling point [h] Anorexia nervosa	[i] Bulimia [j] genitals [k] androgens [l] estrogen [m] progesterone [n] ovulation [o] Masturbation [p] Heterosexuality [q] double standard [r] permissiveness with affection [s] Homosexuals [t] bisexuals [u] need for achievement [v] Thematic Apperception Test (TAT) [w] need for affiliation [x] need for power Concept 3: [a] emotions [b] James-Lange theory of emotion [c] Cannon-Bard theory of emotion [d] Schachter-Singer theory of emotion	Concept 4: [a] stress [b] psycho-physiological disorders [c] general adaptation syndrome (GAS) [d] alarm and mobilization stage [e] resistance stage [f] exhaustion stage [g] cataclysmic events [h] post-traumatic stress disorder, or PTSD [i] personal stressors [j] background stressors [k] daily hassles [l] uplifts [m] learned helplessness [n] coping [o] defense mechanisms [p] Emotional insulation [q] emotion-focused [r] problem-focused coping [s] Hardiness [t] social support [u] inoculation	1. d 2. e 3. a 4. h 5. f 6. g 7. c 8. b 9. b 10. c 11. e 12. d 13. a 14. e 15. d 16. c 17. b 18. a 19. e 20. a 21. c 22. f 23. b 24. d	25. c 26. b 27. a 28. b 29. a 30. c 31. b 32. c 33. e 34. a 35. d 36. c 37. b 38. d 39. e 40. a

Essay Question 9.1: Theories of Motivation

■ Describe each of the main theories: instinct, drive reduction, arousal, incentive, opponent process, cognitive, and need theories.

■ Select an activity—it could be anything from watching television to playing a sport—and describe the behavior involved from the point of view of the motivation theories (no more than one sentence each).

■ Remember, some behaviors, like those satisfying basic needs, will be easier to describe from the points of view of some theories, while others will be easier to describe from other theories.

Essay Question 9.2: Human Needs and Motivation

■ Describe how biological factors impact on eating, including information about the weight set point theory and metabolism.

■ Provide an overview of how social factors relate to eating, including a description of how cultural factors determine the kinds and quantities of the foods that we eat.

Multiple Choice Feedback:

Practice Test I:

1. b   obj. 1   p. 307
a. Incorrect. True, but motives is a more comprehensive choice.
*b. Correct. This defines motives.
c. Incorrect. This is true also, but motives is a more comprehensive choice.
d. Incorrect. These are currently unknown to earthling science.

2. d   obj. 2   p. 308
a. Incorrect. Since we may satisfy our primary drives without much difficulty, they may not hold much importance when compared with other types of drives.
b. Incorrect. Other types of drives may motivate an organism more.
c. Incorrect. They must be satisfied for self-actualization to occur.
*d. Correct. By definition, primary drives are those that have a biological basis.

3. b   obj. 2   p. 309
a. Incorrect. There is no concept of "primary drive equilibrium."
*b. Correct. Homeostasis is the term used to describe a biological balance or equilibrium.
c. Incorrect. Though drive reduction might be used to achieve a state of homeostasis.
d. Incorrect. Opponent-process theory is one of the theories that depends upon the tendency toward homeostasis to account for many phenomena.

4. b   obj. 6   p. 321
a. Incorrect. The views on masturbation in our society are quite mixed.
*b. Correct. And the majority of that number have done it more than once.
c. Incorrect. Masturbation can begin much earlier, and some begin much later than puberty.
d. Incorrect. Masturbation is a normal, healthy activity.

5. d   obj. 7   p. 322
a. Incorrect. However, does this mean that there are a large number of unmarried women or just a few very busy women?
b. Incorrect. This would be a single standard.
c. Incorrect. This would be a single standard.
*d. Correct. A double standard means that one group is held to one standard, and another group is held to another standard.

6. d   obj. 7   p. 322
a. Incorrect. The frequency of sexual intercourse does decline for married couples as they grow older.
b. Incorrect. For most married couples, the frequency is between one and three times a week.
c. Incorrect. There appears to be little relationship between how often a couple engages in intercourse and how happy they are together.
*d. Correct. This may be a result of improved contraception, the change in women's roles, and the presentation in the popular media of the notion that female sexuality is acceptable.

7. c   obj. 2   p. 308
a. Incorrect. A primary drive has a clear biological need that it satisfies.
b. Incorrect. An achievement may or may not have a biological drive.
*c. Correct. By definition, secondary drives are not based on biological needs.
d. Incorrect. An instinct is a species-specific behavior governed by genetics and is thus biological.

8. b   obj. 2   p. 310
a. Incorrect. Instinct theory, not incentive theory, focuses on instincts.
*b. Correct. The characteristics of external stimuli provide the incentive, or promise of reinforcement, that governs incentive theory.
c. Incorrect. Drive reduction is a core concept of drive theory.
d. Incorrect. This refers to arousal theory.

9. a   obj. 2   p. 310
*a. Correct. External stimuli provide for "incentives" to act in a certain way.
b. Incorrect. The drive-reduction model focuses upon internal stimuli.
c. Incorrect. Desirableness would be irrelevant to instincts.
d. Incorrect. While important for this theory, external stimuli would not be the focus.

10. c   obj. 2   p. 311
a. Incorrect. These two factors are taken from two other approaches to motivation
b. Incorrect. Both of these are typically extrinsic.
*c. Correct. Actually, motivations can be only one or the other of these two types.
d. Incorrect. This would have more to do with expectancy-value motivation.

11. c   obj. 3   p. 312
a. Incorrect. Some higher-order motivations may involve extrinsic motivations.
b. Incorrect. Higher-order motivations would include quite

a few intrinsic needs.

*c. Correct. Primary needs must be satisfied before the individual can move on to higher-order motivation.

d. Incorrect. Higher-order motivation includes many secondary drives.

12. c obj. 4 p. 315
a. Incorrect. The cortex plays a role, but it is not central; try the hypothalamus.
b. Incorrect. In the limbic system, but try the hypothalamus.
*c. Correct. The hypothalamus monitors blood sugar and other body chemistry to regulate eating behavior.
d. Incorrect. In the limbic system, but try the hypothalamus.

13. d obj. 5 p. 318
a. Incorrect. Hyperphagia would not account for the refusal to admit to the eating problem.
b. Incorrect. Unlike the anorexic, the bulimic eats - and then regurgitates the meal.
c. Incorrect. This is a deep massage technique.
*d. Correct. Someone suffering anorexia will refuse to eat and claim that she is overweight.

14. d obj. 10 p. 325
a. Incorrect. The SAT measures achievement.
b. Incorrect. IQ tests measure IQ.
c. Incorrect. This test is yet to be developed.
*d. Correct. The Thematic Apperception Test, or TAT, was used by McClelland to determine levels of achievement motivation in his research subjects.

15. d obj. 12 p. 333
a. Incorrect. Try visceral experience.
b. Incorrect. Try visceral experience.
c. Incorrect. Try visceral experience.
*d. Correct. Visceral refers to the internal organs.

16. a obj. 12 p. 335
*a. Correct. Schachter and Singer proposed a theory of emotions that includes the cognitive element of interpretation of surroundings.
b. Incorrect. Cannon and Bard were critical of the James-Lange theory and proposed that exciting information went to the thalamus and then to the cortex and the physiological systems simultaneously.
c. Incorrect. The James-Lange theory is based on the perception of visceral changes.
d. Incorrect. Ekman's theory discusses facial expressions and emotions.

17. a obj. 13 p. 338
*a. Correct. Stressors present threats or challenges to a person and require some type of adaptive response.
b. Incorrect. A mobilization state is not a threat to a person's well-being.
c. Incorrect. A defense mechanism is a mechanism used by the ego to protect against unconscious conflict.
d. Incorrect. An inoculation is a preparation for stress before it is encountered.

18. b obj. 13 p. 340
a. Incorrect. See answer b.
*b. Correct. The stages of Selye's general adaptation syndrome are alarm and mobilization, resistance, and exhaustion.
c. Incorrect. See answer b.
d. Incorrect. See answer b.

19. d obj. 2 p. 340
a. Incorrect. The stage is part of the reaction to a stressor, not just a preparation to react.
b. Incorrect. Increased resistance to the stressor occurs in the next stage, during which the ability to resist disease declines.
c. Incorrect. This describes the final stage of the general adaptation syndrome.
*d. Correct. The "alarm" involves the psychological awareness of the stressor.

20. a obj. 14 p. 341
*a. Correct. Cataclysmic stressors include manmade and natural disasters, like earthquakes and terrorist attacks.
b. Incorrect. Background stressors are the ongoing demands made on the individual all the time.
c. Incorrect. Uplifts are the positive challenges that contribute to a sense of accomplishment or completion.
d. Incorrect. Personal stressors are the demands that are unique to the person and typically not shared with others (like being fired from a job).

21. d obj. 14 p. 342
a. Incorrect. These disorders can appear as a result of the extended operation of the resistance phase of the GAS, and are sometimes called disorders of defense (but not of the psychodynamic ego defense mechanisms).
b. Incorrect. These do not immediately threaten life.
c. Incorrect. Hardy people appear to have fewer of these disorders than the less hardy.
*d. Correct. These disorders often have psychological origins in stress and are thus considered psychophysiological.

22. b obj. 14 p. 343
a. Incorrect. These are described as hassles.
*b. Correct. These minor positive events may be just as demanding and stressful on the individual as are hassles, but they leave the person feeling good rather than drained.
c. Incorrect. Uplifts, by definition, would not be exhilarating.
d. Incorrect. Uplifts, by definition, would not be "major."

23. c obj. 17 p. 345
a. Incorrect. In the psychoanalytic view, "defense" would apply to unconscious events that threaten the ego.
b. Incorrect. Arousal is not the appropriate adjective.
*c. Correct. "Coping" is the term used to describe the ability to deal with stress and the techniques used.
d. Incorrect. However, coping is a form of adaptation.

Practice Test II:

24. d   obj. 1   p. 307
a. Incorrect. It may be focused on alleviating tension.
b. Incorrect. Feelings come from other aspects of behavior, though feelings and motivation may both be processed at least in part in the limbic system.
c. Incorrect. Many survival behaviors do not have to be learned, and many motivations are not survival oriented.
*d. Correct. Motivation guides and energizes behavior.

25. b   obj. 2   p. 307
a. Incorrect. Some animals and some humans may not be interested in power.
*b. Correct. Hunger appears to be a rather universal drive among man, animals, and insects.
c. Incorrect. Cognition is not considered a drive.
d. Incorrect. Achievement is a particularly human drive.

26. a   obj. 2   p. 309
*a. Correct. This is the activity of the parasympathetic system.
b. Incorrect. This new term may soon find its way into scientology.
c. Incorrect. Biofeedback requires intentional activity to control body processes.
d. Incorrect. This is a technical psychoanalytic term that is not relevant to homeostasis.

27. b   obj. 2   p. 308
a. Incorrect. No such instinct.
*b. Correct. Actually, this is true in all approaches to motivation.
c. Incorrect. Sounds good, though.
d. Incorrect. The need for fluid in body tissues is important information for the brain's regulation of fluid in the body.

28. b   obj. 2   p. 308
a. Incorrect. Instinct theory focuses on innate drives and thus would not complement incentive theory.
*b. Correct. Incentives account for external factors, while drive reduction would account for internal factors.
c. Incorrect. Arousal theory says that we actually seek ways to increase stimulation (in contrast to drive reduction).
d. Incorrect. Opponent-process theory identifies opposing processes that together work toward a balanced state.

29. a   obj. 2   p. 310
*a. Correct. Expectancy-value motivation is one of the cognitive approaches, and thus it includes our understanding.
b. Incorrect. Drive reduction is not goal-oriented in this way, and may occur without our awareness.
c. Incorrect. Maslow's approach does not necessarily involve goals and awareness of goals.
d. Incorrect. Extrinsic motivation is driven by external rewards, and we may not be aware of the rewards involved.

30. b   obj. 2   p. 311
a. Incorrect. Instinct theory requires the innate mechanisms known as instincts.
*b. Correct. Cognitive theory applies to understanding of goals, their consequences, and our abilities to reach them.
c. Incorrect. Drive-reduction depends upon the biological concept of drives.
d. Incorrect. Arousal is biological.

31. b   obj. 7   p. 321
a. Incorrect. Masturbation is a healthy behavior, though there are many situations in which its practice would be inappropriate (in public, for instance).
*b. Correct. Men report that they masturbate more often than women report.
c. Incorrect. Masturbation is more common in younger men than older men.
d. Incorrect. Masturbation is an excellent way to learn about one's sexuality.

32. c   obj. 3   p. 312
a. Incorrect. This is a gross overstatement of the idea of self-actualization.
b. Incorrect. Everyone is dependent upon others for some aspect of living.
*c. Correct. Self-actualizers are striving toward goals and seeking to express their potential.
d. Incorrect. Often self-actualizers are not as concerned with the successes of others.

33. d   obj. 4   p. 317
a. Incorrect. The number of fat cells is fixed by the age of about 2.
b. Incorrect. The number of fat cells is fixed by the age of about 2.
c. Incorrect. The number of fat cells is fixed by the age of about 2.
*d. Correct. By 2, the number of fat cells stops declining.

34. c   obj. 5   p. 317
a. Incorrect. Try anorexia nervosa.
b. Incorrect. Bulimia is a similar disorder, but it involves binging and purging behavior to maintain or lose weight.
*c. Correct. Often sufferers of this disorder will not eat or will develop the disorder known as bulimia and then binge and purge.
d. Incorrect. But these females appear to have an extreme fear of obesity, and will perceive themselves as obese even when they are dramatically underweight.

35. a   obj. 10   p. 325
*a. Correct. They are more likely to choose situations that are moderately challenging, not easy.
b. Incorrect. It is learned, or acquired.
c. Incorrect. Individuals with a high need for achievement do find satisfaction from attainment.
d. Incorrect. This is true as well.

36. a   obj. 10   p. 327
*a. Correct. Women tend to find power through socially acceptable ways more often than do men.
b.   Incorrect. The means are rarely questionable and do tend to be socially acceptable.
c.   Incorrect. The quality of aggression is not necessarily a matter of power.
d.   Incorrect. This is much more likely with men than women.

37. a   obj. 12   p. 333
*a. Correct. The perception of a physiological change is the emotion for James and Lange.
b.   Incorrect. However, since they argued that it was the perception of the physiological change that was the emotion, this answer is partially correct.
c.   Incorrect. They did not turn to instinctive process.
d.   Incorrect. The environment does not play a very big role in their theory.

38. b   obj. 13   p. 340
a.   Incorrect. Seligman is responsible for the concept of learned helplessness.
*b. Correct. A Canadian physician, Hans Selye proposed and researched this universal pattern of stress reaction.
c.   Incorrect. Skinner is responsible for operant conditioning.
d.   Incorrect. Freud developed psychoanalytic theory.

39. c   obj. 13   p. 340
a.   Incorrect. See answer c.
b.   Incorrect. The psychological responses vary considerably, but the physiological responses differ only by degree.
*c. Correct. Selye believed and demonstrated through his research that the physiological stress response pattern was pretty much universal.
d.   Incorrect. This happens rarely and with extreme stressors.

40. b   obj. 14   p. 343
a.   Incorrect. This inability depends upon factors other than the presence of background stressors.
*b. Correct. The effect of background stress, and any stress for that matter, can accumulate, with the sum of many small stressors having the same effect as one large one.
c.   Incorrect. This would be difficult to judge.
d.   Incorrect. Background stressors would be unlikely to cause a psychosomatic illness.

41. a   obj. 15   p. 343
*a. Correct. Seligman applied this term to the perception that a situation was beyond the control of the individual.
b.   Incorrect. Hysteria refers to a psychological disorder treated by Freud.
c.   Incorrect. Cataclysmic stress refers to major stressful events that affect many people.
d.   Incorrect. Post-traumatic stress disorder refers to the long-term effects of highly stressful events.

42. b   obj. 17   p. 344
a.   Incorrect. See answer b.
*b. Correct. The two types are emotion-focused and problem-focused coping. Emotion-focused coping is used more in situations in which circumstances appear unchangeable.
c.   Incorrect. See answer b.
d.   Incorrect. See answer b.

43. b   obj. 17   p. 344
a.   Incorrect. Hardy individuals are quite capable of coping with stress.
*b. Correct. The hardy individual is quite resilient to stress and does not get stress-related diseases.
c.   Incorrect. The hardy individual does recognize the challenge of stress.
d.   Incorrect. Everyone is affected in some way by emotional choices, especially if they are difficult.

Practice Test III:
44. d   obj. 3   p. 308
a.   Incorrect. No opponent processes are indicated here.
b.   Incorrect. Arousal motivation suggests that we would seek an exciting job, not necessarily a high-paying one.
c.   Incorrect. However, the money may eventually lead to drive reduction.
*d. Correct. The extrinsic rewards are quite evident.

45. b   obj. 4   p. 315
a.   Incorrect. See answer b.
*b. Correct. Blood chemistry, number and size of fat cells, and weight set point are more important factors than stomach contractions.
c.   Incorrect. See answer b.
d.   Incorrect. See answer b.

46. b   obj. 4   p. 317
a.   Incorrect. See answer b.
*b. Correct. Due to food being an external cue, the obese man is more likely to experience "hunger" as a result of the food, even though he already had lunch.
c.   Incorrect. The thin man is probably not so easily influenced by the external cue of another meal.
d.   Incorrect. Only if the thin man is one of those people who can eat all the time and gain no excess weight.

47. d   obj. 5   p. 318
a.   Incorrect. Medical term dealing with blood flow..
b.   Incorrect. Depression is not the cause of her binge eating.
c.   Incorrect. This type of measurement having to do with volume.
*d. Correct. The disorder is known as bulimia.

48. b   obj. 10   p. 325
a.   Incorrect. A need for affiliation could be at work here if she thought she would be isolated from friends once she began work.
*b. Correct. This sounds most like a need for achievement.
c.   Incorrect. A fear of failure could be operative here if she

is avoiding beginning her career for fear of failure.

d.   Incorrect. Power can be achieved without education.

49. a   obj. 8   p. 321

*a. Correct. Kinsey's view is that everyone falls somewhere on a gradient between complete homosexual orientation to complete heterosexual orientation.

b.   Incorrect. This view would suggest that Seth must be either homosexual or heterosexual, not a mixture.

c.   Incorrect. While this old view did suggest that masturbation led to deviant sexual behavior, it would not account for Seth's mixed feelings.

d.   Incorrect. This is not relevant to Masters and Johnson's conceptualization of the sexual response cycle.

50. c   obj. 11   p. 331

a.   Incorrect. Life would probably be interesting without emotions, but far less so.

b.   Incorrect. Emotion plays a major role in regulating social interaction.

*c. Correct. We are informed of our bodily needs through other mechanisms, primarily those related to motivation.

d.   Incorrect. Emotions are crucial for our preparation for actions, especially emergencies.

51. a   obj. 12   p. 334

*a. Correct. Their position differed from that of James and Lange, who thought it was our perception of the bodily changes that was the emotion.

b.   Incorrect. This suggests that facial changes result in emotional feelings.

c.   Incorrect. Schachter and Singer thought that the emotion resulted from the interpretation of the perception of a bodily change.

d.   Incorrect. James and Lange thought it was our perception of the bodily changes that was the emotion.

52. c   obj. 10   p. 327

a.   Incorrect. Being aggressive and flamboyant is not a typical approach for women who are high in the need for power.

b.   Incorrect. Belonging to a political party in itself is not a sign of a need for power.

*c. Correct. Women tend to display their need for power through socially acceptable methods, like concern for others and nurturing behavior.

d.   Incorrect. Competitive sports are not themselves related to individual need for power.

53. a   obj. 10   p. 327

*a. Correct. Sensitivity to others and desires to spend time with friends are reflective of a need for affiliation.

b.   Incorrect. Membership in a political group is not in itself sufficient to indicate a need for affiliation.

c.   Incorrect. Partying and sports are not themselves signs of a high need for affiliation.

d.   Incorrect. Aggressive behavior does not signal a need for affiliation.

54. b   obj. 13   p. 344

a.   Incorrect. See answer b.

*b. Correct. The shift from intrinsic to extrinsic rewards can undermine the behavior.

c.   Incorrect. See answer b.

d.   Incorrect. The shift from intrinsic to extrinsic rewards can undermine the behavior, but it will not necessarily destroy it.

55. c   obj. 13   p. 338

a.   Incorrect. This is a new stress, so Max is probably at the alarm and mobilization stage.

b.   Incorrect. Exhaustion would appear in this circumstance only after many years of failing to meet goals.

*c. Correct. Since this is a new recognition, Max has mobilized his energies and already begun to cope with the stress of not meeting this year's goals.

d.   Incorrect. In repression, Max would probably ignore his failure to meet this year's goals and make no effort to compensate for next year.

56. d   obj. 14   p. 341

a.   Incorrect. Personal stressors are major life events like marriage or death.

b.   Incorrect. Background stressors include everyday annoyances like traffic.

c.   Incorrect. Daily hassles are also known as background stressors, and include everyday annoyances like traffic.

*d. Correct. The traumatic experience would be classed as cataclysmic.

57. d   obj. 15   p. 343

a.   Incorrect. This does not illustrate the GAS.

b.   Incorrect. Daily hassles will not account for their not taking any initiative.

c.   Incorrect. If they come to believe that they are inferior, then the answer would be "d" anyway.

*d. Correct. They have learned that they are totally under the control of the assistant coaches, thus helpless.

58. b   obj. 14   p. 343

a.   Incorrect. Cataclysmic stress involves many people, such as during war, earthquakes, and terrorist attacks.

*b. Correct. This is considered a major personal stressor.

c.   Incorrect. Post-traumatic stress disorder actually follows a significant period of traumatic stress.

d.   Incorrect. Background stress includes the many small and insignificant worries and challenges one faces each day.

59. c   obj. 14   p. 341

a.   Incorrect. Personal stressors are not shared unless someone seeks out support.

b.   Incorrect. One element of the post-traumatic stress disorder is the failure of the support systems in the first place.

*c. Correct. Since many others have just experienced the same major stressor, the social support group is already defined.

d. Incorrect. Uplifts are personal, background stressors that
    result in the person feeling good.

■ CHAPTER 10: ANSWER KEY

GUIDED REVIEW			MATCHING		

Concept 1:
[a] Developmental psychology
[b] nature-nurture issue
[c] maturation
[d] interactionist
[e] identical twins
[f] Cross-sectional research
[g] Longitudinal research
[h] cross-sequential research
[i] conception
[j] zygote
[k] chromosomes
[l] genes
[m] embryo
[n] critical period
[o] fetus
[p] age of viability
[q] phenylketonuria (PKU)
[r] sickle-cell anemia
[s] Tay-Sachs disease
[t] Down syndrome
[u] rubella
[v] fetal alcohol syndrome

Concept 2:
[a] neonate
[b] vernix
[c] lanugo
[d] reflexes
[e] Babinski reflex
[f] habituation
[g] Attachment
[h] authoritarian parents

[i] Permissive parents
[j] Authoritative parents
[k] temperaments
[l] psychosocial development
[m] trust-versus-mistrust stage
[n] autonomy-versus-shame-and-doubt stage
[o] initiative-versus-guilt stage
[p] industry-versus-inferiority stage
[q] Cognitive development
[r] sensorimotor stage
[s] object permanence
[t] preoperational stage
[u] egocentric thought
[v] principle of conservation
[w] concrete operational stage
[x] formal operational stage
[y] information processing
[z] Metacognition
[aa] zone of proximal development, or ZPD,
[bb] scaffolding

Concept 3:
[a] adolescence
[b] puberty
[c] identity-versus-role-confusion stage
[d] identity
[e] intimacy-versus-isolation stage
[f] generativity-versus-stagnation stage
[g] ego-integrity-versus-despair stage
[h] menopause
[i] midlife transition
[j] midlife crisis
[k] Gerontologists
[l] genetic preprogramming theories of aging
[m] wear-and-tear theories of aging
[n] fluid intelligence
[o] crystallized intelligence
[p] senility
[q] Alzheimer's disease,
[r] disengagement theory of aging
[s] activity theory of aging
[t] Denial
[u] anger
[v] bargaining
[w] depression
[x] acceptance

1. f	30. a	60. c
2. b	31. d	61. a
3. d	32. f	62. d
4. e	33. e	63. b
5. a	34. c	64. e
6. c	35. b	
7. c	36. b	
8. f	37. a	
9. e	38. d	
10. a	39. c	
11. g		
12. h	40. b	
13. b	41. f	
14. d	42. c	
	43. e	
15. d	44. d	
16. a	45. a	
17. e		
18. c	46. d	
19. b	47. c	
20. f	48. b	
	49. a	
21. e		
22. a	50. c	
23. h	51. a	
24. b	52. d	
25. g	53. b	
26. f		
27. i	54. b	
28. c	55. f	
29. d	56. d	
	57. a	
	58. e	
	59. c	

Essay Question 10.1: Nature-Nurture and Childrearing Practices

■ Identify the relative importance of nature and nurture for your views. Do you see them as equal, or is one stronger than the other?

■ Each of the styles may imply a view of the nature-nurture debate. The authoritarian style, for instance, may see children as naturally unruly and in need of strict discipline to come under control. The permissive parent may expect the child to find their own potential, that such exploration is natural.

■ The view that sees nature and nurture as interacting would suggest that the parenting style is the place that an inherited potential can be realized, so child-rearing practices are crucial.

Essay Question 10.2: The Stresses of Adolescence

■ Note that the text considers the notion of excessive stress to be unsupported.

■ Describe specific instances where parents and adolescents have conflicts (rules, self-determination, school performance), and describe the nature of the disagreements. Identify things either parents or children can do to solve the problem. Are some of the problems an effort to assert a sense of self and identity?

■ Home life has changed significantly, and many adolescents are growing up in single-parent homes.

Multiple Choice Feedback:

Practice Test I:

1. a   obj. 1   p. 354
*a. Correct. Maturation involves, to a large extent, the unfolding of genetic code.
b. Incorrect. Nurture refers to the element of environmental influence, not heredity.
c. Incorrect. Environmental factors are not hereditary.
d. Incorrect. Social growth would reveal environmental, nurturing types of factors and some hereditary factors.

2. d   obj. 1   p. 356
a. Incorrect. Identical twins reared apart would probably provide the most information regarding the roles of nature and nurture.
b. Incorrect. This pattern would shed light on how common environments interact with different genetic factors.
c. Incorrect. Siblings reared apart would indicate some aspects of the extent of genetic influence, though the genetic similarity may not be as strong as in twins.
*d. Correct. Siblings reared together share genes and environment, and the ability to separate which factors were influential in which behavior or trait would be very limited.

3. d   obj. 2   p. 359
a. Incorrect. A cross-sectional study examines several groups at one given point in time.
b. Incorrect. There is no type of study called "maturational."
c. Incorrect. A longitudinal study follows a single group through a given span of time, taking measurements at points along the way.
*d. Correct. The cross-sequential study combines longitudinal and cross-sectional approaches by studying different groups in a longitudinal fashion, often allowing for a shorter time frame to complete the study.

4. d   obj. 3   p. 360
a. Incorrect. If longitudinal development referred to a special concept, it would probably mean something like development through time.
b. Incorrect. When people reach middle age, they begin to experience cross-section maturation.
c. Incorrect. This phase occurs in the sexual response cycle but not in human development.
*d. Correct. This phase is called a "critical period" because certain developmental tasks must be achieved during the period or they become very difficult to achieve later.

5. b   obj. 3   p. 361
a. Incorrect. Many sense organs are functional long before the fetus reaches a level of physical maturity that would allow it to survive of born.
*b. Correct. This age continues to be earlier and earlier as medical technology evolves.
c. Incorrect. Viability and learning are independent of each other in that viability depends upon the ability of the fetus to function physically independent of the mother, and this may be highly reflexive.
d. Incorrect. Sexual organs are differentiated long before viability.

6. d   obj. 4   p. 363
a. Incorrect. Junk food might affect some other aspect of development, but this link has not been established.
b. Incorrect. This link has not been established.
c. Incorrect. This is more likely to affect the marriage and the child's later behavior.
*d. Correct. Research suggests that this is true, possibly because the chemicals in the mother's system enter and influence the child's temperament.

7. a   obj. 5   p. 365
*a. Correct. Whenever the baby's cheek is stroked, it will turn its head in the direction of the stroked cheek.
b. Incorrect. The startle reflex is a pattern of actions related to being startled in which the baby flings out its arms, spreads out its fingers, and arches its back.
c. Incorrect. This reflex helps the baby clear its throat.
d. Incorrect. The startle reflex would probably be considered a "surprise" reflex, but there is not a reflex officially named this.

8. b   obj. 6   p. 367
a. Incorrect. Speech development occurs more dramatically in the second year and beyond.
*b. Correct. In the first year, infants triple their birth weight and their height increases by about half.

c.   Incorrect. From birth on, the head decreases in relative size.

d.   Incorrect. Reflexes are modified, but they are modified gradually and disappear gradually.

9.   b   obj. 7   p. 374
a.   Incorrect. It was based on the normal development of normal individuals.
*b. Correct. The eight stages he proposed cover life from birth to death.
c.   Incorrect. As a psychoanalyst, his approach is anything but behavioral.
d.   Incorrect. Actually, Erikson's views predate those of Piaget, and are partially derived from the ideas of Freud.

10. b   obj. 8   p. 375
a.   Incorrect. Only the first stage of Piaget's developmental scheme utilizes perceptual development.
*b. Correct. The child must develop a level of maturation and experience appropriate to the stage he or she is currently completing before moving on to the next stage; in fact, experience and maturation are the forces that give rise to the concerns of the next stage.
c.   Incorrect. Memory organization, not capacity plays a role in Piaget's scheme, and physical growth is only a minor element in the earliest stage.
d.   Incorrect. The social development that is associated with the cognitive development is not one of the necessary elements of cognitive development, rather it is a by-product of it.

11. d   obj. 8   p. 378
a.   Incorrect. Logical and abstract thought do not describe this, the first stage.
b.   Incorrect. Preoperational thought utilizes egocentric and centered thinking, not logical thought.
c.   Incorrect. While logic describes the kinds of operations being learned and tested during concrete operations, the thought is not abstract.
*d. Correct. Formal thought is abstract, and during this stage the adolescent becomes quite capable of identifying and utilizing logical processes.

12. d   obj. 10   p. 381
a.   Incorrect. It would be better described as awareness of one's perception and knowledge.
b.   Incorrect. The ability to be aware of one's cognitive capacity is not common in the preoperational stage.
c.   Incorrect. Metacognition develops with maturation and cognitive skills.
*d. Correct. This is the definition of metacognition, and the awareness improves in the latter stages of cognitive development.

13. b   obj. 10   p. 383
a.   Incorrect. Adulthood follows this period, which is called adolescence.
*b. Correct. The developmental period is called

adolescence, and this phase of growth and sexual maturation is called puberty.
c.   Incorrect. Puberty is the name given the phase of growth and sexual maturation, but the developmental period is known as adolescence.
d.   Incorrect. Childhood ends with the onset of this stage.

14. b   obj. 11   p. 385
a.   Incorrect. In the preconventional stage, people are more likely to be motivated by rewards and avoidance of punishment.
*b. Correct. The conventional stage is marked by a desire to get along socially.
c.   Incorrect. Individuals in the postconventional stage are not likely to be concerned with how others think about them.
d.   Incorrect. Kohlberg did not define a nonconventional stage.

15. d   obj. 11   p. 385
a.   Incorrect. This is not something he did.
b.   Incorrect. He did not collect any survey data of this kind.
c.   Incorrect. This was not his thing.
*d. Correct. Kohlberg was interested in how the person reasoned to solve a moral dilemma.

16. d   obj. 10   p. 383
a.   Incorrect. Preconventional morality is more common in children.
b.   Incorrect. Usually experienced by women who have reached menopause.
c.   Incorrect. Identified with the very elderly.
*d. Correct. Adolescents are very concerned with their self-identity and roles

17. d   obj. 12   p. 388
a.   Incorrect. Many of the other theories are inclusive of both males and females.
b.   Incorrect. Cross-cultural studies have not supported nor rejected a universal application of Erikson's views.
c.   Incorrect. Erikson does not place any special emphasis on understanding infant development in comparison to the rest of the life span.
*d. Correct. Erikson has been a leader in placing emphasis on the entire lifespan.

18. d   obj. 13   p. 393
a.   Incorrect. The detrimental changes are only beginning to occur, and this does not seem to be a major issue during a midlife crisis.
b.   Incorrect. These disappointments can occur at any time, and are not necessarily associated with midlife crises.
c.   Incorrect. For males, the reproductive capability does not end.
*d. Correct. More often than other reasons, the midlife crisis is a result of a recognition of failure to meet many personal goals.

19. c   obj. 14   p. 394
a. Incorrect. This has increased, but not doubled.
b. Incorrect. The number of children under age 5 has not doubled.
*c. Correct. The number has doubled, and the rate of divorce continues to climb as does the number of unwed mothers.
d. Incorrect. This number has fallen dramatically, and only about one-quarter of school-aged children have a mother staying at home.

20. a   obj. 15   p. 396
*a. Correct. The numbers of people in each age group after retirement (70s, 80s, 90s, and 100s) is expected to continue to increase for many decades in the future.
b. Incorrect. Slowed, yes - halted, unlikely.
c. Incorrect. This has been occurring slowly, but it does not account for the increase in the study of gerontology.
d. Incorrect. This is true, but it is not the cause of an increase in the study of gerontology.

21. c   obj. 15   p. 398
a. Incorrect. The genetic preprogramming approach would suggest that this results from genetic programming, but this is not what they would say about the decline.
b. Incorrect. This is the point of view of the wear-and-tear theorists.
*c. Correct. The preprogramming theories suggest that cells can only reproduce a certain number of times, and then they begin to decline.
d. Incorrect. This view is held by many, and not exclusive to the genetic preprogramming theories.

22. a   obj. 15   p. 399
*a. Correct. Fluid intelligence and its adaptive power are most needed during the earlier part of life.
b. Incorrect. Fluid intelligence does begin a decline after middle adulthood.
c. Incorrect. Fluid intelligence actually declines slowly during these periods.
d. Incorrect. Fluid intelligence increases early and declines later.

23. d   obj. 16   p. 401
a. Incorrect. Deactivation theory sounds good, but its actual name is disengagement.
b. Incorrect. Activity theory sounds good, but its actual name is disengagement.
c. Incorrect. Withdrawal theory sounds good, but its actual name is disengagement.
*d. Correct. This defines the disengagement theory of aging.

24. d   obj. 17   p. 402
a. Incorrect. See answer d.
b. Incorrect. See answer d.
c. Incorrect. See answer d.
*d. Correct. Initially the person denies the prospects of death, then proceeds through being angry, bargaining with death (if only I can live until my daughter marries, etc), becoming depressed, and finally acceptance; thought not everyone makes it through the stages.

Practice Test II:
25. c   obj. 1   p. 356
a. Incorrect. Interactionism admits to genetic (not a blank slate) influences.
b. Incorrect. The "nature" element is that of heredity, suggesting some aspects of development are influenced by one's disposition.
*c. Correct. Nurture implies the forces of the environment, including the caregiving and socializing influences, so nurture would be the dominant influence for someone with such a view.
d. Incorrect. Dualism refers to the philosophical perspective of the duality of the mind and body, not the duality of nature and nurture.

26. c   obj. 1   p. 358
a. Incorrect. Only those born of alien parents.
b. Incorrect. Non-twin siblings have shared their lives just as much.
*c. Correct. Having identical genes makes the difference.
d. Incorrect. Most subjects are very highly cooperative in their dealings with psychologists.

27. b   obj. 3   p. 359
a. Incorrect. Chromosomes contain genes, and genes are the basic information units.
*b. Correct. Genes are the basic information units in genetics.
c. Incorrect. Spores are released by fungi.
d. Incorrect. "Somes" is the overgeneralized plural of "some," which would still only be some.

28. d   obj. 3   p. 360
a. Incorrect. At eight weeks, only arms, legs, and face are discernable.
b. Incorrect. At this stage, the face does not have any characteristics of later life to it, and eyes do not open, among many other differences.
c. Incorrect. At this stage, the fetus can move noticeably, the face has characteristics it will have later, and major organs begin to function.
*d. Correct. At 24 weeks, most of the characteristics that will be seen in the newborn are present, eyes will open and close, it can cry, grasp, look in directions.

29. a   obj. 4   p. 362
*a. Correct. Children with Tay-Sachs disease are unable to break down fat, and they die by the age of 4.
b. Incorrect. Down syndrome can occur in any child, but it is more frequent with children of older parents.
c. Incorrect. Meningitis is not a genetic disease.
d. Incorrect. Phenylketonuria, or PKU, is a genetic disease that can afflict anyone, and it does not result in early death; rather, it results in retardation if not treated properly.

30. a   obj. 4   p. 363
*a. Correct. Down syndrome children have an extra chromosome that results in mental retardation and unusual physical features.
b.   Incorrect. Sickle-cell anemia is a recessive trait common among people of African descent.
c.   Incorrect. Children with Tay-Sachs disease are unable to break down fat, and they die by the age of 4.
d.   Incorrect. Phenylketonuria, or PKU, is a genetic disease that can afflict anyone, and it does not result in early death; rather, it results in retardation if not treated properly.

31. b   obj. 4   p. 363
a.   Incorrect. Down syndrome children have an extra chromosome which results in mental retardation and unusual physical features.
*b. Correct. This disease can cause serious malformation and prenatal death.
c.   Incorrect. Phenylketonuria, or PKU, is a genetic disease that can afflict anyone, and it does not result in early death, rather it results in retardation if not treated properly.
d.   Incorrect. Sickle-cell anemia is a recessive trait common among people of African descent.

32. b   obj. 5   p. 365
a.   Incorrect. A neonate is a newborn.
*b. Correct. This is the official term used to refer to newborns in their first week.
c.   Incorrect. A neonate is any newborn.
d.   Incorrect. A neonate is a newborn, and can be early, late, or on time.

33. c   obj. 2   p. 358
a.   Incorrect. Longitudinal method follows one group through many years.
b.   Incorrect. However, the length of funding for the project would probably define the critical period.
*c. Correct. The researcher is comparing different age groups at the same time to compare the different abilities shown by each group.
d.   Incorrect. This combines longitudinal and cross-sectional, following several groups for an extended period of time.

34. a   obj. 6   p. 368
*a. Correct. According to research reported in the text, neonates can imitate the facial expressions of adults (some study-guide authors have not been able to replicate these findings with their own children, however).
b.   Incorrect. Infants have no difficulties imitating facial expressions, and according to research reported in the text, neonates can imitate the facial expressions of adults.
c.   Incorrect. Toddlers have no difficulties imitating facial expressions, and according to research reported in the text, neonates can imitate the facial expressions of adults.
d.   Incorrect. Preschoolers have no difficulties imitating facial expressions, and according to research reported in the text, neonates can imitate the facial expressions of adults.

35. c   obj. 7   p. 373
a.   Incorrect. This concept is not one of Baumrind's parenting styles.
b.   Incorrect. Children of permissive parents tend to be unpleasant and demanding of attention.
*c. Correct. Children of authoritative parents are typically quite well behaved, both with the parents and when they are in other situations by themselves.
d.   Incorrect. According to this view, children of authoritarian parents are well behaved only in the presence of the parents.

36. d   obj. 8   p. 375
a.   Incorrect. This would be common of all children.
b.   Incorrect. This would fall to middle childhood, the era following toddlers.
c.   Incorrect. This describes the concerns of infancy.
*d. Correct. The second stage describes toddlers (ages 18 months to 3 years).

37. c   obj. 9   p. 375
a.   Incorrect. This is secondary to the cognitive development Piaget focused upon.
b.   Incorrect. What is a perceptual decision?
*c. Correct. Cognition's biggest role is understanding reality.
d.   Incorrect. Erikson was more concerned with social responses.

38. d   obj. 11   p. 385
a.   Incorrect. See answer d.
b.   Incorrect. See answer d.
c.   Incorrect. See answer d.
*d. Correct. The three levels are preconventional, conventional, and postconventional.

39. c   obj. 11   p. 387
a.   Incorrect. See answer c.
b.   Incorrect. This is not one of the stages; the stages, in order, are orientation toward individual survival, goodness as self-sacrifice, and morality of nonviolence.
*c. Correct. The stages, in order, are orientation toward individual survival, goodness equated with self-sacrifice, and morality of nonviolence.
d.   Incorrect. See answer c.

40. a   obj. 12   p. 389
*a. Correct. In college, the stage of intimacy versus isolation begins as the individual begins to experience self-defined roles and independence.
b.   Incorrect. See answer a.

c. Incorrect. See answer a.
d. Incorrect. See answer a.

41. b   obj. 13   p. 391
a. Incorrect. Puberty occurs at the beginning of adolescence.
*b. Correct. Menopause is the cessation of menstruation that occurs in middle adulthood for women.
c. Incorrect. Menarche is the onset of menstruation that marks the beginning of puberty for females.
d. Incorrect. Tumescence refers to the readiness for sexual activity that occurs when the sexual organs swell with blood.

42. b   obj. 13   p. 392
a. Incorrect. Most people maintain harmonious relationships with their children.
*b. Correct. It is the prospect that personal goals and dreams may not be completely fulfilled and that there is now less chance for achieving them.
c. Incorrect. All major career advances may no longer be possible.
d. Incorrect. Menopause and physical deterioration may be yet to come, and not all females experience problems with menopause, and certainly physical deterioration is not evident to every 40- to 50-year-old.

43. d   obj. 13   p. 392
a. Incorrect. No evidence of menopause here.
b. Incorrect. The term for this is "midlife crisis," in which one does examine one's identity.
c. Incorrect. This is too traumatic to be considered a mere transition.
*d. Correct. Unlike the milder form of transition, this sounds like a crisis.

44. a   obj. 13   p. 393
*a. Correct. In addition, the conflict between family and career appears to influence the difficulties of developing a clear dream.
b. Incorrect. Timing does not appear to differ significantly for those who experience this crisis.
c. Incorrect. The empty nest can precipitate a crisis, but many women view it quite positively.
d. Incorrect. Menopause does not necessarily precipitate a crisis any more than does the physical change experienced by men.

45. b   obj. 15   p. 398
a. Incorrect. The opponent-process theory does not contribute to the theories of aging.
*b. Correct. Genetic preprogramming theories actually hypothesize the existence of detrimental cells that hasten the end of life.
c. Incorrect. The wear-and-tear theories simply suggest that the body wears out.
d. Incorrect. Gerontology is not a particular theory of aging, but instead is the specialty that studies aging processes.

46. c   obj. 15   p. 398
a. Incorrect. The genetic preprogramming theories suggest that aging results from preprogrammed failures at the cellular level.
b. Incorrect. The genes do not break down, but may actually program the breakdown of cells.
*c. Correct. This is the main thesis of the wear-and-tear theories.
d. Incorrect. This is not a theory of aging.

47. d   obj. 15   p. 399
a. Incorrect. Fluid intelligence declines with age.
b. Incorrect. Verbal intelligence may increase as crystallized intelligence increases.
c. Incorrect. Basic intelligence is not defined adequately to suggest that it exists, much less changes with age.
d. Correct. As described, crystallized intelligence increases as the experiences and memories become more important aspects of intelligent behavior in later adulthood.

48. c   obj. 16   p. 401
a. Incorrect. The wear-and-tear theory suggests that the body wears out.
b. Incorrect. The genetic preprogramming theory suggests that the body is programmed to slow and die.
*c. Correct. The disengagement theory says that people age because they consciously withdraw.
d. Incorrect. The activity theory of aging suggests that people who remain active have a more successful old age.

Practice Test III:
49. a   obj. 1   p. 356
*a. Correct. This statement reflects the interactionist view of most developmental psychologists.
b. Incorrect. Few developmental psychologists take such a strong view of genetics, and most are unwilling to claim genetics or environment as stronger than the other factor.
c. Incorrect. Few developmental psychologists take such a strong view of the environment, and most are unwilling to claim genetics or environment as stronger than the other factor.
d. Incorrect. This is a true statement, and it actually supports the contemporary interactionist view, which is best described in another of the alternatives.

50. d   obj. 3   p. 360
a. Incorrect. See answer d.
b. Incorrect. See answer d.
c. Incorrect. See answer d.
*d. Correct. A rudimentary heart, brain, and intestinal tract are formed during the embryonic stage.

51. b   obj. 4   p. 362
a. Incorrect. While hypertension has some genetic disposition, it is not identifiable enough to be said to be directly transmitted, and it does not cause a short life expectancy.
*b. Correct. This disease results from recessive genes

(passed on by both parents), and the red blood cells have a deformed, sickle shape.

c. Incorrect. Children with Tay-Sachs disease are unable to break down fat, and they die by the age of 4, but they are usually of Jewish descent.

d. Incorrect. Phenylketonuria, or PKU, is a genetic disease that can afflict anyone, and it does not result in early death; rather, it results in retardation if not treated properly.

52. b   obj. 4   p. 363
a. Incorrect. See answer b.
*b. Correct. The mother contributes to problems arising from mother's nutrition and stress level, the mother's drug and medication, and birth complications. These may all be within her control, while hereditary defects are not in the mother's control and require contributions form the father.
c. Incorrect. See answer b.
d. Incorrect. See answer b.

53. b   obj. 6   p. 367
a. Incorrect. And the infant's production of speech sounds and recognition of sounds continues to grow rapidly.
*b. Correct. Infants can recognize their mother's voice as early as three days.
c. Incorrect. This too is true.
d. Incorrect. The sweet tooth must be built-in.

54. a   obj. 7   p. 370
*a. Correct. The style of interaction between mother and child differs from that of father and child.
b. Incorrect. This is reversed.
c. Incorrect. The attachment is not stronger or weaker, but of a different style.
d. Incorrect. Fathers probably spend less time with their children, but this is not universally true.

55. d   obj. 7   p. 370
a. Incorrect. Few would describe the difference as one of superiority.
b. Incorrect. Rather than aloof and detached, fathers are often quite physical and in close contact with their children.
c. Incorrect. While affectionate, fathers do not express this as verbally as do mothers.
*d. Correct. Due to the differences in how fathers and mothers interact with their children, the best description is that the attachment differs in quality.

56. b   obj. 7   p. 373
a. Incorrect. Permissive parents are lax and inconsistent with the discipline of their children.
*b. Correct. Authoritative parents set limits and are firm, but not inflexible.
c. Incorrect. This is not a type of parent, but the very definition of being a parent.
d. Incorrect. Authoritarian parents are rigid and punitive.

57. b   obj. 8   p. 378
a. Incorrect. Reversibility would refer to the ability to reverse an operation.
*b. Correct. This test describes an effort to determine the ability of the child to conserve number even if the objects are arranged differently.
c. Incorrect. A developmental psychologist would not test for spatial inertia.
d. Incorrect. Reorganization is not one of the principles that could be tested by a developmental psychologist.

58. b   obj. 8   p. 378
a. Incorrect. The principle of conservation would be applied to whether a lump of clay were more if it was long, or short and fat - even if it was the same ball of clay.
*b. Correct. As simple as it sounds, Jess is learning that he can reverse his bowl back into a ball of clay.
c. Incorrect. If egocentric thought were at work, Jess might simply decide that the cake Luisa made was a pot of soup for his bowl.
d. Incorrect. Logic will come much later.

59. b   obj. 8   p. 378
a. Incorrect. Reversibility is mastered in the concrete operations stage, not the sensorimotor stage.
*b. Correct. Conservation is one of the major accomplishments of the stage.
c. Incorrect. Object permanence occurs in the sensorimotor stage.
d. Incorrect. Abstraction occurs in the formal stage.

60. d   obj. 8   p. 378
a. Incorrect. This sequential and systematic problem-solving approach is most common of someone in the formal operations stage, not the concrete operations stage.
b. Incorrect. This sequential and systematic problem-solving approach is most common of someone in the formal operations stage, not the preoperational stage.
c. Incorrect. This sequential and systematic problem-solving approach is most common of someone in the formal operations stage, not the sensorimotor stage.
*d. Correct. This sequential and systematic problem-solving approach is most common of someone in the formal operations stage.

61. a   obj. 2   p. 358
*a. Correct. A cross-sectional approach involves investigating how several different groups (they can be differentiated on age, sex, economic status, and other characteristics) responded at one time.
b. Incorrect. A cross-sequential study would follow the development of several different groups through time.
c. Incorrect. A longitudinal study would follow the development of one group for a long time.
d. Incorrect. Archival research would be more appropriate for events occurring in the distant past.

62. b   obj. 11   p. 386
a. Incorrect. Amorality has been used to describe the period prior to when cognitive processes are much involved in behavior, but it does not describe the phase illustrated in the question.
*b. Correct. The preconventional level of morality is driven by rewards and punishments.
c. Incorrect. The conventional level of morality is marked by efforts to please others and become a good member of society.
d. Incorrect. People in the postconventional level of morality make judgments according to moral principles that are seen as broader than society.

63. a   obj. 11   p. 387
*a. Correct. Rape prevention and mutual assistance supports not only the survival of an earlier stage, but also the principle that views violence as immoral.
b. Incorrect. Prevention may be focused on survival, but mutual assistance focuses on higher concerns.
c. Incorrect. Rape awareness does not specifically call upon self-sacrifice.
d. Incorrect. This is not one of Gilligan's stages, and preconventional morality would understand rape through the punishment it deserves.

64. c   obj. 12   p. 389
a. Incorrect. During intimacy-versus-isolation, the individual has a focus upon the self-disclosure and establishing relationships.
b. Incorrect. During identity-versus-role confusion, the individual is focused upon creating a sense of identity and establishing personal roles.
*c. Correct. This describes the components of generativity, in which one contributes to the well-being of others and leads a productive life.
d. Incorrect. Ego-integrity-versus-despair follows this stage.

65. d   obj. 13   p. 391
a. Incorrect. Frank should worry more about how much longer his wife will be able to have children, since he should be able to father children long into his old age.
b. Incorrect. Frank should worry more about how much longer his wife will be able to have children, since he should be able to father children long into his old age.
c. Incorrect. Women lose their fertility in their late forties and early fifties, though many can reproduce into their sixties.
*d. Correct. So he should worry more about his wife's biological clock.

66. a   obj. 14   p. 395
*a. Correct. Working does provide a basis for building self-esteem that is easier to identify than the sense of worth gained form doing the job of mothering.
b. Incorrect. This is not always true.
c. Incorrect. The amount of time spent by husbands with

children does not increase as the time the wife spends working outside the home increases.
d. Incorrect. There is no evidence for this, and given the amount of time required for household work, one wonders where the social life would fit.

67. b   obj. 15   p. 398
a. Incorrect. This would suggest that the loss of hearing resulted from genetic programming.
*b. Correct. The wear-and-tear theory states that the decline of functions is because the parts are, essentially, wearing out.
c. Incorrect. There is no decreased consumption theory.
d. Incorrect. The disengagement theory of aging addresses patterns of social interaction more than the problems of physical deterioration.

68. a   obj. 15   p. 399
*a. Correct. Crystallized intelligence is the intelligence that depends upon memory and experience.
b. Incorrect. Common sense would not have us all informed about Egyptian mummies.
c. Incorrect. Fluid intelligence is that intelligence used earlier in life to help people adjust and adapt to new challenges.
d. Incorrect. Practical intelligence refers to a type of intelligence that helps one survive and thrive in domains like work and social life.

69. c   obj. 12   p. 389
a. Incorrect. The disengagement theory of aging would predict that Dan would withdraw from society.
b. Incorrect. Concrete operations occurs between the ages of 6 and 11.
*c. Correct. Dan is considering becoming productive in a broad sense of making a contribution to society, rather than stagnating in his comfortable position.
d. Incorrect. Conventional morality would be the level of morality focused on getting along with the social group, not necessarily contributing to it.

70. a   obj. 17   p. 402
*a. Correct. She is bargaining with death.
b. Incorrect. The wear-and-tear theory of aging does not address the rationalizations we make in order to finish life.
c. Incorrect. This bargain does not sound like ego-integrity.
d. Incorrect. Alice has not yet accepted her impending death.

71. a   obj. 11   p. 386
*a. Correct. In preconventional morality, children are unable to separate intent from accident, and thus punishment is applied.
b. Incorrect. See answer a.
c. Incorrect. See answer a.
d. Incorrect. See answer a.

72. d   obj. 12   p. 388
a. Incorrect. Kübler-Ross does not have a stage of generativity.
b. Incorrect. Erik has passed the autonomy-versus-shame and doubt stage.
c. Incorrect. While the "Dream" may be appropriate, the conventional stage of morality does not seem to be relevant.
*d. Correct. Erik is defining his life role and engaging in hypothetical thinking.

■ CHAPTER 11: ANSWER KEY

GUIDED REVIEW			MATCHING		
Concept 1: [a] personality [b] Psychoanalysts [c] psychoanalytic theory [d] unconscious [e] id [f] libido [g] pleasure principle [h] ego [i] reality principle [j] superego [k] conscience [l] ego-ideal [m] oral stage [n] Fixation [o] anal stage [p] phallic stage [q] Oedipal conflict [r] latency period [s] genital stage [t] defense mechanisms [u] neo-Freudian psychoanalysts [v] collective unconscious [w] archetypes [x] inferiority complex	Concept 2: [a] trait theory [b] Traits [c] cardinal trait [d] central traits [e] Secondary traits [f] factor analysis [g] Introversion-extroversion [h] Neuroticism-stability [i] Psychoticism [j] Cognitive-social approaches [k] observational learning [l] self-efficacy [m] reciprocal determinism [n] Biological and evolutionary approaches [o] temperament [p] Humanistic approaches to personality [q] unconditional positive regard [r] self-actualization	Concept 3: [a] Psychological tests [b] reliability [c] validity [d] Norms [e] self-report measures [f] Minnesota Multiphasic Personality Inventory-2 (MMPI-2) [g] test standardization [h] Projective personality tests [i] Rorschach test [j] Thematic Apperception Test (TAT) [k] behavioral assessment	1. c 2. b 3. d 4. e 5. a 6. f 7. a 8. e 9. d 10. c 11. b 12. b 13. f 14. e 15. a 16. g 17. c 18. d	19. d 20. b 21. f 22. a 23. c 24. e 25. c 26. e 27. a 28. b 29. f 30. d 31. g 32. f 33. c 34. e 35. b 36. d 37. a	38. a 39. g 40. d 41. c 42. f 43. b 44. e 45. h 46. f 47. d 48. a 49. e 50. g 51. c 52. b 53. d 54. b 55. a 56. e 57. c

Essay Question 11.1: Freud and Female Psychology

■ The weakest area is Freud's developmental stages, particularly with the Oedipus complex. Freud's concept of penis envy is not well accepted by many.

■ Just as Gilligan contests Kohlberg's views of moral development, one could argue that Freud's concept of a genital stage rests on masculine norms.

Essay Question 11.2: Diversity and Norming

■ Some people argue that any kind of separation of a group from the larger society is detrimental.

■ One major problem is the use of norms or averages to prepare job "profiles." These are still average and composite pictures of the individual and may unfairly discriminate against those who do not fit the profile. With these kinds of norms, negative reactions can and have occurred by those excluded from the special normed group. Recent court cases will change how this is viewed as well.

Multiple Choice Feedback:

Practice Test I:
1. a   obj. 1   p. 411
*a. Correct. Repressed wishes, desires, anxiety, and conflict are found in the realm Freud called the unconscious.
b. Incorrect. This was a concept introduced by Freud's follower, Carl Jung.
c. Incorrect. The conscience is found in the superego.

d. Incorrect. The conscious contains our awareness of the world.

2. c   obj. 1   p. 411
a. Incorrect. While important, they are not at the center of his theory.
b. Incorrect. More likely the earlier stages.

*c.   Correct. The mental factors of which we are least aware can have the most grave effects on our personality.

d.   Incorrect. This theory came long after Freud.

3.   b   obj. 1   p. 412

a.   Incorrect. The id is always making demands on the person that are unrealistic, even sometimes dangerous.

*b.   Correct. It is the role of the ego to manage the competing demands of the id and the superego, and it responds according to the reality principle.

c.   Incorrect. The superego's demands of moral perfection and ego-ideal are unrealistic and in conflict with the id.

d.   Incorrect. The pleasure principle is the principle that animates the id, making its demands very unrealistic.

4.   b   obj. 1   p. 412

a.   Incorrect. This describes the id.

*b.   Correct. The ego-ideal represents the internalized expectations of our parents and others for us to act and be moral.

c.   Incorrect. This is the role of the ego.

d.   Incorrect. There is no part of the id that does this.

5.   b   obj. 2   p. 413

a.   Incorrect. The genital stage is the last stage in the sequence and it occurs long after toilet training.

*b.   Correct. During the anal stage, the child learns self-control, and one of the manifestations of self control is toilet training.

c.   Incorrect. The phallic stage is marked by the Oedipal conflict and it occurs after the stage that includes toilet training.

d.   Incorrect. The oral stage is the first stage, and it is marked by a focus upon pleasure taken from the mouth.

6.   b   obj. 3   p. 414

a.   Incorrect. Probably just the opposite.

*b.   Correct. Anxiety is a great threat to the ego, so ego's defense mechanisms help protect it.

c.   Incorrect. The ego, at times, needs protection against the superego as well.

d.   Incorrect. Sometimes, defense mechanisms themselves cause Freudian slips.

7.   b   obj. 3   p. 415

a.   Incorrect. Repression forces conflict into the unconscious.

*b.   Correct. Sublimation converts repressed desire, especially sexual desire, into socially acceptable forms, like work.

c.   Incorrect. Rationalization involves creating self-justifying reasons after the fact.

d.   Incorrect. Projection places unacceptable impulses onto a safe object.

8.   a   obj. 5   p. 419

*a.   Correct. For most trait theorists, everyone has the major traits to some extent, and the amount of these traits tends to be stable through time.

b.   Incorrect. For most trait theorists, everyone has the major traits to some extent, and the amount of these traits tends to be stable through time.

c.   Incorrect. For most trait theorists, everyone has the major traits to some extent, and the amount of these traits tends to be stable through time.

d.   Incorrect. For most trait theorists, everyone has the major traits to some extent, and the amount of these traits tends to be stable through time.

9.   a   obj. 5   p. 420

*a.   Correct. Albert Bandura is the leading social learning theorist.

b.   Incorrect. Allport is known for the cardinal, central, and secondary traits.

c.   Incorrect. Cattell is known for the 16 factor theory, distinguishing source from surface traits.

d.   Incorrect. Eysenck proposed three main trait characteristics: extroversion, neuroticism, and psychoticism.

10.   c   obj. 5   p. 420

a.   Incorrect. It is an analytic technique, and it requires no special equipment.

b.   Incorrect. Used by trait theorists, this use is unlikely.

*c.   Correct. Factor analysis is a method that identifies common patterns in data and was used by Cattell to identify the source traits in his theory.

d.   Incorrect. While it might help identify personality traits in a group (if that is possible), it is only a statistical technique.

11.   c   obj. 6   p. 422

a.   Incorrect. This terminology is that of the trait theorists.

b.   Incorrect. This terminology is from the psychodynamic perspective.

*c.   Correct. As Skinner is a behaviorist, "traits" are explained in behavioral terms.

d.   Incorrect. This terminology is from the humanistic perspective.

12.   c   obj. 8   p. 428

a.   Incorrect. Humanistic theories tend not to judge the unconscious as evil.

b.   Incorrect. Society is not generally viewed by humanistic theories as a corrupting force.

*c.   Correct. Humans have within themselves the ability to heal their own psychological disorders and resolve their conflicts.

d.   Incorrect. No psychological view holds to this thesis of fundamental depravity.

13.   c   obj. 8   p. 428

a.   Incorrect. Learning theory depends upon conditioning and reinforcement.

b.   Incorrect. The psychodynamic theory focuses upon unconscious forces.

*c.   Correct. The humanistic approach focuses upon the abilities of the individual to engage in self-actualization.

d.   Incorrect. The trait theory searches for long-term, consistent behavior patterns.

14. c   obj. 9   p. 431
a.   Incorrect. It is a standardized test, but the scenario does not support this notion.
b.   Incorrect. Indeed, it is supposed to be an academic ability assessment tool, but this scenario does not question that.
*c. Correct. Since it measured her performance and knowledge the same in both circumstances, the assessment is quite reliable.
d.   Incorrect. It may be valid, but this story does not support that claim.

15. b   obj. 10   p. 435
a.   Incorrect. The MMPI asks for the test taker to respond to questions concerning items of which the test taker has an awareness.
*b. Correct. The Thematic Apperception Test (TAT) asks that respondents tell a story about a picture and through that story they may reveal unconscious concerns.
c.   Incorrect. The California Psychological Inventory is a self-report test, thus it reveals only items about which the test taker has awareness.
d.   Incorrect. This is probably another self-report instrument.

16. d   obj. 10   p. 435
a.   Incorrect. The TAT is, but the MMPI is not a projective instrument.
b.   Incorrect. The TAT is, but the 16 PF is not a projective instrument.
c.   Incorrect. The Rorschach is, but the MMPI is not a projective instrument.
*d. Correct. Both of these instruments require that the subject express feelings about pictures or inkblots that are ambiguous, thus projecting their own feelings and anxieties into the picture.

Practice Test II:
17. c   obj. 1   p. 411
a.   Incorrect. Humanistic theory is concerned with the person recognizing their own potential and finding ways to achieve self-actualization.
b.   Incorrect. Learning theory is concerned with the kinds of reinforcements and punishments that have contributed to the formation of the current patterns of behavior of an individual.
*c. Correct. Psychoanalytic theory considers the hidden content of the unconscious to be a powerful force in the shaping of personality.
d.   Incorrect. Trait theory seeks to identify and measure the consistent patterns of traits manifest by people.

18. a   obj. 1   p. 412
*a. Correct. The libido is psychic energy and not a part of Freud's structural model of the personality. The three parts of Freud's structural model of the personality are the id, ego, and superego.
b.   Incorrect. See answer a.
c.   Incorrect. See answer a.
d.   Incorrect. See answer a.

19. b   obj. 1   p. 412
a.   Incorrect. The id seeks to satisfy the pleasure principle and is not concerned with thought, decisions, or solving problems.
*b. Correct. The ego is responsible for balancing the demands of the id and the superego, and thus must solve problems, think, and make decisions.
c.   Incorrect. The superego seeks to present a moralistic, ego-ideal and a judgmental conscience to the ego.
d.   Incorrect. The conscience is one of the two components of the superego; the other is the ego-ideal.

20. d   obj. 2   p. 413
a.   Incorrect. See answer d.
b.   Incorrect. See answer d.
c.   Incorrect. See answer d.
*d. Correct. This child is seeking pleasure from the mouth, and is thus in the oral stage.

21. c   obj. 2   p. 413
a.   Incorrect. The child is only about 6 during this stage, and thus unlikely to participate in mature sexual relations.
b.   Incorrect. The child is less than 2 years old during this stage, and thus will not be engaging in any mature sexual relations.
*c. Correct. This was the name Freud gave to the stage in which sexual maturity develops.
d.   Incorrect. This stage occurs when the child is between 2 and 4 years of age, and thus mature sexual relations are unlikely.

22. a   obj. 3   p. 414
*a. Correct. Defense mechanisms operate below the level of awareness as part of their role in protecting the ego form anxiety and conflict.
b.   Incorrect. There are two instincts (drives) in Freud's view: eros and the death drive.
c.   Incorrect. Freud did not describe whether the defense mechanisms were learned or innate.
d.   Incorrect. After they have been utilized, they may become reflexive, but they respond to complex stimuli rather than the simple stimuli typically associated with reflexes.

23. b   obj. 3   p. 414
a.   Incorrect. Sublimation does not apply here.
*b. Correct. Repression is a form of intentional forgetting.
c.   Incorrect. Denial is one means of dealing with this kind of trauma, but the core mechanism is repression.
d.   Incorrect. After repression, the victims of child abuse may project fears onto other people.

24. d   obj. 5   p. 419
a.   Incorrect. Allport did not identify any traits as "general."
b.   Incorrect. Allport's concept of secondary traits is that people have many of these, and they govern such things as the style and preference of many everyday behaviors.
c.   Incorrect. In Allport's view, everyone has several central traits, but these do not dominate the personality.

*d. Correct. Allport called these cardinal traits, and they dominate the personality of the individual.

25. d   obj. 5   p. 419
a. Incorrect. Try again.
b. Incorrect. Try again.
c. Incorrect. Try again.
*d. Correct. The cardinal trait controls and dominates the personality, while at the other end, secondary traits define style and preferences.

26. a   obj. 5   p. 419
*a. Correct. If traits exist, then by definition they need to persist.
b. Incorrect. Trait theories did not commonly offer a theory for the existence of traits.
c. Incorrect. To only a few are traits learned in the traditional operant conditioning approach.
d. Incorrect. People do not choose to apply traits.

27. d   obj. 6   p. 423
a. Incorrect. This is Freud's idea.
b. Incorrect. This belongs to other drive theorists, like Clark Hull.
c. Incorrect. Bandura may agree that psychoanalysis will modify our personality, but not by using any of Bandura's concepts.
*d. Correct. Self-reinforcement is an important component of the social learning theory of Bandura.

28. d   obj. 7   p. 425
a. Incorrect. Since it appears long before the child has an opportunity to form interests, this answer is incorrect.
b. Incorrect. Temperament might itself be considered a source trait.
c. Incorrect. Temperament is present prior to the opportunity to have early learning experiences.
*d. Correct. This is the current view of temperament, that it is genetically disposed.

29. c   obj. 9   p. 431
a. Incorrect. If the test does not measure what it should, it would not be very accurate.
b. Incorrect. If the test made the same measure each time, it would still have to measure what it is supposed to measure to be considered valid.
*c. Correct. Even if the test failed to be measuring what it was supposed to measure, yet it made the same measurement each time, then the test would be reliable.
d. Incorrect. A statistical test would have to measure some kind of statistics, would it not?

30. a   obj. 9   p. 433
*a. Correct. The MMPI measures tendencies toward a number of psychological difficulties, but it can be taken by anyone and it does produce meaningful results for people who do not have psychological problems.
b. Incorrect. The MMPI is a self-report test, and thus unlikely to reveal many thoughts that are not within the awareness of the test taker.
c. Incorrect. The MMPI does not locate traits and is not specific to any trait theory.

d. Incorrect. The MMPI is a self-report test, and thus it cannot be used for a behavioral assessment except for the selection of true or false on the test.

31. c   obj. 10   p. 435
a. Incorrect. The TAT uses ambiguous pictures, but they are not as ambiguous as the inkblots used on the Rorschach.
b. Incorrect. The California Psychological Inventory and the MMPI both use statements that require a direct and unambiguous response to a rather unambiguous item.
*c. Correct. The Rorschach inkblots are probably the most ambiguous test stimuli used in this manner.
d. Incorrect. The California Psychological Inventory and the MMPI both use statements that require a direct and unambiguous response to a rather unambiguous item.

32. a   obj. 10   p. 435
*a. Correct. This is the famous inkblot test.
b. Incorrect. The 16PF uses a paper and pencil test.
c. Incorrect. The TAT uses a series of ambiguous scenes of people.
d. Incorrect. The MMPI uses true-false questions.

Practice Test III:
33. c   obj. 1   p. 412
a. Incorrect. The ego does operate on the reality principle as it tries to balance demands of the id and the superego.
b. Incorrect. Sigmund Freud was a Viennese physician.
*c. Correct. The ego, not the superego, is considered the executive of the personality.
d. Incorrect. The id follows the pleasure principle as it seeks to satisfy desires and wishes.

34. c   obj. 1   p. 412
a. Incorrect. The concept of unconditioned positive regard is from humanistic theory, and the rapist is the last person who would have such regard for another person.
b. Incorrect. Only if the ego-ideal was that of a rapist.
*c. Correct. The superego provides a sense of right and wrong, and a rapist is clearly missing this dimension of morality.
d. Incorrect. A psychoanalyst would not attribute the behavior of a rapist to brain damage.

35. b   obj. 2   p. 413
a. Incorrect. This is unusual, yet not abnormal for a child of this age.
*b. Correct. Thumbsucking is an oral behavior, so the youngster must be fixated in the oral stage.
c. Incorrect. Breastfeeding is not relevant to later thumbsucking.
d. Incorrect. The child is probably already in the phallic stage, but the fixation or regression to the oral stage is present.

36. a   obj. 2   p. 413
*a. Correct. The extremes of neatness and messiness have been associated with the anal stage, with the neat person overdoing anal retention and the messy person rejecting order.

b.   Incorrect. The messy person could be fixated in the oral stage, but not the neat one.

c.   Incorrect. Fixation in the phallic stage does not result in messiness or neatness.

d.   Incorrect. Freud did not describe what fixation would be like for stages in which we are currently occupied.

37.   b   obj. 3   p. 415
a.   Incorrect. Rationalization would involve making an explanation that would protect the self through after-the-fact justification.

*b.   Correct. The young woman is denying that she had any interest in the young man in the first place.

c.   Incorrect. Regression would require that she regress to an earlier developmental stage.

d.   Incorrect. Repression requires that she force her anxiety and anger into the unconscious.

38.   c   obj. 8   p. 430
a.   Incorrect. The biological view would not be that interested in conscious decisions.

b.   Incorrect. The trait approach does not consider traits within the person's ability to choose, and the humanistic approach certainly focuses upon conscious behavior.

*c.   Correct. The humanistic approach rests on the person's ability to be rational and self-motivated, while the psychodynamic approach assumes the power of the irrational and unconscious forces in the person.

d.   Incorrect. The trait approach does not consider traits within the person's ability to choose, and the humanistic approach certainly focuses upon conscious behavior.

39.   c   obj. 2   p. 412
a.   Incorrect. Many researchers in addition to Freud saw earlier childhood as critical for the development of the personality.

b.   Incorrect. The first in the sequence, but highest only if you stand up.

*c.   Correct. Infants, children, and adults seek physical pleasure.

d.   Incorrect. Piaget's sensorimotor stage is quite similar to Freud's oral stage, but the others differ.

40.   d   obj. 5   p. 420
a.   Incorrect. Jung proposed the idea of a collective unconscious.

b.   Incorrect. Horney argued that women do not have penis envy.

c.   Incorrect. Adler did develop the idea of an inferiority complex.

*d.   Correct. Striving for superiority is Adler's idea, not Cattell's.

41.   d   obj. 5   p. 418
a.   Incorrect. Sounds psychoanalytic.

b.   Incorrect. Sounds like Adler's idea of inferiority complex.

c.   Incorrect. Sounds like Maslow's hierarchy of needs.

*d.   Correct. A trait theorist would describe someone in terms of traits, like warm and considerate.

42.   b   obj. 8   p. 428
a.   Incorrect. This is unlikely, except if she compromises her own desires.

*b.   Correct. The incongruency between Stephanie and her parents could lead to anxiety.

c.   Incorrect. If this incongruency becomes a condition of worth, then Stephanie cannot become a fully functioning person.

d.   Incorrect. Unconditional positive regard requires more acceptance than this.

43.   d   obj. 8   p. 430
a.   Incorrect. Trait theory does propose that traits can be assessed and a picture of the person be composed.

b.   Incorrect. Learning theory does suggest that the environment is a major force in shaping the personality.

c.   Incorrect. Skinner is associated with learning theory.

*d.   Correct. While psychoanalytic theory would suggest that behavior would be consistent across situations, this is a major issue for trait theorists.

44.   d   obj. 9   p. 431
a.   Incorrect. This suggests that the test was a valid measure of pilot potential.

b.   Incorrect. This suggests that studying is a valid means of preparing for an exam.

c.   Incorrect. The test has validated the suspicion.

*d.   Correct. Repeating a test and getting the same or nearly the same score on each administration demonstrates reliability.

45.   b   obj. 7   p. 428
a.   Incorrect. This statement cannot be made based on the evidence reported in the text.

*b.   Correct. Believe it or not, the extent to which a person is traditional and the manner in which the person responds to stress are highly heritable.

c.   Incorrect. Alienation and absorption were moderately high.

d.   Incorrect. The research did not judge which traits were important and which were not.

46.   c   obj. 7   p. 428
a.   Incorrect. Traditionalism itself has been shown to be heritable.

b.   Incorrect. This would actually indicate something about the dependent variable, not a confounding variable.

*c.   Correct. When trying to separate parental genes from environmental forces, one must accept the confounding aspect of the parent's role in shaping the environment.

d.   Incorrect. This is not a confounding element.

47.   a   obj. 7   p. 426
*a.   Correct. Kagan has argued that the higher reactivity in children makes them be inhibited as a protection against the stimulation.

b.   Incorrect. This is reversed.

c.   Incorrect. They are genetically disposed to high physiological reactivity, not social closeness.

d.   Incorrect. Uninhibited children are not necessarily disposed to greater social closeness.

48. d   obj. 7   p. 428
a. Incorrect. While it is important evidence, no one has accepted it as conclusive.
b. Incorrect. The general view is that both are quite important, and making one more important than the other is meaningless.
c. Incorrect. Inhibited children are genetically disposed to greater physiological reactivity, not social closeness.
*d. Correct. This claim does seem to be shared by quite a few of the theorists, especially the psychoanalytic and the trait theorists.

■ CHAPTER 12: ANSWER KEY

GUIDED REVIEW			MATCHING	
Concept 1: [a] medical model of abnormality [b] psychoanalytic model of abnormality [c] behavioral model of abnormality [d] cognitive model of abnormality [e] humanistic model of abnormality [f] sociocultural model of abnormality [g] *Diagnostic and Statistical Manual of Mental Disorders, Fourth Edition (DSM-IV)*	**Concept 2:** [a] anxiety disorder. [b] Generalized anxiety disorder [c] Panic disorder [d] panic attacks [e] Phobic disorder [f] phobia [g] Obsessive-compulsive disorder [h] Obsessions [i] Compulsions [j] Hypochondriasis [k] somatoform disorders [l] conversion disorder [m] Dissociative disorders [n] Dissociative identity disorder [o] Dissociative amnesia [p] Dissociative fugue	**Concept 3:** [a] mood disorders [b] Major depression [c] Mania [d] bipolar disorder [e] learned helplessness [f] Schizophrenia [g] hallucinations [h] Process schizophrenia [i] reactive schizophrenia [j] Negative symptom [k] positive symptom [l] dopamine hypothesis [m] Personality disorders [n] antisocial or sociopathic personality disorder [o] borderline personality disorder [p] narcissistic personality disorder	1. d 2. a 3. e 4. c 5. f 6. b 7. c 8. e 9. b 10. d 11. a 12. d 13. e 14. a 15. c 16. f 17. b	18. e 19. b 20. d 21. a 22. c 23. c 24. b 25. d 26. a 27. a 28. d 29. c 30. b

Essay Question 12.1: Defining Mental Illness

■   The Rosenhan study suggests that mental health workers label their clients with rather unshakable labels. The labels also lead to interpretations of behavior that continue to confirm the diagnosis (note that some stayed for many weeks even though they only complained of the symptom once on admission to the hospital).

■   The issues of deception and the use of subjects who had not given their consent are major issues.

■   A brief examination of the study does not explain the contexts involved: Few people voluntarily walk into a mental hospital and complain of a major symptom. The sudden disappearance of the symptom could be considered abnormal as well.

Essay Question 12.2: Schizophrenia

■   Describe the major symptoms (see pages 463 and 464 in the Text).

■   Distinguish process and reactive, and examine the list of types on page 463 of the Text.

■   Discuss the biological and psychological components.

Multiple Choice Feedback:

Practice Test I:
1.   c   obj. 1   p. 443
a.   Incorrect. It probably was not different from how people would behave on average.
b.   Incorrect. Such behavior is quite sane.
*c. Correct. The ideal was for men to sacrifice themselves for their wives and children.
d.   Incorrect. Though many were probably uncomfortable after the fact, they were still alive.

2.   c   obj. 1   p. 442
a.   Incorrect. While there are always new treatments being devised for psychological disorders, the prologue does not illustrate this.
b.   Incorrect. While this is true, it is not the point illustrated by the prologue.
*c. Correct. Lori kept the voices she heard to herself, and her thoughts of suicide were not revealed: Some

disorders are not accompanied by obvious behavior difficulties.

d. Incorrect. While this is true, it is not the point illustrated by the prologue.

3. a   obj. 2   p. 445
*a. Correct. The medical model views abnormal behavior as arising from organic, physiological conditions.
b. Incorrect. The psychoanalytic view of abnormality depends upon the extremes of conflict in the unconscious and the adequacy of ego development.
c. Incorrect. The behavioral model of abnormality views abnormality as a result of inappropriate, learned behaviors.
d. Incorrect. The sociocultural view of abnormality views abnormality as the result of sociocultural forces, often with the view that social systems are themselves abnormal.

4. b   obj. 2   p. 445
a. Incorrect. The humanistic view would understand abnormality as the self in conflict.
*b. Correct. The medical approach seeks to understand abnormality as a result of organic, physiological causes.
c. Incorrect. The psychoanalytic view of abnormality depends upon the extremes of conflict in the unconscious and the adequacy of ego development.
d. Incorrect. The sociocultural view of abnormality views abnormality as the result of sociocultural forces, often with the view that social systems are themselves abnormal.

5. a   obj. 2   p. 456
*a. Correct. Psychodynamic views depend upon hidden or unconscious conflicts as the cause of most behavior.
b. Incorrect. The humanistic view would embrace the notion of "open" rather than hidden conflicts.
c. Incorrect. The cognitive model would accept the idea of strange beliefs, but it would focus on the irrational conscious thoughts.
d. Incorrect. The behavioral model would suggest that all the strange behaviors were learned.

6. b   obj. 2   p. 457
a. Incorrect. The behavioral model utilizes a behavioral expert who can help modify behavior.
*b. Correct. The humanistic model views the client as the person capable of effecting a cure. The humanistic therapist is there to facilitate.
c. Incorrect. The medical model depends upon a medical professional.
d. Incorrect. The psychoanalytic model requires a trained psychoanalyst.

7. d   obj. 2   p. 450
a. Incorrect. However, a behaviorist should be able to identify the system of rewards and punishments that contribute to these patterns.
b. Incorrect. The psychoanalyst is unlikely to be concerned with the socioeconomic status in which the conditions occur.

c. Incorrect. The humanistic model would not be interested in the socioeconomic conditions in which the abnormality occurs.
*d. Correct. The sociocultural model emphasizes the contributions made by social and economic factors such as income and broken homes.

8. c   obj. 3   p. 450
a. Incorrect. Try 200.
b. Incorrect. Try 200.
*c. Correct. The 200 categories suggest an increasing attention to differentiating a wide range of diseases.
d. Incorrect. Try 200.

9. c   obj. 5   p. 456
a. Incorrect. Phobic disorder is a fear of a specific event or stimulus.
b. Incorrect. This is the disorder in which psychological problems are manifest as physical symptoms.
*c. Correct. Hypochondriacs suffer every ache as a major disease.
d. Incorrect. This is a form of somatoform disorder.

10. c   obj. 4   p. 452
a. Incorrect. A psychosomatic disorder involves a physical symptom with no apparent physical cause.
b. Incorrect. A personality disorder involves a long-standing, habitual, and maladaptive personality pattern.
*c. Correct. This describes an anxiety disorder.
d. Incorrect. The term "neurotic disorder" is no longer used.

11. b   obj. 4   p. 453
a. Incorrect. In obsessive-compulsive disorder, the sufferer has uncontrollable thoughts and compulsions to act.
*b. Correct. The panic attack can be without warning and without apparent cause.
c. Incorrect. A personality disorder involves a long-standing, habitual, and maladaptive personality pattern.
d. Incorrect. A generalized anxiety disorder involves long-standing, consistent anxiety without an apparent cause or source.

12. d   obj. 6   p. 457
a. Incorrect. Schizophrenia involves disordered thought, not multiple personalities.
b. Incorrect. Not sure what this is, but Sybil didn't have it.
c. Incorrect. This is not an official diagnostic category.
*d. Correct. Once called "multiple personality," this problem is increasingly common.

13. b   obj. 6   p. 458
a. Incorrect. A dissociative identity disorder is marked by the presence of two or more personalities, not the dissociative fugue described.
*b. Correct. In dissociative fugue, the individual disappears, often just wandering off, and later reappears, often without any knowledge of why he or she left.
c. Incorrect. Someone suffering hypochondriasis has symptoms without physical illness.

d.   Incorrect. Panic attack is marked by feelings of impending doom or even death paired with sudden and overwhelming bodily reactions.

14. b   obj. 7   p. 461
a.   Incorrect. Or maybe, alternating fears of penguins and polar bears?
*b.   Correct. The "bipolar" aspect is the swing from the high mood of mania to the depths of depression.
c.   Incorrect. The "bipolar" aspect is the swing from the high mood of mania to the depths of depression, not between aspects of the personality.
d.   Incorrect. The "bipolar" aspect is the swing from the high mood of mania to the depths of depression, not between panic and phobia.

15. c   obj. 8   p. 464
a.   Incorrect. A compulsion is an idea that seems to have a life of its own - the sufferer gets up every night to hide the remote.
b.   Incorrect. The hallucination is just seeing Bigfoot.
*c.   Correct. Very delusional. Everyone knows Bigfoot belongs in garages.
d.   Incorrect. Only if you are Bigfoot.

16. c   obj. 8   p. 464
a.   Incorrect. Paranoid schizophrenia is characterized by delusions of persecution or grandeur.
b.   Incorrect. Catatonic schizophrenia os characterized by waxy flexibility and autistic withdrawal.
*c.   Correct. This statement describes process schizophrenia.
d.   Incorrect. Reactive schizophrenia usually has a quicker onset and has a better prognosis than the process schizophrenia described in the item.

Practice Test II:
17. d   obj. 2   p. 445
a.   Incorrect. Centuries ago, maybe.
b.   Incorrect. Rogers never intended this to be a meaning of his concept.
c.   Incorrect. The person may have bizarre behavior as well.
*d.   Correct. The notion of a psychological disorder being an "illness" suggests the medical view.

18. b   obj. 4   p. 453
a.   Incorrect. Panic is probably the more intense.
*b.   Correct. Panic involves symptoms that last for a brief period and then disappear until the next incident.
c.   Incorrect. Generalized anxiety disorder is not caused by alcohol.
d.   Incorrect. Panic disorder is not schizophrenic, though persons suffering from schizophrenia may experience panic.

19. a   obj. 2   p. 445
*a.   Correct. If disease is organic and physiological, then abnormal behaviors are beyond the individual's control.

b.   Incorrect. The sociocultural model would accept that the individual has control over his or her actions, even though they may be present due in part to sociocultural forces.
c.   Incorrect. The behavioral model allows for the individual to take control of his or her actions through behavior modification and self-regulation.
d.   Incorrect. The humanistic model suggest that ultimately the individual must take control and responsibility for his or her actions.

20. c   obj. 2   p. 446
a.   Incorrect. This explanation is more consistent with a cognitive model.
b.   Incorrect. This explanation is more consistent with the medical model.
*c.   Correct. Unresolved childhood conflicts would be repressed in the unconscious, and their efforts to be expressed and the costs of keeping them repressed can lead to abnormalities.
d.   Incorrect. The unconscious is confused and confusing for both healthy and psychologically disturbed individuals.

21. d   obj. 2   p. 447
a.   Incorrect. The medical model is currently focused on treatment through medication, and the only role the patient has is to take the drugs.
b.   Incorrect. The psychoanalyst directs the analysand toward an understanding of the problem.
c.   Incorrect. The behavioral model depends upon the application of different reward systems to alter the problem.
*d.   Correct. The humanistic model views the client as capable of self-healing and control and responsibility over his or her own actions.

22. a   obj. 2   p. 448
*a.   Correct. Some proponents of the sociocultural model claim that it is the society that is sick, not the individual.
b.   Incorrect. See answer a.
c.   Incorrect. See answer a.
d.   Incorrect. See answer a.

23. c   obj. 3   p. 448
a.   Incorrect. Treatment is not part of the manual.
b.   Incorrect. The causes of abnormality are identified with specific theories, so they have not been addressed in the manual.
*c.   Correct. The purpose of the manual is classification and description without implied theories.
d.   Incorrect. The manual does not offer treatment.

24. c   obj. 3   p. 451
a.   Incorrect. While this may be true in some cases, it is not the conclusion of the Rosenhan study.
b.   Incorrect. This may be true, but it was not addressed by the Rosenhan study.
*c.   Correct. Labeling carries a stigma that is difficult to erase.

d.   Incorrect. The *DSM-IV* categories have little to do with stability and change.

25.   b   obj. 3   p. 449
a.   Incorrect. Some prefer a continuum approach and are critical of the category approach.
*b. Correct. The manual is updated with greater frequency, and the update is highly sensitive to changing views of society about mental disorders.
c.   Incorrect. This is a common complaint, especially among psychologists who prefer a less medical orientation.
d.   Incorrect. Often, the diagnosis is viewed as if it provided an analysis of the cause of a disorder.

26.   d   obj. 6   p. 457
a.   Incorrect. The anxiety that gives rise to them is environmental, but the cause of the illness remains open.
b.   Incorrect. Not so.
c.   Incorrect. They are equal opportunity disorders.
*d. Correct. They all have some form of escape from anxiety.

27.   a   obj. 5   p. 456
*a. Correct. These include hypochondriasis and conversion disorders.
b.   Incorrect. The item describes a psychological disorder known as somatoform disorder, and not all psychological disorders have these symptoms.
c.   Incorrect. A disorder related to the study of psychophysics?
d.   Incorrect. No such disorder has been recognized.

28.   d   obj. 6   p. 457
a.   Incorrect. Depressive disorders include major and minor depression.
b.   Incorrect. Schizophrenia does not share these disorders with the dissociative category.
c.   Incorrect. Somatoform disorders involve a physical symptom without a physical cause, not the dissociation of part of the personality.
*d. Correct. Each of these disorders involves the separation of some part of the personality or memory.

29.   c   obj. 7   p. 461
a.   Incorrect. Bipolar disorders appear in men and women.
b.   Incorrect. Both can have either origin.
*c. Correct. In mania, the state remains high-pitched all the time.
d.   Incorrect. Both are mood disorders.

30.   c   obj. 9   p. 469
a.   Incorrect. They feel stress and anxiety to the same extent that normal individuals experience stress and anxiety.
b.   Incorrect. A rare sociopath has bothered to study the *DSM IV.*
*c. Correct. Guilt or remorse are necessary to trigger the physiological reaction that the polygraph measures.
d.   Incorrect. They are quite in touch with reality.

31.   a   obj. 8   p. 463
*a. Correct. Some people with schizophrenia have their own private language.
b.   Incorrect. People with dissociative identity disorder appear quite normal on the surface.
c.   Incorrect. The fugue state results in wandering off, not incoherence.
d.   Incorrect. Depressive individuals can become incoherent, but not because of unconventional language use.

32.   b   obj. 8   p. 464
a.   Incorrect. This is one of the major symptoms.
*b. Correct. Dissociative identity disorder, also known as multiple personality disorder, is not associated with schizophrenia.
c.   Incorrect. This is a common symptom of schizophrenia.
d.   Incorrect. This is a common symptom of schizophrenia.

Practice Test III:
33.   c   obj. 2   p. 448
a.   Incorrect. This statement is consistent with the sociocultural model.
b.   Incorrect. This statement is consistent with the sociocultural model.
*c. Correct. The sociocultural model recognizes that many aspects of abnormal behavior arise from the conditions of society. Even psychic forces within the individual would reflect conflicts in society.
d.   Incorrect. This statement is consistent with the sociocultural model.

34.   a   obj. 2   p. 448
*a. Correct. The sociocultural model of abnormality emphasizes the interactions between people as well as the conditions of society as contributors to abnormal behavior.
b.   Incorrect. The behavioral model would attribute abnormal behavior to faulty learning.
c.   Incorrect. The humanistic model would attribute abnormal behavior to conflicts within the self.
d.   Incorrect. The psychoanalytic model would attribute abnormal behavior to inner psychic conflicts.

35.   b   obj. 4   p. 453
a.   Incorrect. A phobic disorder is an irrational fear of a specific situation or object.
*b. Correct. This describes a panic attack.
c.   Incorrect. Generalized anxiety disorder is very similar to this condition, but it occurs without the rapid heartbeat, shortness of breath, and becoming faint (that is, without the panic).
d.   Incorrect. Obsessive-compulsive disorder is marked by uncontrollable thoughts and compulsions to carry out ritualistic behaviors, not by panic.

36.   b   obj. 4   p. 452
a.   Incorrect. It is possible for someone with schizophrenia to have irrational fears of water, but this kind of fear is more likely a phobia.

*b. Correct. A phobia is a persistent, irrational fear of an object or situation.
c. Incorrect. While the psychiatrist is more prone to using a medical model, the term "organic reactions" is not used to describe any known ailment.
d. Incorrect. Obsessive-compulsive disorder is marked by uncontrollable thoughts and compulsions to carry out ritualistic behaviors, not by panic.

37. a   obj. 4   p. 452
*a. Correct. A phobia is a persistent, irrational fear of an object or situation.
b. Incorrect. Panic disorder involves extreme anxiety and a sense of impending, unavoidable doom accompanied by rapid heartbeat, shortness of breath, and becoming faint and dizzy.
c. Incorrect. Obsessive-compulsive disorder is marked by uncontrollable thoughts and compulsions to carry out ritualistic behaviors, not by panic.
d. Incorrect. There is no category called tension disorder.

38. c   obj. 4   p. 453
a. Incorrect. Panic disorder involves extreme anxiety and a sense of impending, unavoidable doom accompanied by rapid heartbeat, shortness of breath, and becoming faint and dizzy.
b. Incorrect. A phobia is a persistent, irrational fear of an object or situation.
*c. Correct. Obsessive-compulsive disorder is marked by uncontrollable thoughts and compulsions to carry out ritualistic behaviors, like counting the number of times the professor says "the" in the lecture.
d. Incorrect. Generalized anxiety is the feeling that something bad is about to happen without any direct object causing the fear or anxiety.

39. b   obj. 5   p. 456
a. Incorrect. This does fall in the class of somatoform disorders, but another choice offers the specific disorder.
*b. Correct. In a conversion disorder, psychological problems are converted into physical problems, often without the sufferer showing the concern one might expect if the situation were a truly serious physical condition.
c. Incorrect. Panic disorder involves extreme anxiety and a sense of impending, unavoidable doom accompanied by rapid heartbeat, shortness of breath, and becoming faint and dizzy.
d. Incorrect. Obsessive-compulsive disorder is marked by uncontrollable thoughts and compulsions to carry out ritualistic behaviors, not by loss of voice.

40. d   obj. 10   p. 472
a. Incorrect. Less than one percent at any given time.
b. Incorrect. Less than one percent at any given time.
c. Incorrect. Less than one percent at any given time.
*d. Correct. There may be as many as 7 percent of the population experiencing alcohol dependence each year.

41. c   obj. 6   p. 458
a. Incorrect. Drugs are not typically used in this state because the condition is not typically recognized until the memory is recovered.
b. Incorrect. In dissociative amnesia, the loss can be permanent.
*c. Correct. The fugue state helps the person escape an anxiety-producing situation, and sometime after the escape, memory can be recovered.
d. Incorrect. In dissociative amnesia, the memories are considered still to be present, but psychologically blocked.

42. d   obj. 8   p. 464
a. Incorrect. Disorganized schizophrenia involves inappropriate laughter and giggling, silliness, incoherent speech, infantile behavior, and strange behaviors.
b. Incorrect. Catatonic schizophrenia involves disturbances of movement, sometimes a loss of all motion, sometimes with the opposite extreme of wild, violent movement.
c. Incorrect. Paranoid schizophrenia is marked by delusions and hallucinations related to persecution or delusions of grandeur, loss of judgment, and unpredictable behavior.
*d. Correct. Residual schizophrenia displays minor symptoms of schizophrenia after a stressful episode.

43. a   obj. 8   p. 465
*a. Correct. Reactive schizophrenia also has a better treatment outlook.
b. Incorrect. Though process schizophrenia is marked by gradual withdrawal, a reactive schizophrenic can be just as withdrawn.
c. Incorrect. No type of schizophrenia is necessarily aggressive or abusive.
d. Incorrect. Neither type has been shown to be more hereditary than the other.

44. d   obj. 8   p. 466
a. Incorrect. Learned helplessness is used to explain other problems (like depression) more than it is used to explain schizophrenia.
b. Incorrect. The dopamine hypothesis relates schizophrenia to an excess of dopamine.
c. Incorrect. The predisposition model suggests that a genetic predisposition exists for developing schizophrenia.
*d. Correct. This attention to inappropriate social stimuli is the foundation of the learned-inattention theory.

45. c   obj. 9   p. 468
a. Incorrect. This sounds like paranoia.
b. Incorrect. Personality disorder is not considered a mix of schizophrenic symptoms.
*c. Correct. Personality disorders are marked by inflexible, maladaptive personality traits, and these can take several forms.
d. Incorrect. An extended sense of euphoria and elation is found in the manic state of bipolar disorder.

46. b   obj. 8   p. 465
a.   Incorrect. Negative-symptom schizophrenia is marked by withdrawal and loss of social functioning.
*b.   Correct. Positive-symptom schizophrenia is marked by added symptoms, like hallucination (hearing voices) and delusions (fears of persecution).
c.   Incorrect. Process and reactive schizophrenia are differentiated on the basis of the onset of the disorder, not its characteristics.
d.   Incorrect. Process and reactive schizophrenia are differentiated on the basis of the onset of the disorder, not its characteristics.

47. a   obj. 9   p. 468
*a.   Correct. Pat's apparent action without conscience and manipulation of the system are hallmarks of the antisocial or sociopathic personality disorder.
b.   Incorrect. This does not describe someone who is self-defeating.
c.   Incorrect. Since this is not cyclic behavior, it could not be considered premenstrual dysphoric disorder.
d.   Incorrect. While having multiple personalities is not ruled out, the condition is better described as sociopathic personality disorder.

48. d   obj. 10   p. 472
a.   Incorrect. See answer d.
b.   Incorrect. See answer d.
c.   Incorrect. See answer d.
*d.   Correct. Koro, anorexia nervosa, and amok are disorders that appear to be culturally based.

■ CHAPTER 13: ANSWER KEY

GUIDED REVIEW			MATCHING	
Concept 1:	[r] modeling	Concept 3:	1. e	17. b
[a] psychotherapy	[s] token system	[a] drug therapy	2. a	18. c
[b] Biomedical therapy	[t] cognitive-behavioral	[b] antipsychotic drugs	3. d	19. e
[c] eclectic approach to	approaches	[c] Antidepressant drugs	4. c	20. f
therapy	[u] Rational-emotive therapy	[d] Lithium	5. f	21. a
[d] Psychodynamic therapy	[v] cognitive therapy	[e] Antianxiety drugs	6. b	22. g
[e] defense mechanisms		[f] Electroconvulsive	7. g	23. d
[f] psychoanalysis	Concept 2:	therapy (ECT)		
[g] free association	[a] Humanistic therapy	[g] Psychosurgery	8. c	24. f
[h] dream interpretation	[b] Nondirective counseling	[h] prefrontal lobotomy	9. e	25. c
[i] manifest content of dreams	[c] client-centered therapy	[i] community psychology	10. b	26. e
[j] latent content of dreams	[d] unconditional positive regard	[j] deinstitutionalization	11. d	27. b
[k] Resistance	[e] existential therapy		12. a	28. d
[l] Transference	[f] Gestalt therapy			29. a
[m] behavioral treatment	[g] Group therapy		13. b	
approaches	[h] Family therapy		14. d	
[n] aversive conditioning	[i] spontaneous remission		15. a	
[o] systematic desensitization	[j] eclectic approach to therapy		16. c	
[p] hierarchy of fears				
[q] Observational learning				

Essay Question 13.1: The Effectiveness of Psychotherapy

■ Identify the reasons you think psychotherapy works. These may include: psychotherapy offers a chance to reflect on life's problems in a safe environment, it offers a sense of control over one's problems, it provides a new ways of coping with and understanding stress.

■ Select at least two of the previously discussed concepts and describe their roles in depth.

■ Remember Eysenck's early study that suggested that psychotherapy was no more effective than being on a waiting list.

Essay Question 13.2: Should Electroconvulsive Therapy Be Banned?

■ Describe your response to the idea of electrical shock being passed through your brain as a means of therapy. Would you want this to be done?

■ What assumptions are made about the harm or benefit of using ECT? Do we assume that it must have some unseen long-term effect?

Multiple Choice Feedback:

Practice Test I:

1. b   obj. 1   p. 481
a. Incorrect. A sociocultural approach may seek to reintegrate an individual into society, but not all the therapies are oriented toward this.
*b. Correct. The common, shared goal of therapies is the relief of the symptoms of psychological disorders.
c. Incorrect. Some of the therapies are focused more on fear and anxiety than others.
d. Incorrect. Only therapies working with disordered personalities would have this as a goal.

2. c   obj. 1   p. 481
a. Incorrect. Eclectic therapy may utilize approaches that do not involve discussions and interactions.
b. Incorrect. There is not a major therapy called semantic therapy.
*c. Correct. Psychotherapy specifically involves this kind of direct interaction and discussion between the client and the psychotherapist.
d. Incorrect. Also known as ITP, this approach does involve interaction, but psychotherapy is the larger category described by this item.

3. c   obj. 1   p. 481
a. Incorrect. A psychiatric nurse may provide some support in a nursing role, but the psychiatrist conducts the therapy in these cases.
b. Incorrect. A counseling psychologist is not involved in medical treatment.
*c. Correct. A psychiatrist is a medical doctor who administers medical treatment for psychological disorders.
d. Incorrect. A clinical psychologist does not administer medical treatments.

4. d   obj. 2   p. 483
a. Incorrect. Transference occurs in therapy, and it involves transferring emotional energy from other relationships into the therapy relationship.
b. Incorrect. Aversive conditioning utilizes behavioral techniques.
c. Incorrect. Systematic desensitization utilizes behavioral techniques.
*d. Correct. They are called defense mechanisms because they defend the ego from anxiety arising from unconscious conflicts.

5. a   obj. 2   p. 484
*a. Correct. A hierarchy of fears is used in the behavioral technique known as systematic desensitization.
b. Incorrect. Neurotic symptoms, defense mechanisms, and transference are all psychodynamic concepts.
c. Incorrect. Neurotic symptoms, defense mechanisms, and transference are all psychodynamic concepts.
d. Incorrect. Neurotic symptoms, defense mechanisms, and transference are all psychodynamic concepts.

6. b   obj. 3   p. 485
a. Incorrect. The psychoanalytic approach is keyed to the problems caused by unconscious causes of abnormal behavior.
*b. Correct. The behavioral approach is concerned with only the observable causes of behavior, like the reinforcements or stimuli associated with learning.
c. Incorrect. An eclectic approach draws upon the most appropriate technique for the problem being treated.
d. Incorrect. The humanistic approach is concerned with how the individual views him or herself, and this may include causes beyond the person's awareness.

7. c   obj. 3   p. 486
a. Incorrect. Biofeedback uses signals from the body to help the person control physiological functions and achieve states of relaxation.
b. Incorrect. Behavior modification includes classical and operant conditioning techniques to change undesirable behaviors.
*c. Correct. Systematic desensitization utilizes classical conditioning techniques by having the person imagine a hierarchy of fears and gradually become desensitized to the frightening stimuli.

d. Incorrect. Aversive conditioning uses both classical and operant principles to get the subject to avoid certain responses.

8. d   obj. 3   p. 489
a. Incorrect. See answer d.
b. Incorrect. See answer d.
c. Incorrect. See answer d.
*d. Correct. Perhaps stimulus substitution, but not symptom substitution. Aversive conditioning, systematic desensitization, and modeling are all behavioral techniques.

9. c   obj. 4   p. 490
a. Incorrect. This may be a rational approach to problem solving, but it is not the approach of rational-emotive therapy.
b. Incorrect. Love and approval are not part of rational-emotive therapy.
*c. Correct. This is the goal of rational-emotive therapy.
d. Incorrect. This may be part of the theory behind rational-emotive therapy, but it is not the therapeutic goal.

10. d   obj. 5   p. 492
a. Incorrect. Rational-emotive therapy is a cognitive therapy, and thus it incorporates what the person thinks about themselves.
b. Incorrect. Gestalt therapy is a humanistic approach that requires the person to accept parts of him or herself that he or she has denied or rejected.
c. Incorrect. Systematic desensitization utilizes classical conditioning techniques by having the person imagine a hierarchy of fears and gradually become desensitized to the frightening stimuli.
*d. Correct. Client-centered therapy assumes that the client has the potential to handle his or her own problems.

11. d   obj. 5   p. 493
a. Incorrect. All therapies involve, in one way or another, helping the client get in touch with reality.
b. Incorrect. The psychoanalytic approach is focused upon understanding the unconscious.
c. Incorrect. Cognitive therapies, like rational-emotive therapy, are focused upon the person taking control of his or her thoughts.
*d. Correct. Humanistic therapy strives to help the client achieve some form of self-actualization, or at least move toward realizing his or her potential.

12. a   obj. 5   p. 493
*a. Correct. The psychodynamic approach focuses on control of unconscious impulses, and the humanistic approach focuses on self-control and responsibility.
b. Incorrect. The behavioral approach is entirely focused on outer forces.
c. Incorrect. The behavioral approach is entirely focused on outer forces.
d. Incorrect. The behavioral approach is entirely focused on outer forces.

13. b   obj. 7   p. 496
a.   Incorrect. This would be called unethical.
*b. Correct. Sometimes, simply allowing time to pass cures a psychological disorder.
c.   Incorrect. This may be a spontaneous emission, but not a remission.
d.   Incorrect. This is not remission.

14. b   obj. 8   p. 500
a.   Incorrect. Antipsychotic drugs block the production of dopamine.
*b. Correct. Unfortunately, this is not a cure for the problem.
c.   Incorrect. Antipsychotic drugs block the production of dopamine.
d.   Incorrect. Antipsychotic drugs block the production of dopamine; tranquilizers sedate the patient.

15. a   obj. 8   p. 502
*a. Correct. How this mineral salt works remains a mystery.
b.   Incorrect. Valium is an antianxiety drug.
c.   Incorrect. Chlorpromazine is an antipsychotic drug.
d.   Incorrect. Librium is an antianxiety drug.

16. d   obj. 8   p. 500
a.   Incorrect. Psychosurgery has always been a method of last resort.
b.   Incorrect. ECT has become less common than it once was, but even in its heyday it was not the most common.
c.   Incorrect. Genetic engineering has not yet been applied to direct treatment of psychological disorders.
*d. Correct. Even general practitioners will prescribe psychoactive drug therapies.

17. a   obj. 9   p. 504
*a. Correct. The original psychosurgery was the prefrontal lobotomy, where the frontal lobes are destroyed.
b.   Incorrect. Electroconvulsive therapy, also known as shock therapy, does not destroy any tissue.
c.   Incorrect. Electroconvulsive therapy, also known as shock therapy, does not destroy any tissue.
d.   Incorrect. There is not a group of therapies or an approach to therapy known as "personality" therapy.

Practice Test II:
18. d   obj. 1   p. 481
a.   Incorrect. Clinical psychologists cannot prescribe dugs.
b.   Incorrect. Drug therapy is used for almost every disorder.
c.   Incorrect. This may be part of the view, but the predominant view is that the disorders are medical in nature.
*d. Correct. Biomedical therapy uses medical interventions.

19. c   obj. 1   p. 481
a.   Incorrect. That is not what eclectic means.
b.   Incorrect. It is not connected to the paranormal.
*c. Correct. The therapist chooses the technique best matched to the client's needs.
d.   Incorrect. It was actually his long-lost brother, Homer Simpson.

20. c   obj. 2   p. 483
a.   Incorrect. In the psychoanalytic view, abnormal behaviors do not suppress normal behaviors.
b.   Incorrect. The ego does not repress the superego.
*c. Correct. The focus in psychodynamic therapy is on past, unresolved conflicts, often going back to childhood.
d.   Incorrect. The ego always has access to consciousness.

21. b   obj. 2   p. 483
a.   Incorrect. Defense mechanism may play a role when they fail to protect the ego from anxiety.
*b. Correct. Anxiety is the main cause of neurotic symptoms, and the anxiety arises because of undesirable motives or repressed conflicts.
c.   Incorrect. Inappropriate choices would be the cause of symptoms as viewed by humanistic theory.
d.   Incorrect. Contingency contracting might be found in behavior therapy, but not as the cause for neurotic symptoms in Freud's view.

22. b   obj. 2   p. 484
a.   Incorrect. Try transference.
*b. Correct. Transference brings the emotional energy of the past relationship into the current therapeutic relationship.
c.   Incorrect. Try transference.
d.   Incorrect. Try transference.

23. a   obj. 3   p. 486
*a. Correct. The response to alcohol after successful aversion therapy is to avoid alcohol because it is linked to the aversive stimulus.
b.   Incorrect. The craving is probably still there.
c.   Incorrect. No fear of alcohol should develop.
d.   Incorrect. Properly undertaken, alcohol should not become a source of anxiety.

24. d   obj. 5   p. 492
a.   Incorrect. This is the behavioral approach.
b.   Incorrect. This is the psychodynamic approach.
c.   Incorrect. This is the cognitive approach.
*d. Correct. Humanistic approaches focus on personal responsibility and self healing.

25. d   obj. 4   p. 490
a.   Incorrect. The views may be defensive, but those challenged are the irrational views held by the client.
b.   Incorrect. The views may be self-centered, but those challenged are the irrational views held by the client.
c.   Incorrect. The views may be paranoid, but those challenged are the irrational views held by the client.
*d. Correct. The therapist is attempting to get the client to eliminate faulty ideas about the world and himself or herself.

26. c   obj. 5   p. 492
a.   Incorrect. The therapist is primarily responsible for establishing a program of stimuli or reinforcement that will retrain the client in behavioral therapy.

b. Incorrect. The rational-emotive therapist is attempting to get the client to eliminate faulty ideas about the world and him or herself.

*c. Correct. Humanistic therapy attempts to help the client gain insight into his or her responsibility for the need to make changes.

d. Incorrect. The psychoanalytic approach seeks to understand the unconscious forces at work.

27. c   obj. 5   p. 492
a. Incorrect. Reinforcement would be used in behavioral therapy, not humanistic therapy.

b. Incorrect. A contingency contract is used in behavioral therapy, not humanistic therapy.

*c. Correct. Unconditional positive regard is the basis of any therapeutic relationship in the humanistic view.

d. Incorrect. The psychoanalytic approach is aimed more at inner conflicts.

28. d   obj. 5   p. 494
a. Incorrect. Behavioral therapy is not interested in human freedom and other concepts related to existence and the meaning of life.

b. Incorrect. Rational-emotive therapy is focused upon changing the client's way of thinking about the world.

c. Incorrect. Humanistic therapy is focused upon helping the client take responsibility for his or her actions.

*d. Correct. This describes the goals of existential therapy, a type of humanistic therapy.

29. c   obj. 6   p. 494
a. Incorrect. Psychodynamic group therapy will focus on this aspect of the client.

b. Incorrect. This is not possible in any kind of therapy.

*c. Correct. Others in the group have had similar experiences, and the client learns that he or she is not alone.

d. Incorrect. Only in cognitive group therapy.

30. c   obj. 8   p. 500
a. Incorrect. Antidepressant drugs are used for many mood disorders.

b. Incorrect. Antianxiety drugs, like Valium and Xanax, are used for anxiety disorders.

*c. Correct. Chlorpromazine is an antipsychotic drug used to treat schizophrenia.

d. Incorrect. Lithium is used to treat the mania of bipolar disorders.

31. b   obj. 8   p. 502
a. Incorrect. Valium is an antianxiety drug without any preventive characteristics.

*b. Correct. Lithium is one of the few drugs that appears to provide a degree of cure.

c. Incorrect. Chlorpromazine does not cure schizophrenia or any of the other disorders it is used to treat.

d. Incorrect. Librium is an antianxiety drug without any preventive or curative characteristics.

32. d   obj. 8   p. 502
a. Incorrect. Antidepressants do not increase the activity of the autonomic system.

b. Incorrect. Antipsychotics decrease the production of dopamine, but antidepressants actually increase the concentrations of some neurotransmitters.

c. Incorrect. Drugs do not increase the speed of neural transmission.

*d. Correct. Antidepressants, like Prozac and tricyclic, increase the concentration of neurotransmitters.

33. d   obj. 9   p. 502
a. Incorrect. Electroconvulsive shock therapy is commonly used today.

b. Incorrect. Antipsychotic drugs continue to be relied upon by the medical community.

c. Incorrect. Psychotherapy is very common.

*d. Correct. The use of psychosurgery, especially the lobotomy, is used less and less for treatment of psychological disorders.

34. d   obj. 10   p. 506
a. Incorrect. If you are afraid of your therapist, it will be difficult to establish a good therapeutic relationship.

b. Incorrect. Therapy will work only if you put effort into it; there are no easy fixes.

c. Incorrect. You should have a sense of progress after several months in therapy.

*d. Correct. Being involved in your therapy is a good sign that you have made a good selection of a therapist.

Practice Test III:

35. d   obj. 1   p. 481
a. Incorrect. A psychiatrist would probably be inappropriate for this kind of short-term problem.

b. Incorrect. A psychoanalyst would probably be inappropriate for this kind of short-term problem.

c. Incorrect. A psychiatric social worker is trained to deal with other kinds of problems and would probably be inappropriate for this kind of short-term problem.

*d. Correct. A counseling psychologist is especially prepared for dealing with problems of adjustment such as this one.

36. b   obj. 1   p. 481
a. Incorrect. Someone with a degree in psychiatric social work would be more appropriately placed in a community health center.

*b. Correct. This is the most appropriate degree for this kind of position.

c. Incorrect. A clinical psychologist could hold this position, but a counseling degree would be more suitable.

d. Incorrect. An educational psychologist would not be suitable for this position.

37. d   obj. 2   p 483
a. Incorrect. Some, but not all, existential therapists use psychodynamic techniques.

b. Incorrect. Cognitive therapy would have the client explore conscious thoughts.

c.   Incorrect. Behavioral therapy would not have the client think much at all.

*d.   Correct. Dream interpretation is a core technique for psychodynamic therapy.

38.   b   obj. 3   p. 486
a.   Incorrect. Aversive conditioning works well with habits that are being broken, like drug habits, smoking, and alcoholism.

*b.   Correct. Aversive conditioning works well with habits that are being broken, like drug habits, smoking, and alcoholism, but not with psychological problems like depression.

c.   Incorrect. Aversive conditioning works well with habits that are being broken, like drug habits, smoking, and alcoholism.

d.   Incorrect. Aversive conditioning works well with habits that are being broken, like drug habits, smoking, and alcoholism.

39.   d   obj. 3   p. 485
a.   Incorrect. Behaviorists are not that interested in self-perception.

b.   Incorrect. Humanistic approaches focus on personal responsibilities.

c.   Incorrect. Psychodynamic approaches focus on the unconscious mind.

*d.   Correct. These new habits are meant to replace the old, malfunctioning ones.

40.   b   obj. 4   p. 490
a.   Incorrect. In behavior therapy, other avenues would be explored, like the reinforcements that were being sought.

*b.   Correct. In rational-emotive therapy, this expectation of perfection would be viewed as irrational and thus in need of being altered.

c.   Incorrect. In humanistic theory, the concern would be more about the issue of personal responsibility rather than thoughts about how others would view one.

d.   Incorrect. In existential therapy, Dr. Ertle might have asked Peggy to consider what it means to be perfect in such an imperfect world.

41.   d   obj. 5   p. 493
a.   Incorrect. Behavior therapy does not ask clients to act out past conflicts.

b.   Incorrect. Existential therapy is much more focused on the meaning of life than past conflicts.

c.   Incorrect. Rational-emotive therapy is focused more on the client's irrational ideas about the world.

*d.   Correct. Gestalt therapy seeks to have the clients integrate and "own" these conflicts to be able to resolve them for themselves.

42.   a   obj. 5   p. 493
*a.   Correct. The gestalt therapist is trying to integrate the nonverbal message with the verbal message and thus reduce Helen's conflict.

b.   Incorrect. A psychoanalytic therapist might be interested in the nonverbal cues as efforts of the unconscious to get a message across.

c.   Incorrect. A client-centered therapist would attempt to mirror Helen's concerns back to her so she could hear what she was saying.

d.   Incorrect. A behavioral therapist would suggest that the reinforcement for being perfect needed to be reevaluated.

43.   a   obj. 7   p. 493
*a.   Correct. These two approaches require much discussion and insight, so a verbal client will do well in these approaches.

b.   Incorrect. Severely disordered patients should probably be treated with drugs and some psychotherapy.

c.   Incorrect. People with sexual disorders would be best served if they sought a sex therapist.

d.   Incorrect. People reluctant to converse with others would have difficulty talking to a psychoanalytic or humanistic therapist.

44.   a   obj. 8   p. 502
*a.   Correct. These are symptoms of anxiety.

b.   Incorrect. She is not depressed.

c.   Incorrect. She is not psychotic.

d.   Incorrect. She does not need an aspirin.

45.   b   obj. 8   p. 501
a.   Incorrect. Antipsychotic drugs only suppress the symptoms.

*b.   Correct. After taking a regimen of antidepressant drugs, depression tends not to return.

c.   Incorrect. Antianxiety drugs suppress the response to anxiety, but they do not remove the cause of the anxiety.

d.   Incorrect. Chlorpromazine is an antipsychotic drug and it suppresses psychotic symptoms, but they return if the drug is stopped.

46.   c   obj. 9   p. 503
a.   Incorrect. ECT is used for severe depression when other treatments do not work.

b.   Incorrect. ECT is used for severe depression when other treatments do not work.

*c.   Correct. ECT is used for severe depression when other treatments do not work.

d.   Incorrect. ECT is used for severe depression when other treatments do not work.

47.   a   obj. 9   p. 503
*a.   Correct. It does seem to relieve depression.

b.   Incorrect. It was introduced in the thirties.

c.   Incorrect. Drug therapy is much preferred.

d.   Incorrect. Clinical psychologists are not licenced to administer drugs or ECT.

48.   d   obj. 5   p. 493
a.   Incorrect. A psychoanalyst would be interested in what the house symbolized for Richard, not the unfinished business it entails.

b. Incorrect. A group therapist would not likely be
    conducting individual dream therapy.
c. Incorrect. An existential therapist might be interested in
    the dream as it provides insight into the client's concerns
    about life and existence.
*d. Correct. The gestalt therapist is attempting to get
    Richard to recognize and integrate the unfinished
    business that his dream home represents.

49. c   obj. 5   p. 493
a. Incorrect. These are not the concerns of a behavioral
    therapist.
b. Incorrect. These are not the concerns of a
    psychoanalyst.
*c. Correct. Existential psychotherapy is concerned with
    important religious and philosophical issues, especially
    the meaning and purpose of life.
d. Incorrect. A group therapist would probably not bring
    these kinds of issues to a group.

50. b   obj. 3   p. 486
a. Incorrect. The procedure is called systematic
    desensitization, and the list is called a hierarchy of fears.
*b. Correct. This list is called a hierarchy of fears, and the
    behavioral approach is based on classical conditioning
    principles.
c. Incorrect. This would not be done by a humanistic
    therapist.
d. Incorrect. This would not be done by a humanistic
    therapist.

51. a   obj. 7   p. 497
*a. Correct. However, they all are beneficial if applied to
    the appropriate kinds of problems.
b. Incorrect. Behavioral therapy does not work on the most
    serious problems.
c. Incorrect. This is reasonably true, but humanistic
    therapy will work if the client is not economically
    advantaged.
d. Incorrect. This was originally thought to be true when
    studies were first conducted regarding the effectiveness
    of psychotherapy, but now evidence suggests that they
    are all effective to some extent.

■ CHAPTER 14: ANSWER KEY

GUIDED REVIEW			MATCHING		
Concept 1: [a] Social psychology [b] Attitudes [c] ABC model [d] affect component [e] behavior component [f] cognition component [g] vicarious learning [h] Central-route processing [i] Peripheral-route processing [j] Psychographics [k] Cognitive dissonance [l] social cognition [m] Schemas [n] Impression formation [o] central traits [p] Attribution theory [q] Situational causes [r] dispositional cause [s] fundamental attribution error [t] halo effect [u] assumed-similarity bias	Concept 2: [a] social influence [b] Conformity [c] status [d] social supporter [e] Groupthink [f] compliance [g] foot-in-the-door technique [h] door-in-the-face technique [i] that's-not-all technique [j] not-so-free sample [k] Obedience Concept 3: [a] Stereotypes [b] prejudice [c] discrimination [d] self-fulfilling prophecy [e] social learning approaches [f] social identity theory	Concept 4: [a] interpersonal attraction [b] Proximity [c] Mere exposure [d] Similarity [e] reciprocity-of-liking effect [f] need-complimentarity hypothesis [g] Physical attractiveness [h] passionate (or romantic) love [i] companionate love [j] intimacy component [k] passion component [l] decision/commitment component [m] Aggression [n] catharsis [o] Frustration [p] Prosocial behavior [q] diffusion of responsibility [r] Altruism	1. b 2. c 3. a 4. f 5. d 6. e 7. g 8. c 9. b 10. d 11. e 12. a	13. b 14. d 15. c 16. a 17. c 18. b 19. d 20. e 21. a	22. e 23. d 24. b 25. a 26. c 27. g 28. d 29. b 30. f 31. e 32. h 33. a 34. c

Essay Question 14.1: The Consistency Between Attitudes and Behavior

■ Situations that might be relevant are those in which you did something, like go on a date with someone, that you really were not that interested in doing. The mismatch between the attitude (lack of interest) and behavior (going out), while not that great does illustrate the problem.

■ Describe how you felt after the specific incident or act and whether you changed your attitudes (she/he is actually pleasant to be with). Or perhaps, you wait until after the behavior to form your attitude (consistent with the self-perception theory).

Essay Question 14.2: Conformity and Violence

■ Provide an example of recent violence against an ethnic group (or even an episode identified with a particular group).

■ Gang violence is a clear application of the ingroup-outgroup bias. The recent riots in Los Angeles suggest that many today have very strong stereotypes about the groups represented in the violence, including African American, Hispanic, and Asian.

■ Describe how each of the factors of conformity, compliance, and obedience could work toward increasing prejudice and following group behavior.

Multiple Choice Feedback:

Practice Test I:
1. c obj. 1 p. 513
a. Incorrect. This is the behavioral component.
b. Incorrect. This is the cognitive component.

*c. Correct. Affect means "feeling."
d. Incorrect. There is no anxiety component.

2.   d   obj. 1   p. 513
a.   Incorrect. The affective component is the feeling component of attitudes.
b.   Incorrect. In the ABC model, there is no "manner" component of attitudes, though there should be.
c.   Incorrect. In the ABC model, the behavioral component includes the actions that relate to the attitude.
*d. Correct. In the ABC model, the component that includes our thoughts and beliefs is called the cognitive component of attitudes.

3.   a   obj. 2   p. 514
*a. Correct. Linking the product to a positive event originates with classical conditioning.
b.   Incorrect. They seek to link the product to a pleasant stimuli, like a feeling or event.
c.   Incorrect. The peripheral route is one of the methods of communicating in persuasive communication.
d.   Incorrect. A dissonant stimulus might be one that does not fit with the others or causes some kind of conflict.

4.   a   obj. 2   p. 516
*a. Correct. Otherwise, they are simply frightening.
b.   Incorrect. Defense mechanisms may make them ignore the warnings.
c.   Incorrect. Indifferent audiences are no more receptive to fear-based messages than any other audience.
d.   Incorrect. This would be the measure of their effectiveness.

5.   a   obj. 3   p. 520
*a. Correct. A schema is an organizing framework.
b.   Incorrect. Schemas actually serve as the foundation for stereotypes.
c.   Incorrect. Schemas are not communicators.
d.   Incorrect. Schemers maybe, but not schemas.

6.   b   obj. 3   p. 521
a.   Incorrect. Central tendencies are the measures like mean, median, and mode that are produced using statistics.
*b. Correct. Apparently we utilize major, evident traits that are central to the personality of the individual about which we are forming impressions.
c.   Incorrect. The term is "central traits."
d.   Incorrect. The concept "schematic tendencies" is yet to be developed.

7.   d   obj. 4   p. 525
a.   Incorrect. This must have been a later study.
b.   Incorrect. This would be market research.
c.   Incorrect. This kind of perception study was being done in the fifties, but not by Asch.
*d. Correct. They were asked to match a line to one of three other lines.

8.   b   obj. 3   p. 523
a.   Incorrect. The ingroup-outgroup bias (not error) may follow the fundamental attribution error, but its role is in determining the boundaries between groups and strengthening the sense of identity with the ingroup.

*b. Correct. The fundamental attribution error is quite common and may be understood in that we do tend to see the person's behavior more than the environment in which it occurs, and we see our own environment and not so much our own behavior.
c.   Incorrect. There is no dispositional attribution error.
d.   Incorrect. There is no stereotypic attribution error.

9.   b   obj. 4   p. 525
a.   Incorrect. Skinner did not conduct conformity experiments.
*b. Correct. Solomon Asch performed a number of experiments throughout the 1950s on conformity.
c.   Incorrect. Zimbardo conducted experiments on compliance and obedience.
d.   Incorrect. Milgram conducted a now famous experiment on obedience.

10. d   obj. 5   p. 526
a.   Incorrect. Inoculation occurs when the person is deliberately exposed to conformity pressures in order to be better at avoiding conformity.
b.   Incorrect. Obedience requires more direct pressure.
c.   Incorrect. Forewarning is a technique for developing the ability to resist pressures to conform.
*d. Correct. In ambiguous circumstances, social pressure is more likely to have an effect on conformity.

11. a   obj. 5   p. 527
*a. Correct. Buy a small item, and then get committed to another, larger purchase.
b.   Incorrect. This is when after the inflated offer, the salesman lowers the price.
c.   Incorrect. This politically incorrect insult would not be allowed to remain a technique.
d.   Incorrect. This is when after refusing something large, then it is easier to accept something small.

12. c   obj. 6   p. 530
a.   Incorrect. Albert Bandura is known for his study of violence and the Bobo clown doll.
b.   Incorrect. Solomon Asch is known for his experiments on conformity.
*c. Correct. Stanley Milgram asked the subject to give an electric shock to other subjects, and he was able to get most to comply to the point of the highest shock level.
d.   Incorrect. Skinner did not perform any human conformity studies.

13. c   obj. 6   p. 530
a.   Incorrect. Profitability leads to compliance.
b.   Incorrect. Conformity is more critical here.
*c. Correct. Obedience is usually to authority.
d.   Incorrect. Conformity, even the extreme of groupthink, is likely in this situation.

14. b   obj. 7   p. 533
a.   Incorrect. We are all interdependent.
*b. Correct. Self-fulfilling prophecies are a danger to underprivileged groups because they sustain the circumstances.

c. Incorrect. Reverse discrimination occurs when one is making efforts to avoid a stereotype.

d. Incorrect. In this bias, stereotypes are applied to help differentiate the two groups.

15. c   obj. 7   p. 533
a. Incorrect. This discrimination is not reverse but is instead quite direct.
b. Incorrect. Individualism is not a concept relevant to active genocide.
*c. Correct. Not only is this a manifestation of extreme prejudice, but it is also an extreme form of discrimination.
d. Incorrect. Deterrence is a concept that would prevent the actions of a group by threatening retaliation.

16. c   obj. 7   p. 533
a. Incorrect. These are stereotypes, and stereotypes can become self-fulfilling prophecies.
b. Incorrect. Culture is the shared beliefs and practices of a group.
*c. Correct. This defines stereotypes.
d. Incorrect. These are not called contingencies; they are called stereotypes.

17. d   obj. 8   p. 533
a. Incorrect. Economic class can be a basis for prejudice, but it is not as common as racial, ethnic, and religious categories.
b. Incorrect. Prejudices may be based on attitudes of superiority that a group has, but not on jealousies that occur because of a perceived superiority.
c. Incorrect. Interdependence may contribute to the reduction of prejudice.
*d. Correct. The most common source of prejudice is visible characteristics that are used to distinguish one group from another.

18. d   obj. 9   p. 537
a. Incorrect. See answer d.
b. Incorrect. See answer d.
c. Incorrect. See answer d.
*d. Correct. Living nearby, similarity, and frequent contact are the foundations of friendship, and exceptional attractiveness is not.

19. b   obj. 9   p. 538
a. Incorrect. Most view love as a different state than friendship.
*b. Correct. Most view love as a different state than friendship.
c. Incorrect. Most view love as a different state than friendship; both love and liking are emotions.
d. Incorrect. Most view love as a different state than friendship.

20. d   obj. 9   p. 538
a. Incorrect. See answer d.
b. Incorrect. See answer d.
c. Incorrect. See answer d.

*d. Correct. To being nearby, sharing interests, and being similar, love adds the component of physical attraction and arousal.

21. d   obj. 9   p. 539
a. Incorrect. See answer d.
b. Incorrect. See answer d.
c. Incorrect. See answer d.
*d. Correct. Sternberg's triarchic theory of love has three components - intimacy, passion, and commitment - that can be combined in different ways.

22. c   obj. 10   p. 541
a. Incorrect. Phase 1 involves a personal focus on the partner's behavior.
b. Incorrect. Phase 2 involves confrontations with the partner.
*c. Correct. Phase 3 involves negotiation on dissolution and face-saving behavior.
d. Incorrect. Phase 4 involves ending the relationship physically and psychologically.

23. d   obj. 11   p. 544
a. Incorrect. This was one of the earlier formulations, and it suggested a need to vent the frustration or anger before it is expressed.
b. Incorrect. The earlier theories suggested a need for catharsis or release of pent-up aggression.
c. Incorrect. This view is similar to the social facilitation view.
*d. Correct. Aggression leads to anger, and opportunities to be aggressive and express the anger can lead to aggression.

24. a   obj. 12   p. 545
*a. Correct. Prosocial behavior is altruistic helping behavior.
b. Incorrect. Insofar as helping another is cathartic, this could be a good answer, but the term "prosocial" typically refers to helping behavior.
c. Incorrect. Some biosociologists argue that prosocial behavior is innate because it promotes the survival of the species.
d. Incorrect. Prosocial behavior is altruistic helping behavior.

Practice Test II:
25. c   obj. 1   p. 513
a. Incorrect. In the ABC model, the component that includes our thoughts and beliefs is called the cognitive component of attitudes.
b. Incorrect. In the ABC model, there is no "intentional" component of attitudes.
*c. Correct. In the ABC model, the affective component is the feeling component of attitudes.
d. Incorrect. In the ABC model, the behavioral component includes the actions that relate to the attitude.

26. b   obj. 2   p. 514
a.   Incorrect. Peripheral-route processing is not a learning principle.
*b.   Correct. Both classical and operant conditioning principles are involved in the formation of attitudes.
c.   Incorrect. Central-route processing is not a learning principle.
d.   Incorrect. Punishment on its own cannot account for the richness and variety of our attitudes.

27. d   obj. 2   p. 524
a.   Incorrect. Social psychologists, some of who are experimental psychologists as well, have made contributions that are useful to the advertising industry.
b.   Incorrect. Psychometrics is an important technique that probably was used by social psychologists as they developed key ideas that are now being used in the advertising industry.
c.   Incorrect. Of all the branches of psychology, abnormal psychology has probably made the smallest contribution to the advertising industry.
*d.   Correct. Social psychologists, some of who are experimental psychologists as well, have made contributions that are useful to the advertising industry.

28. a   obj. 2   p. 519
*a.   Correct. The conflict between two cognitions becomes cognitive dissonance when this conflict is accompanied by an affective state.
b.   Incorrect. No such thing.
c.   Incorrect. If anything, it would heighten tension.
d.   Incorrect. It may lead to frustration but probably not aggression.

29. a   obj. 3   p. 520
*a.   Correct. Social cognitions refer to the thoughts we have about other people and the causes of their behavior.
b.   Incorrect. Social cognitions are schemas, but schemas–the cognitive units of organization–refer to other cognitive categories as well.
c.   Incorrect. Central traits are the traits we choose to make early impressions about people, and they may be included in our social cognitions.
d.   Incorrect. Stereotypes are forms of social cognitions (but not all social cognitions are stereotypes).

30. d   obj. 3   p. 520
a.   Incorrect. Someone is unlikely to exaggerate the good qualities of a stranger without a reason for doing so.
b.   Incorrect. This is not impression formation, though it sounds interesting.
c.   Incorrect. Impression formation occurs very soon after first meeting someone, so this comprehensive picture would not be created.
*d.   Correct. An overall impression is made very quickly about the individual.

31. b   obj. 3   p. 521
a.   Incorrect. These attributions have serious impact, and they must then be central traits.

*b.   Correct. Because of how significant these traits can be, psychologists consider them to be central traits.
c.   Incorrect. They apply equally to men and women.
d.   Incorrect. As central traits they could contribute to the distinction between ingroups and outgroups, but warm and cold might not be specific enough.

32. c   obj. 3   p. 521
a.   Incorrect. There is no "discrimination theory" that applies to this issue.
b.   Incorrect. In the broadest sense this is true, but another alternative is more specific and thus a better choice.
*c.   Correct. Attribution theory involves the efforts people make to understand the causes of their and others' behavior.
d.   Incorrect. There is not a "directive-behavior" theory.

33. b   obj. 4   p. 526
a.   Incorrect. More knowledge would not necessarily lead to conformity; it could just as well lead to nonconformity.
*b.   Correct. Conformity is to the pressures of the group, and it is accomplished by accepting the attitudes and behaviors of the group.
c.   Incorrect. The intense pressure to be an individual would be counter to the pressure to conform.
d.   Incorrect. People with very secure self-images may be highly conforming individuals.

34. d   obj. 4   p. 526
a.   Incorrect. The tendencies for a male or a female (based primarily on gender) to conform depend greatly on the circumstances.
b.   Incorrect. The tendencies for a male or a female (based primarily on gender) to conform depend greatly on the circumstances.
c.   Incorrect. Someone familiar with the task at hand is likely to be more independent.
*d.   Correct. The more unfamiliar someone is with the task at hand, the more likely they will turn to others present to find someone to imitate.

35. d   obj. 5   p. 527
a.   Incorrect. Conformity results from indirect social pressure and a desire to be part of the group.
b.   Incorrect. Congruence is a concept used in humanistic psychotherapy to describe different aspects of the self-concept.
c.   Incorrect. A commission is an amount of money received for a specific task, like a sales commission.
*d.   Correct. This is the definition of compliance.

36. c   obj. 5   p. 529
a.   Incorrect. This is called the door-in-the-face technique, and it is the opposite of the foot-in-the-door technique.
b.   Incorrect. But it is a form of social compliance.
*c.   Correct. This technique is the opposite of the foot-in-the-door technique.
d.   Incorrect. It is the opposite of this, and called the door-in-the-face technique.

37. c   obj. 5   p. 530
a.   Incorrect. The sample does not cost any money, but there are psychic costs.
b.   Incorrect. But this is the technique used by book and record clubs.
*c. Correct. While you do not think you have to buy the product, you do develop a psychological "debt" that you may try to repay by buying additional products.
d.   Incorrect. Your do not resist the sample; you take it, though it may cost you psychologically later.

38. b   obj. 6   p. 530
a.   Incorrect. They had been assured that the learner would not be hurt, but they did hear him pounding on the wall and screaming.
*b. Correct. Apparently, the presence of the authority figure (the experimenter) gave the impression that the subjects were not responsible for what happened.
c.   Incorrect. They did not know the learner.
d.   Incorrect. They were assured that they would not be punished for stopping.

39. d   obj. 7   p. 532
a.   Incorrect. These would be called traits.
b.   Incorrect. Discrimination is an action taken against members of a group.
c.   Incorrect. Prejudice is the set of judgmental attitudes one has about a person or group.
*d. Correct. Stereotypes are beliefs based upon perceived group characteristics.

40. b   obj. 7   p. 533
a.   Incorrect. Stereotyping applies to attitudes, not behaviors.
*b. Correct. Discrimination is the negative action taken against members of a group.
c.   Incorrect. Prejudice is positive or negative attitudes toward a group or member of a group.
d.   Incorrect. A self-fulfilling prophecy is an expectation about the occurrence of an event or behavior that increases the likelihood that the event or behavior will occur.

41. b   obj. 8   p. 533
a.   Incorrect. This is the claim of social learning theory.
*b. Correct. Social identity theory states that the group to which we belong is a source of pride and self-worth.
c.   Incorrect. This is not the claim of social identity theory.
d.   Incorrect. This describes a self-fulfilling prophecy.

42. a   obj. 9   p. 536
*a. Correct. Physical proximity is nearness to another person, and it is a major factor in both friendship and love relationships.
b.   Incorrect. This defines the effect of reciprocity on us.
c.   Incorrect. This defines the effect of reciprocity on others.
d.   Incorrect. Distance is the opposite of proximity.

43. c   obj. 9   p. 538
a.   Incorrect. Proximity could be tested by asking how close you live or work to your friends.
b.   Incorrect. Companionate love is based on the long-term commitment to being with someone and counting on their companionship.
*c. Correct. These questions could test both love and liking because they share the features addressed in the questions.
d.   Incorrect. Need complementarity would be revealed through other kinds of questions.

44. d   obj. 10   p. 539
a.   Incorrect. This is from Sternberg's theory, and is separate from passion.
b.   Incorrect. This is from Sternberg's theory, and is separate from passion.
c.   Incorrect. This type of love is seen in contrast to passionate love.
*d. Correct. Sounds like "romance."

45. b   obj. 10   p. 541
a.   Incorrect. Phase 1 involves a personal focus on the partner's behavior.
*b. Correct. Phase 2 involves confrontations with the partner.
c.   Incorrect. Phase 3 involves negotiation on dissolution and face-saving behavior.
d.   Incorrect. Phase 4 involves ending the relationship physically and psychologically.

46. c   obj. 10   p. 542
a.   Incorrect. This phase is called "grave dressing."
b.   Incorrect. This phase is called "grave dressing."
*c. Correct. This phase is called "grave dressing," and the couple is engaging in exactly that.
d.   Incorrect. This phase is called "grave dressing."

47. a   obj. 11   p. 544
*a. Correct. Aggressive cues increase the likelihood of aggression (which initially creates a readiness to act).
b.   Incorrect. Aggressive cues increase the likelihood of aggression (which initially creates a readiness to act).
c.   Incorrect. Aggressive cues increase the likelihood of aggression (which initially creates a readiness to act).
d.   Incorrect. Aggressive cues increase the likelihood of aggression (which initially creates a readiness to act).

48. c   obj. 12   p. 545
a.   Incorrect. Aggressive cues are unrelated to the concept of diffusion of responsibility.
b.   Incorrect. Catharsis is not related to the diffusion of responsibility.
*c. Correct. Helping behavior is less likely in the presence of more than one bystander because of the diffusion of responsibility.
d.   Incorrect. Innate behaviors do not appear to affect the diffusion of responsibility.

Practice Test III:

49. b   obj. 1   p. 513
a.   Incorrect. This is an affective component.
*b. Correct. This is a cognition about the vitamin quality of the beans.
c.   Incorrect. This is a neutral, non-attitudinal statement about beans.
d.   Incorrect. This is a behavioral component of an attitude about beans.

50. c   obj. 2   p. 514
a.   Incorrect. Only a few products can sell themselves.
b.   Incorrect. Most people know that the beautiful people associated with the product probably did not buy it.
*c. Correct. The classical conditioning element of association of the positive feelings with the product is what companies are counting upon.
d.   Incorrect. They may think this, but it is not why they create these kinds of advertisements.

51. b   obj. 2   p. 515
a.   Incorrect. Direct reinforcement would require that he express the attitude and then be reinforced for doing so.
*b. Correct. This is an example of learning through observation, or learning vicariously.
c.   Incorrect. Cognitive dissonance involves contradictory thoughts or beliefs that then cause tension (of course, the 5-year-old may have a friend who is a Southerner).
d.   Incorrect. Persuasive communication usually involves a more direct message.

52. d   obj. 2   p. 516
a.   Incorrect. The appearance of being thoughtful actually strengthens this kind of two-sided message.
b.   Incorrect. People will believe that the communicator is trying to give a fair presentation of both sides.
c.   Incorrect. People can actually grasp rather sophisticated messages (it is the industry that is unable to produce them).
*d. Correct. The two-sided approach will be more effective than a one-sided approach in this circumstance.

53. c   obj. 2   p. 516
a.   Incorrect. The approach known as peripheral-route processing is being used.
b.   Incorrect. This applies only to well-rounded messages.
*c. Correct. The peripheral route is one that avoids presenting much reasoning or detail about the product itself.
d.   Incorrect. But it is!

54. a   obj. 2   p. 516
*a. Correct. When the recipient puts effort into cognitively analyzing the message, as would be required in central-route processing, the change in attitude will be the greatest for the situations given here.
b.   Incorrect. Being male does not make the message any more or less effective.
c.   Incorrect. The recipient will do little work in appraising a message that is peripheral.
d.   Incorrect. Intelligence does not affect attitude change.

55. b   obj. 2   p. 519
a.   Incorrect. See answer b.
*b. Correct. Cognitive dissonance would lead to modifying one of the cognitions, making them consistent, or revaluing them, but it is unlikely to make the person enter a program to stop smoking (this requires additional pressures).
c.   Incorrect. See answer b.
d.   Incorrect. See answer b.

56. c   obj. 2   p. 519
a.   Incorrect. This is simply a sexist position.
b.   Incorrect. This is simply typical of salespersons.
*c. Correct. Here, two thoughts are opposed to each other and will certainly result in tension.
d.   Incorrect. This is simply being prejudicial.

57. d   obj. 3   p. 522
a.   Incorrect. John's behavior is explained according to the situation.
b.   Incorrect. The decision to attend the party comes from dispositional forces.
c.   Incorrect. Anxiety is explained in terms of what others do (thus situational).
*d. Correct. The disposition of conscientiousness is used to account for staying up all night.

58. a   obj. 3   p. 522
*a. Correct. Barbara is engaging in a behavior because of the situation, not her disposition to keep the room messy.
b.   Incorrect. Thoughtfulness is Chris's disposition.
c.   Incorrect. Grumpiness is John's disposition.
d.   Incorrect. Punctuality is Mindy's disposition.

59. b   obj. 3   p. 523
a.   Incorrect. It is frequently expressed, but we tend to see it in things like the Ann Lander's column.
*b. Correct. This common tendency is really only visible when we see it in others, such as in the advice columns so many people read every day.
c.   Incorrect. It may be found in them, but it is a normal phenomenon.
d.   Incorrect. We are more likely to make attribution errors with acquaintances than with close friends, since we have more information about our close friends.

60. a   obj. 3   p. 523
*a. Correct. This is one of the few truths you can count on in psychology.
b.   Incorrect. This is known as the assumed-similarity bias, not the fundamental attribution error.
c.   Incorrect. This is opposite the case.
d.   Incorrect. This is opposite the case.

61. a   obj. 4   p. 526
*a. Correct. The individuals in Asch's study should have felt rather confident about judging and comparing the lengths of lines.
b.   Incorrect. But they were all subjects in a psychology experiment.

c.   Incorrect. Subjects were speaking the answer aloud, so all could hear it.

d.   Incorrect. In the first experiment, all members of the group, except the real subject, were instructed to agree with the first person in the sequence.

62. d   obj. 4   p. 537

a.   Incorrect. The more the group members value the group, the stronger will be the pressures to conform.

b.   Incorrect. The larger the group, the more likely conformity becomes.

c.   Incorrect. Public statements increase the pressure to conform.

*d. Correct. Secret ballots remove pressure to conform because other members will be unaware of how the individual votes are cast.

63. b   obj. 4   p. 526

a.   Incorrect. This factor was not studied.

*b. Correct. The more ambiguous the task, the more likely conformity will be.

c.   Incorrect. Dress may reflect the unanimity of the group, but it certainly must be a weak force.

d.   Incorrect. Leadership is less important for conformity than are other pressures from the group.

64. a   obj. 7   p. 533

*a. Correct. Stereotypes are applications of category knowledge, and prejudices involve using stereotypes to make judgments about people.

b.   Incorrect. Neither stereotypes nor prejudices require action.

c.   Incorrect. Neither stereotypes nor prejudices require action.

d.   Incorrect. This is reversed.

65. a   obj. 9   p. 537

*a. Correct. Similarity is the best early predictor of attraction.

b.   Incorrect. Mere exposure is probably the weakest predictor of attraction.

c.   Incorrect. Similarity is the strongest predictor.

d.   Incorrect. Need complementarity is an inconsistent predictor of attraction.

66. d   obj. 9   p. 539

a.   Incorrect. See answer d.

b.   Incorrect. See answer d.

c.   Incorrect. See answer d.

*d. Correct. Sternberg's triarchic theory of love has three components - intimacy, passion, and commitment - that can be combined in different ways.

67. c   obj. 11   p. 544

a.   Incorrect. Sports are not typically considered prosocial.

b.   Incorrect. Lorenz was referring to civilized, game-oriented sports like football.

*c. Correct. Since aggression arises from an instinct, in his view, it needs some form of release.

d.   Incorrect. This is from a different aspect of the frustration/aggression hypothesis.

68. a   obj. 10   p. 541

*a. Correct. This marks the first stage or phase of the decline of the relationship.

b.   Incorrect. This is not one of the phases of the breakup (it sounds a bit like, when did you stop beating your wife?).

c.   Incorrect. This is not one of the phases Levinger describes, though it does happen.

d.   Incorrect. This happens following the shift in judgments about the partner.

69. c   obj. 12   p. 546

a.   Incorrect. Fundamental attribution error accounts for attributing the bombers' acts to their own evil nature.

b.   Incorrect. Diffusion of responsibility would have left many standing by and watching.

*c. Correct. This prosocial behavior demonstrates that more must be involved than mere rewards.

d.   Incorrect. Only if they were angels.

NOTES

NOTES

NOTES

NOTES

NOTES

NOTES

NOTES

NOTES

NOTES

NOTES